Praise for *Mob Boss*

"A gripping, novelistic biography . . . the authors score a bull's eye." —*The New York Times*

"Al D'Arco was the quintessential wiseguy—and the mob's worst nightmare. Capeci and Robbins have used Little Al's incredible insight about 'the Life' and their own reporting skills to write a compelling book about the rise and decline of the American Mafia, from the days of Al Capone and Lucky Luciano to the heyday of Chin Gigante and John Gotti. It's a true crime story that reads like a novel."
—Nicholas Pileggi, *New York Times* bestselling author of *Wiseguy* and *Casino*

"For authors Jerry Capeci and Tom Robbins, the long road to their fascinating new book about Mafia boss Alfonso D'Arco, who became the federal government's most successful cooperator, began a decade ago." —*Village Voice*

"A raw and fascinating account of one mobster's daily activities and career." —*Kirkus Reviews*

"This gripping biography [is] recommended to fans of Nicholas Pileggi's *Wiseguy*, Philip Carlo's *Gaspipe*, or coauthor Capeci's own *Gotti: Rise and Fall*." —*Booklist*

"Just a superb book. This is a powerful addition to the true history of the United States. Through hard, relentless reporting, Capeci and Robbins strip away the dark glamor and wormy movie myths about the American mob and come as close to the truth as any outsiders might ever get. It's a dirty story about corruption and brutal power. The authors take us to many dirty places in our politics, trade unions, and ideals, and make clear that mob power was too often enforced through a bullet in the skull. They also narrate the squalid tale of how mob power declined and fell. The soundtrack for the dying version of the mob was usually loud with the squealing of rats."

—Pete Hamill, *New York Times* bestselling author of
Forever and *North River*

"Tom Robbins and Jerry Capeci have written a fascinating, inside look at the mob . . . Even mob cognoscenti will learn all sorts of things they never suspected. By turns horrifying, suspenseful, and darkly hilarious, *Mob Boss* is a terrific read."

—Kevin Baker, author of *The Big Crowd*

"If you read one book about the decline and fall of the Mafia in America, let it be *Mob Boss*. Capeci and Robbins, two first-rate reporters at the top of their game, present an unforgettable portrait of Little Al D'Arco, who presided over the last big Mafia war in New York, then took the stand in court to once and for all obliterate the Honored Society. An astounding read that belongs in the upper tier of organized crime literature."   —T.J. English, author of
The Savage City and *Havana Nocturne*

"Al D'Arco loved two things: His wife and his gangster life, not necessarily in that order. This book makes me wish I'd known him better. This is a genuinely great mob story about a genuine New York gangster told by two of the city's best reporters."   —Jimmy Breslin, author of *The Good Rat*
and *The Gang That Couldn't Shoot Straight*

"This is the dramatic story of the most important mobster to testify against the Mafia since Joe Valachi, as told by two of New York's top investigative reporters. This is a must-read for anyone concerned about the connection between organized crime and labor racketeering."

—Robert M. Morgenthau,
longest serving Manhattan District Attorney

"Little Al D'Arco had to choose between which family he would forsake. The mob family he commanded as boss, or his own family, including the son who had succumbed to the very drugs the mob helped move onto the streets. When D'Arco made his choice, it shocked Cosa Nostra to its core. Never before had the "Boss" of a mob family decided to break the "code of omerta." The secrets that "Little Al" could reveal were not just the secrets of the Luchese Crime Family—he knew the secrets of the bosses of all the families. No two reporters have ever navigated the secret world of the Mafia more adeptly than Jerry Capeci and Tom Robbins. This book is their masterpiece."

—John Miller, senior correspondent at
CBS News and former deputy in the FBI and NYPD

"Not since Abe Reles first identified Murder Inc. before dropping to his death from the Half Moon Hotel has someone 'in the Life' made such a gift to law enforcement as when Little Al D'Arco called the FBI to keep his real family safe from the criminal one in which he'd served as boss. This account treats its subject as an entirely believable human being, and not just a figure out of bloody folklore. Only a few mob books achieve that. Capeci and Robbins have told D'Arco's story but in their own way. Well done."

—Nathan Ward, author of *Dark Harbor:
The War For the New York Waterfront*

Also by Jerry Capeci

The Complete Idiot's Guide to the Mafia

Wiseguys Say the Darndest Things

Gang Land: Fifteen Years of Covering the Mafia

Mob Star: The Story of John Gotti (coauthor Gene Mustain)

Gotti: Rise and Fall (coauthor Gene Mustain)

Murder Machine (coauthor Gene Mustain)

MOB BOSS

The Life of

Little Al D'Arco,

the Man Who Brought

Down the Mafia

Jerry Capeci
and Tom Robbins

St. Martin's Paperbacks

MOB BOSS

Copyright © 2013, 2015 by Jerry Capeci and Tom Robbins.

For information address St. Martin's Press, 175 Fifth Avenue, New York, NY 10010.

EAN: 978-1-250-06078-5

Printed in the United States of America

St. Martin's Press edition / October 2013
St. Martin's Paperbacks edition / March 2015

St. Martin's Paperbacks are published by St. Martin's Press, 175 Fifth Avenue, New York, NY 10010.

10 9 8 7 6 5 4 3 2 1

For Hap Hairston and Bill Boyle,
two great tabloid editors
who taught us a lot
and who would have liked this story

CONTENTS

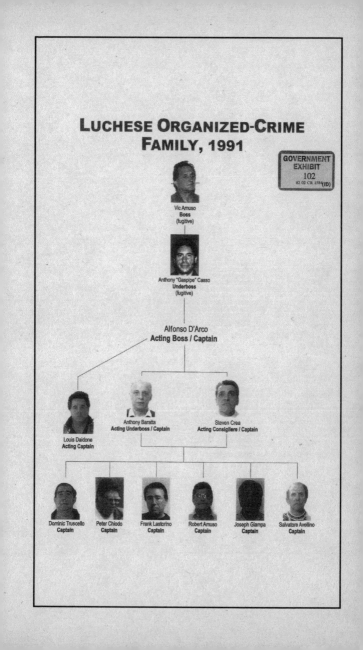

PREFACE

Alfonso "Little Al" D'Arco was the most important mob witness in an era that saw the Mafia slide into a long and bloody decline. As an acting boss of his crime family, he was the highest-ranking mobster ever to share Mafia secrets when he changed sides in 1991. His decision opened the door for others to make the same choice, including John Gotti's top aide, Salvatore "Sammy the Bull" Gravano. Collectively, their testimony helped send the mob spiraling into near collapse.

We got to see him a lot while covering organized crime for the *New York Daily News* and other papers, where we broke many of the stories of his cooperation and revelations. He was the most effective and compelling witness we ever saw take the stand. He gave no excuses for his own conduct, offering a riveting account of a life of crime. What was also impressive about Al D'Arco was that he knew not only his own criminal story, but the history of the mob. He clearly had been a careful student of knowledgeable tutors.

So when the opportunity arose a few years ago to tell his story, we were immediately interested, provided that we could set the ground rules. First, the book would be written by us. D'Arco would have no right to review the manuscript, or declare any areas of his life off-limits. Second, he would

have to make himself available, not always an easy prospect
for someone in the witness protection program.

He agreed, submitting to hundreds of hours of interviews.
He also made his wife of fifty-eight years and his oldest son,
who followed him into the mob, available as well.

Like the FBI agents and prosecutors who debriefed him
for even more hours, we never caught him in a lie. Telling the
truth was a point of pride with him. We were steadily amazed
at his accuracy. One example: When he told us how a young
Jewish gangster he had known on Mulberry Street more
than forty years ago had been stabbed to death in a Bronx
park by Lucky Luciano's former right-hand man, we were
skeptical of being able to confirm it. The murder was not only
unsolved, it wasn't even listed anywhere. But after digging
out the facts, the details dovetailed exactly as he had described
them.

This book is based on those interviews, along with thousands of pages of court transcripts, FBI memos, affidavits,
and other documents. We also interviewed more than three
dozen agents, detectives, prosecutors, and defense attorneys.
Any mistakes here are our own, no one else's.

Al D'Arco's story is many things. It's a true inside account
of what was supposed to be a secret society. It's also the
story of a killer whose crimes were unforgivable, no matter
how much they were part of "the Life," as he and his fellow
mobsters dubbed the world they inhabited.

It's also a story of New York, its streets, its neighborhoods,
and its residents, some infamous, some long forgotten. At
one point, when Al D'Arco's career goal to become a "made
member" was being blocked, he was offered a chance to skip
the wait and join another family. He'd instantly have a lot of
money and a big house. The catch was he would have to
move to Pittsburgh. No thanks, he said. He was a New Yorker.
He wanted to stay that way.

I

La Scuola delle Strade

1

THE CALL

On the evening of September 21, 1991, a veteran agent of the Federal Bureau of Investigation named Robert Marston got a call at his home in the Connecticut suburbs. It was seven o'clock on a Saturday night and Marston and his family were just headed out the door. Neighbors were picking them up to drive them to a local church fair.

The phone rang just as the neighbors arrived. Marston picked it up in the living room as his wife and two young children went outside.

On the other end was an operator from the bureau's New York switchboard, which handled after-hours calls to the agency.

"I have a call for Agent Marston," a nasal-toned operator said. "Will you accept it?"

He said he would. He waited a moment for the call to be patched through. On the line was someone involved in an investigation that Marston was conducting into an illegal landfill. He'd spoken to the man several times, but he couldn't imagine why he would be calling him on a weekend evening. Whatever it was, he hoped it wouldn't take long. He could see his wife chatting with their friends, casting anxious glances at the living-room window.

The caller sounded nervous and rushed. He was speaking almost in code.

"There's this guy I know and he's involved with things. I'd like you to speak to him. I think he can tell you a lot," he said.

Marston asked who it was.

"His name is Al D'Arco," said the caller.

The agent had to skip a few beats to catch up with that one. For the past year he had been trying to wrap up his probe into a dump along the Delaware River in Pennsylvania. It had started as a routine environmental-crime case. That was Marston's beat. He chased illegal dumpers, the corner-cutting trash haulers who tossed medical waste into the ocean, and toxic garbage down open mine pits.

He was part of what the bureau called "a white-collar squad." They pursued crooks who stole with pen and paper, not guns. It was why the bureau's elite mob-chasing agents referred to them as the "sharp-pencil guys." They were smart investigators, very good at deciphering financial records, but lacking in the street savvy needed to handle real wiseguys.

Marston wouldn't have disagreed with that analysis. He had an MBA and had been on the verge of becoming a certified public accountant when his application to the FBI had been accepted. But despite the white-collar nature of his work, several authentic wiseguys had walked into the landfill case just the same. One of them had ended up dead in the trunk of his late-model Jaguar, his blood leaching out onto the Bronx street where the car was abandoned.

On court-ordered wiretaps, Marston's team had heard dump operators voice greatest concern about someone in lower Manhattan's Little Italy named "Al." Whoever "Al" was, he was a mobster with high-level clout in the Luchese crime family, one of New York's five Mafia clans. They'd eventually learned Al's last name: D'Arco. He had done two terms in prison, one for stock theft and another for heroin sales.

Their interest had soared when they'd learned earlier that year from the bureau's Mafia specialists that D'Arco was serving as his crime family's acting boss. He was the pinch hitter for the family's two top figures, boss Vittorio "Vic" Amuso and underboss Anthony "Gaspipe" Casso. Both men had gone into hiding just before their indictment on racketeering charges the year before.

That was where the intelligence had stopped. They had never heard his voice on the wiretaps or spotted him in a meeting. Al D'Arco was someone hidden in the corners.

And now he wanted to talk to Bob Marston?

He said that of course he would speak to him. The caller said he'd have D'Arco call Marston right back on the same number. Then he hung up.

A few moments later, the phone rang again. Outside on the lawn, his wife looked up at the sound of the ring. She gave an exasperated shrug. He held up a finger. He'd be a minute.

"Agent Marston, I have someone on the line who doesn't want to say who he is," said the high-pitched operator.

"That's all right," he said. "Put him through, please."

He heard a voice with a deep Brooklyn accent. "Mr. Marston? My name is Al." The caller paused. "Do you know who I am?"

"Yes, I think I do," he said.

"Okay, good. I was told you were someone I could talk to."

This is how Hollywood would have a wiseguy sound, the agent thought. Street-tough and tense. It suddenly flashed through Marston's mind that this was a gag, a couple of co-workers jerking his chain. In his office in New Rochelle just north of New York City, everyone knew he'd been hammering away at the landfill case. And everyone knew that he'd lately been chasing his own white whale, a mobster named D'Arco.

On the other hand, if the caller was who he said he was, this could be a very significant phone conversation. Robert Marston was thirty-nine years old. He'd been with the FBI for twelve years, long enough to know that agents spent entire careers hoping for calls like this.

If I screw this up, he thought, how am I ever going to explain it?

Marston's wife was now waving her hands, beckoning him to come on. She cupped her hand to her mouth. "Will you please hang up the phone and get into the car?" she yelled. He waved back just as urgently, signaling her not to wait for him. She shook her head.

"I'd be glad to talk," said Marston. They were both silent for a moment. This is like an awkward first date, the agent thought. "How can I help?" he added.

D'Arco began to talk. His words spilled out in a fast, agitated flow. Marston couldn't understand everything he said. It was a mob stream of consciousness, as though he had come in halfway through a conversation the gangster was having with himself.

People had tried to kill him, he got that much. And D'Arco wanted to retaliate. He heard that as well. He had weapons at his disposal, and he was prepared for anything that happened, he said. "I never broke the rules," the mobster kept saying.

Marston just listened. This had to be authentic. His agent pals could never be this creative. He made sympathetic sounds. His chief goal, he decided, should be just to keep Al D'Arco on the phone, to keep him from bolting.

"Tell me what's going on," he said, trying to sound encouraging.

D'Arco told him he was in a house on Long Island. His son Joseph was with him. He didn't give an address, and Marston didn't press him.

Marston couldn't tell whether the men D'Arco said were after him were right outside the house or far away. If the threat was imminent, he said, they might be better off just dialing 911. "We could have police cruisers there in a couple minutes if you want."

"No," responded D'Arco in a low voice. "It's not that imminent."

He next sounded almost embarrassed for having raised an alarm. "I don't need any help protecting myself," he said loudly. "And I can take care of my family. I've been doing it all my life."

All he wanted to do was talk, he insisted. "I'm willing to do this for a few minutes right now," he said. "But that's it. Nothing else," he said.

"That's fine," said the agent. "Let's just talk." He looked outside. The car was gone. So was his family.

Again, there was silence on the other end of the line. Marston started filling in the space. He told D'Arco a little about himself. He was from upstate New York, he said. He told him where he worked and the kind of cases he did.

As he spoke, Marston tried to keep his own voice as normal as possible, as though he were talking to a neighbor at the church fair he now knew he'd miss. He was trying to avoid being pulled into the undertow of the tough Brooklyn accent. It was something he had seen other agents lapse into when talking to hoods from the street. In a bid to gain their confidence, they imitated their language, their gestures, even their dress.

Marston had no illusions about who he was. He was a suburban WASP. If he was to start talking like a tough guy, Al D'Arco would instantly spot him as a fake. Worse, he would consider it condescending. He'd hang up and go a million miles away.

D'Arco sounded somewhat reassured by what he heard. He said he was glad to know that Marston wasn't one of the FBI men that followed the Luchese family. "Those guys have been harassing me," he said. An agent had recently stopped him in the street, he claimed, loudly thanking D'Arco for helping them, making it appear as though he were cooperating.

"He was trying to get me killed," said D'Arco.

The rant against the bureau continued for several minutes. He began a new tirade against those who were after him. Then he paused and seemed to take a breath. "If I was to come with you," he said, "what could you do for me?"

Marston felt a slight panic as he realized he had no idea what the answer was. He'd never handled a mob cooperator. Instinct told him to be honest about that.

"Well, I don't know exactly, Mr. D'Arco. I've never done this kind of thing before." He said he'd quickly find out though.

And then he added some reassurance about some things he knew he could honestly pledge. "What I will tell you, though, is that I will never lie to you. I won't make any promises I can't keep. And I'll never mislead you. If I don't know the answer to something I will tell you I don't know."

D'Arco seemed to appreciate his honesty about his ignorance. "Well, I got an idea of who you are," he said. "And I think maybe you are someone I can talk to."

Marston said he felt the same way. What they should do, the agent said, was talk again in a little while after he'd had a chance to speak to his bosses, who would have a better idea of how to proceed.

He looked at his watch. It was 8 p.m. "Why don't you call me back at eight thirty?" he said. As he said it, he wondered if he was making a huge mistake. He might never hear from Al D'Arco again. Maybe the people who had tried to kill D'Arco, whoever they were, would find him before the FBI did. But he didn't know what else to do.

"Okay," said D'Arco. "I'll call you then."

Marston hit the switch hook on the phone and began dialing. He couldn't reach his supervisor, but he found Mike Flanagan, the assistant special agent in charge of his squad, the ASAC in the bureau's shorthand. Flanagan lived nearby. His brother John was also an agent and a member of the unit that chased the Luchese family that Al D'Arco had just told him he loathed.

Breathlessly, Marston told Flanagan he had just been on the phone with the acting boss of the Luchese crime family. He was talking about cooperating.

"Okay," the squad leader said calmly, as if this happened every week.

"We're going to talk again," said Marston. "This could lead to something."

"Get as many agents as you need, Bob," Flanagan told him. "See if you can bring him in. Spend what you have to spend. Let's hope it works out."

That was easy, Marston thought when he got off the phone.

His next call was to his partner, Jim O'Connor, who had been working the landfill case with him.

"You're kidding," said O'Connor.

"I thought maybe someone was kidding me," said Marston.

He made a few more calls to agents he knew would be eager to interrupt their Saturday nights for a mission like this. The bureau had a SWAT team, and Marston was friendly with a couple of its members. He asked everyone to just stand by. He wasn't sure they were going anyplace. Yet.

His phone rang again a little after 8:30.

The operator knew the routine. "I have your party, Mr. Marston," she said.

"How are you doing, Mr. Marston?" came the voice.

He told D'Arco that he had been authorized to bring D'Arco to a safe location. He asked if any other members of his family were with him.

"No, it's me and my son Joseph," said D'Arco. "We're out at my mother's place on Long Island."

Marston asked how many were in his family. D'Arco seemed to be counting. "Including my mother, my kids, my sister, my nephew, it's twelve," he said. He had sent his wife, his daughters, and another son away that morning, he added. "I know they're safe. I don't have to worry about them right now." He started to ramble again about how the rules were being broken. Mobsters were now going after families. "That was never allowed," he said.

Marston waited for another opening. One thing at a time, he thought. "We're going to start with you and Joseph," he said. "Why don't you give me the location of where you are right now. We will come and get you."

There was silence on D'Arco's end. I lost him, thought Marston. He's going to back off.

Then he heard the Brooklyn accent giving him an address on the North Shore of Long Island.

Late that night, Alfonso D'Arco, a balding fifty-nine-year-old lifelong gangster, known as "Little Al" for his modest height, became the highest-ranking member of the Mafia ever to defect to the government.

Other than sounding like one of the Dead End Kids, circa 1935, he wouldn't have been anyone's idea of a mob boss. He didn't smoke or drink, aside from an occasional glass of wine. He had been faithfully married to the same woman since 1955. There were no mob girlfriends tucked away on the side. He didn't gamble or bet on the races. He was a vegetarian, shunning meat on the advice of a prison doctor.

And he was a true workaholic. His greatest satisfaction was staying busy, running a pair of restaurants and overseeing the extensive holdings of his crime family.

But he was a mobster by both choice and conviction. "I was born made," he liked to say of a life of crime that began as a teenager in the streets near Brooklyn's Navy Yard.

Closing the door on that life was like stepping into a void. He was entering a world he had always viewed with suspicion and loathing. It was a core belief in gangland: There was no honor among cops and agents. They were capable of anything. They were as crooked as the criminals they chased, only less honest about it.

The problem for Al D'Arco was that he had no place left to go. He had become an orphan in his own crime family. Terrified as he was of the new world he was entering, he was certain of the fate awaiting himself and his loved ones if he stayed where he was.

A few nights before, he had sat in a hotel room in midtown Manhattan surrounded by his Mafia colleagues. It was supposed to be a mob business meeting. Gambling, loansharking, labor shakedowns, even a plan to grab control of the market for cardboard at produce stores, were all on the agenda. Toward the end of the meeting, he had spotted a concealed gun tucked in a member's waistband. He then realized something else was planned as well. His partners were going to kill him, right there in the hotel room.

He had been hearing the whispers all summer. "Al is no good," was the word being spread on the Little Italy streets. "Be careful with Al." Men he had known for years, longtime associates he considered good friends, were keeping their distance. He had been labeled an informant, a rat.

It wasn't true, but he knew the truth wouldn't help. Over the past two years, at the direction of his mob bosses, he had helped kill other men about whom the same claim had been made. He had harbored strong doubts about the accusations. But he had gone along. It was part of his mob oath, following orders.

He had also watched as the retribution was extended to families as well. That was also supposed to be against the rules. You didn't punish personal family members for the alleged sins of sons or fathers. But everyone, it seemed, had changed their minds about that one.

Before he had fled the hotel room, he had listened to an acting boss of another mob family, an old-school gangster, loudly insist that the way to end the threat of mob cooperators was simple: kill their entire families.

Listening, Al D'Arco felt like he was looking in a mirror. Now they were doing it to him.

He was not the first Mafia defector. A handful of other sworn members before him had made the same abrupt turn in their careers, including a trio of mob captains and a small squad of soldiers. But as a former acting boss, Al D'Arco was several notches higher than those who had preceded him.

He was different for another reason as well. Earlier mob turncoats had suddenly seen the light and agreed to cooperate when facing long prison terms or seeking to reduce sentences they were already serving.

The night D'Arco dialed the FBI's number in New York, he had no legal matters pending against him. No one was even close to having a criminal case that they could prove. Even Bob Marston wasn't sure his investigation of the crooked landfill would ever be able to tie D'Arco close enough to the scheme for an indictment.

Nor had he been caught in any parole violations, usually the soft underbelly for even the shrewdest mobsters. He had been on a special ten-year parole since his release from prison in 1986. All the government had to do was catch him meeting with any of the convicted felons who made up his circle of friends and associates. It would be enough to put him back behind bars for years.

He had protected himself by carefully avoiding all the easy targets. He shied away from weddings, funerals, social club meetings, all those surveillance opportunities for agents and police. Out of an abundance of caution, he had even skipped his younger son John's wedding in June. It meant he missed the congratulations and good wishes offered by representatives of all five crime families who were present largely out of respect for the groom's father. He had to satisfy himself with hearing the stories later.

In some ways he was like the first government cooperator. Back in 1963, Joseph Valachi had broken the mob vow of *omerta*—silence—by acknowledging the existence of something he identified as "Cosa Nostra." It was a crucial breakthrough for law enforcement.

Like Al D'Arco, Valachi also believed he was marked for assassination when he turned. In prison in Atlanta, he had been so rattled that he had murdered another inmate he mistook for a potential assassin.

But there were differences as well. Valachi's testimony before a U.S. Senate committee made riveting television. Charts of Mafia family hierarchies compiled with his assistance served as investigative road maps for years to come.

But aside from the publicity, Valachi's effectiveness was limited. He testified only once, sending a single mobster to prison. In contrast, ten years after Al D'Arco decided to change teams, the scorecard compiled by prosecutors showed that his testimony had helped win convictions of more than fifty mobsters.

Among them were the bosses of four crime families. One of them was the legendarily elusive leader of the Genovese crime family, Vincent Gigante. D'Arco's testimony helped prove that the "Chin's" bathrobe-clad saunters through the Greenwich Village streets were a feigned effort to pretend insanity and avoid prosecution.

All told, Al D'Arco took the stand sixteen times over the next fifteen years. He was listed as a potential witness in more than forty other cases that never went to trial. Defendants, including some of the most powerful members of Cosa Nostra, threw in the towel and accepted plea deals rather than have juries hear what D'Arco had to say about them.

"He was the best," said Michael Campi, a former FBI supervisor who headed the elite 150-member squad pursuing organized crime in New York. "Al D'Arco was the most significant made member to cooperate," said Campi, who spent twenty years hunting wiseguys. "He really built that bridge for others to cross."

He was equally convincing to juries. "He was one of the toughest, most difficult witnesses I ever faced," said Gerald Shargel, the noted criminal defense attorney who saw two clients, including Luchese boss Vic Amuso, convicted after D'Arco took the stand against them.

He had an uncanny memory. FBI agents who spent months debriefing him found him to be a kind of Mafia Rain Man.

Asked for details about Italian crime syndicates, he ticked off the names of twenty-six different mob factions on the island of Sicily. He then listed the cities and neighborhoods where their American representatives could be found. He sketched out a twelve-page history of the roots of the American Mafia for the Italian counterpart of the FBI, the Direzione Investigativa Antimafia, identifying two dozen American mobsters who had originated in Italy.

He walked agents through the mob's business dealings, ranging from which crime family had the rights to sell bread to vendors at the San Gennaro festival on Mulberry Street in Little Italy, to how the Mafia had made fortunes on the demolition of the old West Side Highway in Manhattan and the construction of a Long Island nuclear power plant.

He listed the trade unions under mob control, identifying by number and location which locals fell under the sway of which crime families and which members.

Despite romantic claims that drug dealing was banned

within the mob, he identified a roster of more than forty Mafiosi actively dealing narcotics.

He provided the answers to more than a score of unsolved homicides, some of them long ago abandoned in the cold-case files.

He was also a repository of mob lore. He had been taught by a succession of old-school Mafia mentors. They had passed along their oral history, like tribal chieftains teaching pupils without books.

Mafia soldiers had fought alongside Sicilian sheepherders in the range wars in Colorado at the turn of the century, he told the agents. He had known ancient veterans of those battles, he said.

He told the story of how auto magnate Henry Ford had traded the once legendary Mafia powerhouse Joseph "Joe Adonis" Doto a lucrative contract to transport cars from plants in New Jersey in exchange for mob muscle to help with his labor problems. When the agents went to check, they saw the record of Adonis's contract.

"You're a walking crime encyclopedia," one of New York's most knowledgeable mob investigators, Kenneth McCabe, told him.

He was that, but he was something else as well. He was also a murderer. He confessed his own role in a dozen killings and the unfulfilled murder plots against many more.

He expressed regret about many of the deaths he had helped arrange. Not because of any compunction about the snuffed-out lives, but because he ultimately realized his mob bosses had concocted allegations against those victims just as they had against him. But regret wasn't the same as guilt.

He expressed more remorse about having once shot a German shepherd guarding a warehouse he was robbing than about the man he had helped bludgeon to death in a vicious assault in a Queens bagel bakery.

Death came with the territory mobsters inhabited, he firmly believed. "It's blood in, blood out," he said repeatedly of his chosen vocation. He had simply dodged his own bullet, he believed, in a bid to save the lives of his wife and family.

2

KENT AVENUE

When he took the stand in court as a government witness, Al D'Arco was asked how he became involved in the mob in the first place.

"Well, it was always around my neighborhood, in my family," he began. Then he paused and offered a notion he'd been playing around with in his head. It was a kind of mob poetry.

"It's like you're in the forest," he said. "The neighborhood is the forest and all the trees in it, well, a lot of the trees, were organized-crime men. It was a way of life."

"Objection for relevance," immediately barked the lawyer for the mobster on trial.

"I'll allow it," said the judge, who didn't get to hear much poetry in his job.

The forest was north Brooklyn, the neighborhoods surrounding the old Navy Yard. In the 1940s, when Al D'Arco was growing up and as America rushed into and out of a world war, the yard was a roaring industrial engine. At its peak, more than seventy thousand workers, armed with rivet guns, torches, and lathes, assembled the nation's ships of war on piers jutting into Wallabout Bay off the East River.

At shift change, those workers poured out onto Flushing

Avenue. They took throats parched from heat and grit into the taverns lining the streets. Crap games sprouted in every doorway. For those whose luck ran bad, men in overcoats and black fedoras, men who didn't go to work every day in the plants, were ready with cash for quick loans. The men in hats walked in and out of storefronts that had windows opaque with whitewash. Inside, operators worked phones not listed with the telephone company taking bets from around the city. It was a small empire of crime and it required its own small army to run it.

The Navy Street Gang, as the tabloid papers dubbed the crew controlling those streets, earned its first headlines in the late twenties. On trial for the shooting deaths of two men gunned down at the corner of Johnson and Navy Streets, "Tony the Shoe Maker" sat confidently in the dock. Witnesses against him suddenly remembered nothing. Didn't he recall, a witness named "Buffalo Mike" was asked by a prosecutor, telling a grand jury about his initiation into the secret society called the Camorra? How his initiator had slit open a vein in his arm and sucked a small taste of blood from the wound? How he had explained that this was the "Brotherhood of the Blood"?

"*Wasn't that your testimony*?" commanded the prosecutor. "I can't remember," said Buffalo Mike. The next day's newspapers explained his forgetfulness: a spectator in the gallery had silently drawn an index finger across his throat, the Camorra death threat.

That was one tale Al D'Arco heard as a boy. There were many others. Big shots in the gang included the Lauritano brothers, who ran a café and pastry shop on Navy Street. For special customers they also served assassination. Murder could be arranged for as little as $10, more if it involved travel, which the brothers did often, leaving a trail of more than two dozen bodies behind. They were particularly effective during a civil war that raged between the Naples-based Camorra organization and the Sicilian Mafia, two factions vying to take over from those who invoked the dreaded Black Hand.

Despite their lethal activities, the brothers had powerful

connections. Authorities had a difficult time putting them away. Convicted of murder, Leopoldo Lauritano inexplicably won early parole. Re-indicted on a new murder charge, a judge dismissed the case. Lauritano went back to his café.

The brothers were friendly with the D'Arco family, especially with Al's grandfather, who received special respect. The grandparents often brought little Al to the pastry shop. "Take this, Sonny," said the man in an apron behind the counter, handing him a creamy confection. Such nice people, said his grandparents.

Everyone called him Sonny.

"I was born in 1932; it was the Depression. My family listened to Al Jolson on the radio. He sang this song everyone loved, 'Sonny Boy.'

> " 'Climb up on my knee, Sonny Boy,
> Though you're only three, Sonny Boy.' "

The name on his baptismal certificate was Alfonso. Joseph and Anna D'Arco named their first child after Joseph's father. There were a lot of Als around. In addition to the grandfather, who lived with the family, there was an uncle of the same name. The baptism was held at St. Michael's, then a little storefront church off Myrtle Avenue. The elderly priest had performed the same rites thirty-three years earlier for yet another baby named Al, another gangster-to-be born just down the block. That innocent child, washed in the blood of the lamb as parents and godparents rejected sin and the prince of darkness, was baptized Alphonse Capone.

Sonny's own godparents didn't last long. His father's teenaged sister, Jenny, stood proudly as godmother at his baptism. She was one of seventeen children in the family. By the time Al was born only ten had survived. The rest, including a pair of twins, perished to the ailments of poverty.

"My aunt Jenny gave me a little bank when I was a baby. It was like a little safe with a dollar sign on it and a slot for coins. I treasured it, still got it with me." But he never got to know her. Within a year, Jenny was dead of pneumonia and heart problems. She was seventeen. "Those days, you got pneumonia, you died."

His godfather, a family friend named Arrigo, succumbed to a different neighborhood disease. Arrigo was a barber whose shop was in the Brooklyn Paramount Theatre building on Flatbush Avenue. A sideline there was bookmaking. A few months after little Alfonso's baptism, a dispute arose. Arrigo was shot and killed.

The family grieved but still needed a godfather, someone who could look out for baby Sonny should some similar fate befall Joseph. They turned to Anna D'Arco's eighteen-year-old brother, Leo. Uncle Leo was doomed as well, but he lived just long enough to figure in an early memory for his godson.

It was just before Thanksgiving. Uncle Leo was ill, stretched out in the single bedroom in a crowded railroad flat. Sonny, three years old, stood in the small living room, staring at the family's pride, a Stromberg Carlson radio. It was beautiful and enormous, made of brown curved Bakelite. Sonny clicked the switch to watch the lights twinkle on. He fiddled with the dials. The gigantic sound made him jump.

His grandmother came running. "She said, 'Don't you see your uncle's sick? What's the matter with you?' She's pulling me by the ear away from the radio."

Uncle Leo died Thanksgiving Day. "He'd bought this nice duck for the family to have for Thanksgiving dinner. Shows you how superstition works: we never had duck after that."

The family lived in a walk-up tenement on Apollo Street in north Brooklyn's Greenpoint when Sonny was born. The extended family—parents, grandparents, a couple of uncles and aunts—moved often for the same reason as many Depression families: landlords offered a month or two of free rent with a new lease. They squeezed into a series of floor-through apartments on North Oxford Street, then North Elliott Place near the Navy Yard.

The family stopped moving in 1940. Sonny's aunt and

grandparents chipped in to buy a building from a neighborhood physician, Dr. John McCabe. They paid $4,000 for the four-story redbrick house with a high stoop at 961 Kent Avenue between DeKalb and Willoughby Avenues. Dr. McCabe had used the four floors for both office and residence, living there in sprawling luxury with only his wife, his son, and a maid.

The D'Arco clan filled every square foot. On the ground floor lived Al's father's parents with two of their younger children. The parlor floor housed his cousin Gino Crisci, who was in the upholstery business, and his family. The third floor held a great-aunt, ZiCarolina, her husband, Don Ottaviano DeCaro, and a daughter. They were Italians by way of Marseille, France. Most impressive for nine-year-old Sonny was the little nickel-plated .38-caliber pistol that Otto DeCaro carried in his pocket. He went nowhere without it.

On the top floor lived Sonny's family and his mother's parents. There were two sisters now as well: Leona and Maryann. They slept in the back with their parents. Sonny slept in the front room, which doubled as his grandparents' bedroom. His own bed was a foldaway cot. "My grandmother called it a *branda*. At night, my grandmother would put a blanket over it. In the morning, we'd fold it up and put it away."

He called her "*Nonna*"—Grandmother. She spoke only the Calabrese dialect of her birthplace. That was the language spoken whenever she was in the room. The boy and his Nonna were close. "Your Nonna really loves you," other family members would tease him.

She was the first to warn him about the menacing trees in the forest around them: "*Attenzione della Mano Nera*," she told him with a shaking finger. "She'd tell me that all the time. If I wasn't a good boy, the Black Hand would get me."

The blocks surrounding the Navy Yard were lined with flophouses, tenements, diners, pawnshops, and bars, all the basic amenities for those living life on the margins. The area was originally called Irish Town; Italians began arriving in large numbers just before World War I. Those lucky enough to have work labored at tough, low-wage occupations. They were longshoremen, truck drivers, factory hands, clerks, messengers, floor girls, and dressmakers.

The Italians included a large contingent of families from Bari, the province near the heel of southern Italy's boot. Barese men were famed as the city's ice and coal delivery workers, trooping up and down steep tenement stairs with a yoke across their shoulders carrying heavy containers. "They used to have these contests for cash prizes, see who could carry a five-gallon can of kerosene and a bin with coal on each shoulder. They'd race each other up and down the stairs. They were crazy, but strong as oxen, all of them."

Beneath the rumbling elevated train on Myrtle Avenue, vendors sold fruits and vegetables from pushcarts. The Navy Street Gang exacted a tax on each one. "You'd see the old-timers in their big black hats waddling down the street, the guys from Italy, shaking down the pushcarts. They'd sound real friendly. '*Come sta? Sta bene?*' Then they put three fingers against their chest, which meant gimme three dollars or else."

A notorious shakedown artist was Manarillo—the little sailor. "He was like a fop, a little fat guy, all fancy with a carnation in his coat and these little pince-nez glasses. There was a pizzeria guy opened up near Vanderbilt and Myrtle. He wouldn't pay Manarillo. And he got a bomb in his place. It didn't go off, but he got the message."

It was a neighborhood of grinding poverty, despite the wartime employment boom spilling over from the Navy Yard. Across the street from Casa D'Arco on Kent Avenue was a massive seven-story manufacturing plant. Among its tenants was Selchow and Righter, the board game company that manufactured Parcheesi. From his window, Sonny watched the owner's wife visit the factory. He thought of her as a character in one of her own board games. "She came in this long green limousine, wearing fancy green dresses, green coats, green hats. We called her 'Mrs. Green.'"

The plant also housed a lingerie manufacturer, a dress-

maker, and a furniture company. When the war began, it
switched to making wooden frames for army trucks. All night
long, the machines blared, the sounds serenading Sonny as
he lay on his *branda*. "*Eooowwwrr, eeoowwr*, you'd hear the
saws going. Never stopped. Drove my grandmother crazy."

Yet the saws provided a vital harvest for families on the
block. Sonny's job was to collect wood to fuel the furnace in
the basement, to keep it stoked and the building warm.
"They'd shout to me, 'Go down, Sonny, bank the stove!'" The
closest and richest source of wood was the lumber scraps from
the factory across the street. He'd fill a barrel, wrestle it up
the street, and dump it into the cellar. There was fierce competition. "I had to fight the Irish kids down the block for the
wood. Sometimes their mothers, too. Everyone wanted it for
their stoves." When the factory supply was exhausted he'd rise
at 5 a.m. with his mother and head for the Navy Yard, pounc-
ing on whatever scraps they found.

There was no complaining allowed. Sonny's father insisted
they'd never had it so good. He was born Giuseppe D'Arco
in the town of Cava dei Terreni, near Salerno on southern
Italy's western coast. Families there scratched a meager living out of the hillsides. "My father talked about having rock
soup when he was little. I always thought he was kidding.
Then I found out they really did eat it. When they had nothing else, they'd put the rocks in the pot with whatever vegetables they had, for the minerals."

Giuseppe arrived in New York in April 1914 at the age of
five aboard the SS *Verona*, a steamship out of Naples packed
with a thousand other mostly Italian immigrants traveling
third-class steerage. Giuseppe's father had emigrated to the
U.S. a year earlier, preparing a home for the family in a tenement on Park Avenue, a desolately poor stretch a block from
the Navy Yard. The family lived just a few doors down from
where that other Al was born, Capone.

Giuseppe D'Arco arrived with his mother; a three-year-
old little brother, Luigi; and an uncle and an aunt. Immigration forms called for identifying any immigrants who arrived

with less than $50. The manifest of passengers arriving on the *Verona* showed that Giuseppe's mother, Anna Abate, could give account of only the $40 she had in her purse.

The entire family worked. Within a year, Giuseppe, renamed "Joe" in the New World, was plying the streets of Manhattan's financial center, selling shoeshines for a nickel. He knew it was a job for the destitute. Boarding the trolley car, he'd wrap his shine box in newspaper so riders wouldn't spot it. "My father didn't like to talk about it. But he kept the box. I had it till a few years ago. You could see where it said 'Five Cents' scratched into the wood."

In between shines, Joe D'Arco earned money prizefighting. "He was a club fighter, fought bare-knuckles. He was strong, built like a Neanderthal, had this big barrel chest, huge hands. He'd take soda bottles, pop the tops with a spoon, send them flying."

He fought for the Brooklyn Navy Yard Club. Bouts were held twice a week against other clubs from south Brooklyn and Coney Island. The average purse was $25. "It would be $15 for my father if he won, $5 for the club, $5 for the manager. My father won most of his fights. He'd knock them out."

In New York, Joe's father, the first Alfonso, started a small fabric-dyeing business, or, as the family proudly pronounced it, a "biz-a-ness." By the time the D'Arcos became landed gentry with a home of their own on hardscrabble Kent Avenue, Joe D'Arco and younger brother Luigi—now Louis—were running the little firm. They dyed thread and skeins of cotton for the many clothing jobbers dotting north Brooklyn. It was hot, dangerous, and noxious work. Sonny hated it.

"It would be a hundred-something degrees everyday in there. You had to have boards on the floor so you didn't walk on the ground. When they spilled hot water from the vats, it would go under the boards to run to the sewer. That hot water had sulfuric acid and everything else in it from all the dyes."

Joe D'Arco rented space for the plant on Adelphi Street near the Navy Yard. Adept at machinery and construction, Joe kept the plant going. Louis was expert at matching colors. "My uncle would make the proper mixture of the chemicals. If you gave him a piece of red thread, he could match it. The colors had to be the same because they used that to sew the dresses."

Sonny was pressed into duty as well, before and after school. "I'd be threading these giant spools right next to some open barrel of caustic soda or hydrogen cyanide, the stuff they used to bleach and dye the threads. That stuff will kill you."

Eventually, it did kill Uncle Louis, who died in his early fifties. "It was from the dye. It got in his blood. It's worse than cancer. He used to break out in rashes all over his body."

It was a fate Sonny vowed to avoid. "I knew I wasn't going to starve to death, and I wasn't going to work in no fuckin' dye house like killed my uncle either."

More enticing were the men he saw coming and going from the cellar beneath the plant. To help make the rent, Joe D'Arco rented the space to a local bookmaker. The operation was under the auspices of a racketeer named Vincent Alo, who had grown up with Sonny's dad. Known as Jimmy Blue Eyes, Alo was a young mobster on the rise: he later gained mob fame helping to run gambling operations in Florida, Cuba, and Puerto Rico.

Also stopping by regularly to attend to the action was a dapper gent named Anthony Ricci. "They called him Tony Goebels. A big gangster back then, close to the Chicago Outfit. He'd pull up in a big black Cadillac. Everyone treated him like royalty, and he looked like it."

The regal gangster took a liking to the little boy upstairs in the dye shop, tossing him quarters, asking him to pick up sandwiches and coffee from the deli on the corner. Sonny watched him, fascinated. "The guys downstairs started kidding him about me. They called me his *napoti,* his nephew."

The father watched the son watching the gangsters. Joe D'Arco grew up in the same forest but managed to avoid the clutches of the trees. He simply wasn't interested. "He was legitimate. He just wanted to make a living." It didn't hurt that his father carried himself like a tough guy, wearing a look suggesting that those who crossed him would do so at their peril.

"He had these steel-gray eyes, looked right through you. My friends took him for a cop when he came around. They'd tell me, 'Look out, the bulls are looking for you.'"

Decades later, sitting far away in his self-imposed exile from the Brooklyn streets, Al D'Arco went to the movies to see a picture called *Road to Perdition*, a film about gangsters in the 1930s. He looked at the Tom Hanks character with his fierce visage, long black coat, and fedora pulled down over his eyes. "That's my father!" he said aloud in the theater.

Sonny went to the movies often as a child, usually with his mother's father, Luigi, who enjoyed westerns. Grandfather and grandson would ride the trolley down to Flatbush Avenue. They'd park themselves in the balcony of the cavernous Subway Theater for a double or triple feature. The audience was filled with men like his grandfather, older Italians puffing away on de Nobili and Parodi cigars, the strong-smelling cheroots favored by their countrymen.

"We'd watch three shoot-em-ups, back-to-back. You couldn't even breathe in there from the cigar smoke. But we had a good time."

Most of the audience, Sonny noticed, rooted for the bad guys.

His own favorite was James Cagney. He sat through repeat showings of *Angels with Dirty Faces* and *The Roaring Twenties*, stories of tough, clever street urchins who graduate into big-shot gangsters. To Sonny, it sounded like a plan. He developed his own little Cagney routine, imitating the wiseguy corner-of-the-mouth snarl. He did the act often to the delight of friends and family.

At the dinner table, there were intriguing morsels. His aunt Mildred, his father's sister, worked in a dress factory. She would talk about her boss, a grand and famous man named Mr. Luchese. Sometimes she'd call him "Three Finger Brown." When she said it, Sonny giggled and the grown-ups looked nervous. She had the job because of a cousin named Joseph Schiavo who also owned a share in the factory. Cousin Joseph and Mr. Brown were in the same "family," she said. Sonny wondered what she meant. Was he related to Three Finger Brown?

Other hints about life on the far side of the law came from the steady stream of relatives who visited the house on Kent Avenue. Cousins, great-aunts, uncles, and in-laws arrived from Newark, Boston, Pittsburgh, and Chicago, the greater diaspora of southern Italian immigration. Some of the relatives, he noticed, were treated with unusual respect. "You could tell there was something special about them. The way everybody waited for them to talk, brought them their coffees."

From Somerville, Massachusetts, came cousin Angelo Spero with his heavyset wife and their pampered young son, arriving in a late-model car and expensive clothes. Cousin Angelo had a successful wholesale grocery business. He was also devoutly religious. "Every time he came, we had to wait an hour before we ate because he'd have this long prayer first." But he kept his religion carefully separated from his business. Sonny picked up from family whispers that his cousin's good fortune stemmed less from commercial expertise than from his active bootlegging operation during Prohibition and the stolen goods filling his warehouses.

Equally high regard was accorded a cousin on his mother's side of the family named Joseph Sica from Pittsburgh. The same age as Sonny's father, Sica was already a man of means, pulling up on humble Kent Avenue in a bright blue Cadillac.

"He wore this nice jacket with big black buttons on the sleeves. Later I find out they were painted black. Underneath they were real gold. My cousin Joe Sica was the number two in the Pittsburgh mob and him and his boss had the same buttons on their jackets, in case they had to go on the lam."

He watched Sica seated in his great-aunt's parlor, sipping coffee, the family clustered around. "He's talking about someone they all knew who had been killed. And he says this thing I always remember: 'When you come right down to it,' he says, 'the only thing you can expect from this life is here to-day, gone tomorrow.' "

It was something he thought about sometimes at night, stretched out on his folding cot. He'd stare at the long shadows on the ceiling as the streetlights shone through the wooden venetian blinds. "I'd lie there, look at those shadows, and think how they looked just like prison bars and wonder what it would be like to be in prison."

Reminders of how easy it would be to get there were right outside. "On the corner at DeKalb Avenue was this bar, Archie's Tavern. I could see it from my window. All the guys from the Navy Yard and the docks would go there. Sometimes when they were drunk, I'd hear them singing and sometimes I'd hear fights and gunshots."

One night when voices rose especially loud he looked out his window and saw two men outside on the sidewalk, nose-to-nose. He recognized one of them as a cousin on his mother's side, a longshoreman named Toddo. He was pointing his finger at an Irishman named Frankie Clark. "Frankie was a little guy but a big hoodlum. He always wore the same clothes, a brown fedora with a green band, a brown suit, and a green tie. My cousin Toddo is teasing him, saying how come he's always wearing that dirty old hat and that puke green tie. And Frankie Clark just pulls back his coat and shows a pistol. 'You guinea bastard,' he says, 'I'll buy and sell you five hundred thousand fuckin' times.' My cousin Toddo just walks away."

There were different lessons taught in school. He started at PS 67 on St. Edwards Street. When the family moved to Kent Avenue Sonny was switched to St. Patrick's Academy, a Catholic parochial school just a block away from home. The school was in a stately three-story brick building, its name chiseled into the parapet. Next door on the corner of Willoughby Avenue was the Romanesque church with a bell tower where his grandmother attended early mass every morning at 6:30, often tugging her grandson along with her.

Nonna also made sure young Sonny said his prayers

every night. The habit stuck with him all through his years, even at the end of days spent plotting murder. "I always said my prayers, every day. It's how I was taught."

Prayer was a major part of the drill at St. Patrick's Academy as well. Instruction there was provided by Irish Christian Brothers who cut fearful figures in their monk's robes. His name was spelled incorrectly, the monks quickly decided. "Alfonso" became Alphonse in the books at St. Patrick's.

The monks were fierce believers in the power of physical discipline to reinforce the need for learning. "They had these bamboo sticks they carried. You said something they didn't like, it was stick your hand·out, palm up, whack you with that bamboo. Stung like a bastard. If you flinched, they made you turn your hand over, gave you another shot on your knuckles."

For those students who still fell short, there was the wastebasket. "They'd put you right in the metal basket, your legs hanging out, the dunce cap on your head. You sit there long enough, it cuts off the circulation in your legs."

Girls were taught by the Sisters of Mercy from the convent next to the church. The nuns were equally strict. Sonny's sister Leona, a few grades behind him, ran afoul of a teacher and received a slap with a strap. "The strap had this little button and it caught my sister in the eye. So Leona smacked the nun right back. She got thrown out of school for that. Had to go to public school."

One of the monks stalked past Sonny's home every day. "I'd be at the window, watching him. He'd walk by straight as a statue. He had this white, white hair, the ropes on his robe hanging down, this big cape thrown around him. He had these spooky eyes, looked like a ghost. Every time he's walking by, he'd look up, spot me at the window. I'd try to duck but he'd always catch me. Scare me half to death."

Yet some parts of school were to his liking. He surprised himself to find he was a good speller. He enjoyed sounding out the words, figuring them out letter by letter. Already fluent in the Calabrese dialect he spoke at home with his Nonna, he mastered the basic rules of English. He excelled at writing as well, his script flowing smoothly across the pages.

At home, he supplemented his lessons with a chemistry set, a gift from a Jewish garment-shop owner who was a client of his father's. "I'd be mixing these things up in vials, potassium nitrate, whatever I could concoct. My father would be standing there watching. He'd call me 'professor.' He loved to break my balls."

He looked somewhat professorial. At the age of nine, Sonny was prescribed glasses. "I always had trouble with my eyes, an astigmatism. My mother took me to an eye specialist in the Albee Building downtown. He gave me exercises for the eye muscles. Look this way, look that way." Even here, gangland connections followed. The same doctor, he learned with interest, was treating Joe Bonanno, the Mafia dignitary who lived up DeKalb Avenue in Bushwick.

He wasn't a big boy. He eventually topped out at five foot seven. But he was wiry and he made up with muscle what he lacked in height, hitting a punching bag and doing calisthenics, trying to bulk up like his tough-guy father.

And his chief extracurricular activities emphasized brawn over brains. "Back then I was always in trouble."

He ran with a gang of friends in the neighborhood, some of them fellow students at St. Patrick's, others who had already dropped out of school. There was his best friend, Tommy Ryan, from Classon Avenue, and Junior D'Urso, whose father was a racketeer in Joe Bonanno's outfit. Willie Albergo was from Bari, his dad one of the neighborhood's many ice haulers. The Luca brothers, Blackie and Gerald, lived a block over.

Another pal, Nicodemus, was known for his brute strength, always winning the fights that broke out constantly among the friends. Nicodemus's father worked in the old Wallabout fruit and vegetable market along Flushing Avenue before an expanding Navy Yard swallowed it during the war. The father put his son's broad shoulders to work at the age of twelve, unloading freight cars at the market.

"Nicodemus is down there working around the clock while his dad is sitting in Rocco's grocery store on Kosciuszko Street, drinking wine and playing cards. One day Nicky comes up from the market, tells his father he's sick. He's pissing blood he's been working so hard. His father wore a fedora, had these gold teeth. He starts yelling at his son to get back to work. Then he picks up an iron bar and hits him with it. We're standing there watching this, can't believe it. Nicky just takes it. So I grabbed the bar out of his dad's hand and heaved it at him. I missed. It went through the window of the barber shop next door. I had to pay for the window, but I didn't care."

The little gang clung together, seizing any opportunity to flex their muscles, to make a few dollars, or simply to make mischief.

In the rear yards of the factories lining the nearby side streets were long-abandoned wooden stables. The boys first used them as hangouts, then recognized their moneymaking potential.

"Across from St. Patrick's were these six-story tenements. They were mostly Irish families in there and all they had for heat was stoves in the apartments, so they always needed lots of wood. We'd break up the stables, selling the wood to them for twenty-five cents for two bushels. We chopped those stables right down to the ground."

The factories hired guards to keep the neighborhood riffraff away. But the boys easily slipped past, taunting them as they ran.

Prowling through a three-story abandoned building on a late-summer day, Sonny and his pal Willie Albergo spotted a pear tree in the backyard. When they went out to grab the ripe fruit, a watchman for the factory next door began shouting at them.

"This Italian guy comes running at us, swinging a big two-by-four. We ran back into the building." The avenging security guard chased after them as the boys raced upstairs. The guard cornered them on the top floor. "He's still swinging at me, trying to brain me. I pick up this old chair to fend him off. I'm like a lion tamer. But he won't quit." Behind him, Willie was at the window. "Jump!" Willie yelled as he leaped. "I went out right after him. Three floors down. Hit my chin, bit through my tongue. My legs felt like they were paralyzed. I'm crawling away, this crazy bastard is up there heaving things at us, still yelling."

His first foray into crime was at the factory across the street from his house. "I was twelve years old, scheming how to make money. I watched all the workers going into the furniture factory. They had money in their pockets, I figured, so all I had to do was slip into the locker room while they were working. I was in and out, no problem. I got about ten bucks and I took all my friends to Coney Island. We were gone the whole day. We rode the Steeplechase, the merry-go-round."

When he got home his father was seated on the stoop waiting for him. "I saw him and I froze. He says, 'Get over here.' I said, 'No!' I took off. He came flying off the stoop and caught me. He was *fast*. I got my ass kicked all the way to the house. He says, 'You robbed the factory!' I said, 'What are you talking about?' He says, 'People saw you go in there.' I stuck to my story. 'What are you talking about?' I never admitted it. For years after that, my father would try to slip it in when he thought I didn't care anymore. 'You robbed the factory that time, didn't you?' I'd say the same thing. 'What are you talking about?' It drove him nuts."

He didn't always get away with it. Dispatched by his father one day on a shopping errand, Sonny ran into his pals, who were just squaring off for combat with a rival gang. "I had this short little billy club I'd been carrying. My cousin Gino who lived with us had given it to me. I pulled it out and was whacking away at these kids when the cops showed up." Sonny tossed the billy club and ran. When the cops caught up to him, one of them had retrieved the club. "This is yours, right?" said a heavyset detective.

"No, I never saw it before," answered Sonny. The detective rammed the short club into Sonny's stomach. He bent over, retching. "Yeah you did," the cop said. "It's yours. We saw you toss it."

He was handcuffed and thrown into the back of the detective's car. The cop drove toward the Eighty-Eighth Precinct, a fortresslike building topped by a tall brick turret a couple of blocks away on the corner of Classon and DeKalb Avenues.

Outside the precinct, the detective pulled over to the curb. He leaned over the front seat and slammed Sonny in the face with his fist. Then he hit him again. "He's hitting me over and over and I was spitting blood." Then the detective climbed into the backseat. Sonny grimaced, expecting further beating. Instead, the detective took off the handcuffs and pushed him out the door. "Get the hell out of here," he said.

Sonny stumbled away. "I think he didn't pinch me because he didn't want to have to explain why he'd given this thirteen-year-old kid such a beating."

At home, Sonny's father stared at his son's battered face. "I said, 'Oh, I was getting you the razors and this big fight with all these kids started.' I don't think he believed that either, but he didn't push me."

Nonna and his mother looked at him and shook their heads. In Italian, Nonna lamented: "My dear son, if you don't stop what you're doing you're going to wind up in the electric chair."

He did have one positive interest. It was a notion that had begun when he was little and had steadily grown, a dream that soared far beyond the streets of north Brooklyn.

He wanted to fly. And he wanted to build the airplanes he'd fly in. The dream started with a bird's-eye view of Brooklyn. A friend of his father's in the Army Air Force had been made a captain. One day the friend came by in his glittering uniform, asking Joe D'Arco if he and his son would like to take a ride out to the air base at Floyd Bennett Field in the borough's southeast corner, on Jamaica Bay. Who knows, they might even take a spin in a plane. A few hours later, Sonny was perched at his father's side looking out the window of a tiny Piper Cub. He was all of five years old. He'd barely traveled in a car more than a few times and here he was in an airplane. "I remember it like it was yesterday. We're in this little plane, flying over the water, over Coney Island, up so high I couldn't believe it, gliding around."

Visions of airplanes began fueling his fantasies. He'd sit in his classes at St. Patrick's sketching them, trying to get the details of a wing or a tail fin just right. "I'd be drawing a plane, and—bonk!—the teacher would smack me. I didn't care."

At home, he got his grandmother to buy him balsa-wood model planes, powered by wind-up rubber bands. "I'd work on them for hours, glue all the different colored tissue paper on them."

Added fuel came from one of his father's brothers, Philip, who was drafted into the Army. The uncle returned from basic training with pictures of the silhouettes used to spot enemy aircraft. Sonny stood on the roof on Kent Avenue, silhouette sketches in hand, watching the planes above float past.

As luck would have it, New York City had a special school for boys with dreams like his. The Manhattan High School of Aviation Trades was located on East Sixty-Third Street. Students studied aeronautics, mechanics, electrical wiring, carpentry, and metal fabrication, everything they might need for a career in aviation.

"So that's where I applied, of course. I was all set. I knew the curriculum, what I would study. You got to go in ninth grade, and soon as I could I went down and handed in the application."

He was rejected. Not for poor grades, but because, by the rules of the city's board of education, he fell outside the zone from which Aviation drew its students. The rules made no sense to a fourteen-year-old boy.

Flying was his first legitimate ambition. And his last. Telling the story a lifetime later, he pounded the arm of a wing-chair in frustration. "Explain this to me: My friend Blackie Luca lived one block away from me—*one block*—and he got to go. But I can't? These were supposed to be educated people? Who made these rules? What for?"

A friend of the family, a local doctor, tried to pull some strings. The answer was still no.

"They had me zoned to go to Haaren High School. It's all the way on the West Side in the city, up by Columbus Circle. They said I was supposed to learn radio. I never wanted to learn radio."

He showed up for a few classes and then stopped attending altogether. His parents found out when a truant officer knocked on the door on a spring Sunday in 1947.

"My father gave me a hard time. He says, 'You gotta go to school.' He hounded me. Said I had to learn a trade. So I said, okay, I want to take pictures. I don't know where it came from. I just said it. I'd heard about this school, the New York School of Photography. It cost $15 a month. My father paid and I went for about a month. That was it."

The family had limited experience with education. His father's own schooling had ended in the eighth grade; his mother hadn't made it that far. "My father wanted me to help build the biz-a-ness, so I'd take it over. That's the way it worked. Like his father started the dye house, then my father took it over. He thought if I went to school I'd make it bigger."

But there was little support for educational ambition in the house on Kent Avenue. His Nonna could neither read nor write. Nor could Uncle Otto downstairs, or his aunt Carolina. None of them saw themselves as worse off for their lack of schooling. Nonna viewed it as a waste of time. "My grandmother says, 'Get a job. *Fangul* the school.' In other words, screw it. Never mind the book learning. The old-timers didn't believe in school. A trade for them was a good shoemaker, a good carpenter, a good painter—that's what counted."

He didn't take much convincing. If he couldn't go to aviation school, Sonny decided, then he would pursue life on the streets. He'd rub up against those trees in the forest he had admired mostly from afar.

He was smart, fast, and strong, and the neighborhood's criminal masters viewed him as a ripe potential recruit for their schemes. One of them was the proprietor of a candy store named Dominick Citera. "Dom Citera was like a Fagin. He'd get kids to do crimes for him, send them out to steal, then give them just a little piece of what they took. Very sneaky, greedy guy."

The candy-store schemer dispatched Sonny and his friends to break into the neighborhood dress factories. But there were usually slim pickings. "The garment shops were all owned by these smart Jewish guys. They never left anything out to steal after they closed up shop. You were lucky to find a dead moth in a drawer in those places."

No burglary was too small. Citera directed his youthful bandits to Cascade Linens on Myrtle Avenue when he heard that a new load of sheets had been received. "He had us lifting crates of brand-new sheets. He'd give us fifty cents apiece when we brought them in. What a fucking sport. He's selling them for hundreds of dollars."

After Sonny dropped out of school, the candy-store operator directed him and his friend Tommy Ryan to a factory at the northern end of Greenpoint. The company manufactured a special and expensive form of graphite used in machinery, carefully packed in boxes inside the plant. "He says, 'You go there, it's easy. You grab these boxes. They're worth a lot of money.'" Citera pulled out a .38 snub-nosed revolver and pushed it into Sonny's hand. "You take this, just in case," he said.

Sonny and Tommy Ryan set out at night for the factory. They had made it past the first gate and were prying open another door when a watchman spotted them. They ran out to the street, the watchman on their heels. "I'm running for all I'm worth along this brick wall. All of a sudden, *peeoow*, this bullet hits the brick right over my head. I look over my shoulder and the guard's shooting at us. I couldn't believe it. So I duck around the corner, pull the .38 out of my pocket, and start shooting back. The guard dives to the ground." It was a satisfying feeling. The failed robbers jumped on a trolley car and got away.

It was the first time he'd been shot at, and one of the only times in a long criminal career that he ever fired a gun at anyone. He acted like it was no big deal.

He was coming to realize that the local gangsters were checking him out, seeing if he measured up to their standards. Part of the qualifying test, he knew, was to see if he balked at tough assignments.

One such exam came from a neighborhood old-timer, the owner of the Pastime Pool Hall on DeKalb Avenue. Sonny knew him only as "Pop," a veteran of the old Navy Street mob who handled stolen goods and helped set up robberies. "He looked like a walrus, had a big drooping mustache, and went about three hundred pounds." The walrus was a bit of a dandy. He spent his days perched on a stool in the back of the pool hall wearing a flat-topped straw boater, a white jacket, and black-and-white saddle shoes.

One day he pulled Sonny aside to tell him he had a job for him. "Your friend Tommy Ryan is going to come by soon," the dandy said in Italian. "When he comes I want you to punch him out real good. Then you go away and don't come around for a while." He handed Sonny a different kind of weapon, a pair of heavy brass knuckles. "You hit him hard with these," Pop said. "*Fatto na buona jobba*." Do a good job.

Sonny took the brass knuckles and sat down on a bench outside the pool hall. He wasn't reluctant to fight his pal Tommy Ryan. The friends fought often. But they remained friends. Brass knuckles, however, were for serious damage, something he didn't want to inflict. On the other hand, if he faked it, pulling his punch, the walrus in the straw boater inside would know it. Word would circulate in the neighborhood. He imagined himself blackballed in the local hangouts.

He was still considering his options when Tommy Ryan came strolling up. Tommy was greeting him when Sonny stood up, pushed the knuckles into his fist, and slugged his friend on the side of the head as hard as he could. Tommy fell back against the wall and slipped down. His eyes were wide open but he was unconscious. He was out cold. Sonny quickly walked away, his friend sprawled on the sidewalk.

He later learned the reason for his assignment. The pool hall owner had paid Tommy Ryan for a load of stolen goods, but Tommy had sold part of the load to someone else. The brass knuckle beating was the payback, a revenge made sweeter because Pops had gotten Tommy's best pal to deliver it.

Sonny had passed another milestone: asked to choose between his budding gangster credentials and his loyalty to a friend, he'd chosen the mob. It was a choice he confronted repeatedly over his career. He chose the wiseguys every time.

He tried to patch things up with his friend, but things were never the same between them. Tommy Ryan later spiraled downward into drug addiction, dying at a young age. Sonny often thought about the day he'd coldcocked Tommy outside Pop's pool room. It was one of the few events he admitted he wished he'd handled differently. "It is one of my biggest regrets to this day."

Every Sunday afternoon, a steady line of men filed into the State Theater on DeKalb Avenue near Franklin, the neighborhood's biggest movie house. The pictures weren't running. The theater was closed on Sundays. Instead, the theater's manager, Blackie Garafalo, hosted a major crap game in the balcony hallway. Any given Sunday, thousands of dollars were strewn across the floor as men praying for the help of Lady Luck tossed dice against the wall.

The game was run under the auspices of a pair of up-and-coming local hoods. One was Armando Bartolillo, who had already demonstrated his own remarkable good luck. Arrested in connection with the murder of a state trooper who had pulled over the stolen car he and a pal were driving in 1946, Bartolillo managed to get off with a plea to possession of stolen property.

Bartolillo's partner—Sonny knew him only as "Larry"— wasn't as lucky. One Sunday, someone in the game threw weighted dice. The game was challenged and the crooked dice were spotted. "Larry was gone the next day. He disappeared. There's no cheating in organized-crime crap games. You can have razzle-dazzle games, where you have con artists who rent a room and bring suckers up to gamble. But games like this when there's wiseguys playing? Not allowed. And Larry was responsible for that. So he was just gone."

It was another lesson learned. Bartolillo, however, was allowed to continue running local gambling. He took the eager young D'Arco under his wing.

Among the chores assigned to Sonny was to help with a numbers and bookmaking operation that Bartolillo ran out of a luncheonette across from the movie house. The card games were played in the back room. A row of pay phones were used for taking bets. "Customers were lined up. When it got too obvious, the cops would come in and raid the place. When they did, they'd make us walk this gauntlet. They'd be whaling away at us with their nightsticks. *Whap! Bing!* They'd hit you pretty good. By the time you got out the door you were half falling down."

After Sonny made it through the police gauntlet a few times, Bartolillo paid him the ultimate compliment. "You got the stuff, kid," he told him. "You've got the grit."

The gangsters' biggest complaint wasn't the police raids but having to make big payouts to occasionally lucky customers. "They had to pay. That was the rules. But if a guy hit the number big it threw the business off. They hated that worse than anything."

They would plot how to retrieve the money. One day, after a fortunate numbers client scored a $9,000 win, the gangsters summoned the kid with the grit. Sonny's instructions came from Louie the Butcher, one of Bartolillo's partners, who operated a meat shop down the block from the theater.

"He says to me, '*Sienta me*, listen up. Out there is a guy wearing a black overcoat. I am going to point him out to you. When he comes outta that door,'" Louie said, looking at the luncheonette down the street, "'I want you to watch him. You follow him and grab the money. Don't get caught.'" The butcher handed Sonny a .45 revolver. It felt huge in his hand. He stuffed it in his jacket pocket.

Sonny stationed himself on the sidewalk outside the luncheonette, waiting for Louie the Butcher to nod when the winner emerged. "Sure enough the guy comes out wearing this big black overcoat. Louie nods to me and I start following. First thing he does is head across the street right into the State Theater."

It was a weekday afternoon and the movie house was showing the matinee feature. The theater had just raised its price from a dime to eleven cents. "That was the big talk in the neighborhood. They raised it a penny." Sonny handed over his change and followed the man into the theater. Inside, after his eyes got used to the dark, he saw the winner. A fat woman was sitting next to him. Sonny sat down on the other side. "There was a shoot-em-up playing, which I figured was good for me. I take a minute to look around to spot the exit door which goes to an alleyway out to Franklin Avenue. That's my way out, I figure."

Sonny sat for a while fingering the pistol in his pocket. "Then I put the .45 in his side. I whisper to him, tough as I can, 'Give me the fucking money.' The cocksucker looks at me and starts hollering. Now the fat lady sees what's going on and she jumps up. She's screaming, 'Murder! Murder!' Son of a bitch. I don't know what to do, but I know I gotta get the dough."

Sonny slammed his victim with the pistol. "I hit him in the head. But he still don't give it up. So I'm tearing at his big coat now, hitting him with the other hand and telling him to give me the money." The woman beside continued to scream. "He's got a gun! He's got a gun!" Al finally managed to rip the money out of his coat pocket. "I hit him so many times I think it was just the fear holding him up."

The movie house was now in chaos, the audience stampeding for the exits. Sonny joined the throng. "I just run with the crowd. They were running so fast I'm lucky I didn't get trampled."

He ran down the alley to Franklin Avenue and into the butcher shop. Louie the Butcher led him to the back of the store and pointed down a cellar stairway. He told him to go downstairs and wait. Sonny sat in the dark, his heart pounding. After a few minutes, he was summoned back up. "Now give me the money," the butcher said. Sonny pulled the wad out of his pocket and handed it to him. In return, the butcher gave him an apron and gestured to the van used for deliveries that was parked outside. "You get in the back of the truck," Louis told him. "Anyone asks you anything, you don't know nothing. You work for me. That's all you know."

The butcher drove him out of the neighborhood. He handed Sonny $500. "Don't come around for a while," he was told.

It wasn't much for having risked an assault and armed robbery charge, but still more money than he could imagine. The money, however, wasn't the important part. "What counted for me was the respect. Like Armie said, 'You got the stuff, kid.'"

When he wasn't busy as a gangster in training, he worked with his father and uncle in the dye shop. His father insisted. "You got to work," he told his son. Actually, Sonny liked to work. "I always wanted to keep busy, be doing something, making a few bucks, whatever it was. I hated doing nothing, sitting around." But he still loathed the dye shop and the foul chemicals running under the floorboards. When an opportunity to both work and practice his gangster trade appeared, he grabbed it.

The chance came when Dom Citera was forced to go to prison and needed someone to run his candy store while he was away. "Dom Citera got caught with a load of swag and was sent up to Dannemora. He asks me to take over the shop for him."

Why not? he reasoned. He'd be running his own business. Make his family proud. He threw himself into the shop's operations, both legitimate and illegitimate.

He hired a friend from the neighborhood, a young Irish girl named Rita, to help run it. They stocked the shelves with candy, cigarettes, and magazines. On a rack out front, he sold the city's papers: the *Brooklyn Eagle*, the *Daily News*, the *New York Evening Post*, the *Mirror*, the *World-Telegram and Sun*, *Il Progresso*, the *Irish Echo*, the *Racing Form*.

Right away, he had a problem, one he hadn't anticipated: kids in the neighborhood, rascals very much like himself just a few years earlier, stole the coins customers left in the change bowl on the rack. Sonny was outraged. He was being robbed. "I'd stand in the corner of the door, try to spot them. If I caught them, I'd grab them, throw them right into the street. I didn't care if the DeKalb Avenue bus was coming down."

While he was defending nickels and dimes at the front of the shop, the store's real profits were being earned in the back room. There, two of his friends, Charlie Dima and Freddy "Momo" Venturino, ran dice and card games and took bets over the phone. Among the budding gangsters, Momo Venturino ranked highest. Momo was already hooked up with an authentic wiseguy, a wealthy and good-looking gambler named John Robilotto. Known as Johnny Roberts, Robilotto was a soldier under Albert Anastasia, the waterfront racketeer dubbed the "Lord High Executioner" of Murder Inc., and the undisputed crime boss of Brooklyn.

Johnny Roberts operated out of a clubhouse at St. Marks and Grand Avenues. Momo regularly reported there, sometimes accompanied by his envious neighborhood pals, who loitered outside on the sidewalk while Venturino conducted business inside with his crew chief. Johnny Roberts was one of the tallest trees in the forest. A key suspect in the murder of Willie Moretti, a top gangster whose mental problems had made him untrustworthy, Robilotto had beaten the rap. "We all looked up to Johnny Roberts. We all wanted to be like him."

Or at least to live like him. A few years later, shortly after Anastasia was famously gunned down in the barbershop at the Park Sheraton Hotel in Manhattan in 1957, Robilotto was also killed, his body dumped in the Brooklyn streets.

Shopkeeping wasn't for Sonny either, he decided. It wasn't as bad as his father's dye plant, but when his friends weren't around, he was immensely bored. To pass the time, he did calisthenics behind the counter. "I'd boost myself up, do lifts, dips, anything to keep myself going."

A little over a year after taking over the candy store, he'd had enough. "I got disgusted staying put. I hated being inside all the time. I wanted action."

The biggest action was the war in Korea. Sonny pored over the stories in the tabloids, reading them as he leaned against the counter in the candy store.

War fascinated him, the same way airplanes had. His father's brother Philip had landed at D-Day and fought his way across Europe. "He was like a big brother to me. We were always building things together in the backyard, making these chairs out of the scrap wood from the factories. Then he was drafted and we didn't see him till the end of the war."

When Philip returned he didn't talk much about what he'd seen and done. His uncle, once so carefree, was now quiet and somber. But Sonny listened in awe when one of his uncle's Army buddies, a gum-chewing sergeant from Georgia, visited the Kent Avenue house and regaled the family with tales of Philip's heroics. The sergeant produced a photo of his uncle clutching a machine gun on a field in France. He also had a Nazi flag he said Philip had captured. "Your uncle pulled this right down from the Reichstag," he told Sonny. His uncle just smiled. The flag went into a trunk in the basement. The story went deep into Sonny's memory bank.

So did other tales of military daring. A cousin, Toddo, his mother's sister's son, drove an ammunition truck in the American Army in Europe during the war. "He'd tell about the German dive bombers coming at them, how they'd have to drive off the road into the woods to get away."

Other family members had fought in other wars. A great-uncle, ZiMiguel, fought in World War I. It was the price of citizenship. "They told him if he joined the Army, he could become a citizen." Then there was Sonny's namesake, his grandfather Alfonso, who was among the Italian troops who landed in Tripoli in 1911. "He got a medal there for bravery fighting the Turks. My grandmother would take it out and show it to me."

In the fall of 1951, Sonny D'Arco stood in his candy store on DeKalb Avenue reading about the monthlong Battle of Heartbreak Ridge ten thousand miles away on the Thirty-Eighth Parallel on the Korean Peninsula. He read about the U.S. Second Division Infantry and allied troops battling endless waves of North Koreans and Chinese soldiers sweeping down steep hillsides turned into moonscapes from constant shelling. He saw the stories about the Medal of Honor awarded to an Army private killed while covering his company's retreat when it ran out of ammunition, taking forty North Koreans with him before he went.

"That was it. I was out of there. I might have been a gangster, but my country was at war."

He called in a friend named Sammy Fillipelli who lived across the street on DeKalb Avenue. "I said, 'Here's the keys, it's yours.' I had maybe two or three hundred dollars' worth of cigarettes in there, plus deposits on the *Daily News* and the *Mirror*, the other papers. I said, 'Pay me when I get back.'"

On December 5, 1951, he rode the train to lower Manhattan to the Whitehall induction center near Battery Park. He told the recruiting officers he wanted to go to Korea. "They looked at me funny but approved me fast, before I could change my mind."

He went home to pack a bag and say good-bye to his parents and family. His father wished him luck. His mother was upset. Nonna didn't understand what was happening.

He walked out the door and down the long stoop, a small duffel bag with a few belongings over his shoulder. On the top floor, his grandmother threw open a window.

"Dove stai andando, Sonny?"

"Essere un soldato, Nonna."

"Tu sei pazzo? Torna a casa!" Are you crazy? Come home!

Sonny waved and blew her a kiss.

3

THE ARCTIC CIRCLE

His grandmother wouldn't have been the only one to wonder about the sanity of someone happily marching off to battle in late 1951. The war Sonny was eager to fight was bogged down in bloody stalemate along the frozen hills of the Thirty-Eighth Parallel. Americans at home were war-weary and divided. Many liked former general Douglas MacArthur's plan to cross the Yalu River into China, blasting the Reds with nuclear weapons if necessary. Even more thought President Harry Truman was right to fire him for trying to start a third world war. But few were volunteering to fight in what was seen as a losing cause. The military was relying on those who didn't have a choice, calling up reservists and National Guardsmen. Enlistments were extended and the draft age was dropped to eighteen.

The debate bypassed Sonny entirely. He just wanted to fight.

As things worked out, his mother and Nonna needn't have worried. Keen as he was to get into the battle, the Army had other plans for him.

"First they sent me to Fort Kilmer in New Jersey. I told them straight up: I want to go to Korea." Officials told him that was just fine and sent him south to Fort Jackson in South Carolina for basic training.

He had never been farther from home than Pittsburgh. Or farther south than Philadelphia. "They had me crawling through the swamps with snakes and all. They took us swimming in a lake and there's alligators in there."

In addition to the perils of the southern countryside, there was the challenge posed by the heavy drawl of drill sergeants and officers. "There were all these rebel types and half the time I couldn't understand a word they said. They couldn't understand me either. They said I had the worst accent they'd ever heard. They're telling *me* I had an accent?"

There was another misunderstanding. When he signed up, Sonny was under the impression he would be granted leave to spend Christmas with his family. At Fort Jackson he was told he'd have to wait. He wasn't about to do that. "I had that kid's attitude: nobody's gonna screw with me. So I talked my way onto a Constellation plane out of the base back to New York and flew home." He had been back on Kent Avenue for two days, showing off his uniform to family and friends, when someone spotted MPs coming up the block. He ducked down the rear fire escape and got away. "I headed straight back to the base. I went to the captain and told him the story, how I'd just wanted to see my grandmother for Christmas. He said he appreciated that I'd returned. He gave me company punishment, putting me on extra duty, instead of a court-martial, which he could've done."

Aside from the clashes with Army culture, he was a willing soldier, happy to comply with the rigorous training. "I liked all the workouts, the running, the exercise. I was good at it."

He did well enough to be placed in a regimental combat team, a battle-ready unit including troops and artillery. His instructor was a Filipino who had fought the Japanese in the jungle during World War II. "He taught us all these guerrilla moves, like how to live off the land and how to stab someone so they can't call out. I figured, Great, now I'm finally going to Korea."

Instead, along with a squad of other soldiers, he was loaded on a huge prop plane in the fall of 1952 and flown 4,300 miles northwest to Ladd Army Airfield near Fairbanks, Alaska. He got off the plane and met the only enemy he'd fight for the next twelve months: frigid cold.

"I got to the Arctic Circle it was thirty degrees below zero. Then they had a cold snap. Hit sixty-two below. They gave us a card, said we were members of the Sixty Below Club."

He was outdoors a lot of the time. The Army detailed him to the Air Force, which assigned him to a military police unit. His job was to guard a three-and-a-half-mile-long airstrip used for long-range planes and bombers of the Strategic Air Command. Although the bombers' specific task was supposed to be secret, the soldiers in his barracks talked openly about it: they were carrying the Big One. The Bomb. The planes circled the Bering Sea and the frozen north, ready to deliver their deadly cargo when ordered.

The mystery planes would taxi down the long airstrip into an enormous hangar. "Soon as the doors closed, these armored vehicles would circle the hangar. There were fifteen of us always outside standing guard. Only officers could go inside where the plane went to load and unload the A-bombs." He was ordered to sign papers pledging never to discuss anything he saw at the air base. "They'd tell us every day, 'One word about this and it's straight to Leavenworth.'"

The would-be gangster from Kent Avenue found himself standing on the tarmac, shivering, a nine-and-a-half-pound M1 carbine on his shoulder. "I said, 'How the hell did I end up here? I'm a military policeman. I'm guarding the atom bomb.' I kept saying, 'Hey, I signed up to go to Korea!' But it didn't matter. The Army did whatever it wanted with you."

The fight against the cold was a daily battle. "You'd just freeze your ass off. We only had the uniforms left over from World War II, these cheap pants. No matter how many layers you added on you were still cold."

In the mail pouch one day came a letter from Blackie Luca, the pal from the neighborhood who had made it into Aviation High School when Sonny was rejected. Blackie's luck was still holding: after being drafted, he'd been shipped to Germany. "He sends me this picture of him in a beer garden someplace, drinking with these girls. He's got 'Wish you were here' on the back. Yeah, I wished I was there."

Although the war was sputtering to a close, the steady drumbeat delivered by officers to Sonny and his fellow soldiers in the remote post was that they were on the front lines of the inevitable next war against the Soviet Union. "They'd tell us the Russians were probably going to invade soon, and when they did, they'd be headed straight for us because we were closest."

The soldiers cheered themselves up by noting that the enemy would have a tough time parachuting into the frozen wilderness. "We figured their lungs would freeze up so they couldn't jump out of their planes to get us." On the other hand, the troops glumly noted that devices were rigged all along the airstrip to destroy it with explosives should enemy forces attempt to seize the base. "In other words, there was no way out for us. We were like a suicide squad, just stuck up there if anything happened."

At least there were kindred spirits around to share the pain. Shivering alongside him was Oscar Feal, a guitar-playing Puerto Rican who hailed from his own tough turf. Sonny marveled at the long, angry scar on Feal's arm where he'd almost sliced off his limb with a machete while harvesting sugarcane back home as a boy. Another close friend was Tony Verni, a second-generation Barese whose father was an iceman. He'd grown up just two miles from Sonny on Union Avenue in Williamsburg. The three soldiers grew identical pencil mustaches and sang tunes that Feal picked out on his guitar. "We were either the Three Amigos or the Three Amici, depending on who was talking."

In back of the barracks, they hung a heavy boxing bag. They took turns holding the eighty-pound sack while one of them flailed away with his fists. When summer came, they raised a basketball hoop outdoors. At night they shot craps on the floor between the bunks. "We did everything we could to stay busy, to keep from thinking about the cold and about being a million fucking miles from nowhere with a giant target on our backs waiting for the Russians to hit us."

For all his earlier training as a street hoodlum and his disappointment at being cheated out of battlefield heroics, Sonny made a pretty good soldier. In 1953, as his tour was coming to a close, he was asked if he wanted to take an entry test for Officer Candidate School.

"I handled myself pretty good so they told me I should take the test. I figured what the hell. I took it and passed pretty high. When they saw my grade, they didn't believe it. Thought I must've cheated, that a guy from Brooklyn who talked like me couldn't have the brains."

He was asked to retake the exam, this time by himself in an office with a corporal watching. He did better the second time. Al cackled in delight when he saw his grade. "I learned from those Irish Christian brothers. When they taught you, they *taught* you."

After he passed the test, the Army handed him an agreement to sign. The good part was that officer training would take place at Fort Benning, Georgia. At least it would be warm there. The bad part was that the extra hitch required a minimum of six more years. "I decided that was too long. My grandmother was getting old. I'd never see her."

The Army wasn't happy when he turned down the offer. "They stuck me with extra duty for the rest of my tour. That was how they picked on you. But I wasn't changing my mind."

In late 1953, Private First Class D'Arco was shipped back to Fort Kilmer in New Jersey. "They gave me my honorable discharge and my mustering-out pay, which came to about $600."

On Kent Avenue, he got a big hug from his Nonna, who told him all over again how crazy he'd been to try to go to war in the first place. His mother and sisters admired his uniform, while his father told him there was a job back at the dye shop for him. Sonny said he'd think about that, but first he wanted to check in with his old gang.

  With his Army payroll in his pocket, he headed to Ally's on Fulton Street, the clothing store where he and his teenaged buddies had shopped for zoot suits and peg pants. "I bought some new clothes and picked up where I left off: shooting craps with the guys in the neighborhood and looking for scores."

He was a good-looking young man, in trim shape thanks to his Army workouts and his steady bouts with the heavy bag behind the barracks. He had a thick brush of dark wavy hair that he combed straight back and a bright impish smile that made him look a little like his old movie idol, Jimmy Cagney, at least when he grinned, which was often.

He'd never had a serious girlfriend but now everyone wanted to fix him up. He briefly went out with a girl named Jay, who lived on Clinton Avenue. Her father owned a local carting firm. "Her dad threw me the keys to his black Cadillac and we went to the Copacabana. We parked right out front. Jerry Lewis and Dean Martin were playing. I even got to talk to Dean Martin. But there was no fire there with me and Jay. She later became a nun."

A few weeks later, he was riding even higher when he got a car of his own, his first. It was a gray 1949 Buick Super with split windshield and portholes on the side. His grandmother chipped in a big chunk of the purchase price. Red Cacace, a local wiseguy who lived on Waverly Avenue and had grown up with Sonny's father, took Sonny to Mid-County Buick on Empire Boulevard across from Ebbets Field to pick it out. "Mid-County was run by Mike Miranda, who was big with the Genovese family. Red Cacace was pals with him so I got a good price." Coming along for the ride to the dealership was Red's then twelve-year-old son Joel, who was destined for his own eventual Mafia stardom under the moniker "Joe Waverly," for the street where he'd grown up.

Touring down DeKalb Avenue behind the wheel of his big Buick, tooting his horn at friends as he passed, Sonny felt the many months on the frozen tarmac in Alaska melt away, even if it was December. "This ain't winter," he laughed at those who complained about the weather.

He was "Al" now to anyone who asked. He'd forever be

"Sonny" to his family. But the ex-GI with the new car and a growing swagger decided it was time to put the little boy in the Jolson song to rest. "Call me Al," he told those he met.

There were a lot of introductions being made. His Army buddy, Tony Verni, was back in Brooklyn as well, and one evening Sonny's sister, Leona, talked Tony and Al into going out with her and her boyfriend. It was to be a triple date, a big night out. They were headed to Brooklyn's most lavish nightclub, the sprawling Town & Country on Flatbush Avenue near Marine Park. It was a vast club, seating two thousand customers. Tony Bennett had made a name for himself there a couple of years earlier, playing to sold-out crowds. That night, jazz singer Dakota Staton was playing with an orchestra. Al's date was a pretty girl named Mary, a friend of Leona's. "I knew her a long while. We were just friends, having a good time."

Tony Verni was looking to be more than friends with his own date, a slim, raven-haired nineteen-year-old from Mulberry Street in Manhattan. Dolores Pellegrino had dark eyes and a mischievous smile. She was going to school to be an airline stewardess. Her friends had convinced her that she was a natural for a job whose qualifications included "near-Hollywood" looks. That night she wore a black dress and her hair up in curls. Al D'Arco got one look at Tony's date and decided he didn't have to look any further. The tough guy dissolved on the spot. "We looked at each other and that was the end. Nobody was there but me and her."

Dolores felt the same way. "It was such a funny thing. I was with Tony and Al was with this girl," she recalled years later. "But as soon as our eyes met I knew I wanted him and he wanted me. It was crazy. Crazy love I guess."

The next day Tony called Dolores. "I saw you making eyes at Al," he told her. "I guess you don't want to go out with me anymore." He told her not to worry about it. "Al's a good guy," he said.

Tony went over to his Army friend's house to tell him there

were no hard feelings. He gave him a card with Dolores's
name and phone number on it: Barclay 7-8568. Al took the
card. He still had it in his wallet sixty years later.

The next thing Dolores knew, Al was on the phone. "I said,
'What took you so long?'"

A couple of nights later, he went to meet her in the city at
the drugstore and soda fountain on the corner of Canal Street
where her uncle Julius worked. Al was wearing a new double-
breasted suit, trying to look like he did this all the time. He
chatted with the uncle for a while and then a girl walked in.
She looked like Dolores, except shorter and younger. "Are
you Al?" the girl asked. "I'm Theresa, Dolores's sister. She'll
be right down." That's fine, Al told her. Forty-five minutes
later he was still holding down a stool at the counter, talking
with her uncle, when Dolores finally arrived. "She looked
like a million dollars, so I had no complaints. Her mother
explains to me later that Dolores doesn't like to do things in
a rush."

They went to dinner at a restaurant on Hester Street. "What
do you do?" Dolores asked Al. "I drive a truck," he told her.

It was almost true. Shortly after getting out of the service,
Sonny had gone on a few truck hijackings with Momo Venturino and Charlie Dima, his old gambling pals from the
candy store on DeKalb Avenue. With this latest addition to
his gangster résumé he'd decided to buy himself a good pistol. He paid $200 for a Spanish-made Llama 9 mm automatic
with chrome plating. Hefting it in his palm brought a thrill
of power. He had no place to hide it at home, so he kept it in
the trunk of his new car, wrapped carefully in a rag and hidden under the spare tire. Which is how Dolores found out what
he actually did for a living.

"Our third date, I took her to the Sign of the Dove on the
Upper East Side. I had a friend, Bootsy, he was just getting
big in narcotics, said he had a piece of the place, and told me
to take her there, that it's the best place for a date.

"So I get all dressed up. I pick her up and I swing up
Sixth Avenue, headed uptown. I am on top of the world.

Dolores looks beautiful next to me in the front seat. Then I get a flat tire."

Making matters worse, it had begun to rain. Dolores climbed out of the car and offered to help. "I say, 'No, no, I can do this.' But I like that she offers, you know? So I walk Dolores over to a building canopy where she's out of the rain. I go back to the car and I have to pull off my jacket, my tie. Then I go into the trunk and pull out the spare."

As he pulled out the tire, the rag hooked on the rim. The 9 mm came flying out of the trunk, skittering along the wet street. "I don't look at her, but I know she can't miss it, since it made a big clatter when it fell."

Al quickly scooped up the piece and placed it back in the trunk. He finished changing the tire and walked Dolores back to the car. After they'd driven few blocks, Dolores spoke. "Get rid of that," she said. Al didn't look at her. He just nodded his head.

"It killed me to do it, but I did it. It was some nice piece but I got rid of it. She was asking me to. That was enough for me."

He soon discovered that Dolores knew all about guns and the wiseguys that used them. Her information came from an excellent source: her father.

Joseph James Pellegrino was in semi-retirement by the time his daughter started dating Al. But among Little Italy's Mafia elders, his reputation was secure. "I asked around about him, about who he was with. I found out he was so tough he didn't have to be with anyone. He was with himself."

Back in the 1930s, Joe Pellegrino had been partners with a mobster who went by the name of Terry Burns. Born Dominic Didato, Burns grew up on the Lower East Side with Lucky Luciano. He rose in the Mafia pantheon alongside Luciano, and among his prizes was control of a major trucking firm that served the city's massive garment industry. Somewhere along the line, he and his boyhood chum had a serious business disagreement, and in 1936 Burns was gunned down outside a bar on Elizabeth Street.

After his partner's demise, Pellegrino refused to follow normal mob protocol by realigning himself with the winners. But he was considered a fearsome enough foe that Luciano's crew simply left him alone.

Al was in awe of him. Joe Pellegrino was fifty-six years old by the time they met, but built like a solid block of Italian marble. "His nickname was Joe Lefty because he'd had polio. His whole right side was screwed up, but his left was strong enough to take care of business. That's why they called him Joe Lefty." He'd had some tough schooling: At the age of eleven he and a friend were arrested for gun possession. "They were eleven years old and they were sticking up people already." He was sent to the New York Catholic Protectory, a vast facility teeming with juvenile delinquents and children cast off by families too poor to raise them.

The first time Sonny sat down for coffee with his future father-in-law he was stunned to see him snap the handle off of a coffee cup. "He wasn't even upset. He just closed his hand on the cup and—bang—the handle went flying."

Joe Pellegrino asked if Al had a job. The way he asked it made Al think there was only one answer he wanted to hear. "I said sure I was working, but it wasn't regular. I fibbed a little. I didn't want him thinking I was just a street guy." Dolores's dad said he might be able to help. A few days later, Al had a job at the Fulton Fish Market on South Street in lower Manhattan. The employer was a place called Teddy's House of Seafood, a major purveyor of fish to city hotels and restaurants. Managers assured Al that any friend of Joe Lefty's was a friend of theirs. The fish market was firmly under wiseguy control, so the job reference was crucial. The fish market operated at night. Al worked through until morning, unloading trucks and making up orders of fish for the restaurants.

"I didn't mind the work. There were a lot of guys from the neighborhood working down there so it was like old home week every time I pulled into a loading dock." But it left little time for extracurricular activities with his crime partners. And he wouldn't leave the house without scrubbing out the seafood smell that clung to him after a night at the market.

He found a new day job with an export-import firm called Theodore Ficci and Sons that shipped machinery and other goods. The company was on Dover Street, at the base of the Brooklyn Bridge. Across the street was the old *Police Gazette* building, soon to be demolished to make way for traffic ramps to the bridge. Once again, Al was driving a truck, this time as a card-holding member of Local 807 of the Teamsters. He picked up loads at the piers. The freight didn't smell. Yet there were other hazards.

He was resting on the loading dock on Dover Street idly watching another trucker park his rig at the top of a small rise by a garage. The trucker got out and walked away. "I'm looking and I see the truck is rolling. He forgot to set the brake."

Al leaped from the platform, chasing the truck. He was tugging on the door when the rig hit a fire hydrant, sheering it off. The lurch from the impact almost knocked him under the truck's wheels but he somehow managed to heave himself into the driver's seat. The truck, he realized, was headed straight for a police officer.

"The cop is standing there with his back turned in front of a bar on Water Street. He has no idea what's happening— then he turns around and this truck is almost on top of him. I think he got diarrhea when he turned around. It would've flattened him, but I hit the air brake just in time."

The cop staggered away without saying anything. "So I save this cop's life and of course never even get a thank-you for it."

For a straight job, he made good money. More important, he proved to Dolores's father he was a hard worker. His gangster apprenticeship was put on hold for the time being.

He wanted to get married right away. "I never even thought of marriage before I met Dolores. Then I didn't want to take any chances."

Dolores felt the same way, but she had told her parents she was going to be a stewardess. "The rules were you couldn't be a stewardess if you were married, and so we waited."

Dolores had graduated from Seward Park High School on the Lower East Side, and had been accepted at the Grace Downs Air Career School. Located in the old Bernard Baruch mansion on Fifth Avenue, it was a charm school, a place for young women to burnish ladylike skills that airlines insisted their hostesses possess. Al would drive up to the school, wait for Dolores outside, then bring her home. "She had the uniform, a special hat, everything she needed."

On weekends, they went for drives in the country or to the shore, out to Oyster Bay on Long Island Sound. Dolores was shy about having her picture taken in a bathing suit, but Al talked her into it a few times. One photo captured them on the beach, Dolores leaning into Al, her elbow bent over his shoulder, his arm around her waist. He had his father's barrel chest; Dolores looked like the alluringly perfect stewardess. The look on their faces suggested they needed no one else for anything.

Some evenings they'd go up to the Italian Riviera, the roof of Dolores's building at 78-80 Mulberry Street. It was a high six-story walk-up tenement, towering over Canal Street and bustling Chinatown below. "Dolores would walk right to the edge of the parapet and look straight down. I'm worried just looking at her, but I don't want to say nothing. She'd turn around and smile, give me a 'What's the big deal?' look. She had nerves of steel."

At Dave's Corner Luncheonette at Canal and Broadway, the couple squeezed into the photo booth, shooting cheek-to-cheek pictures of themselves, like teenagers.

Al's constant attention to his new girlfriend brought him gibes from his friends in Brooklyn. They teased him about being led around by the nose. He brushed it off. He rejected this part of wiseguy culture outright. "I never was interested in anyone before Dolores, and never since. I didn't need a go-matta or anyone to fool around with on the side. She was the one and that was plenty for me."

Eventually, the couple decided they didn't want to wait. Al spoke to Joe Pellegrino, who gave his blessings.

"We had a big party to celebrate our engagement on Grand

Street, above Ruggiero's Restaurant, across from Ferrara's. There was a hall up there you could rent." Between her family and his and their friends, they packed the house.

Six months later, on June 4, 1955, they were married. The wedding was at the church attended by Dolores and her family, Transfiguration in Chinatown, just past the bend in Mott Street. Joe Lefty, somber in a black tuxedo, walked his daughter down the aisle. Al's friend Charlie Dima was his best man, his uncle Philip standing alongside. Dolores wore a gown of white silk, complete with bridal veil and long fingerless gloves.

After the ceremony, the wedding party piled into cars and drove out to Coney Island. The feast was at Villa Joe's on West Fifteenth Street, famous for its Neapolitan cooking. "We had probably 150 people, all this fresh Italian food." Al's friends and the old-timers got a kick out of the place. "We were right next door to where Joe the Boss got whacked by Lucky Luciano, right in the middle of his pasta."

4

MOTT STREET

The new couple took an apartment in Brooklyn, just down the street from Al's family. The three-story brick house at 847 Kent Avenue between Myrtle and Park Avenues came with its own ready-made mob heritage: the landlord was Al Capone's aunt. Rosa Lisena lived on the ground floor with her husband, Belfronte. Rosa was from the Fischetti side of the Capone clan. Two other nephews, Charlie and Joe Fischetti, had also gone west to make their gangster careers alongside their famous cousin in Chicago. Charlie became "Trigger Happy" Fischetti; Joe became close friends with Frank Sinatra.

Rosa's life was less eventful. "She was a caterer, she'd make sandwiches for all the parties and weddings. A nice lady, she talked about how sweet her nephews were."

Al still drove a truck occasionally for Theodore Ficci and Sons, the firm in lower Manhattan. But having passed muster with his father-in-law as a hard worker, he was focused now on trying to come up with money-earning scores. He lucked into one such opportunity after a cousin introduced him to an enterprising hustler who went by the name of Willie Dumps. The hustler hung out on Mott Street in the city and was expert at selling stolen merchandise. One of his hustles was the sale of pharmaceuticals like penicillin on the black market.

"This Willie Dumps put out word that he is looking for a connection to get hold of penicillin." As it turned out, Al had just such a hook. The E. R. Squibb Corporation was one of the largest employers in downtown Brooklyn, operating out of a pair of towering manufacturing plants near the Brooklyn Bridge facing the East River. "I knew a couple guys from the neighborhood who were working there, and when I asked if they could get penicillin they said they could get as much as we wanted."

The problem was how to get large quantities of the capsules, which were stored in five-gallon glass jugs, out of the plant. Entry doors were well guarded. But the north side of one wing of the massive Squibb complex was adjacent to a narrow cobblestone alley that ran behind an old brick warehouse once home to the *Brooklyn Daily Eagle*. Al hatched a plan that called for him to park his car in the alley, then casually saunter away. Several floors up, one of his pals in the plant used clothesline to lower the jugs to the street below. Another Squibb insider hauled them in, placing them carefully in Al's trunk. When the coast was clear, Al strolled back to his car and drove away.

The scheme worked fine the first few times. No one spotted the jugs, containing more than four thousand capsules each, as they were gingerly lowered from an upper floor. Managers noticed that a chunk of inventory had somehow gone missing, but were mystified about how it had disappeared.

Meanwhile, Willie Dumps lived up to his reputation, clearing a profit of sixty cents per pill. One customer was a New Jersey fence named Peter LiButti, who was tied into Vito Genovese's crime family, the city's most powerful mob outfit. Known as "Hoboken Pete," LiButti had a contact who was a legitimate pharmaceutical salesman for drug firms who was eager to buy all the cut-rate capsules he could get.

LiButti lamented that he wasn't allowed to water down the drugs to boost his profits. There was a strict mob edict issued against it, he explained, after a group of thieves had adulterated stolen pharmaceuticals to hike their earnings. "They got stopped because a wiseguy's kid or mother could wind up with the drugs. No bootleg medicine allowed. That came from the top."

After a few weeks of the lucrative thefts, however, the thieves solved the mystery for the puzzled Squibb managers. One evening, as Al waited on the corner, a jug slipped loose of the line and plummeted seventy feet straight down, smashing on the cobblestones below. "It was like a bomb went off. The capsules go exploding everywhere up and down the alley." Workers in the plant rushed to the windows to see what had happened. Al raced to his car and sped away.

The penicillin caper was Al's introduction to a network of accomplished thieves friendly with Willie Dumps. One of them was Columbo Saggese, a burglar who operated out of a small café at 113 Mott Street in Little Italy. Saggese lived in a top-floor apartment, while his brother Moe, his legs crippled from birth, ran the café. While Moe worked the espresso machine, Saggese and his associates sat perched at the small tables discussing opportunities and strategy.

Their specialty was robbing commercial lofts in the garment and fur districts. The burglars tried to ensure success in their enterprise by bribing detectives in the police department's Safe and Loft Squad, which was charged with protecting industrial spaces in midtown and lower Manhattan. Garment-shop owners also paid the cops for protection, upping the ante after major thefts.

"The detectives on the squad were always coming by Moe's place looking for bigger envelopes. You couldn't tell these cops from the gangsters. They wore flashy clothes and had big pinkie rings. They were like their own wiseguys. They had their own rules."

Bribe-wise, the burglars were often outbid by the shop owners. At those times, the corrupt cops would deliver a stern lecture. "They'd say, 'If we catch you up there, you ain't coming out. We'll kill ya.' They'd do it too. Throw you right out the window, say you fell getting away. The message was that they're getting their grease from the owners, and you'd better not embarrass them by pulling a job there."

Al took to sitting in the café on Mott Street soaking up gangster lore with his new friends. The café actively discouraged paying customers. "Any time someone they didn't know came in off the street to ask for a cup of coffee they were told the machine was broken. We could be sitting there, steam coming off the top of our cups, and Moe would tell them, 'Sorry, no coffee.' They got the idea."

The rear of the café was an even more important locus for crime. Behind a narrow partition was an active bookmaking operation and organizational headquarters for some of the neighborhood's most venerable gangsters. One of them was a distinguished-looking man in his sixties with dark hair graying at the temples. Slightly shorter than Al, he showed up every day at the café impeccably dressed in tie, jacket, and fedora. In whispers, Saggese informed Al that this was an important old-time Mafioso named Jimmy Alto. Al had never heard of him. Neither had most people. In a decades-long run, Vincenzo "Jimmy Alto" Altomari successfully kept his name out of both police blotters and newspapers while ranking in the highest order among Little Italy's gangland fiefdoms.

Born in the city of Mangone in Calabria, Italy, in 1894 of Albanian parents, Jimmy Alto was a swashbuckling battler as a young man. Part of his legend was that after arriving in the U.S., he made his way to the Southwest, where he joined the Mexican rebel army of Pancho Villa, who at one point had crossed the border into New Mexico. If so, he was in good company. Giuseppe Garibaldi II, grandson of the Italian liberator, led a contingent of Italian volunteers who fought alongside Villa during major battles. Alto later joined the American Army during World War I. His soldiering experiences gave him bragging rights few other mobsters could match. "Mob big shots would come by the café asking to see him. Jimmy Alto would sit in the back and say in his heavy Italian accent, 'Do they know him in Albuquerque? Let him wait.'"

In New York, Alto joined a Masonic lodge where he forged close connections with politicians and judges. Crime-wise, he was allied with the family headed by Vito Genovese. But his association went back to Genovese's predecessor, Lucky

Luciano, recognized as the founding father of the modern American Mafia. Luciano had operated out of his own social club a block away on Mulberry Street.

But from what Al could tell, Jimmy Alto answered to no other boss. His chief dominion was control over gambling in a choice swath of Little Italy. "He had the floating crap games, the faro card games, and the ziginette games that had hundreds of thousands of dollars changing hands every night."

Despite his influence, Alto lived modestly. He and his wife resided in an apartment above the Fretta Brothers pork store on the corner of Hester and Mott Streets. His one indulgence was fine clothes. "He'd shop at Kaplan's on Canal Street, buy expensive suits. If he got a spot on a necktie, it came right off. He'd tie it around a lamppost and leave it there."

In the café's back room, Alto surrounded himself with a small group of close associates. There was Sammy Chillemi, a big man of few words; Vito Truppiano, considered a tough guy in a neighborhood filled with them; and Paul Della Universita, who helped Alto brainstorm his schemes. Al already knew Della Universita, who was known as "Paulie Lefty." "Paulie lived down the block above Vincent's scungilli place with his wife, Anna. She was friendly with Dolores. They played bingo together at Transfiguration Church."

Alto's single most lucrative enterprise, Al learned, was the ziginette games. The game was wildly popular and the mob collected 25 percent of every winning pot, the biggest cut the house took on any of its gambling operations. "When the ziginette was running, all other dice and card games were shut down. If you wanted to gamble then, it was ziginette or nothing."

Gamblers were still eager to play. To win a game was like hitting the lottery. Cards were dealt out of a faro box allowing players to see only one at a time. Bets were made as each card was dealt. There was no real skill involved, just luck. But the game drew big crowds. "The money builds up. You hit one card, then you pile the money on top. If you run nine hands, you're rich."

The right to operate the game was reserved for mobsters.

"You couldn't just open a ziginette game. If you did, the wiseguy who controlled that area would send one of his men to put his own faro box on the table. That meant you had a new partner. It was either that or a trip to the hospital, or worse."

Games changed locations regularly to thwart the occasional stickup crews that preyed on gambling clubs. The police were less of a problem, since the nearby Elizabeth Street precinct was provided with a share in the winnings. Still, some detectives prowled Little Italy basements looking for signs of gambling. "You were supposed to sweep up all the cigarette butts after the game so the cops couldn't spot where guys had been standing around."

One evening Al and Saggese were at a crap game in an upstairs apartment around the corner from the café when detectives burst in from the fire escape. Others poured in from the hallway. "They crashed the door in and took a bunch of us to the precinct. But that was nothing. You wait for night court, it gets dismissed. The big thing was the cops took the bankroll on the table. It was more than ten grand including the house's share. That was a problem."

Federal agents were another headache. "They weren't reachable the way the cops were. And if you had guys at the games driving in from Jersey and Connecticut or Pennsylvania, then they could nail you on interstate gambling, a federal charge."

Jimmy Alto's clout gave him control of all such games operating in a two-block stretch between Mott and Mulberry Streets, from Canal to Hester. It was the heart of Little Italy and prime gambling territory. Running the games required a string of clever and dependable assistants, and Alto soon singled out Al D'Arco as a potential recruit.

Al didn't feel very clever at first. "One day me and Columbo are sitting in the café talking and one of us mentioned the word 'combination.' That's what they called the mob in Chicago and it was a word—like 'Mafia'—you were never supposed to say out loud." They realized their mistake when Sammy Chillemi and Vito Truppiano stepped out from the back of the café to glare at them. "I froze. So did Columbo. You weren't supposed to say those things."

The lapse was forgiven. A few days later, Chillemi summoned Al behind the café's partition. There, Jimmy Alto looked him up and down and asked if he would like to handle a few things for him. "Whatever you need," said Al, thrilled to be asked.

The first task involved a visit to a Times Square shop called Ace Novelties. Alto introduced him to the owner, a Jewish craftsman named Abe who handmade the dice used in Alto's crap games. "They weren't just any pair of dice, they were 'perfect dice' because they were perfectly square on all sides with a special beveled edge you couldn't get with machines."

Al's assignment was to go up to Ace Novelties every few weeks and pick up new sets when they were ready. The dice came in matching sets of five, tightly wrapped in tissue paper and sealed with tape. Al noticed that the color of the tissue paper changed with each delivery. He realized it was to spot any tampering and to keep him from switching the sets. "Jimmy had strict rules about the dice. I wasn't supposed to bring anyone with me when I picked them up, or even tell anyone where they came from. After I got them, they were to go to Jimmy, no one else."

Recalling the fate of the crap-game operator at the State Theater on DeKalb Avenue who went missing after loaded dice surfaced in his own game, Al understood Jimmy Alto's caution.

Al would chat with Abe on his visits. The dice maker said that he crafted products for several Las Vegas casinos, as well as for mob-run gambling joints in places like Hot Springs, Arkansas, and Covington, Kentucky, across the river from Cincinnati. His connections, Abe told him, stemmed from his good friend Abner "Longie" Zwillman, the ex-bootlegger who had used his wealth to become one of New Jersey's biggest political powers.

Al enjoyed the trips and the conversation. "I was attending *la scuola delle strade*, the school of the streets. I was a good student."

* * *

School never recessed. One hot afternoon, Al stood on the sidewalk in front of Moe's café, leaning against the wall, smoking a cigarette. He had a handkerchief tied around his neck and wore sunglasses against the glare of the day. It was a pose struck up and down the gangster boulevards of Mott and Mulberry Streets by young men trying to look both dangerous and idle at the same time. Jimmy Alto stepped out of the café looking annoyed. "What are you, an actor?" he snapped. "Take off those sunglasses." Inside, there was a further scolding. "Don't be standing out there like you got nothing to do in the middle of the day," Alto told him. "Be low-key. Don't stand out. Don't do anything to get noticed."

Low-key. It applied to everything Alto's men did. Considering the amount of money hauled in from their gambling rackets alone, Al knew they could easily afford Cadillacs, the car he had hoped to get once he could swing it. But Chillemi and Truppiano both drove old heaps. Chillemi had a Buick older than the car Al bought when he got out of the Army. Truppiano, considered one of the toughest men in the neighborhood, drove an old Pontiac.

"Nothing flashy," they explained.

Vito Truppiano handled another profitable gambling enterprise for Alto, one Al had never heard of before starting to hang out on Mott Street. Gee-far was a kind of Chinese lottery. Players bet on one of three dozen different symbols—frogs, rats, fire, even coffins. Like many of those who bet regularly on the numbers racket, bettors tried to interpret dreams and other signs to help them pick winners. Unlike the numbers, however, which were based on a single daily figure such as the handle at the racetrack or stock market volume, gee-far paid off nine times a day. All day long, runners raced through the streets collecting bets and delivering payoffs.

It was hugely popular in the Chinese community, located mainly south of Canal Street. But it caught on as well among their Italian neighbors, since the odds, 36–1 less the house percentage, were good. Bets were mainly nickels and dimes, but profits added up.

It was enough to make competitors jealous. "Vito and Jimmy Alto were making huge money off the gee-far, and some guy, they called him Feets, made a play to try to get a piece. Vito told him to mind his own business."

The man named Feets continued to press. Truppiano, with Alto's approval, pushed back harder. In a tense meeting over the game, Feets slapped Truppiano in the face. "Vito didn't do anything. He just walked away. The next day this Feets is crossing Canal Street and a car goes by and someone gives him three blasts with a shotgun. *Boom, boom, boom.* Everyone in the neighborhood heard it. That was the end of Feets and no one bothered the gee-far game after that."

At the café, no mention of the incident was made other than a comment by Jimmy Alto that Al often heard him offer in such situations. "All the tough guys are in the graveyard," he croaked.

Al knew he was being watched by Alto and his crew to see how he handled himself, the same way the mobsters back in Brooklyn had tested him. A few months after he had started running errands for the gangsters, Al was again summoned into the back room. They were starting a new café and club a few doors down the block, Alto told him. It would be in the basement of Mike Lubrano's drugstore at 109 Mott Street. "He says they are going to run a big ziginette game there."

Alto asked if Al would like to be part of the operation and share in the game's earnings. Al restrained his excitement. "Whatever you want, Jimmy," he said. "I will be glad to help."

He was honored to be asked, even though he knew he'd have to do most of the work, everything from keeping track of their earnings to making coffee for players and getting supplies.

It started with securing cards for the game. They had to be Bicycle brand only, red and blue decks, purchased from a friend of Alto's in sealed cartons. He had to keep a record of the house's cut of the winnings. When players wanted coffee, he would make black espresso in a Neapolitan Maganetta pot.

It was served only at the counter. "If you give it to someone while they're playing and it spills, then they'd say it messed up their hand."

There were two dealers, a doorman, and someone to clean the café and the bathroom. "We called him 'Filthy Pants Dom,' or 'Dirty Dom,' since he was a mess. But he didn't care, since he got tips, which came to quite a bit."

Tips also went to the doorman, who was responsible for making sure no one got inside who wasn't known. "His name was 'Chuch' and he was very valuable because he knew the name and face of every wiseguy and big gambler."

Even before the space was ready to open, detectives from the Elizabeth Street precinct came to look the spot over. "They told Jimmy they'd be back in a couple of weeks, which meant everything would be okay as long as they were on the pad and collecting a payoff."

The partners also had to pay homage to local mob politics. In a nod to the branch of the crime family based in Manhattan's Fourth Ward on the Lower East Side, Alto put an old-timer from that group named Don ZaZá on the game's payroll.

Rosario DiMaggio was a caricature of the fast-disappearing generation of the original Black Hand. Every day he dressed as if for a funeral. He wore the same crumpled black jacket, black tie, black vest, and pants with a Charlie Chaplin–style hat with the brim turned up. Although only in his late fifties, DiMaggio walked like a much older man, slowly and bent over, as though the earth were already calling him to ground. He was also less than helpful. "Don ZaZá would sit in a chair inside the door, smoking the stump of his stinking cigar. He'd toss the matches on the floor and then spit. When he went to the bathroom he'd piss all over the seat and the floor."

The old man made a point of goading Al. "He'd tell me to bring him a box of matches when he's got a box sitting right in front of him. I know he's waiting for me to tell him that so he can scream that it's none of my business, and to shut up and bring him what he asked for. He was looking to bait me into saying something out of line to a made man." The way Al figured it, the aging gangster was scheming to get him removed from the club so he could fill Al's slot with one of his own cronies.

Al wasn't the only one annoyed by the antics. "Gamblers would use the toilet after Don ZaZá and come out complaining that someone had pissed all over everything. This happens one night when Jimmy Alto is there. He goes in the bathroom to take a look and comes out steaming. I told him I'd handle it and got Filthy Pants Dom to clean it up fast. But I see Jimmy sitting at the bar eyeing Don ZaZá."

DiMaggio didn't seem to notice or care. "He just sits in his chair, throwing matches on the floor and spitting like he did every night." After a while, Don ZaZá rose. He stepped to the counter and told Al to make him a cup of espresso, "*forte e dolce*"—strong and sweet. Al nodded and proceeded to make the brew in the Maganetta pot. He carefully warmed up the demitasse with boiling water to make sure the coffee wouldn't get cold. He placed it in front of the old man. "*Favorita*, Don ZaZá," he said. Enjoy.

The gangster reached for the cup, then flicked his finger out, knocking it over. Hot coffee splashed Al and spilled down the counter. Al tried not to flinch. He told DiMaggio not to worry, that he'd make him a new cup. But as he reached for a rag, Jimmy Alto exploded.

"Don't clean that bar," Alto shouted. Then, eyes bulging, he turned to DiMaggio and yelled. "You come in here and spit on the floor, piss all over the toilet, and throw your matches everywhere. Enough. You are barred from the game. I will send Al to you with your pay, but don't come around anymore."

The gamblers in the room went silent. It was the first time Al had heard Jimmy Alto raise his voice, much less at a fellow member of the mob. "Go ahead," Alto added as he waited for Don ZaZá to respond. "See what you have to do about it."

After a moment Don ZaZá heaved a loud sigh. "*Songano stanza*," he said. He was tired. Turning to Al he said, "When the game is over if you would drive me home I would appreciate it." Al looked at Jimmy Alto, who seemed embarrassed to have lost his temper in public. Then Alto nodded. "I would be glad to," Al told the old man. DiMaggio lived on Madison Street, in Knickerbocker Village, near the East River. Neither said a word on the drive over.

Don ZaZá stayed away from the ziginette game. But a few days later, when Al arrived at Moe's café, he was surprised to find the old man in his crumpled black suit sitting on the wooden bench out front. Don ZaZá motioned Al to sit down next to him. Al sat. "*Como te chiama?*" the old man asked. DiMaggio wanted to know his name. He told him. "Ah, I have a brother Alfonso in Sicily. We had a lemon grove together. You know," DiMaggio said, "I have never been home to see my brother or my lemon grove."

Al sat there not saying anything, wondering what the old man wanted. "Alfonso, I would like you to take me home," he continued, "but please stop at the fruit stand. I want to get some fruit." Al went to get his car and then helped DiMaggio, who seemed more bent over than usual, get in. At the fruit stand, the vendor quickly filled a small bag with grapes and peaches and handed it to Don ZaZá, who didn't offer to pay. Al noticed that the vendor didn't seem surprised.

At DiMaggio's apartment building, Al helped him out of the car and walked him to the door, his hand on the old man's elbow. Don ZaZá turned toward Al and straightened himself as much as he could. "Alfonso, you are a good young man," he told him in Sicilian. "You have learned well the lessons of the school of the streets." He started to go inside, then paused and turned back. "*Ricordo Don ZaZá con na buona cuore,*" he said as he kissed Al on both cheeks. "He told me to remember him with a good heart. I didn't see him again after that."

Al's ability to keep his rage in check with the abusive gangster won him more high marks in Jimmy Alto's school. Not long after the incident with Don ZaZá, Sammy Chillemi asked Al to help him with a different scheme, one that was a few grades higher up on the mob curriculum.

Chillemi explained that he was an official of a union

representing workers who made toys. This was news to Al, who couldn't imagine how Chillemi found time to run a union, since most of his days and evenings seemed to be taken up with the bookmaking business and other crimes being hatched in the back of Moe's café.

The union job didn't require that much work, Chillemi told him. In fact, it wasn't much of a union. Its labor contracts were tailored to suit the needs of employers, not members. What it did require, however, was making regular rounds of the city's toy manufacturers to collect payoffs and find out if there were any problems. Al was fascinated. It was a level of crime he'd never seen in action. "Anything I can do for you, Sammy," he said.

The job entailed driving around the city with Chillemi to the various firms. Many of the manufacturers had offices in the Toy Center on West Twenty-Third Street across from the Flatiron Building. Al would ride the elevator to the top floor and stop off at a half dozen or more companies on his way down.

In between pickups, Chillemi explained the economics of the arrangement. "The way it worked, he told me, was that they'd have a contract that says the employer is supposed to pay pension, welfare, etcetera for all their workers. But if they had maybe a hundred workers, they'd pay for like ten of them. So they'd give Sammy a cut of what they were saving. There was a lot of money in that."

The agreement with the bogus union was even more important, Chillemi explained, if a legitimate labor group came around trying to organize the workers. "The owners get to say they've already got a union, so get lost. Everyone knows it's a sweetheart deal, but there's nothing anyone can do about it. That's the law. You can only have one union."

Even better, the seasoned racketeer explained, it was hard to get caught. As long as you weren't exceptionally greedy, employers were glad to go along. The workers, most of them among the city's poorest, rarely questioned things. If they did, they were usually easy to intimidate.

Al listened carefully. The labor racket seemed promising.

* * *

It was a good time for finding new earning opportunities, since his own responsibilities were growing. On July 4, 1956, Dolores gave birth to a son. They picked Joseph as the baby's name. It was an easy call. Following the same Italian tradition that Al's father had practiced when he was born, the new baby was named after his father's father.

The baptism was held at St. Lucy's, a Roman Catholic church down the street on Kent Avenue. Afterward, family and friends celebrated at a club next door to their apartment. "We had a big party, we went late that night." Everyone complimented the food. The chef was Rosa Lisena, the landlady with the famous nephew.

The new father took his work seriously. He occasionally rolled the dice at a game of craps, but when his luck ran bad he stopped before digging himself into a hole. He wasn't much for drinking either, taking a glass of wine and an occasional brandy, but that was it. As much as he could, he stayed out of bars. "That's where trouble starts. My father taught me that. Guys get drunk, your friends become your enemies. I stayed away."

Instead, he was home most nights on Kent Avenue for dinner with his wife and baby boy. Some friends poked fun. "You sure you're a gangster?" Columbo Saggese asked one night when Al begged off a night of gambling.

He focused on learning his trade.

"Every day was crime day. You got up, it was 'How you going to make money today?' It was a job you went to, and you couldn't slag off."

Some crimes weren't to his taste, however. A tip from a gambler at the ziginette game led him to a Lower East Side butcher-shop owner who was cashing checks for people. "He was an old German guy and he kept the money in a shoebox behind the counter. Him and his wife were in there, and I went in and stuck them up." The shop had a walk-in refrigerator. Al pointed his gun at them and told them to get inside. "The guy got all afraid. He's shaking. He says, 'Please, don't hurt my wife.' I said, 'I won't hurt your wife.' I felt bad, the guy was really scared. And then I realize if the guy fights back I'm going to have to hurt him. And some of these jerks, they just shoot the guy. That was it for me with stickups."

There were plenty of other opportunities.

One of Al's new acquaintances was a moonfaced young man from the Red Hook section of Brooklyn named Albert Gallo. He and his brothers Larry and Joe were part of an ambitious crew affiliated with Joseph Profaci's crime family. Al didn't much care for Joe Gallo's nonstop chatter, but he liked Albert, who, in sharp contrast to his older brothers, was a man of few words. "I knew him as 'the Blast.' They said he was so quiet he wouldn't blast a mosquito."

Together with the muted Blast, Al embarked on a series of hijackings and warehouse burglaries around Brooklyn. "We stole everything: TVs, dresses, meat trailers. Whatever we could get." Some paid off nicely, others not. One tip Gallo relayed was about a garage on Franklin Avenue. He had learned that trucks were loaded there with merchandise the night before they headed out to department stores around the city. "It was supposed to be a place filled with expensive stuff. We could get in easy, snatch the truck keys, and just drive right out."

They drove the load to an isolated spot by the East River where they climbed in the back to examine the loot they'd grabbed. "The whole back was filled with cartons of these new chrome kitchen trash pails made by Beautyware, the ones you step on to lift the lid. They were pretty popular items, but still, they were trash pails. We figured, What the hell? We sold what we could and spread the rest around. Everyone in our families got one."

While Al was risking life and liberty for a stolen load of shiny trash cans, a bloody battle for control was being waged in the upper echelons of organized crime. In May 1957, a gunman followed Mafia boss Frank Costello into the lobby of his fashionable Central Park West apartment building and fired at him almost point-blank. He missed, just creasing the gangster's skull.

The attempted assassination wasn't discussed openly in Jimmy Alto's crew, but there was no hiding the jitters on the street. Costello was Lucky Luciano's closest ally. After Luciano's deportation to Italy in 1946, Costello had taken his spot as the leader of his crime family. With it came the de facto leadership of the Commission, the assembly of Mafia bosses created to smooth out intramob disputes and enhance profits. Costello was such a strong influence in New York politics that he was perceived as having made one mayor, William O'Dwyer, and helped control his successor, Vincent Impellitteri.

"It was like they'd tried to kill the president. Everyone was keyed up. There wasn't a lot of hanging out for a while."

There also wasn't much mystery about who was behind the attempted rubout. The bullet that nicked Costello's head was fired by one of Vito Genovese's chauffeurs and enforcers, a lumbering ex–light heavyweight prizefighter named Vincent Gigante, known on the street as "Chin."

Al often saw Genovese walking in the neighborhood. "You always knew he was coming up Mulberry Street to the Alto Knights social club on Kenmare where he hung out because he'd have wiseguys on each side of the street guarding him. There'd be gunmen posted on the corners."

It was like watching a general on military parade. Genovese's own reputation for violence preceded him. In order to marry his wife, he'd had her first husband strangled, the body left atop a six-story building on Thompson Street. "People were very afraid of him. They knew he'd kill you for anything."

Around the same time, Al got a chance to see the other big name in New York's gangland, another five-star Mafia general who made his own headlines a few months after the Costello hit attempt.

"It was at a big crap game on Columbia Street in Red Hook. I was there with Al 'the Blast' Gallo. The game was run by Aniello Ercole, Mr. T they called him, a big man in the Anastasia gang. There was a lot of money on the floor, guys were losing $50,000 in a roll."

Al was impressed with the layers of secrecy required to gain entry. "You met them in a café and then they'd take you in a car to the game. They kept the location secret because they knew the cops would steal the money if they could find it. Then when you got there, you had to slide the card of the day under the door, like the ace of spades."

When Al and the Blast finally gained access to the game, the room was dark, smoke-filled, and noisy. "The place is packed and we're watching the action. There's a bunch of guys shooting dice and going wild. They had on long leather coats went right to the floor. One guy hollers, 'Ah, we lost again! Who the fuck we gonna kill now to get some more money?' Then one of them looked up and he goes pale. There's Albert Anastasia leaning against the wall right across from him, staring."

Anastasia didn't do anything, but his look of irritation at the gangsters publicly bragging about murder was enough. "Those guys cleared right out of there, and they were tough guys too."

The chief of what became known as Murder Incorporated was then heading the second-biggest crime family in New York, rivaling Vito Genovese's fiefdom. But the rivalry wasn't to last. On October 25, 1957, a few months after Al spied the mob boss through the haze at the crap game, Anastasia was gunned down in the barbershop inside the Park Sheraton on Seventh Avenue in Manhattan. He was just sitting down for a morning shave when two men in suits and fedoras walked in and opened fire. The shooters got away. No one was ever prosecuted. The word on the street was that the Blast's brother, Joe, was part of the hit team. Actually, he had nothing to do with it. The killers were gunmen from Anastasia's own crime family. But Gallo relished the notoriety just the same, dropping broad hints that he had been there.

"It went around that Joe Gallo was part of the hit. But you didn't talk about it." The next time Al saw his friend the Blast, they acted like nothing had happened.

The friends stayed similarly mum a few weeks later when headlines blared about the police discovery of a secret meeting of nearly a hundred top mobsters in upstate Apalachin, New York. It was a dramatic and public confirmation of the Mafia's existence. Al tried to read Jimmy Alto's reaction. The old man didn't say a word.

Al was hunting for new moneymaking opportunities when he first met another future mob chieftain, one who was to play a major role in his own future. At the time, Vittorio Amuso didn't look anything like a boss.

"On Mulberry Street I ran into Archie Mannarino, who is from my neighborhood in Brooklyn. He told me he knew about some guys who were doing a bust-out on a grocery wholesale outfit on Flushing Avenue near the Navy Yard. He said, 'Come down. Maybe we can make a few bucks.'"

The bust-out was already well under way. A pair of brothers had gotten hold of a firm doing business out of one of the stalls in the old Wallabout market. Trailerloads of groceries were being ordered, filled with butter, eggs, and meat. "Waldbaum's supermarket was their big customer. They were selling so much merchandise that the vendors were giving them all the credit they wanted. They're ordering more and more, and it's all going out the back door while they get the cash. Then they stick the company with the tab."

While Archie was introducing Al to the brothers and discussing ways they could participate, Al saw a young man his own age pushing a hand truck. "One of the brothers turns to him and says, 'Kid, go get us a cup of coffee.'" The young man dropped the hand truck and went next door to a luncheonette. When he returned with the coffee containers, he was introduced. "Al, this is Vic Amuso," he was told. The young man was slightly shorter than Al, with a wide jaw and a crop of curly hair. They shook hands. Al didn't give him another thought. "He was like a lobby boy, a gofer." A few years later, he got to know him better—in prison. "I didn't even remember anything about him till I ran into him in Sing Sing."

* * *

He remained an attentive student of "the Life," as Jimmy Alto and others referred to their chosen calling. He also took lessons from a new tutor. At a family wedding he met Joseph Schiavo, the cousin by marriage who was the co-owner of the garment factory where his aunt Mildred had worked. Tall and totally bald, Schiavo was an imposing figure. "He reminded me of that actor, Erich Von Stroheim. He had that look." Schiavo's connections were equally impressive. His partner in the garment plant was Thomas Luchese, the crime boss whose nickname of "Three Finger Brown" had made Al snicker when he was a boy.

The boyhood snickers were long gone. The name Luchese, he now understood, ranked alongside Luciano, Costello, Genovese, and Anastasia in the Mafia pantheon. Even more impressive, his cousin Joe was a top member of Luchese's family. Known among wiseguys as "Joe Reese," Schiavo lived in the Canarsie neighborhood of south Brooklyn near the Queens border.

When Al met him, Schiavo was in his late forties. He was partners with Luchese in more than a dozen garment shops, as well as trucking firms and supply companies. Each had its own favorable union contract and a market niche that no competitor dared challenge. Another part-owner in the shops was an old man of the mob named Torrido Curiale, who presided over the family's Brooklyn crew with Schiavo as his top lieutenant.

"I learned a lot from Joe Schiavo. He knew the whole history of the mob. He could trace back the families to where they started and the wars they had."

Among the history lessons he imparted to the young student was that the first American-based mob family had originated in Newark, not in New Orleans, as is generally believed. "It was called *La Chiesa,* the Church. The family that Tommy Luchese headed was the descendant of that first group."

The American mob had fought its own war of independence, Schiavo told him. "It was decided back under Luciano that the old Italian crime gangs, the Camorra, the Sicilian

Mafia, and the 'Ndrangheta from Calabria, wouldn't have any control over the American mob. They killed a lot of old-timers, Mustache Petes, who didn't want to go along with that."

The revolution was viciously enforced. "They had killers who went around the country taking out the old guys who wanted to stay aligned with the Italian families."

One of those traveling executioners, Al was fascinated to learn, was Leo Lauritano, the smiling baker at the Navy Street café he'd visited as a small child with his grandparents. Another was his other mentor, Jimmy Alto, who had also been a traveling hitman, enforcing the new regime's rules, he was told.

Schiavo imparted tips as well as history lessons. "He knew a lot of places we could knock off if we were careful and smart. We started making good scores through him, hitting dress rooms, and factories."

Schiavo never asked for a share of the proceeds, Al noted, even though he was rightfully entitled to one. "I'd bring a couple cases of good olive oil as a thank-you. He never asked for more than that."

But the older mobster did stake his claim. He informed Al that he was now "with" the Luchese family. It was like putting the family brand on the budding mobster. Any future criminal enterprises Al launched would be under the Luchese umbrella.

Al had no objections. In fact, he was delighted.

In his workaday crimes, he was trying to be careful, steering clear of deals that sounded too good to be true or too dangerous, and hoodlums too loud or clumsy to be trusted. But there were so many heists and hijackings with so many partners that he had to trip up. And he did. Not once, but twice.

The first time was a load of stolen men's overcoats. They were cheap coats as well. Initially, that made the foul-up even more embarrassing. Later it proved a blessing.

It started by trying to help out a neighbor.

"Tony Billeci ran the butcher shop across the street from us on Kent Avenue and he kept telling me he wanted to get into the action. I told him, 'Hey, stay a butcher, it's safer.' But he kept pushing."

Billeci excitedly reported that he'd met a crew of burglars who were looting stores in south Brooklyn. "He tells me these guys have a load of coats they took from a Robert Hall store in Bay Ridge. They wanted someone who could help sell them."

Al did know someone he thought might be interested. "Buddy Garaventi had been coming around Mott Street and he was pretty active as a fence." Al knew that Garaventi, a swaggering, outgoing man, was someone he could trust. For one thing, Garaventi had endless opportunities for moving stolen merchandise through his job running a crew of longshoremen on the docks in Hoboken for a major freight company. It also didn't hurt that he was a first cousin to Frank Sinatra. "Buddy didn't brag about it, but he seemed to be pretty close to his cousin. I know he could get guys tickets to shows anytime."

On February 17, 1961, Al and Tony Billeci rented a small van at an Avis car rental in midtown and drove out to Union City, a couple of miles north of Hoboken on the New Jersey side of the Hudson River. There, they met Garaventi and a shop owner named Louis Parisi who dealt in stolen merchandise. After agreeing on a price, they returned the next night with the coats loaded in the back. There were 260 of them, all with labels for Robert Hall, the cut-rate clothing store where the "values went up, up, up, and the prices went down, down, down," according to the chain's incessant TV jingle.

"First thing, we had to strip out all the labels so there wouldn't be any proof they were hot." They were working away inside the store on Hudson Boulevard when police burst in the door.

"The cops are all over the place before we can do anything. They had to be tipped because it was the middle of the night."

At a Union City police precinct, Al was handcuffed to a chair, his arms tethered to the bottom rung. A detective stood behind him. Another sat atop a desk in front of him, thumbing through Al's wallet. He pulled out a driver's license. "What's your name?" the detective with his wallet asked.

Al told him.

"Where do you live?"

"Brooklyn, New York."

"What were you doing in there?"

"I got nothing to say," said Al. The detective behind him slammed him in the neck.

"Where'd those coats come from?"

"Nothing to say." The detective in front lifted his leg and kicked him hard in the chest. The blow knocked Al over backward. He lay on the floor, pinned to the chair. The detective who had been standing behind him aimed a kick at his head. Al swerved and the blow landed on his shoulder. The detective moved closer and stomped him in the ribs. Then the cops propped him up again and it started all over.

The beating and questioning continued much of the night. When the detectives gave up trying to get him to talk they told him to sign a statement. Al refused that too. "Boom, the same detective starts hitting me from behind."

He was arraigned late the following day. A bail bondsman from Centre Street in Manhattan, one used regularly by Alto's crew, rushed over to post bond.

At home, Al limped upstairs, where Dolores put him to bed. The next morning he couldn't move. "It was like I was paralyzed. My neck was killing me, I couldn't move my head." Dolores called Columbo Saggese, who drove out to the house from Mott Street. They draped a blanket around Al, who was only half-dressed, and took him to Brooklyn Hospital on DeKalb Avenue.

"What happened?" asked a nurse.

"He fell," answered Saggese.

The nurse looked him over. He was covered in dark bruises. "That was some fall," she said.

It was Al's first major arrest. It felt like a badge of honor. At Moe's café, there were slaps on the back. Several friends counseled him not to worry, that so many cops and judges were on the take in Hudson County, New Jersey, where the arrest had taken place, that the problem could probably be taken care of with the right bribes to the right people. That might've been true, except the case was quickly taken over by federal prosecutors.

"The FBI got into it somehow and it became a federal case. They wanted to make it into a big deal, interstate trafficking in stolen goods."

With Jimmy Alto's help, he got a local New Jersey lawyer who went to work finding out how the cops had been tipped off to the meeting.

Al went right back to work. "I figured, Why should I slow down? I'm going to need more money for legal bills." He was also by now feeding a family of four, a daughter, Ava Marie, having been born in 1958.

As penance, he vowed once more to steer clear of crimes involving people he didn't already know and trust. The resolution lasted less than five months. The rule quickly went out the window when someone approached him with a scheme worth a lot more than a pile of overcoats from a discount clothing store.

"It was $500,000, that's what turned my head." The tantalizing offer came from a gangster in the Profaci crew who went by the name of Paulie "Guns" Bevacqua. "I knew him from Albert the Blast. He told me that they had these stolen stocks and bonds lifted from a big brokerage company worth half a million dollars. They were looking to unload them but they couldn't line up a fence who could handle that much."

Al was more than glad to help out. "I knew Tommy Kapatos, this Greek guy from the West Side, had been around a long time and understood about fencing stocks and bonds." Known as Tommy the Greek, Kapatos was forty-six years old and, despite his nickname, half-Irish. That was enough to make him a senior member of a mainly Irish gang that ruled Hell's Kitchen, midtown's far West Side near the Hudson River waterfront. Kapatos was out on parole having served twenty-two years for killing a rival hood named Albert "the Ape" Dillulio in a fight on Tenth Avenue. Excited about the stock deal, Kapatos pulled in three other friends. "Next thing I know this Irish kid, Jimmy McKay, from Tommy the Greek's neighborhood, is in it, along with two other guys." The added gang members included Robert Raymond, another ex-con from Brooklyn who had done time for murder, and a stickup man named Armand "Frankie" DeCicco. The expanded group made Al nervous, but he figured there would be plenty to go around once they pulled off the sale.

After a few days of nosing around, Kapatos and McKay announced they had a buyer. Al asked what they knew about him. "His name was Spiro and they said he was legit, meaning he wasn't a cop or a snitch. They said he had dealt with people they knew in Jersey who vouched for him." Al let it go at that. The would-be buyer wanted to see the stock certificates to assure himself they were genuine. That sounded reasonable enough to the partners. Since Al was holding the stocks for safekeeping, it was agreed that Al would conduct the show.

It was his first mistake. He had the stocks hidden at home in Brooklyn in a hiding place he considered secure. "There was this walk-in closet and I had built this trapdoor in there where I could hide whatever I needed. No one knew it was there but me." As for hiding the loot at home, it seemed eminently sensible to him. "Where else am I going to hide half a million bucks in stocks? I couldn't take them with me and I didn't want to put it on someone else to hide."

Mistake number two came when he invited Spiro to visit him on Kent Avenue to see the securities. He thought he was covering his tracks by instructing him to sit in a single spot at the dining-room table and to touch nothing else in the apartment. Al retrieved the certificates and fanned them out on the table. It was a dizzying array of corporate riches: There were hundreds of shares in blue-chip stocks in firms like Gulf and Western, National Steel, Sperry Rand, and Trans-Lux. Each was embossed with an official seal designating its bona fides. Spiro examined them closely and announced himself satisfied.

"Soon as I got him out the door, I wiped down the chair

where he sat, the table, and anything else I thought he might've touched."

The next step was to make sure the buyer had the money. A date was made to meet a few days later. Spiro said he would bring someone with him, his "investor," he called him. Al agreed but insisted on a public spot. "We wanted it out in the open in case anyone tried to pull something." They chose the Taft Hotel on Seventh Avenue and West Fifty-First Street, then a bustling 1,400-room mecca for tourists near the old Madison Square Garden and Radio City Music Hall. The meet was scheduled for late Friday afternoon, July 14.

The five partners waited upstairs in the hotel's mezzanine seated at a table overlooking the lobby so they could see who was coming in the door. Al nudged Kapatos when he spotted the buyer with another man carrying a briefcase. The two men came upstairs and joined them around the table. The briefcase was opened. Kapatos and McKay both inspected the contents and nodded to the others, indicating the cash looked right. As a good-faith offering, Al had brought $40,000 worth of the stock certificates with him in a zippered airline flight bag. Trying to look inconspicuous, the group sat chatting for a few minutes. Then Kapatos got up and walked a few feet away to make a call from a nearby telephone booth.

"Soon as he steps into the booth we see this big guy charging at us with a revolver in his hand. He lets loose a shot at Tommy the Greek." Al was stunned to see the shot hit the phone booth, just missing Kapatos's head.

Bedlam erupted as gang members tried to flee. Detectives surrounded them, pointing drawn guns. Jimmy McKay made a break for it. The detective who had fired at Kapatos now leveled his revolver at McKay as he tore down a mezzanine corridor. "He fires another shot. I'm thinking, These guys are trying to kill us. So I don't move. I just stand there and let them grab me."

It made the front page of the next day's New York *Daily News*. "HOTEL SHOOTING: NAB 5 IN 45G HOT STOCKS DEAL," ran the headline. Journeyman reporter Joseph McNamara wrote about how when McKay took off, veteran detective William McCartin calmly pumped a couple of warning shots into the ceiling to stop the fleeing felon. McCartin then "flushed McKay from under a bed in one of the rooms."

It wasn't the way Al saw it go down. He heard several shots, not two. From his view, the guns were aimed straight ahead, not up. "The way they were shooting," he thought, "they were looking to take one of us down."

But there was no disputing the rest of the facts as to how the gang had been snookered: In all, there were a dozen plain-clothes officers from the district attorney's squad posing as tourists in the hotel lobby that afternoon, three of them policewomen. Spiro and his investor were also detectives. They were on the case of more than $200,000 in securities looted in April from a brokerage firm on Liberty Street in lower Manhattan.

It was a big story. "It was on the radio all that night and the day after. They made out like we were John Dillinger or something."

The hot-stocks quintet were first taken to the Fifth Precinct on Elizabeth Street. Then they were brought over to police headquarters, on Centre Market Place, just two blocks from Moe's café. On the Broome Street side of the elegant Beaux-Arts building, they were led down a ramp once used for horse-drawn police wagons. "They took us into the cellar where they had the holding pens. Walking in, we scared all these hookers down there waiting to be let out. They went, 'Ooh, gangsters!' Like we were real dangerous criminals. We got a laugh out of that at least."

Al was placed alone in a cell for several hours. Then a pair of detectives led him in cuffs outside to an unmarked sedan. He rode in the back, a detective beside him. The car headed across the Manhattan Bridge to Brooklyn. The detective in the back asked him where the rest of the stocks were stashed. Al looked at the floor of the car, waiting for the beating to begin. He was surprised when they pulled up in front of his apartment building on Kent Avenue. No one had laid a hand on him.

"They took me out and I said, 'Do you gotta walk me down

the street in cuffs?' " He was surprised again when they took them off. "If you take one step we'll shoot you," the detective assured him. Al believed him.

Dolores was ironing when they came in. Joseph, five years old, was playing with toys in the living room. Ava Marie was in a high chair. "Dee just froze. She looks at me and she looks at the detectives. She didn't know what to do." The police told Al he should just tell them where the stocks were. Al didn't say anything. They began tearing the house apart, pulling out drawers in the kitchen, tossing over chairs and tables.

Terrified, Dolores went into the living room and sat down with Joseph and Ava on her lap. She had no idea what was going on.

Al tried not to look as they neared his stash. "Almost right away, the cops went straight to the closet. The guy Spiro must've seen me. They started banging on the walls and floor, and found where the stocks were hidden." So much for that, Al thought.

He was in jail for two weeks before he made bail. It was $10,000. Again, a bail bondsman pal of Jimmy Alto's helped him out. He went home thinking about how he now had two lawyers and two bail bondsmen to pay. At home, there was worse news: Dolores had been pregnant with what would have been their third child. Instead, rattled by the raid, she'd had a miscarriage.

"It was my fault. I kept apologizing. She said, 'Just leave it alone.' I felt terrible."

Manhattan district attorney Frank Hogan took the stock case to a grand jury. It quickly returned indictments for burglary, grand larceny, and criminal concealment of stolen property. Even for someone like Al, who had no prior convictions, it was enough to win him a ten- to twenty-year sentence. For convicted felons like Kapatos and Raymond, both of whom were on lifetime paroles for their murder convictions, it likely meant life in prison.

Al's Mott Street friends brought him to a criminal defense

attorney then making a name for himself among organized-crime figures in need of talented legal help. Maurice Edelbaum had won an acquittal for Vincent Gigante when he was charged with putting a bullet through Frank Costello's hairline. It helped, of course, that Costello testified he'd never seen Gigante before. But Edelbaum didn't hold out much hope for this one: Al had the stolen stocks with him at the hotel, and more hidden at home. "It's going to be very tough," he told his client.

If that was the case, Al decided, he didn't need to spend a fortune on legal help. Thanking Edelbaum for his honest assessment, he found another, less pricey attorney. For the next few months, the defendants tried various delaying tactics. Tommy the Greek had his own lawyer file a motion for dismissal, claiming he had just run into Raymond, an old friend, at the Taft. The two friends were catching up on old times when the detectives opened fire. Motion rejected.

Kapatos, desperate to avoid a life sentence, next turned to Al. After one of the court hearings, he leaned over and grabbed him by the shoulder. "Tommy says, 'Can you help me out kid? I'm looking at life here. Would you cop out and say I had nothing to do with this?'"

Al looked at him, slightly stunned. Kapatos wasn't a close friend. But he also understood. Tommy the Greek was almost twenty years older than Al. He'd already done more than twenty years in prison. The evidence against Al was dead-cinch certain. Kapatos had a chance, with some help, to beat the rap. Al wondered: Would I ask the same favor if the tables were turned?

On January 9, 1962, Al stood up in General Sessions Court in Manhattan. The judge presiding was Thomas Dickens, a former state assemblyman from Harlem and one of a handful of black judges on the bench at the time. Dickens owed Tammany Hall, the Democratic machine where organized crime still retained strong influence, for his judgeship. But no one Al knew had a clue about whether Dickens would be amenable to a bribe.

And it might not even be necessary. Al's new lawyer told

him that as a first conviction, he was, at worst, looking at a year in prison. With luck, he could get even less.

At home he assured Dolores that they'd be okay. And he tried to explain things to his son. All the five-year-old boy picked up was that his father was leaving him. It was an early painful memory for Joseph. "I remember him tying my shoe and telling me that he was going away and that I wouldn't see him for a long time. That was it. I got really upset and started crying."

In court, Al confessed to the judge that he was guilty of criminally buying and receiving stolen property. He added that it had been his idea, that Kapatos and the others had just happened into it. The judge sentenced Al to two and a half to five years at Sing Sing.

"I wasn't sure I heard right. I looked at my lawyer, he doesn't look at me. And there's this loud whistle behind me. I turn around and there are some guys from Tommy the Greek's gang in court there to support him. Sonny 'Machine Gun' Campbell, the boss of that outfit, was shaking his head saying, 'Wow.'" The gangsters were amazed at the length of Al's sentence.

Al was immediately remanded into custody. Dolores was in court with her father. He waved. "My father-in-law says, 'Don't worry, son, we'll be here for you when you get out.'"

There was one reprieve. Back in Newark, in federal court where the stolen-coats case was still pending, Buddy Garaventi's lawyer, himself a former United States attorney, had been working hard on the matter. Several months after Al was sent up the river to Sing Sing, federal marshals came to fetch him for a court hearing in Newark.

On the drive to New Jersey, Al braced himself for another stiff sentence, one likely to be consecutive to the state term he was already serving. A marshal turned around from the front seat to ask if he wanted something to eat. "No," Al snapped.

"How about a cigarette?" said the marshal affably.

"I don't want nothing from you," he shot back.

"What's your fucking problem?" said the marshal. Al didn't respond. He just stared out the window.

In court, however, the scenario that played out was dramatically different than he'd expected. He listened with growing amazement as he heard the judge accept a motion from the federal prosecutor to dismiss the charges.

Al thought Garaventi must have bribed the U.S. attorney's office *and* the judge. But that's not what had happened. It turned out the Robert Hall jingle was correct: the store's prices really had gone down, down, down. The wholesale value of the 260 stolen overcoats, Garaventi's attorney had adeptly proved, was less than $5,000, the statutory minimum needed to prove a violation under federal interstate commerce laws. "Case dismissed," said the judge.

On the way back to Sing Sing that night, Al couldn't stop humming. "Knock it off," snapped one of the marshals. Al grinned.

5

SING SING

He knew Sing Sing from the movies, the ones he'd watched as a child with his grandfather through clouds of cigar smoke at the Subway Theater. Sing Sing was the Big House, where his hero, James Cagney, framed for murder, landed in *Each Dawn I Die*. It was where John Garfield, the hood with the good heart, was sent up the river in *Castle on the Hudson*.

It looks just like the movies, he thought as he passed through the towering redbrick walls on a plateau above the Hudson River. There were the endless tiers of gray cell blocks packed with prisoners in gray uniforms. There was the din of 1,800 inmates and 500 guards trying to keep them in line. There were the glimpses of the Hudson, a reminder that home and family lay just thirty miles down the river.

But the movies had left much out, he discovered, both bad and good. The bad was that much of the prison was a damp dungeon, beset with rodents, roaches, constant filth, and predators. The good almost made up for it: Sing Sing was one big graduate school for gangsters.

"They throw you in quarantine for fourteen days when you get there to make sure you're not bringing any diseases inside. I don't know why. They didn't have to worry about bringing anything in—they had plenty of their own."

His first breakfast, Al spotted black flecks in his oatmeal. Rat feces, he learned. Some prisoners simply flicked them aside and continued eating. Al threw his away. Handed an orange in his first week, he figured things were looking up. But that was it, a single orange, once a month to keep inmates from getting scurvy. In his bunk, he slept crushed up against a freezing steel wall, feeling the chill from winds on the river. He'd wake up and his legs would be numb from the cold. He could see his breath, even inside.

He was given a uniform with a number. His was 128968.

For the prison's receiving blotter, he was asked the basics of his crime and background. A clerk typed in his responses.

Reason for crime? "Needed money at the time."

On friendly terms with accomplices? "Doesn't know accomplices."

Occupation? "Odd jobs."

Employer? "No verifiable employment."

Social Security number? "?"

Family left behind? "Father, 53. Mother, 49. Two sisters. Wife, 29. Two children."

Grade reached? "Two years high school."

Well, close enough. No one cared how much high school he had.

Moved into a cell on an upper tier in B-block, a vast warren of caged men, Al kept to himself, alert to any challenges headed his way. He bought Pall Mall cigarettes at the commissary. When an inmate asked him for one, he said sure and in a friendly gesture, shook a half dozen out of the pack. "Soon as I did, these other guys come over demanding the whole pack. I said, 'Come by tomorrow, I'll give you a carton.' I was ready for them too, I was going to bust them up. But they didn't show."

It was the first prison lesson learned: kindness spelled weakness, which was to be avoided at all costs.

A few days out of quarantine, Al spotted a friendly face. Sal Scarpa was from Bensonhurst, Brooklyn, and had worked with Al's cousin Gino Crisci. Al also knew Scarpa's brother Greg, a swaggering member of Joe Profaci's crime family.

Sal Scarpa was just one year into a fifteen-year stretch for armed robbery, assault, and kidnapping. With a partner and a revolver, he had hijacked a tractor-trailer carrying $12,000 worth of cheese and tomato paste. The heist was a side job. At the time, Scarpa was a $110-a-week organizer for an upholsterers workers local that practiced unionism the same way as Al's own labor tutor, Sammy Chillemi.

The two cons greeted each other as long lost friends. "Sal told me to come by the 'Italian table' and he'd introduce me around."

The Italian table turned out to be a spot in the cavernous recreation hall where inmates with mob connections ate and talked. It was an exclusive club, criminals of Italian descent only. Next to it was the Irish table, where hoods from Manhattan's West Side and the Bronx gathered.

The recreation room included a long row of gas burners where inmates could set their pots and cook a quick meal. The Italians made a tomato sauce with pepperoni sticks from the commissary or goods brought by family members. "They had it down to a science. They'd get the tomatoes going, drop in the pepperoni and some salt and pepper everyone kept in their pockets or anything they'd scored from the mess hall. Then set it on the table, where everyone scoops it out of the pot with some bread crusts. It doesn't sound like much, but in there it was heaven."

It was a multiethnic food fest. "The Puerto Ricans made rice and beans. The Irish had some kind of stew. You were only allowed twenty-five minutes to use the burners so everyone was rushing to get their sauces going."

In addition to Scarpa, the regulars at the Italian table included Frank Aliventi, another gangster from Brooklyn. Known as "Frank the Sheik," Aliventi was doing thirty years for a shooting death during a stickup. The difference in the Sheik's case was that he was innocent. "Everyone knew he'd taken the rap for a friend of his who pulled the trigger. That's the way it was. You got caught, you did the time. You couldn't finger someone else."

Another regular was Vincent Caserta, a soldier in Vito

Genovese's family known as "Jimmy Red," who was doing a three to five year term for loan-sharking. Then there was Salvatore "Babe" Vario, another Brooklynite doing time for robbery. He was one of five brothers. His older brother, Paul, was a power in the Luchese crime family. More important to Al, they were protégés of his cousin, Joe Schiavo, who had sponsored them as soldiers in the family.

Not that those ranks counted behind bars. Mafia prison etiquette required that the dividing lines between mob families and crews be suspended, Al learned. It didn't matter what group you belonged to, or what grade you'd achieved. "Everyone was the same, on an equal level. What mattered was that you watched each other's back, and took care of any guys who turned rat."

The power assembled around the Italian table was acknowledged throughout the prison. "Even the hacks paid us respect. When we were together, they couldn't touch us. Alone, they'd make a run at you sometimes. But at our table? We were like bosses."

Other inmates also paid homage. Convicts were not permitted to approach the group unless invited. Seated at the table one afternoon, Al watched as a compact black inmate in his thirties with a large scar on his neck walked toward them. The inmate stopped several feet away as if at an invisible fence. "Come on over, Reggie," said a regular, waving. The inmate stepped forward. Reginald Seaborn, Al was told, was a well-practiced killer. He had served as an assassin for Bumpy Johnson, the Harlem drug czar allied with the Genovese family's branch in Italian East Harlem. Seaborn was doing a five to seven-year hitch for one of his few mistakes. His pistol had failed him as he was trying to gun down a rival in a Harlem bar. "I think he must've killed forty or fifty guys out there. But he was a very honorable guy. Everyone liked him."

Despite the gangland bravado, there was a steady reminder of the consequences they faced. The Italian table sat in the shadow of Sing Sing's most famous landmark, its electric chair.

"Our table was right across the alley from the death house,

where they kept Old Sparky. You'd look right out on where
they walked convicts inside, the Last Mile. There were a lot
of stories about guys who took that walk."

Executions had long been a booming business at Sing Sing.
By 1962, the year Al arrived, 613 people had been put to death
there, receiving the fatal 2,000-volt jolt through moistened
electrodes attached to leg and head. Court appeals and growing sentiment against the death penalty had slowed things considerably. There were no executions at all during his first year
in prison. But Al was there when the electrodes were strapped
on for the last time on August 15, 1963, for the execution of
Eddie Lee Mays, who had killed a woman during the robbery of a Manhattan bar.

By that time, Al was friendly with a few inmates who had
once sat on death row before their sentences were commuted.
"I remember how spooked everyone was that night, how quiet
the place got."

One of the most popular men in the rec hall was a garrulous
older Jewish inmate who had been behind bars for decades.
Nathan Goldstein was an honorary member of the Irish table. That was thanks to his past close association with Owney
Madden, the former beer baron and gangland potentate pushed
aside by the Mafia.

"They called him Sonny Gold. He had already done
twenty-five years for a hit he did for Madden. He did his first
few years in the old cell block by the river, the one where Warner Brothers shot the movie with Spencer Tracy, *20,000 Years
in Sing Sing*. They had a plaque up there about it."

Sonny Gold was filled with tales of prison life that hadn't
made it into the Warner Brothers version. "He told how the
old cells, you could barely fit in there with a bunk and be able
to turn around. They had no running water. They'd slide a
rusty pie plate of drinking water under the door. You and your
cellmate would crap in a night bucket. You had to live with
that stinking bucket all night and most of the day. Then they'd
march you down by the river to empty it. Cons had to walk
single file in chains, with a hand on the shoulder of the guy

in front of you. Then you'd fling your bucketload in the river. Sometimes the wind would blow it right back at you."

Sonny Gold had persevered, thanks in large part to a strong-willed wife who stood by him through his sentence. The wife worked hard, earning enough money to allow her husband to buy himself considerations not allowed other prisoners.

"Sonny had all the top hacks on his payroll." The most influential was the principal keeper, the prison's top disciplinarian. While wardens came and went, Al learned, the PK remained. "PK Kelley had been there for years, and he was the one who really ran the place. When Sonny wanted something done, that's who he went to."

Gold took a liking to Al and offered to help get him a job as a clerk in the administration office of the hospital prison. Traditionally, well-educated Jewish inmates had a lock on the post. But thanks to his tough schooling by the brothers at St. Patrick's Academy, Al was a good candidate. "There were a lot of guys in there couldn't read or write, so they picked me for the file job. It was a nice soft spot."

To make sure his friend obtained the slot, Sonny Gold met with the principal keeper. "He's with PK Kelley and he tells him he has three hundred reasons why I should get the job and never get transferred out of there. As he's talking, he's counting out $20 bills and dropping them in the wastebasket by Kelley's desk."

It was the perfect prison job. He did nothing. "I sat in a little room, every once in a while you had to file a chart or sign out a piece of equipment. That was it."

Sitting in the office, Al became friendly with Herbert Russell, an older black inmate who worked in a small hospital kitchen next door preparing meals for diabetic prisoners.

"The day I met him he was fixing fresh coffee, which you never got in stir, but he could get it for his patients. He sees me and asks if I'd like a cup. I says, 'I'd kill for one,' which was almost true. He laughs and pours me one."

Russell had spent his own quarter century behind Sing

Sing's walls thanks to his association with another gangland legend. In 1933, Dutch Schultz was expanding his criminal empire to include Harlem's lucrative numbers rackets. A key obstacle in his path was a prominent member of the Elks club and a congregant at the Reverend Adam Clayton Powell's Abyssinian Baptist Church named Martin Harris, who was known as Harlem's "policy king." Harris publicly vowed to resist the white intruders.

Posing as police, Russell and three others forced their way into Harris's West 130th Street apartment. He was shot dead in front of his wife. The allegation, widely trumpeted in Harlem's much-outraged black press, was that Russell had done the deed at Schultz's behest. Russell suggested otherwise to Al. "Herbie always said the real story never came out."

Russell's first conviction for first-degree murder was dismissed on appeal. A second ended in mistrial. The third time his luck ran out and he was sentenced to die in Sing Sing's electric chair. On the eve of his execution, however, Governor Herbert Lehman commuted his sentence to life imprisonment, saying there were still doubts about Russell's role in the slaying.

The two convicts enjoyed the relative freedom their prison assignments brought them. "Herbie was in his little kitchen right across from me. We'd just sit and talk about the rackets, about our families, our neighborhoods. I learned a lot talking to him. He was a great guy."

Not all prisoners were eager to gab. Coming and going in the hospital was an elderly Mafioso named Antonio Russo. Then in his late seventies, Russo kept to himself, speaking to no one. A native of Sicily, Russo had been in prison more than fifty years. As a young man he had been a combatant in the battle between the Camorra and the Mafia for supremacy in the years before World War I. Convicted of three separate murders, one in New Jersey and two in New York, Russo had served twelve years in Trenton State Prison followed by forty-one years in Sing Sing when Al encountered him.

Al would see him each morning when Russo, assigned to

work as a hospital gardener, approached his desk to sign out a pair of pruning shears. Each evening he returned them. "He never said a word, but his eyes had this 'I'm already dead and I got nothing left to lose' look. It made you not want to bother him. When guys would try to engage him a little, he always said the same thing back: 'If I no talk to you, you no talk to me, *capice*?' Then he'd turn away."

When Russo's sentence finally ended in 1964, the state moved to deport him back to his native Sicily. The exit of one of their longest-serving prisoners was a noteworthy event for Sing Sing's administrators, if not for Tony Russo.

"On his last morning, we're standing on the breakfast line, and this screw named Garland comes up to him. 'Russo,' he says, 'I'm here thirty-six years and you were already here when I got here. Come in the kitchen and I'll cook you whatever you like on your last day.' Tony Russo just points to the table in the dining room. 'For forty years,' he tells the guard, 'I sit at that table and eat what they give me. This morning, I stand on this line, I take what they give me and sit at that table.' "

Stung, the guard turned red and walked away. After watching the exchange, Al decided to say something. "I expected to get the same 'If I no talk-a to you, you no talk-a to me,' he always said. But I wanted to wish him well. So I tell him in Sicilian, 'Tony, tonight you will breathe *aria fresca*—fresh air—in the land where you were born. *Buona fortuna*, good luck to you.' He looks at me and answers back: 'Yes, I leave today, and I will breathe the *aria fresca*. But what good will it do me now? *Tutte le rose sono lasciato la faccia.*' All the roses have left my cheeks."

Later that morning, a line of prison officials stood at a side exit near the hospital to say good-bye to the old man. "They were all there, the old-time hacks, the doctors in the hospital, PK Kelley, even Warden Denno. Tony Russo just walks right by all of them. He never even looks in their direction. The warden has his hand out to shake, and Tony goes right past. That was some kind of tough guy."

*   *   *

Many old-time gangsters had washed up behind Sing Sing's high walls and were now fading away. Mike Basile had been a bodyguard for Vincent Coll, the freelance enforcer who worked all sides of New York's bootleg wars. Basile was with Coll when he earned his tabloid tag as "Mad Dog" by strafing an East Harlem street corner with machine-gun bullets, felling a five-year-old boy. A few months later, Coll met his own end, gunned down while sitting in a drugstore phone booth on West Twenty-Third Street. Basile retreated with the remaining gang members to an upstate hideaway in Colonie, New York, near Albany. There, he was wounded in a shoot-out with detectives. Sentenced in 1933 to seventeen to thirty-five years for attempted first-degree murder of a policeman, Basile served the full term.

By the time Al met him, Basile was due to be released. But like aging tough guy Antonio Russo, it wasn't going to do him much good. "Mike was dying of cancer. They'd never done anything for him in the hospital. He was an attempted cop killer so they wouldn't really treat him. They just let him get sicker."

Knowing he was soon to die, Basile told the younger gangster that when he went, Al should help himself to a tin box he kept under his bunk in his cell. "He said, 'There's a box there. When they take me outta here, do whatever you want with it. It's yours.'"

Basile finally did make it out of Sing Sing, only to die in an ambulance on his way to an outside hospital. After he left, Al retrieved the old tin box. "It was filled with newspaper clippings about his life. All the old stories about him and Mad Dog Coll. Them and a couple of prayer cards. That was it."

As the months ticked by, Al did his best not to worry about his own fate and that of his family back in Brooklyn. Dolores visited every week. Sometimes her father drove her up to Ossining. He'd wait outside in the car for her. As a former felon, he wasn't allowed in the visiting room.

More often, Dolores came by public transportation. She rode two buses and a subway to get to Grand Central Station in Manhattan, then took the New York Central line, which dropped her a long walk away from the visitors' entrance to the prison. The first few times she came, she brought Ava Marie, who had just turned four, and Joseph, who was six.

"Joseph didn't know what the word 'prison' meant," Dolores said of her visits. "I told them this is where their father worked. They didn't know for a long time." But Joseph soon started to figure things out. "He started to ask me questions. I thought this wasn't for a little boy. He didn't need this."

Al agreed. "I wanted to have the kids come visit, but after a while I felt like this was something they shouldn't see."

For Joseph, the trips in the car with his grandfather to Ossining were an adventure. "There wasn't much happening in our lives. We had no money to go anywhere. A long ride in a car was a big deal." He was fascinated by the looming high walls, the gates that buzzed as they approached, and the strange uniformed men everywhere. "I remember sitting in this big room at these long tables, my father on one side, us on the other." Surveying his surroundings, he looked up and was surprised to see men standing in the corners above them holding guns. "They were standing up above us, like where the priest stood in the pulpit in church, except they all had these big guns."

He took all of it in. Leaving the prison after a visit, Joseph walked beside his mother as they passed a sunken, fenced-in area where inmates were playing baseball. As they walked, a ball came rolling through the fence. He ran to grab it. "It was like a hard rubber softball. I took it home with me. I had it for years."

The ball was his one happy souvenir from his father's prison days. Back in Brooklyn he began to piece things together. "I'd see a movie on TV about prison, and I'd say, 'Hey, that's where Daddy is.'" Other reminders came from kids in the neighborhood. "They'd shout, 'Your father's in jail. We saw the cops come to your house.'" He didn't know what they were talking about, but it was enough to start a fight anyway. Like his dad, he was fast with his hands and fast to use them. "I'd be fighting with these kids, even if I didn't really know why."

There were occasional letters from his father, decorated with drawings of cars and dinosaurs for the children. "They were few and far between, but my mother would read them to us, show us the pictures. He was pretty good at drawing things."

On her visits, Dolores assured Al that things were fine at home. Both her parents and his were helping. As proof, she brought sacks of groceries—loaves of Italian bread, cheese, salami, tomatoes.

But things weren't fine. Without telling him, she applied for welfare. "I had to. No one else had any money. My parents tried to help, but they didn't have much either." Welfare brought another official intrusion into the house. "They'd come and look everywhere in the apartment. They'd walk right into the bedroom, look all around. What did they think? I was hiding something?"

Approved for public benefits, she was told her telephone was an unallowable luxury. "Don't ask me why, but they said I had to get rid of it. So we had no telephone for years."

In the neighborhood, the visits from the welfare inspectors to the D'Arco household were no secret. It became another taunt Joseph heard in the street, and another cause to use his hands. " 'Your mother's on welfare,' they'd yell at me. *Pow*, right away I'm in another fight, no idea why."

Al heard about none of this. "Dolores never complained once. She didn't say nothing about going on welfare to me. She just did it."

He had an outside chance to get home much earlier and help lift his family out of the hole he'd dug. With good time—months lopped off his sentence in exchange for staying out of trouble—Al was eligible for parole as early as September 1963.

But he had a hard time being good.

"The first time I got tossed in the hole was after I hit a guy in the head with a bucket. I did thirty days for that. But it couldn't be avoided. I had to fight him."

The battle erupted when a guard ordered Al to make the rounds of the cell blocks distributing slices of a single-layer sheet cake. The cake had been baked in the kitchen as a treat for prisoners who were too old to leave their cells. "These guys were invalids. They wouldn't take them in the hospital, so they just stayed in their cells. But you'd try and take care of them. They were our senior citizens."

He walked around handing out the little cakes, making conversation with the elderly inmates. In prison, sweets of any kind were as good as cash, and like everything else in Sing Sing, the slices were counted. Al was responsible for any shortage. For keeping things orderly, his reward was supposed to be that he got his own slice when he finished.

"I get to this old Italian guy, Frank, on the bottom floor. He had twenty-nine years in and was not in good shape. He says, 'Al, give me another piece.' I says, 'Frank, I can't, they're counted. If I give you another piece, I'm going to have to beat somebody else out of a piece.' He's looking at me and I say, 'Okay, I'll tell you what, I'm gonna give you the one that's supposed to be for me.' So I gave him another slice."

As Al turned toward the next cell, three tall black inmates blocked his path. "They were big, like basketball players. They seen what I did. But they mistook kindness for weakness. It's all predators in there. One of the big guys says, 'Hey, mother-fucker, give me some of that cake. I want two slices for me too.' I said, 'You want some cake? All right, I'll give you some cake.' And I swung the bucket up and smashed it in his face."

The bucket was steel and the tall man collapsed with a groan, blood spurting from a gash in his head. His two friends grabbed for Al. He tried to fend them off. "I was swinging at the other two guys when the screws jumped us and I got pinched."

In solitary confinement, the only furniture was a concrete slab covered by a thin horsehair mattress. "Down there, if you give them trouble—any little thing they don't like, just talking back will do it—first thing they do is take the mattress away. Now you're sleeping on concrete. Then if they think you're a real prick, they spray the concrete with a hose to wet it down.

You learn fast why they do that. Concrete burns the skin. You get a bad rash. It stings like a bastard."

It was the first of four trips Al was to make to the hole during his time at Sing Sing. Other infractions earned him a secondary-level punishment known as keep-lock. "They just lock you in your cell. They hang a sign on the outside, 'Keep Locked.' You don't come out for nothing till they're done with you." Keep-lock sentences often lasted two weeks, sometimes longer.

With little else to do locked in his cell, Al fashioned a physical regimen. "I had a little metal desk about three feet tall and a wooden chair. I'd take that, lift it up, put it on the bunk. Then I had that much more room and I'd do my exercises, put my feet on the bars and do push-ups, sit-ups. All day long."

When he'd had enough of his workouts, he'd lie on his bunk and listen to the guard pacing up and down the tier. "The hack on our block was Mr. Johnson, not such a bad guy. He sat in a little office down at the end of the corridor with his desk. Every half hour, he'd come out and walk this way and that way. The hacks had this routine, they'd take their billy clubs and brush them up against the bars as they walked. Made this *ratatat-tat* sound. It wasn't to make a racket, but to see if the bar makes a different sound, like a *ping*. Then they'd know the bar's been cut."

There hadn't been a successful breakout from Sing Sing since 1941 when three convicts killed a guard as they made their getaway. But escape remained a topic of discussion, most of it fanciful. "There were plots, but no one ever made the move. They watched you too close. They'd do a head count every few hours. Wherever you were, everyone froze in place until the count was done. If the number wasn't right, the hacks would be running all around. The warden would come down. But always it would turn out someone screwed up."

Inmates had their own communications systems. To stay in touch while locked in their cells, prisoners tapped runners in each block who relayed messages along the tiers and to friends gathered in the yard and the rec hall.

"The runner on B-block was a little guy everyone called Jerry the Jew. If you needed to tell someone anything, you passed the word down the tier to send up Jerry the Jew. The screws used him too, to pick up coffee from the kitchen, whatever they wanted. He pretty much had the run of the place. He knew everything that was going on. You wanted to check out a rumor, you asked Jerry the Jew if he'd heard anything. If he didn't know, he'd find out. He was better than a telephone."

Reading was another kind of escape. "I liked to read. I read *Moby-Dick* in there. And Jack London, and John Steinbeck, his book about the guys in the cannery. I even read dry stuff. Julius Caesar's *The Conquest of Gaul*. I got into it." The problem was the light. After dark, he was allowed only a 25-watt bulb for the little lamp permitted in his cell. "My eyes couldn't take it. You couldn't get bigger lights. The bulb kills your eyes."

But trapped in a seven-foot-by-five-foot cage day and night took its own toll. Lying on his bunk, Al stared at the shadows of the bars on the ceiling just as he'd done as a little boy in his Nonna's bedroom on the top floor on Kent Avenue, imagining what it felt like to be in prison.

So now he knew.

If there was a saving grace it was his constant exposure to the gangsters' version of the social register. In the four years and three months that Al D'Arco was to spend in Sing Sing, a steady flow of mob-connected inmates passed through its gates. It made for musical chairs at the Italian table. It also offered a network of useful contacts in the outside world of crime.

Al became friendly with an ambitious young criminal named Ralph Masucci, doing time for an embezzlement scam. Masucci was thirty-five and from Greenwich Village. Unlike most of the cons in Sing Sing, he had turned to crime less out of desperation than by choice. His family was fairly well off, he told Al. His father was a successful fruit and vegetable vendor whose customers included many of the city's

biggest nightclubs, including the Copacabana and the Stork
Club. His parents wanted Ralph to become a doctor. But like
Al, he had been dazzled by the gangsters he had encoun-
tered growing up. "He lived just a few blocks from Don Vito
Genovese himself and he knew all the guys in the downtown
crew of the family."

Masucci had gone to school with Vincent Gigante, the
boxer whose off-kilter bullet had grazed Frank Costello's
head. "He was a couple of years older than the Chin and he
had a little dice game going in school. Ralph told how the
Chin had come around, all tough talk, trying to shake him
down. Ralph knocked him on his ass."

Masucci sported a boxer's build himself, and Al thought
he looked like he could have done it. But his approach to crime
had so far been more mental than muscle. Before his most
recent conviction, Masucci had done a short federal stretch
for counterfeiting.

The inmates hit it off. "Ralph had ways to make money
I'd never heard of. We'd walk around the yard and the cell
block, gabbing."

Another, nervous new prison arrival was the young man
Al had seen pushing a hand truck on Flushing Avenue in
Brooklyn at the grocery bust-out. He barely remembered Vic
Amuso's name, but he knew the face when he spotted him
on B-block.

"No one else at the Italian table knew Vic, so he wasn't
invited over. He was up on the fourth floor with all the black
and Spanish cons. You could see he was having a hard time."

Amuso needed all the help he could get. He was the elev-
enth of twelve kids from a poor family in south Brooklyn.
He'd won his first prison term at the age of twenty-one when
he served two years in Green Haven prison. A few months
after his release, he was picked up on an assault and robbery
charge. He'd beaten that case, but then he'd tried to pull off
the single-handed theft of a $3,200 payroll at an ironworks
factory in Brooklyn. During the holdup, the factory clerk was
shot and wounded. Amuso had pleaded guilty and been sentenced to a term of two and a half to ten years.

Al told his pals he knew the kid upstairs was okay and that he should be allowed to join them. He brought Amuso over and introduced him around. Amuso was deeply grateful. "Thank you, Al," he told him later. "I'll never forget this."

Other newly arrived wiseguys needed no introduction, but still appreciated whatever assistance they could get. Al became the self-designated welcome wagon. "Fungi Gambino shows up—he was with the Profaci family. I knew him from Albert the Blast Gallo. His real name was Filippo, and he was doing a bid of two and a half to five, same as me, for burglary. They stuck him in a cell where the bed was all caved in. He showed me—you couldn't sleep on it."

Eager to make his friend comfortable in a new place, Al went looking for a better mattress. He found one in an empty cell downstairs. "They'd just shipped out a guy that week so I knew no one was using it. I grabbed the bed outta there and I dragged it around the corner. Fungi is up on the second tier, and I am handing the bed up to him when here comes this hack I knew, his name was Gioia. He says, 'What the hell are you doing there, D'Arco? Put that bed down. Get to your cell.' Right away, I squared off on him. I said, 'You cocksucker,' and raised my fist. He jumped. He says, 'Hey, it's me. I'm a good guy, don't be swinging at me.' I said, 'Okay, you're right.' But next thing I know they have me in keep-lock for fifteen days."

He risked much harsher punishment a few months later over another old acquaintance, one who had been nothing but trouble ever since Al first met him. Patrick Sparks had grown up near Al in north Brooklyn. Al hadn't seen him since the two men had brawled over an unpaid loan beneath the Myrtle Avenue elevated train, grappling for a gun as terrified Saturday shoppers watched. When he heard Sparks's voice echoing down from the tiers where new prisoners were held in B-block he recognized it instantly.

"He lived over near Skillman Avenue. His father was black and his mother was Italian. He was real light-skinned and he used the name Anthony Valenti." Sparks ran with Joe Gallo's gang in Red Hook. When Sparks asked for a loan of $600, Al agreed. The debtor made the first payment, and then went missing.

"I left messages for him all over but he wasn't answering. Then on a Saturday I spot him at Skillman and Myrtle." Sparks was hard to miss. He dressed in the style affected by Joe Gallo's crew, in a black coat, narrow pants, and the wide-brimmed gingerella hat worn by would-be hoods all over Brooklyn. "First thing, I smacked the silly hat off his head and knocked him down. He pulls out a gun and we're grabbing for it. I get it away from him and I pull the trigger to shoot, but nothing happens." Sparks ran. It was the last Al saw of him until B-block.

Al called out to him. "They called him Maverick, because of the dumb hat. I says, 'Hey, Maverick, what happened?' He sees me and he's panicking already. 'I'm sorry, I'm sorry, I was wrong,' he says. He's leaning over the rail looking down at me and I can see how scared he is. I told him forget about it, that I'd see him when he got into general population. I sent him up a care package of shaving cream, soap, some coffee, and a mirror, the way you did for guys you knew when they first arrived. But I don't hear anything back from him."

A few weeks later, he learned why. Sparks had arrived facing a tough fifteen- to thirty-year sentence for having stabbed a liquor store clerk in a $500 robbery. He had promptly sought to make his time easier by offering to be a direct pipeline to the warden's office on the activities of problem prisoners.

"They gave him a special cell in the Number Five building, the best cell block out by the wall. He was allowed to come and go on the grounds without a pass. Even the guards were scared of him because he was squealing on them too and the warden loved him."

Around the Italian table, the informant became an urgent topic of discussion. The issue was raised most forcibly by Freddie Sardo, a tall and gaunt man who was a soldier in the Genovese family originally from Hartford, Connecticut. Sardo's ferocious temper had earned him the nickname of Sudden Death. At the table, and in walks around the prison yard, Sardo loudly announced his hatred of snitches. "It's an insult to all of us. Everyone thinks this kid is Italian," he said.

Al listened to the rants, and waited to hear a plan. "Everyone wanted to see this stool pigeon dead, but all they were doing was talking about it. I said I'd take care of it."

His initial plan was to make his way into Sparks's cell in Number Five building just as the cell doors were opening in the morning and then, amid the clamor of prisoners filing out for breakfast, plunge a shank fashioned from a jagged piece of metal from the machine shop into his neck before he could cry out. As a backup, he carried a guitar wire in his pocket. "I was going to garrote him if I could. This was stuff they trained us to do in the Army. I knew I could do it."

But his dreams of enemy combat were again frustrated. Three times, Al snuck into Sparks's cell block. Three times the informant was not to be found.

Plan number two called for surprising Sparks at the weekly movies shown in the prison hall. This time Al's weapon of choice was a heavy metal bar from the prison repair shop, wrapped in cloth and electrical tape at the bottom so as not to leave fingerprints. He hid it inside his trousers. "I figured when the lights went down and everyone was temporarily blinded, I could smack him in the back of the head hard enough maybe to at least put him out of action for a while."

His co-conspirators were Jimmy Red Caserta and Fungi Gambino, who would surround Sparks so no one could see. "Jimmy was really anxious and wanted to get to the movies early. I said we should wait because he'd see us and get spooked." This proved true. Just before the lights went off, Sparks spotted the three cons headed his way.

"He starts yelling, 'He's gonna kill me! He's gonna kill me!' and he's running and jumping over people's chairs, climbing over their heads. Jimmy Red yells, 'Get him, get him!' Now the whole place is one huge riot, everyone's screaming."

Al chased after Sparks but the lights came back on. He dropped the rod. "Let's get out of here," he said. The three hustled out of the hall. They made it back to B-block without being stopped. Al stretched out on his bunk, trying to look like he'd been there for hours.

A few minutes later, Jerry the Jew came running down the corridor. "Did you hear what happened over in the hall? Someone tried to kill that rat Sparks," he said.

Al looked up. "Jerry, just remember, I was here all night, right?"

The runner's jaw slipped. "Yes you were, Al." He turned to go, then added: "Hey, Al, I'm proud of you!"

For two days, nothing happened. The would-be assassins thought they had gotten away clean. Then the "Keep Locked" signs came out and all three were locked into their cells. They remained there for five days before being brought to a disciplinary hearing. They faced the likelihood of criminal charges with heavy increased sentences if found guilty.

"We're brought into this office. I'm looking around for other guards because usually there are witnesses against you, but there's just us and these two captains in there."

The inmates had nicknames for the top prison officials. "Captain Fitzgerald was heading the hearing. We called him 'Cherry Nose' because he had this big honker with red veins that got redder when he got agitated." Sitting alongside Fitzgerald at a long desk was an especially brutal officer named Captain Taylor. He was dubbed "Captain Munsey." It was an inside joke with the convicts. Munsey was the name of the vicious prison captain played by Hume Cronyn in the 1947 Burt Lancaster film *Brute Force*. The movie, in which an informant is crushed by a huge stamping machine, was a prison favorite.

Captain Fitzgerald confronted the prisoners with the metal rod and shank they had dropped in the movie hall. "Are these yours?" Al was asked.

"No," he said. Fitzgerald's nose began to redden. Taylor stepped out from behind the desk, pounding his baton into an open palm. Photos of Sparks and his friends were presented.

"Do you know these men?"

Al took the pictures and looked at them. "No," he said, passing them to Caserta and Gambino.

"No," they said.

Fitzgerald started shouting. "Don't fool with us. We know you mob guys did it. And we know *why*!"

The inmates said nothing. A frustrated Fitzgerald pulled out another photo. "And I suppose you don't know this guy either?" he said. Al peered at a picture of himself.

"No, but he looks familiar," he cracked.

As he spoke, Captain Taylor punched Al in the side of the head, then jammed his billy club into his stomach. Al doubled over.

Fitzgerald exploded out of his chair. "Stop it, stop it. We're not going to have that." Taylor stiffened, his hands still in fists, his baton poised.

Fitzgerald glared at the inmates. "Look you guinea bastards, I'll not frame you. But we know you did it, and if I see you back here anytime soon, I'll turn this guy loose on you."

Al later learned how they'd beaten the rap. The guards at the movie had been so delighted to see Sparks's panicked rush across the hall that they'd all said they didn't see the attackers. Sparks was placed in special protective custody. It was almost as effective, if not as satisfying, as having completed their attack, since he was now out of the informant business. Sparks was later moved upstate to Clinton prison near Plattsburgh, where his good citizenship helped win him early parole. "I heard after he got out, he stayed up there, which was a smart move on his part."

A few weeks after the hearing, officials moved to break up the trio. Gambino was shipped out to Attica prison, near Buffalo, a tough commute for his family. Caserta was dispatched to Green Haven, a few miles north in Dutchess County.

For Al's part, he had already blown his first parole date. Now a second flew by. Then a third. He steadily lost credit for good time that might have hastened his return to his family.

On the other hand, he savored the applause he received at

the Italian table for having taken the initiative to silence the hated informant.

In Sing Sing, newspapers were handed from cell to cell. "When it was your turn, Jerry the Jew would bring you the *News* or the *Mirror*, whatever we could get." By the time it arrived, the paper was dog-eared and torn. Some articles had been ripped out.

In the fall of 1963, the Italian table inmates pored over the papers. The big news wasn't the death of the president, which came a few weeks later and was of markedly less interest. It was the front-page photos and stories of an unthinkable event: Genovese soldier Joseph Valachi, aka Joe Cago, his hand raised in the air, giving sworn testimony about the Mafia to a United States Senate committee.

"This is gonna be very, very bad," said Frank the Sheik Aliventi, a reaction shared around the table.

No one was more stunned than Freddie Sardo, the mobster who complained loudest about hating snitches. Sardo, Al learned, had been Joe Cago's longtime partner in crime. Before Valachi's photo showed up in the papers, Sardo was under the impression his pal was serving his own stretch in federal prison in Atlanta. But the stories explained how Valachi, fearing he had been marked for death by his boss, Vito Genovese, had split the skull of another convict he believed had been dispatched as his assassin. Except he'd killed the wrong man. And shortly after that mistake, he had fled into the arms of the FBI for protection.

"Freddie Sardo wasn't saying anything, but you could tell he was worried. He was in on a parole violation after serving a long bid for murder in Dannemora prison. He was wondering if anyone was looking at him cross-eyed for what his partner had done. I think he was trying to figure out if he was safer inside prison or out."

Informants at least were a threat that Al and the Italian table understood, much as they loathed them. Far murkier was another prison peril that haunted the gangster convicts almost as much. That was the policy aimed at thwarting prisoner sexual activity by alerting families back home that inmates were associating with known homosexuals.

Sex was common in Sing Sing. But to the outlaws gathered around the Italian table, it was an *infamia*, shameful and unforgivable conduct. The homosexual ban was one law they supported wholeheartedly.

"If the prison saw you even talking with anyone suspected of being a fag, they'd write a letter home to your family saying you were associating with someone suspected of homosexual conduct."

Al made it a point to shun anyone suspected of socializing with homosexuals in the prison. "I maintained myself like a monk in there. I didn't let anyone come near me."

His concern led him to abruptly shut off all contact with a prisoner he'd grown to like and admire.

Morris "Moishe" Malinsky was forty-three years old and serving his fourth term in prison when Al met him at Sing Sing. Another tough kid from Brooklyn, he was the son of Russian immigrants. As a teenager, he did three years at Elmira Reformatory for assault and robbery. Released in 1941, he was arrested with two of his Elmira roommates for the murder of a policeman who had been escorting the manager of the Loews Coney Island theater on Surf Avenue to a bank to deposit $770 in box-office receipts. The bandits gunned down the patrolman and snatched the cash.

Captured and charged with first-degree murder, Malinsky was convicted in 1943 and sentenced to die in the electric chair by Judge Samuel Leibowitz, Brooklyn's most famous jurist. He spent three years on death row at Sing Sing before the United States Supreme Court reversed the decision, citing evidence that cops had beaten Malinsky into confessing. He'd been taken to the sixth floor of the Hotel Bossert on Montague Street in downtown Brooklyn, where detectives stripped him naked, beat him, and threatened to throw him out the window if he didn't tell them what they wanted.

At his retrial, it was revealed that prosecutors had supplied witnesses in the case with hookers and cash. Acquitted, Malinsky sobbed his thanks to the jury.

Granted a second chance at life, Malinsky simply became a more sophisticated criminal. He became manager of the New York Pickle and Condiment Dealers Association, the lead group in what was then a $10 million city industry. In 1956, he was convicted on federal coercion and extortion charges for using a corrupt union to instill "fear and terror" in pickle dealers to get them to join his association. He got three years.

Back on the streets, he was arrested in 1961 while tunneling into a drug-supply warehouse in Long Island City. He was serving that sentence when Al met him.

"Moishe used to come down to my cell to talk. He talked about the death house and how he'd handled that. He could tell a great story, and he knew a lot of wiseguys. He knew the labor rackets and he'd spent time out in Las Vegas."

The storytelling came to an abrupt end one day when Jerry the Jew stopped by Al's cell. "He says, 'Al, can I talk to you? I want to tell you something. Moishe just wrote a letter to this female impersonator who was in here. He's doing some kind of show at this club on Fourth Street in the city and Moishe's writing to him.'"

"Get the fuck outta here," said Al.

"No, I swear it's true," said Jerry.

Al listened. He imagined Dolores getting one of those letters about his socializing habits.

Al told Ralph Masucci what he'd heard. Together they went up to Malinsky's cell. When they got there, Malinsky was fixing himself a lunch of tomatoes and lettuce he had taken from the mess hall.

"Hello, guys," he greeted them. "Help yourself."

Al stood at the door. "You come by my cell again and I'll kill you," he yelled.

"What'd I do?" cried Moishe.

"You want to come near my cell? Are you out of your mind? Stay away!"

His reputation preserved, Al went back downstairs.

* * *

He was marking his fourth full year in prison when inmates went on a sit-down strike to protest parole rules. On January 3, 1966, immediately after breakfast, 1,550 of the 1,821 prisoners in Sing Sing refused to report to their work assignments in the shops and galleys. There was a brief riot in the yard where some inmates started breaking up the ballfield stands. Corrections officers marched them back to their cells. Prisoners locked themselves in and refused to come out.

In B-block, Al was a prime agitator. "We all stuck together. A couple of guys didn't want to do it. In fact, one of them was a Genovese guy from the West Side who was friends with the Chin. We told them either they lock themselves in or we'd do it for them. They went along."

The prisoners were demanding mandatory time off for good behavior of up to a third of their term. That rule was already on the books, but parole officials frequently overruled it, citing prisoners' lack of jobs or housing on the outside.

Word of the protest rippled up and down the prison grapevine, sparking sit-ins at correction facilities around the state. It was an echo of a similar statewide sit-in over parole inequities that lasted for two days in November 1961, shortly before Al's arrival. Sing Sing warden Wilfred Denno had helped end that protest by telling prisoners he agreed with their complaint, and that he'd push for state legislation to remedy the inequities in the system. No one was punished for the protest, but the legislation never passed.

As far as Al was concerned, his parole hearings were just a formality. Even if he'd behaved himself, he was sure he'd have been denied early release. "They would've never let me out. You go to those hearings and the parole commissioners, the top guy was Oswald, would make a big deal about your plans for after prison. He'd go, 'Oh, what are you going to do when you get out? Oh, you don't have a job?' Well of course I don't have a job. I'm stuck in Sing Sing. It was all a fake."

In January, the warden helped end the new sit-in by promising there would be no retaliation against the strikers, and that he'd try again to win the reforms. After two days, the inmates went back to work.

In April, three months after the protest, Al was released on parole. He would serve the last nine months of his sentence at home. "They couldn't hold me any longer. It was mandatory release. I did my time."

Dolores and her father picked him up. It was a sunny spring day in April. "I remember looking at the river and everything outside and thinking, Wow, you could almost forget what the rest of the world looks like in there."

When Joseph came home from school that afternoon his mother was standing in the living room. She hadn't told him his father was coming home that day from prison. But then she hadn't really told him he'd ever gone. "My mother goes, 'Oh, I have a surprise for you!' And then the door swings shut and my dad is hiding behind it." The ten-year-old stared at the father he hadn't seen in four years. "It was like *boom*— there he is. I ran to him and was hugging him and crying." Holding his father, he thought how strange it was that they were in the same spot where his father had tied his shoes years before and said good-bye.

6

MULBERRY STREET

He arrived back on Mott Street to find only poor crippled Moe at Moe's café. Columbo Saggese was in prison. Jimmy Alto had died of lung cancer in 1964. Al had known the old man's prospects weren't good. Before he went away to Sing Sing, he'd driven Alto up to St. Clare's Hospital on the West Side several times, walking him right into the examination room. Doctors told him he had a tumor. It was in his chest, shaped like an egg.

"It was a heartbreak when I heard about him dying. I owed him a lot. He was a good man, and he was good to me."

He paid his respects to Alto's widow and children. He congratulated Jimmy's son, Vincent, who had passed the bar to become a lawyer. He had shortened his name to just Alto, the son told him. Al told him his dad would be proud.

He then considered his own circumstances. The newly minted ex-con was on parole for the next nine months until his full sentence expired. To satisfy regulations, he had to show legitimate employment, or at least that he was legitimately looking. Neither of which he was about to do.

"I wasn't going to get a job driving a truck again. I said, 'How about if I have my own business?' The parole officer thought I was nuts, but I was serious."

He rented a small warehouse just a couple of doors up the

block from his home on Kent Avenue and proclaimed himself a furniture dealer. "I got a few sticks of furniture, some couches and chairs, and stuck them out front. I showed the parole officer. I said I was going to run a furniture sales business."

Al was pleasantly surprised when he sold a few pieces. He ordered more items, and customers started showing up. "I got people asking for mattresses, so I added these Perfect Sleeper mattresses. I joined the Furniture Exchange on Lexington Avenue to get a better price." His little enterprise pleased Al's family, especially his father, who figured it would keep him out of trouble.

He enjoyed learning the trade. Setting himself up in a small office in the warehouse, he rose early, working the phones and handling orders. He hired a helper to move the bigger pieces and rented a truck for deliveries. He solicited orders from his underworld pals. It was the same work ethic he'd brought to his criminal endeavors. "I liked making a business. Just like my father, I liked to stay busy. No sitting around."

At the same time, he had no intention of going straight. He had learned too many angles in prison to waste all his time on a sidewalk furniture outfit. As soon as he could, he headed into Manhattan to see what other business opportunities had opened up while he was away.

One of his first stops was to see Ralph Masucci, his pal from Sing Sing. Masucci had finished up his sentence in Green Haven and had made it back to the streets a few months ahead of Al. They met at the corner of Desbrosses and West Streets in lower Manhattan across from the North River piers. Masucci introduced Al to his sister's husband, a successful carting company operator named Angelo Ponte. Along with his brothers, Ponte was preparing the West Street site for a lavish two-story restaurant. Al was impressed.

Masucci had other connections as well. In Green Haven, Ralph explained, he had met another Mafia old-timer looking for younger recruits to help relaunch his own criminal career. "Ralph said, 'We're going to be bouncing around, do-ing a lot of things. He's got a lot of ideas and connections. You should join up with us."

The old-timer's name was David Petillo. He was fifty-eight years old and looking to make up for lost time. He had spent most of the last thirty years behind bars after being convicted in 1936 as Lucky Luciano's chief accomplice in the business described as "compulsory prostitution" by the state's ambi-tious young special rackets prosecutor, Thomas E. Dewey.

It was the gangster trial of the decade. After beer baron Dutch Schultz was shot to death in a New Jersey tavern, Lu-ciano was declared public enemy number one on the East Coast. Dewey vowed to take him down. Instead of narcotics or gambling, both of which fell under Luciano's domain, Dewey went after what he saw as the gangster's weak spot: his control of the city's $12-million-a-year "vice rackets," including two hundred brothels and two thousand prostitutes.

Indicted under his given name, Salvatore Lucanía, the trial of Charlie Lucky garnered daily headlines. Dewey depicted the crime lord pulling the strings as he strutted around his luxury suite in the Waldorf-Astoria in a silk robe. Luciano's main instrument of terror and control over the prostitution ring was "Little Davie" Petillo, or Betillo as he often allowed his name to be misspelled.

"You guys are through," a brothel operator testified he was told by Luciano. "I am giving the business to Little Davie." Those who resisted suffered beatings, bullets pegged in their direction, and guns and knives in the ribs, Dewey told jurors.

It didn't hurt Dewey's theory of the case that Petillo had previously served as a gunslinger for America's other most notorious gangster, Al Capone in Chicago. Petillo was first arrested at age eleven; his rap sheet included charges of va-grancy, "jostling," robbery, gambling, grand larceny, and nar-cotics possession. He was creative with aliases. Over the years, he had given his name to police as Rose, Rosen, Rossa, Farrara, Slade, Quello, Petrilla, and Betillo.

There was no doubt about his real name, however. His fa-ther, Anthony Petillo, was a hardworking city sanitation worker who later retired to his homeland in Salerno, Italy, with his wife, Michelina. A brother had returned to Italy, where he went missing fighting with the Italian Army during the war. One sister, Anna, lived out her life in a mental institution. Another lived quietly in Stuyvesant Town with a husband who worked for the Internal Revenue Service, hoping each day not to be asked about his brother-in-law.

Little Davie wasn't actually that little. He stood five foot seven, with wavy brown hair and a ruddy complexion. Newspaper writers covering the trial often referred to him as "Handsome Davie" and remarked on his deceivingly boyish good looks.

The case was heard over a three-week span by a special blue-ribbon jury panel carefully culled and selected from respectable citizens. Jurors diligently deliberated over a Saturday night, announcing their verdict of guilty on all counts at 5:25 Sunday morning.

At the sentencing, Supreme Court Justice Philip McCook told Luciano he was "responsible, in law and morals, for every foul and cruel deed" committed by his underlings. Then he gave him thirty to fifty years in prison, a vastly longer term than ever ordered for similar crimes.

The judge then turned to Petillo. "As Luciano's chief and most ruthless aide, you deserve no consideration from this court," he told him. Little Davie got twenty-five to forty.

Both Luciano and Petillo were dispatched to Clinton prison in Dannemora, dubbed Siberia because of the chill of its winters and its location hard by the Canadian border.

In prison, Luciano chafed at his plight. While his true crimes were many, he insisted that his conviction for this one was purchased largely through perjured testimony. Pimps and prostitutes eager to avoid their own jail time had fed Dewey's investigators the evidence they sought to tie the king of the underworld to their own squalid business. Private investigators hired by Luciano's appeals attorneys obtained affidavits from key prosecution witnesses admitting that they had manufactured many of their stories involving Luciano.

Yet his appeals went nowhere. Dewey meanwhile rode into

higher office on his rackets-busting reputation. He was elected Manhattan district attorney, and was on his way to becoming state governor and eventual Republican presidential candidate.

No one had to frame Davie Petillo. There was ample evidence of his brutal handling of the brothel operators. But he eventually came to have his own complaint.

That started a few years later, after World War II began, when U.S. naval officers launched a naive mission to try and use mob influence to safeguard New York's harbors against enemy sabotage. They first approached Joe "Socks" Lanza, a power on the Manhattan waterfront. Lanza told them the person they needed to see was Luciano. Only Charlie Lucky, he told them, had the clout to get them what they wanted. The officers made the long up trip to Dannemora. Luciano told them he was only too glad to help.

To accommodate easier visits from his new military allies, Luciano was moved out of Siberia to Great Meadow prison in Comstock, near Albany. Petillo remained behind. At Comstock, Luciano's underworld cohorts, including Lanza, Frank Costello, and Meyer Lansky, became regular visitors. They were allowed to meet alone in a private office next to the warden's. He needed to consult with them for the war effort, Luciano said.

But if any concrete benefit was derived from the charade, the Navy could never cite it. The FBI later stated that the entire operation was a ruse. "A shocking misuse of Navy authority in the interest of a hoodlum," fumed J. Edgar Hoover in an internal bureau memo.

Yet it paid off well for Luciano. At war's close, Dewey, now governor and eager to put the episode behind him, pushed the envelope in the other direction. In 1946, he agreed to deport Luciano to freedom in Italy as a reward for his patriotic service. On the morning of February 10, Charlie Lucky, again living up to his name, set sail from a pier in Brooklyn on a freighter for Naples. Newsmen who tried to get aboard were blocked by burly longshoremen.

Left behind bars, Little Davie ranted to anyone who would

listen about his old partner's ingratitude. Al was to hear the story often.

"He would say Lucky Luciano was a rat. He was a rat if he helped the government, and he was a bigger rat for not taking Davie with him when he talked his way out. He could've threw Davie in there when he was stringing the government along. Instead, he left him rotting in prison."

By the time Ralph Masucci ran into him in Green Haven, Petillo had bounced around the state prison system. He was a surly, often paranoid, inmate. "He didn't trust anyone when Ralph met him. If you looked at him too long, he thought you were a spy."

One of the inmates who drew Petillo's suspicions was a Profaci crime family member named Eddie Fanelli, who was doing time for murder. One day, Fanelli's glance lingered a moment too long. Petillo began cursing. Then he pulled a shank from his pocket and lunged at him. Fanelli dodged, the blade just grazing his side. He quickly recovered and wrapped the smaller man in a chokehold.

Masucci intervened. "Eddie was choking Davie's lights out. Ralph punches Eddie in the head and knocks him right out. Davie figured Ralph saved his life, which he probably did."

The grateful Petillo told Ralph that when the two of them got out of prison, they would do big things together. He was now "with" him, Little Davie told Masucci.

The same way Al had been bound to his cousin Joe Schiavo's Luchese crime family, Masucci would henceforth have to clear whatever he wanted to do in the world of crime with Petillo. On the other hand, he could now count on the protection and guiding hand of a powerful figure in the most powerful crime family in New York.

Masucci told his new sponsor about his pal from Sing Sing. Petillo said he'd like to meet Al and told Ralph to bring him around when he got out.

Al duly consulted with Joe Schiavo about working with Petillo. For good measure, he checked in as well with his other connected cousin, Joe Sica, whose Pittsburgh crime group was aligned with the Genovese family. Both gave their approval. "If I had problems, they said I should see Joe Schiavo."

Al's employment interview took place in Luciano's old social club at 121 Mulberry Street. The two-room storefront was the one inheritance that Little Davie was able to claim from his former partner after his own release from prison. It was located on the ground floor of a five-story brick apartment house a few doors down from Hester Street, topped with proud lettering proclaiming the owner's name and date, Anna Esposito 1926. The club's exterior had been painted green at one point, but it was chipped and faded by the time Little Davie took over. Inside were a counter, tables, and chairs set on a tile floor. It looked much like Moe's café and a score of other nearby clubs.

Crime-wise, it was in the center of things. Mulberry Street was the main thoroughfare in the still heavily Italian section stretching from Canal Street to Houston Street. There were more mobsters per acre in the neighborhood than anywhere else in America. And it was still something of a free-fire zone for criminal operations. Detectives assigned to the Elizabeth Street station house were still looking the other way under the same pay-and-let-live approach to law enforcement.

One of Petillo's main moneymaking businesses was loan-sharking. Al was assigned to service the loans. "Davie had collected a big nut of money owed him when he got out and went straight into big-time shylocking. At one point, I know he had $700,000 pushed out on the street."

Al had done some loan-sharking of his own before going to prison. But this was a different league, where thousands of dollars had to be collected from businessmen, restaurant owners, and even other wiseguys.

There was an art to the task, his new boss explained. "He'd say, 'I want you to go see this guy over here and don't let him give you any stories. Get the money.'" The threat of violence underscored every exchange, but it was to be avoided whenever possible. "It made sense. If you gotta hit a guy, you might as well kill him, because you're putting yourself in a jam if he goes to the cops."

The best method, Petillo instructed, was to have a set day for collections so that both customer and lender understood the payment schedule. The etiquette of a mob loan officer was also important. "For starters, you didn't loan to guys you didn't trust. You look them right in the face and say, real quiet, 'You know what you're doing here, right? I don't want to have to chase you. No excuses. Otherwise, don't take the money. Do us both a favor and just walk away now. No hard feelings.' But the guy *never* walks away. They always want the money and they always say they understand."

Al found the loan shark's customers easier to handle than the loan shark himself. Petillo was a man of ferocious temper, constant suspicions, and strange habits.

"Davie smoked like a chimney. He'd light one cigarette off of another. But he was also a health nut. He'd take us up to some vitamin wholesale place and buy a shopping bag full of vitamins. He'd be popping the vitamin pills all day long, in between his cigarettes." The health fiend also delighted in showing off muscles shaped by decades in prison. "He'd drop to the floor and do sixty push-ups right in front of everyone. Me and Ralph were in pretty good shape ourselves, but we'd watch this old guy and be amazed."

Petillo brought the same manic approach to his driving, piloting a car as though he were trying to catch up with his lost years. "He'd always be borrowing your car, and he'd bomb along at top speed wherever he went. Meanwhile, he's slouching so far down on the seat that it looks like there's no one behind the wheel."

Petillo kept the two recruits busy. "He had us make the rounds with him every day. You'd take care of some loans, see someone else about a heist and any other crimes he could come up with. He'd say, 'We're going out to shake the trees.'"

One of the crimes that fell from the branches was arson for hire.

Their first target was a trucking firm on Washington Street around the corner from where Masucci's brother-in-law,

Angelo Ponte, was opening his new restaurant. Their instructions were to torch the place, but to make sure no one got hurt. "They asked us to burn this company, Essenfeld Brothers, a big trucking outfit. They had some kind of dispute going on with Ralph's brother-in-law. But they just wanted to send the message, not get anyone killed."

Equipped with several gallon jugs of gasoline, Al and Ralph waited until late at night after the business had closed. "We jimmied our way in and looked around to make sure no one was there. We even banged on the door and no one answered." The crime was a first for the men, but they figured it couldn't be that complicated. They started by pouring a wide trail of gas across the second floor, then down the stairs. Inside the door, they connected a long gauze rag to a pair of open bottles. They lit the fuse and walked quickly away.

A block from the warehouse, they stopped to look back. "We weren't sure if the fuse had gone out. We were wondering should we go back when we hear this *ka-boom* and the windows on the second floor explode." An object came hurtling out to the street. "There was a guy there rolling around. We took off, but we read about him in the newspaper the next day. He was a security guard who was asleep upstairs. He blew right out the window. He only broke his shoulder, but that was close."

Other arsons followed. "There was a wastepaper company out in Jersey that was competing with Ponte for business. It was owned by a politician and he wanted it wiped out. We drove out there and did the job. The place was filled with paper so it lit up like a bonfire. We could still see the smoke halfway back to the city."

Mornings on Kent Avenue, Al was host to regular visits from his skeptical parole officer. "He'd come by to see was I really working, and since I did the furniture business early in the day, I'd be there. I'd say, 'C'mon in, have a cup of coffee.' He'd leave, and then I'd be gone, out doing crimes."

Despite Al's part-time management, the business continued to prosper, fueled by orders from his gangland contacts.

After his parole ended, he merged with another nearby company.

"There was another guy I knew had a business a couple of blocks away on Hall Street and Myrtle that sold appliances, refrigerators, and stuff. I moved in with him."

His need for income similarly expanded. In March of 1967, Dolores gave birth to a second son, John. A year later, the couple had a fourth child, another daughter, Tara. One more daughter, Dawn, arrived in 1970.

Joseph, increasingly attuned now to the nature of his father's business, would sometimes accompany his dad to work. He rode with Al in the truck as he delivered furniture. On occasion he'd go to the other job on Mulberry Street. "They'd put me up on the counter, give me a soda," recalled Joseph.

There weren't many of the father-son get-togethers, on the job, or off. Mostly on his own, Joseph came to love baseball. He was a die-hard Mets fan, attending games with his mother's father. He played ball in a Little League sponsored by local shop owners in Fort Greene. The games were played in the park by Navy Street, beside the elevated Brooklyn-Queens Expressway. His dad didn't make it to the games. But there was a day Joseph remembered when he looked up from the field to see his father sitting in the cab of his furniture delivery truck under the highway watching his son play. "He didn't call out or anything, he was just sitting there, watching me. But I was happy he was there, watching me play."

As far as Al was concerned, his was just an ordinary working-class family, with many mouths to feed and bills to pay. If he didn't make it to the Little League games, he still made it home most nights for dinner with the family, even if he often went out again immediately afterward. He accompanied Dolores and the kids to church on Sundays. They enjoyed big meals on Sunday afternoons with the families. The only difference was the way he made his living.

The daily scheming began at the Mulberry Street club, which had become a gathering spot for many of Petillo's old partners in crime. Over cups of coffee and card games, Al listened to their stories.

Many, he learned, had started out under the wing of an old mob boss from the Fourth Ward on the Lower East Side named Giosue Aiello whose crew included Al's old tormentor at the ziginette game, Don ZaZá. Like Jimmy Alto, Aiello was another powerful mobster who slipped unnoticed past law enforcement and newspapers. After his death, his crew merged into the Genovese crime family, or *borgata*. But the group still maintained a feisty independence.

Among those clustering around the tables at the club was a big, broad-shouldered man named George Filippone, known on the streets as "Georgie Argento." Filippone's sidekick, Philip "Phil Katz" Albanese, controlled a lucrative truck-loading concession on the West Side docks and had served prison time for dope sales.

Another regular was Ottilio Frank Caruso, whose short, barrel-shaped build lent him the nickname "Frankie the Bug." In early 1962, the Bug had jumped bail on a narcotics charge and fled to Madrid, where he tried to hook up with Luciano. The two never got together, however. On January 26, 1962, a few days after Caruso and a cohort contacted the exiled gangster, Luciano suffered a fatal heart attack. The former underworld boss died complaining that Genovese's men were trying to set him up for arrest on drug charges.

There was a lot of it going around. Another veteran who had started out with Aiello was Angelo Tuminaro, a Genovese soldier who had been arrested a few years earlier in a million-dollar narcotics-importing ring. The bust was the first stage in an episode that later became mob history as the French Connection, with its huge cache of seized heroin famously vanishing from police custody.

But the mobster to keep the closest eye on, Al was told, was the smallest man in the group. Charles Gagliodotto was the size of a jockey, barely five feet tall. He had hooded eyes, hair gone gray, and an often ghostly pale pallor. He looked something like a pint-sized Boris Karloff. But no one dared kid him. "They called him 'Chalootz,' and he was a mad hatter. A stone killer. People were deathly scared of him."

For good reason. His killings had begun in 1925 when Gagliodotto, at age eighteen, was charged with shooting a rookie cop who had interrupted the robbery of a Jewish sacramental wine shop on Rivington Street on the Lower East Side. The teenaged Gagliodotto hid behind the cellar stairs, then shot the patrolman in the back of the head as he climbed down to investigate. A few years later, he was back on the street, serving as a proficient hit man for Luciano and others.

Many of Gagliodotto's missions were cross-country jaunts to rub out those who had balked at going along with Luciano's new world order in the Mafia. On those trips, the old-timers told Al, Petillo often accompanied him.

The two slightly built men had a special technique to help them get the drop on their victims. "They'd dress up like women. They'd wear hats and veils and dresses and stick the guns in their purses. That way they could sneak up on people, do the hit, and get away. One time, Davie and Chalootz go to a funeral. They wore black veils. They get in the funeral limousine with the guy they're after, and pop him right there in the car. They did at least a couple dozen hits made up like women."

That estimate meshes with one offered by an FBI informant who told the same strange tale to a bureau agent back in 1960. Referring to Little Davie as "Betillo," the unnamed snitch described him and Gagliodotto as "two of the most feared members of the Italian syndicate." The informant added that "it was common knowledge among the hoodlum element" that the pair had "killed between 20 and 30 persons in Detroit, Cleveland, Chicago and New York." The memo of the interview offered a slightly different wrinkle on the duo's deadly mode of operation: "Betillo often dressed as a woman and Gagliodotto accompanied him as an escort. In this manner, they aroused no suspicion in contacting the victim, and identification was almost impossible once they succeeded in fleeing the scene of the murder."

* * *

As far as Al could tell, the two aging gangsters had abandoned their cross-dressing tactic. But neither one was out of the murder business.

Al found that out when a young Jewish hoodlum from the Bronx named Frank Salzberg who had been hanging around the club suddenly disappeared. Salzberg had done time with Petillo in prison, and had been another willing recruit to the mobster's team. All anyone knew when he went missing was that he had somehow rubbed Little Davie the wrong way.

"Frankie was a pretty decent kid. He would hang around with us on Mulberry Street. Davie got mad at him and claimed he owed him money. Next thing I know, the kid is gone."

The story soon emerged that Petillo had borrowed a car and barreled up to the north Bronx where Salzberg lived, and taken him for a walk in Van Cortlandt Park. The details were whispered around the club. "Davie stabbed him in the head. Killed him."

The body was found by someone out for a Friday afternoon stroll in the park on August 9, 1968. Salzberg was lying face up in the bushes, just east of West 253rd Street, where he had been living. The medical examiner's office determined that he'd been stabbed seven times, including in the neck, face, lung, jaw, and head. An aunt identified him but didn't claim the body. The Hebrew Free Burial Association took care of it, burying Salzberg in Mount Richmond Cemetery on Staten Island.

Soon, another detail of the story tumbled out. Salzberg had been distributing heroin for Petillo. At that point, neither Al nor Ralph had been assigned that task, but it hadn't taken them long to notice that it was all around them. The crew at 121 Mulberry Street was drenched in the narcotics business.

Gagliodotto had been among nineteen gangsters arrested in a 1965 roundup by the Brooklyn district attorney, charged with helping to run a $90-million-a-year narcotics ring. "These are the big boys," said Brooklyn DA Aaron Koota announcing the arrests. Named as leader of the ring was Frank Tuminaro, who was following in his big brother Angelo's footsteps in the dope trade. A host of other Genovese associates were also snared, including Frank Gangi and his nephew, Rosario "Ross" Gangi. The case was made by many of the same investigators still chasing the French Connection, including NYPD detective Eddie Egan, the model for Popeye Doyle in the movie.

Thanks to multiple motions filed by defense attorneys, the case had still not gone to trial three years after the arrests. Defendants were still walking the streets, free on bail. But they were worrying as much about each other as they were about prosecutors. Al noticed Gagliodotto was particularly edgy. Part of the problem was that Chalootz had become addicted to his own product. "He was doing heroin and smoking opium. Some of the old-timers were users. They called it 'kicking the gong.'" Together with Chalootz's suspicious nature, it made for a lethal combination. The same summer of 1968 when Frankie Salzberg disappeared, Charles Gagliodotto went on his own final killing spree.

"Chalootz thought Frankie Tuminaro and Frank Gangi were stealing from him. Considering how crazy Chalootz was, I don't think they would have done that. But he didn't give them any time to explain."

The way Al heard it, Galgiodotto invited the two men to a social club on Elizabeth Street around the corner from where he lived in an apartment on East Houston Street above Bentivegna's Restaurant. "He gives them a drink and then shoots them both. He had body bags ready and he puts them in his car trunk. He dumped them upstate in Monticello in the Catskills where he used to go in the summers."

Actually, Chalootz never made it up to Monticello. He pulled off Route 17 about twenty miles south of his vacation home, and dumped the bodies in the woods outside the village of Bloomingburg in Sullivan County. A few days later, a pair of boys from a nearby American Legion camp spotted the body bags just off a dirt road. The men had been shot once in the head, their bodies trussed in rope and wrapped in heavy plastic. They'd been dead about a week. All identification had been stripped, but it took state troopers and the FBI only a day to figure out who they were.

On Mulberry Street, the reaction to the murders was that crazy Chalootz had finally gone too far. "When people are deathly scared of you all the time, you're gone. Because you're too crazy. No one's safe."

The motion for termination was made by Frankie Tuminaro's outraged big brother, Angelo. "Little Ange got the okay to whack him." Even Chalootz's old killing partner, Davie Petillo, was on board with the decision. The assassination team stealthily tracked Gagliodotto, waiting for an opportunity to take him.

On the evening of August 22, Petillo met his old pal in Astoria, Queens, on Twenty-First Avenue. Chalootz, suspicious of everyone else, figured he had nothing to worry about from Little Davie. Petillo had brought along a younger cousin, Eddie Vassallo, nicknamed "Bullshit Eddie" for his mangling approach to the truth. Petillo managed to slip behind Chalootz and strangle him while Bullshit Eddie held him down. "I heard he used a plastic bag over his head."

Whatever the tool set employed, no discernible marks were left on Gagliodotto's body. After passersby spotted it on the sidewalk where Petillo and Vassallo deposited it, the assumption by police and the responding ambulance crew was that a neatly dressed old man had simply collapsed and died on the street of natural causes. He was still wearing his diamond ring and wristwatch, so he clearly wasn't a robbery victim. At the morgue, doctors concurred. "Arteriosclerotic heart disease," they wrote on the death certificate. Even as he'd been wrestling bodies of full-grown men in and out of his car trunk, the sixty-two-year-old Gagliodotto had apparently been in pretty tough shape.

A day after the murder, a pair of informants whispered in the ears of FBI agents in New York that there was nothing natural about Chalootz's death. Police and the bureau should already have been suspicious. A reputed mob assassin and drug dealer drops dead on a Queens street two weeks after the murders of two members of the same gang, all of whom were indicted in the same massive narcotics case? It was a bit odd.

Chalootz was already being waked by family members at La Vecchia Funeral Home on Mott Street next to St. Patrick's Old Cathedral when the FBI told police what they'd learned. Armed with a search warrant, police went into the parlor and removed the body. The Gagliodotto clan was irate, but there wasn't much they could do. The remains were brought back to the morgue, where a second autopsy produced a new finding: death by strangulation.

FBI memos noted that city police detectives mounted a "major investigation" to find Gagliodotto's killer. No one was ever charged. A month after he'd throttled his former friend to death, Petillo was spotted attending a wake for another old pal, Joe "Socks" Lanza, the waterfront boss who had helped Luciano con the Navy. Unlike Chalootz, Lanza really had died of a natural cause, cancer. Petillo, the FBI's informant noted, attended together with "Angie Tuminaro."

Absent Chalootz's spooky presence, most of the crew at 121 Mulberry Street relaxed somewhat, Al noticed. Little Davie, however, seemed more keyed up than ever. His core industry remained loaning cash. He pushed Al and Ralph to get more money on the street, and collect from those who owed. But every now and again, despite the consequences, a customer would fail to make his payments. "You got a choice then. You kill him or you take his property."

When a loan shark customer who owned a small diner at the corner of Seventh Avenue and Perry Street near St. Vincent's Hospital in Greenwich Village defaulted on a loan, Al and Ralph decided to take over the diner. "The guy who had it went bust. He was a gambler and when he couldn't make the vig, he just handed us the keys."

The little diner had been called the Greenhouse. Al renamed it At Joey's. "You know, 'Where are you?' 'I'm *at Joey's.*'" He enjoyed operating a restaurant. "I liked to cook, so that was part of the reason we took it."

To handle chores at the diner, Al brought in a pal he had met in Sing Sing who was helping him with his furniture business. "His name was Gene Agress. I called him 'Big Gene.'

He was half Irish, half Greek. He'd done time for supermarket stickups. He'd stick a big wad of bread in each cheek to disguise himself, but he got picked up for it a few times."

Big Gene was working in the kitchen of the diner one afternoon while Al was behind the counter when a heavyset man in a suit came in the door. "He introduces himself as Abe something or other, saying he represents the landlord of the building and the old owner owes rent. Right away he's talking tough. I said, 'So what? He's gone and now we're here.' We're arguing, it gets loud, and then he pulls a gun." Al grabbed for the weapon. He was fighting with the collection agent when Big Gene burst out of the kitchen, grabbed the man by the shoulders, and punched him. Together, they wrestled him out a back door.

"We were getting ready to stomp him out back when a cop comes in the front to buy cigarettes from the machine. The guy in the suit takes off. The cop must've heard us because he comes in the back and sees the gun lying in the street where it fell. He says, 'What's this?' Gene and me look at each other. I said, 'I dunno. I think maybe that guy was looking to rob us till he saw you.' The cop couldn't figure out what to do, so he picks up the gun, gets his cigarettes, and that's it. It was close. We almost got pinched."

A few days later, the landlord himself came by to meet his new and uncooperative tenants. "That's how I met Frank Moten. He was a black guy who was big in the numbers, not just New York, but in a bunch of states. He also had a couple of nightclubs uptown."

Moten, it turned out, held the mortgage on the building where the diner was located. He had other properties nearby as well as in Harlem and the Bronx. The two men found they had a lot in common. "We started talking about guys we both knew. We hit it off." Moten, Al learned, was allied with the East Harlem Genovese family faction, which was running a booming narcotics trade out of storefronts along Pleasant Avenue near the East River. Moten was one of their major heroin distributors. But unlike most of the gangsters Al knew, Moten was wisely investing his profits from the numbers business and his dope trade in real estate. Handling the transactions for Moten was a savvy Bronx real estate operative named Morris Skidelsky. "Frank was a lot smarter than most guys. He was figuring out how to save money."

The diner drew a cross section of customers: workers from St. Vincent's up the avenue, jazz musicians playing at the famed Village Vanguard across the street, the occasional cop, as well as more than a few gangsters. The most illustrious of these was Thomas Eboli, known as "Tommy Ryan," a high-ranking leader of the Genovese crime family. Eboli's official title at the time was acting underboss for the still imprisoned Don Vito. But Eboli was widely perceived as caretaking for most of the family's operations in the city. For Al and Ralph, having Eboli stop in for a regular cup of coffee at the counter of At Joey's was better than a four-star restaurant review.

"Tommy Ryan would come by every day. He had a little private café he ran nearby, Napoli di Notte, and he'd stop in on his way there, hang around and chat." Eboli did not adhere to the Jimmy Alto school of keeping a low profile. There was nothing low-key about him. "He rode around in this Cadillac Eldorado with a purple roof and a cream-colored body. He dressed like a million bucks. Everything about him said, 'Gangster.'"

Eboli told Al and Ralph he liked the job they were doing with the diner and for Davie Petillo. And he suggested they might want to branch out. "He had an offer for us. He wanted us to take over this hotel in Texas that he got the same way we got the diner, from someone who couldn't pay a debt. He was telling us it was a nice place and we could make a lot of money."

Al and Ralph told Tommy Ryan they'd think about it. But after Eboli made his pitch and left, they started to laugh. "We couldn't go to fucking Texas. Me? With my Brooklyn accent? Down there? We didn't want to offend Tommy Ryan, but there was no way we were doing that."

The acting underboss wasn't bothered. The next time he

took a stool at the counter the subject never came up. "I liked Tommy Ryan. For a boss, he was an easy guy to talk to."

Far harder to communicate with was the other Genovese power in Greenwich Village. Vincent Gigante, the ex-prizefighter with the bad aim, got out of prison in 1964. He'd served almost five years in Lewisburg federal penitentiary after being convicted alongside Genovese in a major narcotics conspiracy case. Ralph Masucci occasionally saw his old high school acquaintance around the neighborhood, but they didn't spend time together. Gigante was just starting to perform the role he would eventually make famous as the mentally unhinged gangster. He spent much of his time closeted inside his Sullivan Street clubhouse, brooding and saying little.

But when a promising business opportunity developed involving one of Gigante's associates, Al and Masucci went over to Sullivan Street to discuss it.

Masucci had met the captain of a Greek ocean liner docked at a pier on the lower West Side. The captain explained he was unable to depart because of a million-dollar lien that had been placed against the vessel by a downtown travel agency. The lien had been placed by an ambitious travel agent named William Fugazy who had grown up in the Village and who kept an office above O. Henry's steakhouse at Sixth Avenue and West Third Street.

Fugazy was a tireless self-promoter. His name constantly appeared in the press. He could honestly boast of friendships with Bob Hope, Lee Iacocca, and Cardinal Terence Cooke. Along with former federal prosecutor Roy Cohn, he had promoted the second and third Ingmar Johansson–Floyd Patterson heavyweight title matches in 1960 and 1961. Another of Fugazy's influential friends was the local Greenwich Village Genovese capo, Vincent Gigante.

Together with the captain, Ralph and Al hatched a plan for the lien to be lifted and the ship to sail in exchange for letting the gangsters have the vessel's gambling concession. "We knew a casino on the ship would be a big moneymaker.

Ralph knew Fugazy from the neighborhood, and we went to see him and his partner, who ran O. Henry's steakhouse." The deal they pitched was that the travel agents would recruit customers for the gambling junkets and get a percentage of the take. Their next stop was to see Gigante to get his approval.

At the Sullivan Street clubhouse, Gigante looked perfectly normal. He was wearing a gray suit and an open-necked white shirt. He nodded at Al and said hello. Although their trails continued to cross over the years, it was the only word he and Al ever exchanged. Gigante and Masucci then went off to the side to have a whispered conversation.

Outside the club, Ralph relayed the verdict. "Chin was good with it. He gave the okay to do the deal." But the scheme soon fell apart. The ship's captain, possibly thanks to second thoughts about his prospective new partners, found another way to raise the cash for the lien and paid it off. A few days later, the ship sailed without them.

Davie Petillo made his own trips abroad, but in keeping with his restlessly suspicious nature, he said little about them. Al never asked. In fact, he and Ralph knew little about Petillo's life away from Mulberry Street. What they did know was that he was single. His wife had died while he was in Dannemora. For a time after he got out of prison, Petillo lived at the Holland Hotel in Times Square. He also remained deeply embedded in the local narcotics trade, despite the arrests of many around him. It was the one crime in which he hadn't enlisted Al or Ralph, but that day soon arrived as well.

Petillo showed up at the diner one day and announced that he had a large load of heroin he needed to move. They should take as much as they wanted to sell, he told them. They asked him how much he had. "One hundred kilos," he told them.

The partners were amazed. They'd had no idea he was that big in the business. Gangsters all around them were getting nailed as big narcotics traffickers, and here was Little Davie moving mountains of junk and yet no one had laid a glove on him.

They debated what to do. On the one hand, they were deeply envious of the enormous profits they'd seen others make in the dope trade. On the other, they had no idea how to spot a quality product, or how to distribute it.

"We ended up telling Davie we'd take one kilo. We figured that was a good starting point, and if it worked out we'd be back for more."

Petillo was pleased. After he delivered the package he began to talk openly about his heroin importing. "One of the places he got junk from was Afghanistan, he tells us. And he smuggled it into the country by hiding it in these big sheepskin coats." In proof of his claim, Petillo showed up the next day with one of the garments. "He spreads the coat out right there on the counter in the diner, and he starts cutting it open. There's the package of heroin inside, just like he said."

Enthused about their new business, Al and Ralph lined up customers who said they'd be happy to sell some of the heroin. "We didn't know what we were doing. We just gave it to them. We didn't cut it down to make more like you're supposed to." But even at full strength, the product was rejected.

"Everyone we sold to came back and said the junk was no good. So we took what we had left and brought it back to Davie. He asked what was wrong. We said it just didn't work out. He was much too crazy to try and take a chance of telling him his stuff wasn't any good. You never knew what he would do."

Petillo's volatile nature became even clearer a few months later when, in the spring of 1970, the gangster world went almost completely off its axis.

The turmoil began when a gung ho Mafioso from south Brooklyn named Joe Colombo decided to adopt civil rights tactics used by black leaders in defense of Italian Americans being pursued by the FBI. It was an audacious gambit, especially for a second-generation gangster like Colombo. He had ascended to the leadership of the Profaci crime family in 1964 thanks to his skills as a hit man and his cunning as a mob strategist. But when his son Joe Jr. was indicted in April 1970

on federal charges of conspiring to melt coins into silver—
charges he later beat—the father decided to shift gears. He
organized picket lines outside FBI headquarters in New York
at Third Avenue and East Sixty-Ninth Street. The picketers
grew to more than five thousand people, led by cheering members of Colombo's crime family. He took things up several
notches more by calling for a "Unity Day" mass rally for June
29 in Columbus Circle.

The antics struck most top mobsters as a clownish embar-
rassment, and a potential threat to organized crime's well-
being. But the take-it-to-the-streets approach struck a chord
with many younger mobsters. Al and Ralph went up to the
rallies to check things out. So did Al's son, Joseph, then fifteen years old and eager to get his licks in against the hated
FBI. "Joseph went up there and got into a fight with some guy
who tried to pull him out of the crowd."

After Genovese family leaders passed the word to steer
clear of Colombo's activities, Petillo told them to stay away.
Al didn't disagree. "'It was just drawing attention. What are
you trying to do? Prove you're a gangster?"

But few mobsters were more on board for fighting the FBI
than Little Davie. For him, the bureau was the ultimate symbol for the cops and prosecutors who, by his lights, had kept
him unfairly locked in prison for decades and had hounded
him ever since.

The bureau got a taste of that hate when it tried to interview him in his room at the Holland Hotel in 1967. "Petillo
began shouting and using obscene language," reported the
luckless agents who tried to talk to him. He'd been "framed
by Tom Dewey," he said. If the FBI didn't stop "buggin'" him,
he'd "yell harassment to the highest court in the land."

Colombo's civil rights protests a few years later were fuel
for Petillo's fire. "Davie comes to see me and Ralphie. He says,
'There's this thing they're gonna have called Unity Day and
we're gonna do our own protest.' We're listening, since he told
us not to go up there no more."

Petillo then laid out his plan. "I'm getting you a garbage
truck from the company that picks up trash at the FBI build-

ing," he told them. "I got a load of dynamite we're gonna put in it, and you're gonna drive up there on Unity Day, get right close to it, and blow the whole place up."

Al and Ralph listened in wonder. "We're looking at this crazy bastard trying to figure out if he's serious or having us on. We realize he means it. He did thirty years and it did something to his brain. And it's not like he's asking, 'Whaddya think?' He's telling us. He wants us to do it. He was out of his mind."

Petillo may have come to his senses later. More likely, someone else in the Genovese clan spelled out for him why his plan was a dangerous and foolhardy notion. The idea vanished as quickly as it arrived. Al breathed a sigh of relief. He didn't want to have to say no to the lethal Petillo.

But there was more to come. A few weeks later, Petillo announced that he had another important assignment for them: a murder.

The proposed victim was Petillo's own cousin, Edward "Bullshit Eddie" Vassallo, who had helped Little Davie throttle Charlie Gagliodotto to death. Petillo didn't give a reason for wanting his cousin dead. But Al had a general idea. Vassallo was a heavy drug user, a habit that had helped make him notoriously sloppy. The story was widely told on Mulberry Street how Bullshit Eddie, assigned to get rid of a body wrapped in a carpet, had left the back door of his station wagon open, allowing both body and carpet to roll out onto a busy Lower East Side avenue. Not that any of those issues really counted in the end. "Davie was always ready to kill anyone who got in his way."

Vassallo, Al knew, was deeply involved in the pornography business, with Little Davie as his chief backer. Porn was another part of the mob repertoire that Al had so far avoided. "That was something Jimmy Alto taught us to stay away from. He said it was a bad way to make a living."

But it was clearly lucrative. There was a studio in the office building at 75 Spring Street at the corner of Crosby Street where Vassallo and another partner, a hairdresser from First

Avenue named Charlie Pomaro, had workers making and copying 8 mm sex movies. The films were supplied to Times Square peep shows and marketed to customers at adult bookstores throughout the metropolitan area. Vassallo and Pomaro owned a few of the stores themselves.

Al learned something of the problems between the cousins one night when Davie took him and Ralph out to dinner at Paolucci's restaurant on Mulberry Street. "Davie was feeling good because he had this young girl visiting him, and he took us all out to celebrate." At the restaurant, Petillo began complaining about a string of new porn shops that Vassallo and Pomaro had opened uptown. "I couldn't tell exactly what his beef was, but he was pissed off about it."

Whatever the motive, murder had not been among the crimes that Al signed up for when he agreed to work with Petillo. Before things went any further, Al told him, he would have to talk to his own cousin, Joe Schiavo, to make sure the killing was approved by his Luchese family superiors.

"Davie wasn't happy when I told him. He must've thought that all this time we'd been scheming together that I would just do a piece of work for him, no questions asked."

Al contacted Schiavo, who immediately told him not to do anything more involving the plot. "Joe said we would have to have a sit-down to work out this thing and to get Davie to stop trying to order me around."

Sit-downs were the mob equivalent of arbitration sessions, except that the highest-ranking mobster in the room usually got to decide. The one about whether Davie Petillo could have Al D'Arco kill for him was decided at a coffee shop at the corner of Clinton and Grand Streets on the Lower East Side.

Representing the Luchese family's interest in Al were Schiavo and Babe Vario, the gangster from Canarsie in south Brooklyn who had been friendly with Al in Sing Sing. Babe's older brother, Paul, was now the captain of the family's Canarsie crew. But Joe Schiavo was still its senior member. It was understood that the captain's job had been Joe Schiavo's for the asking, but that he had opted to continue handling the garment shops and business interests he ran with boss Thomas Luchese and other elder statesmen of the family.

Petillo came alone to the meeting. But lingering on a corner nearby, and making no effort to hide his presence, was an old friend of Davie's who made an excellent bodyguard. Red Levine lived in the neighborhood, so he had a good excuse to be there. But more significantly, Levine was a veteran and well-known Jewish gangster who had led the hit team that assassinated the most powerful mobster in New York, Salvatore Maranzano, back in 1931. The murder, on an upper floor of a Park Avenue office building, established Lucky Luciano as the unchallenged leader of New York's mobs. Levine and Petillo had been close ever since.

From the coffee shop, Schiavo and Vario watched Levine, who was being greeted on the corner like a celebrity. "Look at all the Jews kissing Red Levine's ring," said Vario. "He's like the pope down here."

Petillo began the discussion. "Right away in the sit-down, Davie tried to get an advantage, throwing some crap out there claiming I had been doing cocaine. At that time, if you were using drugs, you automatically lose the argument, whatever it is."

Al suppressed his anger and simply shook his head. "I didn't want to call him a liar right to his face. I just said that's not true." The discussion moved on, going back and forth until Schiavo announced his findings. "Joe put it on record that I was allowed to keep operating with Little Davie. But I couldn't commit any murders without the approval of the Luchese family, including Joe Schiavo and the captain, Paul Vario."

Schiavo closed the meeting with an instruction for Davie. "When you talk to Al, you are talking to me."

Petillo left the coffee shop fuming. Al felt like a giant burden had been lifted. "I knew Davie wasn't going to want me back to work under him again. Not after he'd been told he couldn't make me do whatever he wanted."

"How's Paulie?" was Petillo's taunt to Al when he next saw him on Mulberry Street. "You still with Paulie?"

Al ignored him. "I didn't care. I didn't have to deal with that loony bastard. That was the important thing."

As for Bullshit Eddie Vassallo, he went on making porn movies, having been granted a stay of execution. But it was only temporary. In February 1980, someone shot him to death as he sat in his New Jersey living room.

The prime suspect in the shooting was the same man who had wanted him dead ten years earlier. David Petillo quickly fled the country. The FBI and Interpol tracked him for the next three years as he moved between luxury hotels in Germany, Greece, Singapore, Bali, Hong Kong, and Hawaii. They never caught up. The trail ended three days after Christmas in 1983 when Petillo collapsed and died while staying in the resort town of Málaga, Spain, on the Mediterranean coast. Little Davie had added one more alias to his roster. The dead guest was registered as James J. Pilone.

7

32 SPRING STREET

On October 6, 1970, the body of a gangster named Salvatore Granello was found in an abandoned car on the Lower East Side. He had been laid to rest in a mob casket: a heavy canvas wrap, a plastic bag over his face. He had four .22-caliber bullets in the back of his head. By the time a passerby finally worked up the nerve to take a good look inside the car sitting at the curb along the Franklin D. Roosevelt Drive at Gouverneur Slip, Granello had been dead at least a week, by police estimate.

The murder generated a day or two of newspaper stories, but the killing was never solved, so that was about it for public notoriety in the case. In terms of mob slayings in New York in the early seventies, it didn't make much of a ripple. The big headlines and permanent historical mob markers went to the sensational cases that came soon after: Joe Colombo, shot in broad daylight in Columbus Circle at the start of his second annual Italian-American Civil Rights League rally in June 1971; the even more cinematic rubout of the man most people blamed for having Colombo hit, Joe Gallo, gunned down while dining with friends in Umberto's Clam House on Hester Street in April 1972.

But for those trying to carve out criminal livelihoods on the streets of Little Italy in those days, it was the execution

of Salvatore Granello—known as Sally Burns—that raised
eyebrows the highest. Granello's mob bloodlines went deeper
and wider than either Colombo's or Gallo's, both of whom,
by the time of their demise, were generally dismissed as
equally *ubazz*—crazy.

On Al's turf, the hit on Granello was the talk of the town.
"Sally Burns was one of the biggest guys around. He was into
everything. He had a racetrack and a casino in Cuba. He had
nightclubs all over. He was big in the unions, had a big shylock book. He lived in this beautiful duplex apartment at 215
Mott Street. The building was just another tenement, but he
spent a lot of money on it, made it into a fancy place."

A frequent visitor to the swank apartment was Granello's
boss, Vito Genovese, who strolled over from his office at
the Erb Strapping Company at 180 Thompson Street. After
Genovese's top lieutenant, Anthony Strollo, vanished in 1962,
Granello took over many of Tony Bender's old chores, including handling bars and nightclubs in the Village and Times
Square. His criminal career began in 1940 at seventeen when
he and a pal, Carmen Di Biase, pistol-whipped a tailor on
Hudson Street in an attempted robbery. He spent two years
in the reformatory at Coxsackie for that. He was charged with
evading the draft in 1946, but it was later cleared up when
he proved he was 4-F and just not up to the task.

He was five foot seven, a stocky 225 pounds. He liked to
dress with flash and flare, drove a light blue Cadillac convertible, and sported a ten-carat diamond ring on his right hand.
There was a vacation home on upstate Greenwood Lake where
he kept a twenty-one-foot Chris Craft speedboat and ran a
club called the Little Copa. He was a mob trend setter. A
leader in the electricians union local representing TV repairmen, he was suspected of having orchestrated the 1953 hijacking of a $500,000 cargo of Sylvania televisions.

Once the FBI started taking the Mafia seriously in the late
1950s, Granello quickly made the agency's "top hoodlum"
list. Agents spent hours surveilling his Mott Street tenement,
quizzing neighbors, and checking out the numbers dialed
from his phone. The checks confirmed a lengthy and varied

list of business interests. Along with another crooked union official, George Levine, Granello had been part owner of the Oriente Park Race Track outside Havana. The duo also ran the next-door casino as well as the restaurant and bar in Havana's Hotel Sevilla Biltmore. After Castro took over, Granello opened a gambling and after-hours club on Collins Avenue in Miami Beach. There, he fleeced exiled supporters of dictator Fulgencio Batista, turning their millions in pesos into dollars at a rate to his considerable advantage.

In New York, his clubs included the El Borracho on East Fifty-Fifth Street, and the Headline Bar and Joey Dee's nightclub in Times Square. At the Café de Paris at Fifty-Third and Broadway, his front man was nightclub impresario Lou Walters, whose daughter Barbara was then writing copy for CBS News. Another illustrious pal was former middleweight world champ Rocky Graziano, who stood as godfather to Granello's youngest daughter.

He ranked high enough on Attorney General Robert F. Kennedy's target list that in 1963 he was hit with tax-evasion charges for failing to disclose $425,000 earned from the sale of Cuban oil shares. That was followed by a state extortion rap for shaking down a Nassau County jukebox distributor. Granello, testimony alleged, threatened to kick the distributor's pregnant daughter in the stomach.

But his most serious difficulties stemmed from his dealings with a fast-talking lawyer named Herbert Itkin, whose past clients included Teamsters union chief Jimmy Hoffa. Itkin told Sally Burns he could help the Genovese organization tap into the vast millions of the Teamsters union's pension funds.

Granello was charmed by the tall, glib attorney and his easy access to decision makers. He brought him to meetings of fellow mob dignitaries, including James "Jimmy Doyle" Plumeri, a Luchese family captain who had graduated from Luciano gunman to major power in the city's garment industry.

Granello also drove Itkin out to western Pennsylvania to meet a pair of friends from his salad days in Cuba. Until their own Castro eviction papers were served, Pittsburgh crime boss Sebastian John La Rocca and a top lieutenant, Gabriel "Kelly" Mannarino, had held a large share in the casino at the Sans Souci Hotel. Both men were also eager to obtain the favorable financing Itkin offered.

Al knew about these meetings because they took place at the Monroeville, Pennsylvania, home of his cousin Joe Sica, the man whose gleaming Cadillac and shiny jacket buttons had dazzled Al as a boy on Kent Avenue.

"Sally Burns brought Herbert Itkin into Joe Sica's house and they scoped out all these deals he was going to do for them. They thought they were all going to make millions with this guy."

Instead, the meetings and ensuing deals became a Mafia disaster. Itkin was a true double agent. He had been a part-time informer for the Central Intelligence Agency before taking his talents to the FBI. Along the way, he was careful enough to win immunity for his own many financial scams while building cases against those he hooked.

More than two dozen mobsters, mob associates, and politicians were indicted for fraud. Among them were Granello, Plumeri, and the entire top shelf of Pittsburgh's mob, La Rocca, Mannarino, and Sica. In a separate case involving kickbacks on a city water contract, Itkin snared a New York trifecta: a top aide to Mayor John Lindsay named James Marcus, Tammany Hall boss Carmine DeSapio, and the heir apparent to Thomas Luchese's crime family, Anthony "Tony Ducks" Corallo.

The Itkin cases caused a mob furor. When the charges came down, Al was asked to hide Joe Sica and a son-in-law, Frank Rosa, who was also indicted. "I picked them up right in front of Macy's on Thirty-Fourth Street. They dove right in the car. We hid them out at my aunt's house and our place for a few weeks till they were ready to surrender."

Granello also went into hiding when his first indictment came down. Law enforcement thought he was only ducking the fraud charges. But given the way Joe Sica talked about him while he was on the lam, he had more to fear from his friends in the mob than the law.

"Sally Burns was the guy who caused the pinch. He was responsible for bringing Herbert Itkin around. Everyone was looking for him."

While Granello was serving his time in Danbury prison, someone killed his nineteen-year-old son Michael with a shotgun. Granello got a one-day furlough to attend the services at Most Precious Blood Church on Canal Street and the burial at St. John's Cemetery in Queens.

After he was released from prison in the fall of 1970, FBI agents warned the mobster that they'd picked up word he was marked for death. Other gangsters, they'd heard, were worried he would seek revenge for his son's killing. They had the right information, but only a partial motive. Granello brushed them off anyway, telling them to talk to his lawyer, Roy Cohn, who was representing him on the fraud charges.

On the evening of September 24, 1970, Sally Burns was spotted at Vincent's Clam Bar at the corner of Hester and Mott Streets. He was seated with his old partner, George Levine, and a couple of other associates. He told them he had an appointment and he'd catch up with them later.

Granello went around the corner, where he ducked into a Genovese clubhouse on Mott Street called the Eighth Ward Pleasure Lounge. Al was later told what happened next.

"The guy that got him was his own goombata, Charlie Brody, one of the DiPalermo boys." The DiPalermo brothers were a notorious band of Little Italy drug dealers. "He was the only one could get that close to him without him worrying. They clipped him right there on Mott Street."

After Granello turned up dead, police and the reporters who quoted them anonymously offered two theories for the hit. One was the concern over vengeance he might seek for his son. The other was that it was part of the fallout from the scramble to succeed Vito Genovese, who had died in prison in February 1969. Granello's death meant one less applicant for the job.

Years later, another theory surfaced after a congressional investigation found evidence that Granello had been one of the mobsters approached by the CIA in 1961 for help with his Cuban contacts in figuring out how to kill Castro. Conspiracy theorists soon added his name to the list of those who died untimely but convenient deaths after the assassination of President Kennedy. Al wasn't impressed. "I know why Sally Burns went, and I know who did it. After he brought that rat around who caused so much trouble, he was not going to last too long."

No matter how steeped in the ways of the mob he was becoming, and for all of his hard work in the crime business, Al still wasn't making much of a living. There was even less money coming in after his split with Little Davie Petillo. He kept up the furniture business, at one point landing a contract to distribute and deliver sofas for Macy's. "Me and Big Gene Agress were humping these big couches up and down flights of stairs. Some of those downtown buildings were six stories, no elevator. It was tough work."

He gave up the company only when police came around pestering him with more questions than he wanted to answer. A rolled-up rug he had sold to one of his wiseguy pals had been found a couple of blocks from his Brooklyn warehouse under the viaduct on Park Avenue. Inside was a body belonging to a local gangster. "The cops came looking for me, breaking my chops. So I gave it up."

At Joey's diner suffered a similar fate. Al met an out-of-work chef who had worked at Rumpelmayer's, the upscale ice-cream parlor at the St. Moritz Hotel on Central Park South. "I said, 'Why don't you come down and make sodas for us? But sodas with a little pop in them.' We called it the 'Drinking Man's Ice-Cream Soda.' He'd put in crème de menthe, or a shot of schnapps, maybe a pineapple liqueur. We put some chairs out on the sidewalk, we were serving those sodas all night."

No one bothered trying to get a liquor license, however, and when spoilsport neighbors complained, a police raid was

staged. "There must have been fifty cops come down on us."
No arrests were made, but At Joey's was shuttered. "I just
walked away."

In 1971, he walked away from the old neighborhood as well.
Looking to save both time and money, Al moved his family
out of the apartment in Rosa Lisena's building on Kent Avenue and into the city. "I was spending most of my day in the
city anyway, and Dolores's family was still there, so we figured, why not?"

Al's own parents were already gone. In 1965, they had
bought a small cottage on Long Island's North Shore in the
town of Bayville. Al tried to visit every weekend with Dolores and the kids.

The new home of the Al D'Arco family wasn't much to
look at. It was four rooms in a row, a railroad flat, one flight
up in a hulking old-law tenement at 32 Spring Street between
Mott and Elizabeth. Across the street was Guidetti's funeral
parlor. "I got a good deal on it. The guy who had it before
me was a hijacker named Sonny and he had spent a few thousand making it tough for the cops to break in. He put in rein-
forced steel doors, and a special rear exit." The hijacker threw
in a new washing machine, and Al covered the bedrooms with
flocked wallpaper with roses. For a seven-member family, the
apartment was a tight fit, but Dolores said it was fine.

The landlord was an electrical contractor named Arnold
Migliaccio who handled all the streetlights for the annual feast
on Mulberry Street. "He didn't do nothing for the place. Left
it filthy. We had to keep it clean." The other downside was
their upstairs neighbor. "This lady lived up there was nuts.
She would forget, leave the water running, we'd get these big
leaks." Solving the problem was complicated, though. The
bothersome tenant was the niece of Pete DeFeo, one of the
grand old men of the Genovese crime family. "I could complain, but it wasn't like we could get her thrown out of the
place. I mean, she was Pete DeFeo's niece."

But the apartment came with a lot of history. "After we
get there, Dolores's father comes by to visit. And he says,

'I was *born* in this apartment.' It was unbelievable. Then, I find
out that Paulie Vario, the guy who was my captain out in Canarsie, lived there too when he was a kid, because his aunt
and uncle had the place. They had the lemon concession for
the feast and he would stay with them, make some extra dough
when he was just a kid." Then there was a darker side. One
night, Dolores dreamed that a woman in a long black dress
came running at her in the bedroom, then flew right out the
window. "Later we find out, that really happened. There was
a woman went out the window there many years ago." He was
to tell the story of the apartment and its many coincidences
over and over, shaking his head. "These are things you can-
not fathom."

Joseph wasn't thrilled with the move. He'd already spent some
time in the new neighborhood, after being forced to hide out
in the Mulberry Street apartment of his father's friend from
Sing Sing, Jimmy Red Caserta, after a gang fight in Brooklyn in which one teenager had died.

   "These homicide detectives were looking for me, so they
sent me to stay with Jimmy Red in the city. I wasn't supposed
to leave the apartment for anything, so of course the first thing
I do is go out. I was walking around, it was mostly a new
neighborhood to me, and I see this ten-speed bike and I
jumped on it and took off. I pedalled it back by Jimmy Red's
house and a bunch of kids are hanging out the window. They
were calling me out, like 'Where'd you get that bike?' and
'Who the fuck are you?' and 'Why are you in our neighborhood?' So I go, 'You want to fight? Or fuck you.' But I didn't
get any takers. Nobody came downstairs. It was like a bullshit thing. That wouldn't have happened in my neighborhood.
They would've come down."

   By the time he got to Spring Street, Joseph was fifteen
years old and had a pretty good grip on what his father's life
was all about. The light had gone on as he was sitting in his
uncle Gino's apartment at 961 Kent Avenue reading the newspapers about Vito Genovese's death in 1969. "I'm looking at
the papers to see 'Who is this guy?' Then I start thinking to

myself, these are not just a bunch of guys. There is this thing
that exists, there actually is a Mafia. I'm thinking about my
father and the things I'd done at that point. I used to steal
things and I'd take them down to Myrtle Avenue and sell
them to the guys who hung out in the Sons of Italy club.
I never thought of them as a mob or the Mafia, but right then
I started to understand what was going on."

For Al, getting straightened out as a full-fledged member of
that secret society was the surest ticket to making the big
money. The status would make him an automatic earner, with
the clout to lend protection to favored businesses, both legitimate and illegitimate, and the power to insert himself into
their profits.

But there were steep obstacles to getting his button, as
mobsters called it. Al understood the term. "It means you're
told to do something and you do it. Whack someone, whatever it is. You press the button, and you go."

One reason was that the leadership of New York's five families had kept their enrollment books closed for new members for the past twenty years. Lucky Luciano's original
Commission had capped the number of members of each family as a means of keeping everyone in line. The Genovese and
Gambino crews were the largest with some 300 soldiers each.
The Colombo gang had about 150. The Luchese and Bonanno
families were the smallest with 125 to 140 members.

There were plenty of vacancies due to deaths, natural and
otherwise. But the bosses couldn't agree on when to fill them.
Jealousy and greed were part of the reason. Why split the take
with new partners when things were going so well? Pride of
position was another. Any expansion of the franchise only di-
luted the product, the thinking went.

The exclusive attitude about the franchise had sparked deep
resentment and rebellion among some younger hoods. "There
were guys got fed up. What was the point in hanging around
and waiting to get made when it wasn't going to happen? They
still had to split part of their scores with the good fellows in
their territory anyway for the right to operate. They were

going around saying, 'Let these guys stick their button up their ass.' "

Some of these rebels had banded together in an effort to resist the shakedowns from the wiseguys in control. "One of them was Tommy Langone from downtown in the Fourth Ward, a very tough, streetwise kid into heists and hijackings. He got together his own crew and stopped sending a piece of his earnings up to the families. He openly told some wiseguys to go and fuck themselves. Next thing we know, Tommy is at the bottom of Canal Street near the bridge, inside a roll of linoleum, cut up in pieces. Like Jimmy Alto said, 'All the tough guys are in the cemetery.' "

Al marked it down as another lesson learned. He figured in three years or so, by 1974 or 1975, the books would open up again. By that time he'd be well positioned, after his years on various farm teams, to join the Luchese family, probably in Paul Vario's Brooklyn crew, courtesy of his influential cousin Joe Schiavo.

That was his game plan, at least until he got an offer to skip the wait and go to the head of the line. The offer came from his other well-connected cousin Joe, the one in Pennsylvania. "Joe Sica tells me he'd like me to come down and join up. He even had a beautiful house picked out for us to live in near him in Monroeville." It was a multigenerational offer. "He says, 'I can straighten you out now, and when your sons are ready, I can straighten them out too.' "

Sica was riding high at the time. He and the other Pittsburgh mob leaders had been acquitted of the charges in the Itkin case. He had a lot to offer. The Pittsburgh crew's area of influence extended over a wide western arc, including Wheeling, West Virginia; Youngstown, Ohio; and Erie, Pennsylvania. The family itself was small, with no more than three dozen members. One of the reasons for its size was that its founding fathers had ruled that only blood members of the same family could be made there. "They had the old rule, 'Sangue del mio sangue,' 'Blood of my blood.' It was sort of like a village in Sicily, or Calabria. The idea was to trust only your own, to keep it all in the family."

Unlike New York, where Luciano's rules held that names of new members had to be circulated to the other families for possible objections, no one else had veto power over the Pittsburgh family's recruits. "They took care of their own problems. If they made a mistake, they corrected it by just taking the guy out to the Monongahela River, and that was the end of it."

As inviting as his cousin's offer was to become a big fish in Pittsburgh's smaller pond, Al decided against it. "It was tempting, with the house and all. But my cousin Joe Sica was a demanding kind of guy. I would have been under him and I don't know if that would have worked out." Besides, he also just didn't want to leave home. "I felt like New York was part of who I was, and what my family knew. I didn't think I'd fit in anywhere else."

With deep thanks, Al told Sica his decision. "He was good with it. He said if I changed my mind, the offer stood."

Al spent his days scrambling for opportunities, with Ralph Masucci still his chief partner in crime. After Al moved to the city he spent more time in Ralph's hangouts. One of them was the saloon downstairs at Ponte's, the restaurant co-owned by Ralph's brother in law, Angelo Ponte, along with his brothers on Desbrosses Street near the river. "They called the bar the Faja Lounge after all the Ponte brothers, Frank, Angelo, Joey, and Anthony."

Al was in the Faja Lounge one evening with Ralph and two of the Gallo brothers, his friend Albert the Blast, and Albert's brother Joe, who was already living on borrowed time after Joe Colombo's shooting. The scene made Al nervous. "His bodyguard, Pete the Greek, is sitting at the bar watching everything, so no one's going to pull anything right there. But Joe is talking about how he wants Ralph to help get him a machine gun. And stupid Ralph is going along with him, saying he knows where to get one."

Upping Al's anxiety level was the presence of two senior powers in the Genovese family, Mike Genovese, Vito's brother, and a powerful capo, Saro Mugavero, who were dining upstairs in the main restaurant. "That was Ralph's family and he wasn't supposed to be taking sides in this war going on with the Colombo family, and here's Joe Gallo talking about getting machine guns. I am trying to tell Ralph, 'What are you crazy? We have nothing to do with this.'"

Al was trying to coax Masucci away when Joe Gallo shifted the topic. "All of a sudden, he starts raging about fat Jimmy Breslin, the newspaper reporter. He is calling him a drunken Irish bum, and saying he is going to get even with him for writing a book making fun of his crew."

Breslin's novel *The Gang That Couldn't Shoot Straight* came out in late 1969. The tale of bumbling gangsters quickly became a bestseller. The movie version, starring Jerry Orbach, was due out in December 1971. Gallo later became friends with Orbach, who played the Gallo character, Kid Sally Palumbo. But Gallo, whose temperature rarely dropped below a boil, was furious, saying that Breslin had demeaned him, portraying him and his crew as vicious lowbrows.

"Joe Gallo is telling us he has a plan. He says he knows where Breslin's kids go to school, because it is the same school as where Angelo Ponte's sons go. He says, 'We're gonna grab his kids. I know just where they are.'"

"What do you mean 'grab them'?" asked Ralph.

"I mean we're gonna snatch them," said Gallo, grinning.

Al didn't say anything for a moment. "I am thinking, This is nuts. This guy might actually kill this guy's kids. So I wait awhile, listening to him go on. Then I tell him, real quiet and serious, 'What are we talking about here? Kidnapping kids? We don't do that stuff.' I look at the Blast after I say it, because he's a good friend and knows how to handle his brother. I go on about how this will just make big trouble for everyone. I tell him, 'That's why we don't hurt newspaper guys, Joe, because it creates bigger headaches than they're worth.'"

After a while, Gallo calmed down and seemed to agree, or at least he dropped the subject. Al finished his drink and said his good nights, pushing Ralph along in front of him. Outside, Al asked Ralph if he thought Gallo was serious or just blowing smoke. Masucci shrugged. "With him, who knows? That's why they call him Crazy Joe."

Years later, Gallo's bodyguard, Pete the Greek Diapoulas, wrote a book. "The writer our crew would have loved giving a beating to was Jimmy Breslin," he wrote.

Breslin himself never heard a word about it. The writer reacted with typical bravado when told of the scheme. "He'd have been dead if he tried it, oh yes," insisted Breslin. His own gangland pals in his home borough of Queens would have taken care of Gallo, he said. But he also acknowledged that Gallo was capable of the escapade. "If he ever meant it, it's dangerous," he said.

Al was just down the block the night Gallo was shot on Hester Street. His chief surprise when he heard that Joe Gallo had been hit in Umberto's was that the forty-three-year-old gangster had been foolish enough to wander into Little Italy in the wee hours of the morning.

The other was that the shooting had taken place right in front of Matthew Ianniello, a wealthy Genovese member built like a tree trunk, who owned a string of bars and restaurants, including Umberto's. "Matty the Horse was right there in the kitchen. They could have shot him too. Now that would have made trouble."

Al steered clear of the shooting scene itself. "It was none of my business so I stayed away. But the place was crawling with police. They start raiding all the clubs and cafés. The next day in the paper, there's a sketch of the shooters. Somebody says, 'Hey, Al, that looks like you.' So I got scarce."

Later, Al learned that he knew two of the men dispatched to take care of Gallo once word circulated that he was in the neighborhood that night. One of them was Filippo "Fungi" Gambino, who had been at Al's side the chaotic night in Sing Sing when he tried to kill the jailhouse snitch in the movie hall.

"Fungi was one of the two guys that went in the side door to Umberto's. The other was Sonny Pinto."

Sonny Pinto was the street name for Carmen Di Biase, who

had been Sally Burns Granello's teenaged robbery accomplice. Di Biase had been a fugitive for seven years after shooting a friend of his in an argument over a card game in a Mulberry Street social club. Di Biase eventually turned himself in. He was tried and sentenced to die in the electric chair in 1959. But his sentence was later overturned, and he got even luckier when he was acquitted at retrial. Long associated with Granello's Genovese family, Di Biase had shifted to the Colombo gang after his friend's death.

"Sonny Pinto never got made, but I know he was very close to Matty the Horse, which was another surprising thing about it, since Matty is right there when it happened."

Di Biase and Gambino were named as part of the hit team by one of the getaway drivers, Joe Luparelli, who turned state's evidence days after the Gallo execution out of fear that his partners were about to kill him.

But all that the district attorney had was a single, uncorroborated witness, not enough for an indictment. Gambino was convicted only of a parole violation for consorting with known felons. Di Biase disappeared again, this time never to resurface. Al eventually heard the last chapter. "Years later, my bosses in the Luchese family told me Sonny Pinto got killed while he was on the lam. So that was it."

Matty the Horse Ianniello told cops he saw nothing that night in his restaurant. The gunfire would hardly have rattled him. Ianniello fought in the Pacific in the war, where he won a Bronze Star. When Al was asked in the summer of 1973 to do a favor to help out the war hero turned mobster, he was glad to help. The favor was to torch Times Square's most prominent topless dancing spot.

"The guy who asked me to do it was a friend of mine from Brooklyn named Frankie Mengrone who was associated with the Genovese crew. Frankie said that Matty the Horse wants this place put out of business. He told me the request for the favor was coming from Chin Gigante. Matty didn't say nothing to me about it, but I figured what he wanted was to close it down, so he could take the place over."

Al wasn't sure why they needed him for the job, but he guessed that word of his earlier arson accomplishments for restaurant owner and waste-carting magnate Angelo Ponte had filtered up the ranks. "I wasn't going to say no. It was coming from the top of the family."

The target was the Metropole Café, the biggest and brassiest of the many Times Square topless joints of the era. Located at the corner of Seventh Avenue and West Forty-Eighth Street, it had a looming marquee of blinking lights and picture glass windows that beckoned passersby to check out the action inside. There was usually a crowd on the sidewalk.

The club had long been a jazz mecca, where performers like Gene Krupa, Dizzy Gillespie, and Roy Eldridge held forth. But in 1970, a new owner kicked the less profitable musicians upstairs to the club's smaller second floor, and installed a large mirror-backed platform for strippers and topless dancers surrounded by plush red sofas and chairs in the main room downstairs. It was a hit with tourists and visiting businessmen.

Al went by to check the place out. "It didn't close until four in the morning, that was one problem. And you couldn't pull it off after people started going to work outside." He figured he needed a timer, a task well beyond the limited scope of his arson know-how. "I asked around for someone knows how to do it, and I am told about an Irish guy in the Bronx who was in the Army and is an expert with bombs and timers. His name was Dailey and I went up to see if he was interested. He said he was."

Al took Dailey on another reconnaissance mission while the club was filled with patrons. "The place was jam-packed. We went up the stairs and there is a cigarette machine on the landing, halfway up to the second floor. Dailey says this is the spot."

They returned the following night, this time posing as repairmen for the cigarette machine. Dailey had obtained a key that opened the rear of the machine. "I stood in front, watching his back while he stuck the bomb in there."

They set the timer for five in the morning. Reports in the

next day's newspapers described how a bomb had shattered walls and furniture, leaving a clutter of debris. Employees were nailing up temporary plywood coverings. "We drove by to see what had happened. We'd blown the front of the place right into the street." Club owners glumly refused to discuss it. Police had no suspects, but described it as the latest in a series of "suspicious mishaps" plaguing Times Square strip clubs. "That was Matty the Horse. He was taking over, and he was letting everyone know it."

The occasional favor for a mob boss came with the territory, Al figured, and would stand him well down the road. But while he waited for the Mafia to open its books to new members, he still hustled for scores.

Al and Ralph made some money helping Venero Mangano, another Genovese captain. Known as "Benny Eggs," Mangano was also a war hero, having won the Distinguished Flying Cross as a tail gunner on B-29 bombers over Europe. He was a member of what was known as the Mozzarella mob, a wing of the Genovese family headed by Vincent Gigante. "Benny Eggs had this big clothing-sales business, and Ralphie and me hooked him up with a lot of customers dealing stolen leather coats, including my relatives in Pittsburgh."

Masucci considered Mangano a loudmouth, however. "One time they got in a fight and Ralph grabbed Benny by the neck. He was choking him." Al pulled his friend off. It was a capital offense to attack a made member. Masucci shrugged. "Ralph never worried about that stuff."

Another friend steered them to the operator of a large Bronx discount store who was in the market for stolen merchandise. "They called him Louie Corners and he had this big place under the elevated train line up on Allerton Avenue. It was giant, with furniture, kitchenware, clothes, electronics, anything he could get. Guys were bringing him swag, doing bust-outs, letting places go bankrupt, and selling all the property to him."

Together with Frankie Mengrone, Al hijacked a truckload of new cameras. It was a good example of the grunt work crime often demanded. "Nice Japanese cameras still in their boxes. But Louie Corners wanted just the cameras, so he could make them look like he got them used. So me and Frankie have to pull every camera out of its box."

Between finding the load, stealing it, and pulling the merchandise out of the containers, Al figured his wages were not a lot better than if he were still driving a truck. And while that might be a decent living, it wasn't his idea of being a gangster. Plus, he had no idea where the next haul was going to be found.

Part of the solution to his problems came when he and Ralph Masucci heard that a small hamburger stand a block away from Ponte's was going out of business. The owner was trying to find a tenant to finish out the lease. "I did pretty good with the diner, so I figured a coffee and burger stand would work out too."

The stand was located at the corner of Laight and West Streets. It was more of a shack than a stand. It was a one-story structure attached to the side of a nineteenth-century brick storehouse, an after-thought constructed to serve fast meals to the factory and dock workers who had once filled those streets. Above it roared traffic on the elevated West Side Highway. Across the street sat the Market Diner, an all-night eatery with a small parking lot.

Al borrowed some cash to fix it up. He named it the Late Laight Stand after the street corner where it stood. He priced his hamburgers at the affordable price of 75 cents apiece. Al often opened the stand himself in the mornings, serving coffee and rolls to people on their way to work. Joseph, ever eager to be beside his dad, came down after school to help.

"West Street had a lot of traffic, and cars and truck drivers would pull over to grab a bite. Our biggest seller was the coffee. We made it fresh every hour. We were doing pretty good. I'm thinking, Here I am trying to be a gangster and I'm making my best money selling java."

The other solution to Al's money problems came from Angelo Tuminaro, one of the powerful men he had gotten to know while hanging out at 121 Mulberry Street. In addition to his extensive dealing in narcotics, Little Ange was deeply involved in the union business. He told Al and Ralph he was looking for organizers.

Al understood the pitch. "I knew what it was. It was shake-downs, it wasn't organizing. It was like what Sammy Chillemi had going with the toy workers union when I used to help him make his collections."

The difference in Tuminaro's case was that he had assembled a team well versed in the law and the labor rackets, men who were aggressively marketing their contracts to companies, willingly or otherwise.

Tuminaro's partner in the union scams was John Dioguardi, a fellow member of the Luchese crime family who managed to be both a major owner of garment sweatshops and a top city union official at the same time. Known as Johnny Dio, he hailed from mob royalty. His uncle was Jimmy Doyle Plumeri, the Luchese captain who had been snookered by Herbert Itkin with Sally Burns's help. Dio had created his own legends. In a deal with Jimmy Hoffa, he had carved up the city's Teamsters locals among different mob factions. He was also alleged to have ordered the acid blinding of newspaper columnist Victor Riesel for writing stories that angered him.

But Tuminaro's senior, day-to-day labor expert was a man named Ben Ross, a New York City racketeer whose antics had plagued businesses and legitimate unions for more than twenty years. Born Benjamin Krakofsky on the Lower East Side in 1916, he received fifteen years for attempted robbery as a teenager. He served most of his sentence in Clinton prison in Dannemora, where his fellow inmates included Charlie Luciano and Davie Petillo. He later changed his name, but his nickname stayed the same. He was known as "Benny the Bug."

"Benny was a stickup guy. He'd done time with Little Ange in prison when he was young. Then he went into unions, with Ange backing him up."

Ross only finished eighth grade, but he was considered a

formidable opponent by law enforcement. In 1959, Johnny Dio and Ben Ross were top targets of Robert Kennedy when he served as chief counsel to the U.S. Senate committee investigating labor racketeering.

One of Ross's associates testified about his organizing tactics to the committee. "He would just walk into the shop and pull the switch, and say, 'Everybody out on strike.' That is all there was to it. Everybody thought he was crazy, and they would walk out, and the boss would sign a contract."

By the time Al met him, Ross had racked up additional convictions for loan-sharking, embezzlement, drug possession, and assault.

Assisting Ross in his schemes were two other veteran union racketeers, a bookmaker named Louis Richko, who had shortened his name to Rich, and Richko's brother-in-law, Nathan Nass. "Their side business was shylocking to all the downtown stores. I helped them out with that too."

Al's first stop was the headquarters of the many catch-all unions that Ross and his crew ran. The largest was Ross's District 5 and Affiliated Unions, which was then battling to get control of maintenance workers at Shea Stadium, even though the three hundred workers there had opposed them in a vote by a margin of six to one. Behind the same doors at 11 East Seventeenth Street were Local 348, International Brotherhood of Trade Unions, the International Jewelers Union, the Allied Crafts Union, and the Allied Guards Union.

Al and Ralph were given business cards declaring them organizers. Al was clear what his job was. "My end was to scare guys."

He was a quick learner. His instructions were to visit hesitant employers and show them a stack of cards that had allegedly been signed by their employees asking to be represented by one of Ross's unions.

"I would go up to the shop and show the guy my business card. Then tell him, 'You know, I represent the union and we got all your workers signed up right here.' But you hold the cards in your hand so he can't see them. And there's not one signed card in the whole stack. You say, 'See, we got them

all signed up, and you know it is against federal law for you
to break the union.' "

Step two was to let the employer know you weren't to be
fooled with. "You get that rough tone in your voice and tell
them to back off. 'Your workers are all signed up, so don't
threaten them, don't talk to them.' "

The third step was to reassure the employer that he was
really getting a gift, a union that was an ally, not a threat.

"I'd say, 'How are you doing with the business? You got a
hundred guys working here? And you're worried about the
union? Listen, you ain't got a union. You know why? Because
I give you a contract and you stick it in your drawer, and you
pay me $100 a year for each worker. And for each worker you
don't want to pay any pension or welfare on, you pay me $100
a month so they never get listed. They don't get this, and they
don't get that.' Then you put your business card right in his
pocket and say, 'Keep this, and if anybody bothers you with
a real union, show it to 'em and call us. We'll come around.' "

Another tactic was to pull a kind of labor razzle-dazzle
on employers. "Nat Nass or Lou Rich would reach out to anyone they had a contact with at a big company, telling them,
in strict confidence, that if they ever had a labor problem, that
they'd be there to help them. Bingo, a month or so later, Benny
would tell me and Ralph to go and give that company a big
headache."

They'd start by setting up an "informational" picket line,
claiming the company was unfair. "A lot of truckers would
see that and not cross, even if they had no idea what was going on. The guy can't get his deliveries, and pretty soon, Nat is
getting an SOS from the guy, saying he's ready for that favor
Nat promised."

Ross's team broke Al and Ralph in on a push to sign up
Cumberland Packing, the company that made Sweet'n Low
and which was located in Al's old neighborhood next door to
the Brooklyn Navy Yard. "They weren't interested until after we released the brakes on a couple of their trucks that were
parked on an incline. The trucks rolled down the hill and
crashed. They got the idea."

Other successful targets included a caviar-importing company, a jewelry chain, and a sporting-goods shop. The shakedown artists' job was made far easier by the fact that there were plenty of legitimate unions around signing up workers and demanding real wages and benefits. One out of three workers in the city belonged to a union in the 1970s, most of them providing real benefits. In comparison, Benny the Bug's crew and their sweetheart contracts didn't look like such a bad deal.

Al felt like a salesman with a good product, even if the customer sometimes needed some tough persuasion. As for the workers trapped by subpar contracts and wages, they weren't his problem.

Sometimes, they found themselves up against legitimate labor organizations. Those fights occasionally got rough. In one contest, Al represented a corrupt electrical workers union in a face-off against Local 3 of the International Brotherhood of Electrical Workers, one of the city's most powerful unions. "Our union, Local 363, was getting the contracts to install incinerators in the big apartment buildings. Our wages were a lot less than what Local 3 was getting, so the buildings that dared to, used our contractors."

The mob was making money on both ends of the deal. Many of the contractors were mob controlled. The lawyer for the union was Richard Oddo, brother-in-law of Luchese captain Paul Vario. The showdown came at a site in Queens where incinerators were being installed.

"Local 3 was run by Harry Van Arsdale and he had members who were cops and firemen, moonlighting as electricians. And he'd turn them out for his picket lines. Big guys. We've got our guys out there too, and we're getting ready to go at it. Their leader is this very big Spanish guy with a fedora. He's got a bullhorn and making a lot of noise. Me and Nat Nass stepped out, and I go over to the guy and say, real quiet, 'I don't care about all these other guys, you're the one that's gonna go.' And I put my hand in my pocket to let him know I had a gun. And I did, too. He waited awhile and he's looking at me, and then he says to his crew, 'Let's go.'"

But there were also times when the racketeers were the ones who had to walk away. One of them was when Al and Ralph went after their biggest shakedown target, the big cosmetics firm Estée Lauder. "We were getting a little greedy. They had their plants out on Long Island and we were way out there trying the informational-picketing scam. We had sandwich boards with different signs on each side. One said just 'Unfair' and the other said 'On Strike,' which was bullshit, since we didn't have any members there to strike. We'd wear the strike signs, then flip them over when the cops came around so we were within the law. As long as you kept walking, you were okay."

Several delivery drivers balked at making deliveries. A representative of the company came out to see the picketers. "We were sure he was going to ask us who to see to make a deal. We'd seen it happen before." Instead, the company official handed them a business card.

"He says, 'This is my lawyer. He'd like to speak to you.' We look at it, and it's the United States Justice Department, attorney general. We scrammed out of there."

They also backed down when faced with an employer who simply challenged them to take their best shot. The company was a food outfit called Meal Mart located on Taaffe Place in Brooklyn, a couple of blocks from where Al was raised. The company's owner was an Orthodox Jewish rabbi. Most of the employees were Orthodox as well, many of them women in traditional long skirts and wearing wigs. "We were picketing and Nat Nass came out. Since he was Jewish, we figured he could reason with the guy. Nat is giving the guy our spiel, how we won't go away, that we're within our rights."

The owner was wearing a long-sleeved white shirt. He rolled up one sleeve to show the tattooed number of a concentration camp survivor. "He looks at Nat and says, 'I lived through Hitler, I'll live through you.' Nat looked like he'd been hit with a rock. He shrugs and says, 'Okay, I guess that's enough for today.' We didn't go back."

* * *

Between his union scheming and the burger stand, he still made time to get out to Long Island to see his cousin Joe Schiavo. "Joe never wanted to say a thing on the phones. But he would call me up, say, 'Hey, you got any olive oil over there?' And that was the code. I'd bring him a bottle of oil from one of the *salumerias*, the Italian delis, on Grand Street."

Sometimes he'd head out to his parents' place in Bayville on a Sunday afternoon, drop off Dolores and the kids, then double back to Valley Stream, where Schiavo lived in a large Tudor home on North Corona Avenue. "He bought it from the guy built all the sewers in Nassau County. He bragged that the walls were so thick a bomb can't blow them down."

Schiavo had a porch in back where the two men sat and talked. Conversations ranged from the long-ago past to the present. Still an eager student of mob history, Al pressed Schiavo for details about the old days, who got made by whom.

"Joe could have been the captain of the Brooklyn crew. He was made by Don Turrido Curiale. Don Turrido was still alive then, even though he was almost a hundred years old. He was from Agrigento in Sicily, 'Grigento' they said it in Sicilian. He was one of the originals from before they made the Commission, when there was just one mob in Brooklyn."

Schiavo's own induction was a small piece of mob history. He was the first American-born member of the Brooklyn crew, he told Al. When Curiale decided to step down, he offered his post as captain of what had become the Luchese family's Brooklyn crew to Schiavo. "Joe didn't ever want to be a captain. He was more like an elder. He had his garment businesses with Don Turrido and Tommy Luchese, and he was more interested in staying out of the limelight."

Schiavo demurred, telling Curiale he should give the job to Paul Vario, an ambitious young mobster that Schiavo had recruited and sponsored into the family, along with Vario's brother Babe, Al's friend from Sing Sing.

Schiavo did a good job of staying out of the limelight. No one kept closer track of New York's mobsters than an investigator named Kenneth McCabe, who spent thirty-five years as a New York Police Department detective and later as a

federal investigator prowling outside of social clubs and
mob meetings. At six foot four, McCabe was a familiar sight
to mobsters, Al included. "Everyone knew Kenny. He was
like a friendly enemy, always out there in his white Dodge
taking notes on us. Guys would wave hello. One wedding
they brought a piece of cake out to him."

But Schiavo slid even below McCabe's keen radar. By the
time McCabe started clocking wiseguys in 1969, Schiavo had
already moved Vario into his slot. McCabe had Schiavo's
name, birth date in 1910, and some hints about a few of his
garment shops in Brooklyn and on Long Island. That was it.
Like Al's other mob mentor, Jimmy Alto, the mob watchers
had barely a clue.

Schiavo's criminal record included a bust for his own
bogus-union scams back in 1943, when he was arrested for
trying to help shake down a Seventh Avenue photo studio.

Five years later, Schiavo successfully played the victim,
claiming he'd been robbed of $5,500 in payroll cash outside his
Hendrix Coat Company in Brooklyn's Brownsville. Schiavo
was quoted in the newspapers as having told police that a
pair of young men had jumped out of a car, brandishing a
pistol and shouting, "Hand over the coconuts!"

Al laughed at the story. "If he got robbed, he'd never tell
the cops anything. And 'coconuts'? That was his word for
dough. It was a scam."

The other topic of discussion on the back porch was when
and how Al was going to get his own button.

"I never paid attention to it that much. I was content to wait
things out because I knew my day was going to come."

He admitted, though, that he didn't much care for being
on the outside looking in with his made-member pals. "Two
guys you know would be talking, and then they say, 'Excuse
us,' and step away so you can't hear their wiseguy discussion.
'Excuse us'? Who the fuck are you? I didn't like that stuff."

Schiavo tried to convince Al that, in some ways, he was
better off not getting made. "He'd say, 'What do you want
that for? This way, you're not responsible. You can always say
you don't know. Say you punch a guy in the mouth, and he's

a made guy? When you're made, you're responsible, whether you know it or not. If you're not in the mob, you can just say you didn't know.'"

Al wasn't convinced. In early 1974, Schiavo put forward Al's name to be included when the books opened up. The Luchese family added twenty members to its membership rolls that year. But when the approved list came back, Al's name wasn't on it. "Politics," Schiavo told him. Al was badly disappointed, but didn't push for more details. He knew his cousin would handle it eventually.

Later, he found out that men he considered less worthy than himself, crime-wise at least, were getting straightened out as made members ahead of him. One of them was a friend of his named Anthony Tortorello who lived on Madison Street on the Lower East Side in Knickerbocker Village, the government-subsidized development complex that was home to Don ZaZá and a score of other mobsters.

"I knew Torty a long time. His brother Richie worked in the fish market with me. Torty hung out at the K & K Luncheonette on Market Street and Monroe, and I'd go by there sometimes, see what was going on."

Tortorello's specialty was shylocking, but he was also adept at handling stolen cars, and had dealt narcotics with the DiPalermo brothers on Mott Street.

"I said, 'Hey, they straightened out Torty. What's the matter with me?'"

Schiavo eventually explained to Al that the "politics" he'd mentioned earlier was the objection of a single member, a Luchese soldier named Frank Manzo. "Joe didn't want to tell me what Manzo said about me, but I found out. He said something like, 'Why are we making him? He's nothing but an ice-cream vendor.'"

Al's nomination had passed muster with all the other families. But the mob demanded consensus. One man's thumbs-down was enough to block a candidate from getting his button.

Frank Manzo was a late import to the American Mafia. Born in Naples, he came to the U.S. at the age of twenty-one after spending two years in the Italian Navy during the war.

His accent was so thick that his nickname was "Frank the Wop." But he'd done well in the U.S. He owned a couple of restaurants on Long Island and was a successful contractor.

The real reason for Manzo's veto, Schiavo reassured him, had nothing to do with Al. "Joe told me it was some old *paisan* stuff. Manzo was mad at Joe for something he did years ago."

Schiavo told Al he'd spoken to the captain of their crew, Paul Vario, about the matter, and that Paul was also annoyed. "Joe said there was nothing they could do for the time being."

If he couldn't give Al D'Arco his button, Paul Vario did the next best thing. On a snowy Sunday in late 1974, the captain told Al to come out to Canarsie to meet him at his headquarters, a bar called Geffken's on Flatlands Avenue.

Vario was fifty-nine years old and feeling all of his years. A bear-sized man with glasses and multiple chins, he was living in an apartment above the tavern because his wife had kicked him out of his home in Island Park in Nassau County after discovering his dalliance with a mistress.

In the past few months, he'd been hit with a torrent of criminal charges. He was looking at six years in prison, having been convicted on federal tax evasion. In state court, he was facing six separate indictments, all stemming from a bug placed by police detectives in a junkyard trailer on Avenue D where he occasionally did business. Dubbed the "Gold Bug" after Brooklyn district attorney Eugene Gold, whose office made the case, Vario had been caught trying to buy a list of informants from a detective posing as a corrupt cop. More embarrassing, he'd been recorded telling the detective, Douglas Le Vien, how he rigorously avoided wiretaps by refusing to have a telephone in his house.

The hardest blow, however, was the death of his youngest son, Lenny, in the summer of 1973. Moments after an arson explosion at a nearby construction company involved in a labor dispute, Lenny, twenty-three, was deposited at the emergency-room entrance of Wyckoff Heights Hospital. He had burns over 90 percent of his body. He lingered for weeks, but true to his dad's ethic, he refused to say anything before he died. The tragedy was compounded by what the son didn't say: that he had been dispatched on the arson mission by his father. "Yeah, Paulie sent him there. But the kid didn't know what he was doing. He went to torch the place and the fumes from the gas ignited on him and he caught fire himself. They had to have a closed casket."

The funeral was held at St. Fortunata's Church on Linden Boulevard in East New York. "There had to be a thousand people there, half of them wiseguys. Some real old-timers went, out of respect for Paulie. We had to park five blocks away, it was so jammed. I went with Joe Schiavo, and he never liked to go to those things because he knew there'd always be cameras and agents."

Cameras and law enforcement agents were on hand for this one as well. But when the crowd spotted cameramen for two local TV stations, they set upon them, beating them furiously. Detective Kenny McCabe was across the street conducting surveillance for the DA's office. He waded into the crowd toward the besieged cameramen. But that afternoon, the rage was so strong on the sidewalk outside the church that even the bear-sized McCabe took a pummeling. "He saved those news guys' lives, but he took some shots, I saw that."

When Al got the summons to Geffken's Bar, Paul Vario was waiting to surrender on a combined sentence of three years. "Paulie had all these things going on with him, but he called me out to Geffken's to tell me that, even without the button, he was going to treat me just as if I'd been made. Then he took me around to the members of his crew and told them the same thing." Leaving the bar, Al told himself he was at least halfway to his goal.

II

—

In the Life

8

FLATLANDS AVENUE

Despite Paul Vario's generous gesture, it was hard to put a label on Al's gangster status. He remained an associate, one of the large crowd hanging around Geffken's, ready and eager to assist the Luchese captain with any chores. But he was also a wiseguy in his own right, with his own underworld connections, running his own legitimate moneymaking business.

The burger stand generated a small but steady stream of revenue. Al added a sideline of taking numbers. Georgie Argento, one of the old-timers from the Mulberry Street club, had control of the numbers action in the territory and suggested to Al that they see how it worked out.

But it was hard to make customers feel safe. "Part of the problem was the cops took a liking to the place. They'd be pulling up, order a cup of coffee, a burger. Then they'd hang out and bullshit with each other. Nobody's gonna come bet a number when you've got a line of cop cars parked out front."

Even the governor liked the coffee at the Late Laight Stand. Al had noticed the dark sedan with official State of New York license plates pulling up almost daily. He had nailed the driver right away as some kind of cop. The officer always ordered two coffees to go. Al stepped outside to see who was getting the second cup. He did a double take. "It's the new governor,

Hugh Carey. He's sipping on my coffee. He looks up and gives me a wave."

Al's regular assistant at the stand was a hard-luck gambler named Pete Del Cioppo. When Al met him, Del Cioppo was badly behind in paying off gambling debts to one of Paul Vario's loan sharks. A big plodding man with a comb-over haircut, Del Cioppo was a sheet metal worker who regularly gambled away his earnings. "Petey Del came from Broome Street. He was a tin knocker working on the World Trade Center when I met him. He'd borrowed a lot of money, but he was broke and ducking payments. Paulie was furious. I heard they had it set up, they were going to toss him off the Trade Center. Make it look like he tripped. That happened more than once on that job."

Al took a liking to Del Cioppo. He persuaded Vario to give him another chance. "I paid the money he owed, then I grabbed hold of Petey and read him the riot act. He must have been grateful because he stood around me after that."

A lot of his gangland pals suddenly became jet-setters in those years, thanks to the big mob fad of the era, counterfeit and stolen airline tickets. Al and Ralph Masucci first learned about the scheme from Anthony Tortorello, the gangster from Knickerbocker Village who had reached his Mafia milestone ahead of Al. Tortorello was selling tickets by the hundreds out of the K & K Luncheonette on Monroe Street.

"It was the hottest thing going for a while. Everybody had a different angle. Some guys were stealing them, other guys figured out how to copy them. And everyone was taking off for wherever they wanted to go."

Airlines and travel agencies were at the mobsters' mercy. Prosecutors brought several indictments of multimillion-dollar air ticket fraud rings. But the tickets were everywhere and the fraud was rampant.

Al scored a few tickets from Tortorello and passed them on to others at a modest profit. But his biggest source was one of his associates from the labor rackets. Julius Angstreich was a gambler with a taste for the good life who had done prison time in the early 1950s. He had gone from counterfeit unions to counterfeit tickets.

"Juicy Angstreich had a connection with a printer who had figured how to knock off thousands of phony tickets. They had the wax backing and everything. Once they were printed up, you couldn't tell them from the real thing."

The bootleg tickets went for 25 percent of the cover price. Angstreich and his confederates peddled them to travel agencies glad to get them at a heavy discount, and shop owners who dealt them to customers under the table. Angstreich cut Al in as a fellow middleman, giving him a commission on whatever he could sell.

Al and Ralph decided to take advantage of the discount airfare and see the sights themselves. "We went and got passports. I was surprised, since we both had records, that we could get them, but it was no sweat." For spending cash on their junkets, Angstreich had access to fake American Express checks as well. "So not only were the tickets free, so was everything else as long as the hotels and stores didn't catch on."

Their first outing was a modest hop down to Mexico City. "That was mainly to score some money. We went to a bank and cashed a stack of the phony American Express checks. Ralph goes up to the counter and I'm standing back watching. There is a Mexican soldier in a *federale* uniform right there, and he's got a gun almost as big as him on his hip giving us the eyeball. I'm trying to look like this is no big deal, smiling at the guy."

From the bank they went to the money exchange and converted their pesos to dollars. They spent a day sightseeing. Al dropped a postcard in the mail to the kids and Dolores. Then they got back on a plane to New York.

Back on Spring Street, Al told his family about the trip, minus the details about the fraudulent tickets and fake money orders. Joseph excitedly asked if he could go with him next time.

"I had to say no, that this was business. Dolores knew what was going on but she never asked and never said anything."

His kids felt left out, but Al wasn't taking chances. "I knew we could get caught and I wasn't going to have my family picked up for some scam I'm running. I said I'd bring them presents and send more postcards next time I went someplace."

The next overseas postcard to arrive at apartment 2B at 32 Spring Street came from Hong Kong. "We heard about these places you could buy gold on the cheap, and we had this idea we could make a big score, bringing jewelry back into the country and flipping it."

But the Chinese dealers they were directed to were slicker than the gangster tourists. "We bought these medallions and half of them turned black. They had just enough gold in there to pass a test we gave, but the rest of it was junk."

To console themselves, they went over to check out Macao, the nearby gambling mecca. While Ralph gambled in a casino, Al took a walk. He asked someone where the border was with mainland China.

"I walked over and there were these soldiers standing on the other side of a swampy area." The ex-GI reflected on his long-missed opportunity to lead an Army charge against Red Chinese troops in Korea. "So I took an American quarter and threw it across and said, 'America has landed!' "

It must have brought them luck. "Back in Hong Kong, we found a place had real gold that we could buy from and got it back into the country. Between the sale of the phony tickets and the gold, we were doing pretty good."

They rested up from their travels for a few weeks, then made plans for one more excursion, this time to Japan. The idea was to scout out more opportunities for buying precious metals and jewelry on the cheap, then smuggling them back into the country. But once they reached Tokyo they found out that the big demand in Japan was for diamonds, not to sell, but to buy.

"The Japanese were desperate to get their hands on them. They wanted big stones, over three carats each." They got the lay of the land from an American contractor named Pepe they met in their Tokyo hotel. Pepe was from California, but he had been living in the Far East for several years. He was a jack-of-all-trades for a large construction company that did work for the American military. Part of his job was entertaining local officials, which was how he'd learned of their craving for big diamonds.

"Pepe told us that if we could get our hands on large stones, he had buyers who would take them for a big profit."

As it happened, Al and Ralph had recently met a dealer in the West Forty-Seventh Street diamond district in Manhattan who handled large pieces. George Solow was a second-generation diamond cutter whose skill was such that he was a sightholder for the De Beers Family, the dominant trader in international diamonds. As a sightholder, he was regularly apportioned a set number of rough, uncut stones, which he would then cut and refine.

The introduction to Solow had come after the cutter went looking for protection from armed, mob-linked thieves preying on small diamond cutters in the district. In 1970, Solow and his father had been pistol-whipped by a pair of men posing as telephone repairmen. The jewelers had managed to activate a silent alarm, and the patrolman who responded had shot one of the holdup men six times, firing directly over the diamond cutters as they lay on the floor.

Al had forged a bond with the dealer by promising he would do his best to make sure he was off the list for future targets.

Returning to New York, Al went to see Solow to ask if he'd let him take a package of stones to Japan on consignment to try and sell them. "We were talking about $150,000 worth of diamonds. It was no small thing we were asking." After hearing about the possible profits, Solow agreed.

"So Ralph and me sew these diamonds into our clothes and go right back to Japan to catch up with Pepe. It was just a little package, so it was easy to make it in and out of customs."

Pepe the hustler was good to his word, and quickly sold

the diamonds for more than twice what Solow had paid for them.

"We did it one more time, in and out, without getting caught. We thought, This is beautiful. Then the whole airline-ticket scam started falling apart and it got dangerous to fly. The airlines had hired these Pinkerton agents and they were snatching people right off the planes. People got arrested right in their seats. The private eyes were watching the passenger lists for guys like us. That pretty much ended a nice thing for a lot of people."

The sudden halt to the bogus-airline-ticket splurge left some promoters high and dry. One of them was Morris Campanella, the printer who was Juicy Angstreich's source for counterfeit tickets. Campanella was a master printer but a failure at business. "Everybody called him 'Moishe,' but he was an Italian. When the tickets scam ended, he was starving to death."

Campanella's printing company was located in an old barn of a building on Imlay Street in Red Hook, a neighborhood of factories, warehouses, and longshoremen's bars strung along an elbow of the south Brooklyn waterfront. Al went down to Red Hook to look at Campanella's operation. "It was a rainy day, and when I got there, Moishe was trying to move his machines by himself to take them out of the place. All he had was a crowbar. He said he hadn't paid rent in a while and the landlord was cracking down. If he didn't get the machines out of the building, the owner was going to seize everything in the place."

The landlord owned a book-distribution business located down the street. Al had a few hundred dollars with him. He told Campanella to call the owner and tell him to come down to get his rent. "Moishe didn't want to do it, but I told him go ahead. He gets off the phone and says, 'He's coming over.' So I go downstairs and wait in the doorway. I get a paper bag and put the money in it and keep one hand inside. The owner, a guy named Goldstein, comes up. I say, 'You're the landlord? How come you're pressuring Morris?' I point the bag at him like I got a gun hidden there. He freezes and starts to put his hands up. I said, 'Relax, I'm Moishe's new partner.' I hand him the bag and the money. I told him I was sure we could work out the rest of it.' He was glad to get out of there alive I think."

Campanella had printing and stamping machines for making cardboard boxes, but no customers. "Moishe was a screwup. He didn't have any credit. I knew from my father's dye business that no one used cash to order supplies. You got a line of credit at a bank and then paid it back when you made and sold your order. You want to order $50,000 worth of cardboard from the mill? You got to have credit to get the loan."

Al's own background was an automatic out at any lender. Only a wiseguy shylock was going to give an ex-con who had done time for stock theft a major loan, and the points charged would make it too expensive. On the other hand, Petey Del Cioppo didn't have a big criminal record. He might get a loan. "I made Petey the president of the Cherokee Box Company. He didn't have a clue but all that mattered was his signature."

Campanella's machines could cut and print small packing boxes for food or other items. The trick was to come up with customers. "I'm thinking about it, and then it hit me that I knew somebody had a company made sausages." The somebody was Anthony "Hickey" DiLorenzo, a freewheeling mobster originally from Avenue A on the Lower East Side who was a high-earning member of the Genovese family.

"Hickey had a company that made Italian sausage. He had the hot sausages in boxes with a red stripe, and the sweet sausages in blue-striped packages." Al went to see him. DiLorenzo said he'd be glad to start buying boxes from Al's company, as long as he could supply them in bulk. He needed no fewer than a half million, he said.

Al the businessman now went into high gear. "This was a big order, but it was all legit. We could take the order to the bank, get the credit, and get the materials." They discovered they also needed a four-color press. "We went out to Edison, New Jersey, and bought one off a company going out of business. We had to get riggers to get it set up in the plant on

Imlay Street. Then we needed a die-cutting machine to cut the boxes. We got one of those, too."

For a gangster-run enterprise, the entire operation so far was remarkably legal. But to keep the machines going, they needed more customers. And here, Al decided, he needed to put his thumb on the scales. "The guy who had control of the big meat suppliers, the bacon and sausage makers, was the head of the butchers union, Frankie Kissel. I went to ask him if he could help."

Frank Kissel Sr. was part of the network of labor racketeers loosely associated with Ben Ross, which was how Al had met him. Unlike Ross's mostly rogue outfits, however, Kissel had a tight grip on a union that was a major member of the dominant AFL-CIO. Despite that official recognition, Local 174 of the Amalgamated Meat Cutters and Butcher Workmen of North America had been under mob control since its inception. Its officers had long used their clout to push meat suppliers and supermarkets to accommodate gangland entrepreneurs. The mob was so closely tied into Kissel's union that one of his top officers was an aging former enforcer for Lucky Luciano named Lorenzo "Chappie" Brescia. Even at seventy years old, the solidly built Brescia cut an intimidating presence, and he often accompanied Kissel to meetings and negotiations as a reminder of the union's backers.

The local had been at the center of a series of corruption scandals for the past decade, including scams that allowed adulterated meat to be sold in major New York supermarkets. Kissel had just finished up a seven-year sentence for extortion. But he'd lost none of his zest for crime or profit. After hearing Al's pitch, Kissel said he'd be glad to help. All he'd charge was $5,000 to start, with a percentage of the profits down the road.

Figuring it would be money well spent, Al scratched around and came up with the cash. He had several meetings with Kissel and his son, Billy, at Pete's Tavern, the saloon on Irving Place near Gramercy Square and around the corner from Local 174's offices. "We talked about what companies they could get for us. It took a while to line things up, but

Frankie came through." Orders eventually came in from a half dozen manufacturers, including a firm called Chef Romeo in the Bronx and a large supplier called White Packaging in New Jersey.

"We were rolling. We had some trouble collecting payment from one of the companies, but I sent Petey Del around to give a pep talk to the bookkeeper and that did the trick."

There was enough money coming in now for some modest luxuries. Dolores's parents had retired to Miami, where they owned a condominium. Al and Dolores brought the family down to Florida for visits. Al still admired his father-in-law. Joe Lefty Pellegrino still projected a fiercely tough image, even in old age. Surrounded by retirees in pastels, he looked out of place in his formal white shirt. The old man was eager for news of New York. "We'd sit by the pool or the beach talking while the kids swam and played around."

Ever cautious, Al left as light a footprint as he could as he moved through the mob world. On a visit to the in-laws, he decided to switch his driver's license to their Florida home. "I just used their address. The less they had on paper about me in New York, I figured, the better."

He was now basically working three jobs. He had the burger and coffee stand on Laight Street, the occasional labor assignment from Ben Ross and his crew, and the box company, which was taking up more and more of his time.

His gangster pals wondered why Al worked so hard. One day in the K & K Luncheonette on Monroe Street, Anthony Tortorello started in. "Al, how come you make money in the street," he asked, "then go and spend it in a straight business you got to work at around the clock?"

Al answered with his father's inflections of the word. "I go into the *bizaness* because I like *bizaness*," he said. Then he added, "Second of all, when you buy something, at least you can show where you got the money, unlike a lot of guys."

Not that his gangster world and the printing operation didn't heavily overlap. In addition to the orders that resulted from strong-arming by Frank Kissel and his crew at the butcher's union, Al was approached by local Brooklyn pizza shop owners, most of them mob-connected, to make boxes for their pies.

"I said we'd make all they needed, but if they wanted their names on the boxes, they had to pay up front. That worked out, except for this one store that made a big order and refused to pay."

Al first sent Petey Del around to collect. Del Cioppo returned empty-handed, sheepishly admitting that the Sicilians who owned the place had tossed him out of the shop. When he'd demanded the money, he said, they told him they were real Mafiosi, unlike him, and to get lost.

"So I go over there myself with Petey to show him how it's done. It's a place in Bay Ridge. They owed us for twenty thousand boxes, a lot of money. I go in there and I'm speaking Italian to them, basically asking who the fuck do they think they are?"

The pizza shop owner tried to pull rank, invoking his own affiliation with the Sicilian Mafia and citing the name of a powerful island chieftain. "This one guy says to me, 'Show me your *moosa*.' It means 'Show me your lip.' It's basically a way of saying, 'Screw you, do something about it.' So I did."

Al smacked the pizza maker, knocking him down. "I hit him hard as I could. When he hit the floor, me and Petey Del gave him a stomping." When they were done, they went in the back and got the unused boxes and carried them out of the shop.

Under normal mob protocol, raising your fist to a made member of the Mafia was a felonious offense, punishable even by death. After they left the shop, Petey Del asked Al if he was worried about that. "Nah," he responded. "They're Italian Mafia. They don't count."

The printing business was proving a growth industry for the hardworking mobster. Looking to expand further, Al started trying to land contracts with fast-food outlets. McDonald's wasn't yet much of a local presence, but White Castle had several popular hamburger outlets in Brooklyn, and he went around trying to line up the business. But obtaining the proper thickness of cardboard demanded by the burger company was difficult. "First thing I find out is they use only ten-point board for their paper burger sleeves. And you can't buy ten-point board. The mills won't sell it to you because the big box companies have a lock on it, and they don't want anyone else getting a piece. I'm thinking, These guys are gangsters too. How you gonna print the boxes? You can't."

There was a gangland solution to everything, however. "I heard about a load of ten-point board coming into the printing company that's got the contract. The shipment is in Connecticut, so I get Petey Del and Ralph and we went out there and hijacked the truck."

They delivered the load to the plant at Imlay Street. "Now we're all set—we got the board, and I can tell the burger joints we're ready to supply them." There was so much business coming in, however, that Campanella's printers were backed up on production.

"Fucking Moishe, he procrastinates. He leaves the board near the heaters, and since it's wintertime they're going full blast to heat the place. And of course they warp the board so now it's useless. It's curved and won't print right."

Such was the life of a small businessman. Frustrated, Al was casting around for a new cardboard source when a different way to make money with Moishe's printing machines was broached by Anthony Tortorello and some of his friends. Their idea was literally to make money. Counterfeit cash.

The plan had started with a Genovese member named Salvatore Aparo who had gotten hold of some samples of bleached dollar bills that, if carefully handled, might be reprinted as larger denominations. Aparo was from the family's East Harlem faction. Known on the street as "Sammy Meatballs," he had been arrested in the same big 1965 narcotics sweep that netted Chalootz Gagliodotto and his victims, Frank Tuminaro and Frank Gangi. Aparo had made it through unscathed, however. A couple of years younger than Al, he was an active hustler and another regular visitor to the K & K Luncheonette.

Aparo was thinking big. "The numbers Sammy threw out were huge. He was saying we could make $20 million if the job was done good enough." Campanella took a look. He said he could do it, but it would take time and investment. He'd need a new printer, a special camera to shoot photos of real $100 bills, plus ink, oil, and chemicals. The tab for the added equipment, he estimated, would come to about $50,000.

Aparo and Tortorello kicked in $13,000 to get things going. As Al was scrounging around for more, Moishe got to work fashioning the plates he would use to make the bogus bills. "I'll say this, the guy was some printer. When we couldn't find the press he said he needed, he just started building his own. Moishe was amazing that way."

But it was a time-consuming process. While Campanella was trying to perfect the machine and the plates, Al got a different pitch involving faked money from another friend in the Genovese family. Ever the nimble businessman, he was all ears.

The pitch came from Frank Caggiano, a close associate of Vincent Gigante and a member of the Mozzarella mob. Known as "Frankie Heart," Caggiano ran a jewelry stand in the Canal Street diamond exchange and had a members-only social club on Prince Street near Thompson, across from Milady's bar. At the box company, he explained his needs to Al. "What he wanted to know was if we could get bundles of paper that would match the exact weight and look of a $10,000 stack of $100 bills. It had to have bank wrappers on them with real bills on top and bottom. He said he needed four hundred stacks' worth."

Al did the math. "I thought, Wow, $4 million." He told Caggiano he would see, but he thought it was possible. "I wanted to help him out. I really liked Frankie. Everybody did." Al checked with Moishe and an agreeable paper supplier. "What you needed was 100 percent rag paper, and this guy said he could get it." Al sent Caggiano word that it would take a couple weeks but they could handle it.

A few days later, Frankie Heart returned, this time with a large blue bag made of heavy canvas cloth. "He says that when the paper is ready, we should see if four hundred packets of the bills fit into this sack." Caggiano warned Al that everyone handling the paper and the sack should wear double sets of latex gloves to avoid leaving any fingerprints.

"I don't ask him what he wants with this, but now it's pretty clear. The bag was like the ones that armored-car drivers use to deliver money to the banks." When the paper had been cut, wrapped, and placed in the bag, Caggiano sent an emissary to collect it. Al received a hefty payment for the work.

"I never asked Frankie about it, but I heard later that a couple of guys who worked for an armored-car outfit had been busted after switching a bag of cash that was headed for a bank in Germany. I heard they almost made it."

It took Moishe Campanella almost a year to get the plates perfected to make the counterfeit $100 bills. On the day he started running them off his homemade press, Sammy Aparo and Anthony Tortorello came out to watch. "It was like we'd just hit the lottery. We're looking at the bills and they look real to us." Moishe printed a quarter million dollars' worth. The stacks of bills filled an entire pallet.

There hadn't been much talk about how the money would be passed off. But Al now learned that Aparo and Tortorello had been planning all along to buy heroin with it. The thinking was that the bills might not fool a bank, but that an eager narcotics dealer wouldn't be able to tell the difference.

Al begged off that plan. Not because he was against selling junk, but because he suspected that Tortorello, who tended to flaunt his crimes, might already be a police target. It turned out he was right to hesitate. Shortly after the phony money was produced, Tortorello was arrested, charged with narcotics trafficking.

"After Torty got picked up we brought the counterfeit cash over to his kid, Joey. We told him not to do anything with it, but keep it in a safe that his family had. Of course, him and his friends immediately go out on a buying binge." Even a friend of the Tortorello family got into the act when she came across the stash, buying herself a new car with a wad of bills she lifted.

The counterfeit money was spotted, and the rest of it became too hot to touch. "Sammy Aparo started complaining that he was out $30,000 between what he laid out for the bleached bills and his investment in the press. I couldn't say he was wrong, but we were all out a lot of dough on this thing."

Moishe's intensive labor on the counterfeit cash had also taken him away from their regular box-printing business. "Suddenly I look around and we owe about $100,000 in bills, with almost nothing coming in."

The yawning financial hole made Al receptive when someone told him about a supply of stolen drums of quinine, used for cutting heroin. "There were ten drums from a shipment from West Germany that had been heisted off a pier in New York. You could gross $22,000 a drum if you had a steady buyer." Despite Tortorello's recent arrest, Al reached out through Torty's network of dope dealers to test the market. He found immediate interest. He sold the first two drums, then two more.

The drug money kept the wolf from the printing company door for a while, but he eventually ran out of options. He looked around and realized he still had one asset: the insurance policy he'd had Del Cioppo take out on the business. Collecting on it was the only possible payday he saw ahead of him.

"It was pretty simple. Petey and me went to Imlay Street one night and went to work. We had these propane tanks to run the fork lifts that we used to move the cardboard pallets around. We also had gasoline in this separate room we used to wash down the printing plates. The gas was permitted as long as we kept it away from everything else. Which we did."

The place was also filled with tinder-dry combustibles. Paper and cardboard were strewn throughout the floor. Al propped up a propane tank and stuck a long, gas-soaked length of gauze tissue in the top of a jug of gas as a wick. "Then I took a lit cigarette and a book of matches, laid them at the end of the gauze, and took off."

He and Petey Del drove away, then looped back on the Brooklyn-Queens Expressway to see what had happened. "The place was roaring."

The arson was successful. The insurance scam, less so. "Petey was the president of the company so he was the one the insurance investigator came to talk to. I told him what to say, but when they asked him if he had gas there, he just said yes. The big dope didn't explain that it was allowed to be there."

The claim was denied. "I think we were out $300,000 on that score."

The setbacks might have gotten him down, if not for his frequent visits out to Geffken's Bar on Flatlands Avenue, where he had become an increasingly popular figure. Even without his button, Al was treated as an accepted member of Paul Vario's crew.

Among the tavern regulars was Jimmy Burke, a wild Irish gangster who was feasting on the freight going to and from nearby John F. Kennedy Airport. "Jimmy Burke and his crew were hijacking everything they could. I couldn't tell how much he was passing up to Paulie, but I know he was getting a share." One day, Vario turned to Al and asked if he could handle a dispute between Burke and two other men over a hijacking that was threatening to get out of control. "I said, 'Sure, I'll listen to it,' but what I was thinking was, Why does Paulie want me to handle a sit-down with Jimmy Burke?"

At a nearby coffee shop, Al heard them out. The dispute centered on a $300,000 tractor-trailer load of Bic lighters that Burke had snatched. The other two men claimed that they were owed half the earnings because they had told Burke about the load. Burke said he was willing to give them a third, but no more. "I asked the two guys claiming a bigger share if they'd shopped the deal around to others before bringing it to Jimmy. They said yes. So I said, 'That's it. You get the third. He helped you out here.'"

Burke apparently thought even a third of the profits was unreasonable. "Both those guys turned up dead a few nights later. He shot them right in their own car. Jimmy'd kill you in a minute for nothing. He didn't give a fuck."

Al was around to notice all the furtive whisperings after Burke's biggest and most famous score, the $6 million Lufthansa heist from a Kennedy Airport terminal a couple of weeks before Christmas in December 1978. "It was none of my business so I never asked a thing, but it was hard to miss."

A few days after the robbery, he accompanied Paulie to Vario's mother's house for a small Christmas celebration. Burke was there, as were Frank Manzo and Peter "Rugsy" Vario, one of Paulie's two surviving sons. The group talked about the robbery with Al in the room. "I'm trying not to listen. It's something I don't need to know about."

As members of Burke's crew who had participated in the heist started turning up dead over the following months, Al had good reason to be glad he'd steered clear of it.

The closest he came to being pulled into Burke's robberies was when Paul Vario asked him if he could have a diamond ring he'd received from Burke reset. "I had told Paulie about my friend George Solow in the diamond district, so he knew I had a connection who could handle it." The ring was an expensive trophy, possibly a championship ring. It was clear from the engraving that it had once belonged to New York Jets football star Joe Namath. There were several large diamonds on it arranged in the shape of a football. Vario wanted it redone so he could wear it.

"I took it to George and he did a beautiful job. Paulie was very pleased. I don't know how he got it to begin with, but I heard that Joe Namath was a gambler, so maybe it had something to do with that."

The other big diamonds he saw out at Geffken's were on the cuff links of Jimmy Burke's friend and hijacking partner, Tommy DeSimone, the model for Joe Pesci's character in the movie *Goodfellas*. "Tommy was just as wild as Jimmy. The mob had a strict rule that you never carried a gun unless you were going to use it. But Tommy always had two guns on him and he wasn't afraid to flash them."

The night DeSimone was killed, Al saw him come into Geffken's. "He was all dressed up. He had on this nice suit and diamond cuff links and everything. The word was around he was going to get made." Everyone in the bar seemed to know about it. In addition to Paul Vario, there were his sons, Peter and Paul Jr.; Pete "the Killer" Abinanti, who was another of Joe Schiavo's protégés; and Angelo Sepe, part of Burke's hijacking crew. "Even the barmaid, this Sicilian girl, was congratulating him."

Al saw DeSimone leave the bar with Peter Vario and a member of the crew named Bruno Facciola. About an hour later, Al went to a pizza parlor that Facciola owned. DeSimone was seated at a table inside, with Facciola and Peter Vario. They seemed to be waiting for someone. "I remember Bruno was standing up and both him and Petey were wearing nice sports coats like they were going out somewhere."

It was DeSimone's last dinner. "They brought him to the place he was supposed to get made, then pushed him in and whacked him." The reason for the murder was that DeSimone had killed a Mafia member without permission. Al understood the rule, but was disturbed by the ruse. "I didn't like the way they did it. It was dishonorable. They told him they were going to make him. Then they kill him."

He got his own invitation to murder one day while sitting at Geffken's. The bar was almost empty and Al was seated next to Paul Vario when the crime chief leaned over the counter, picked up a kitchen knife, and handed it to Al. "He says he wants me to go out and kill Red Gilmore."

Al barely knew Tommy Gilmore. He knew he made his living as a burglar and that a lot of people in the Vario crew didn't like or trust him. But Al neither liked him nor disliked him. He didn't care one way or the other. "I took the knife from Paulie and it was almost automatic. Red had been in the bar just a few minutes before, having a beer. He'd said he was going out to work on his car. He had an antique Chevy he liked to tinker with. I figured he was in the alley out back."

Al stood up, slipped the knife down along his pants leg, and headed out the side door. He was going to do what Paul Vario had told him to do. Kill Red Gilmore.

Just as Al got to the door, Vario called him.

"Okay," he said. "That's enough. C'mon back."

Al went over to Vario, who took the knife and patted his shoulder. "Good," he said.

"That's all he said. It was some kind of test, I guess. But if he hadn't called me back, I know I would have done what he asked."

In March 1979, Al's best friend, Ralph Masucci, died. He was just fifty-three years old, but it was natural causes, not the gangster virus going around. "He died of cancer, Hodgkin's. It came on real quick. The doctors told him, 'Don't go in the sun no more, and stop smoking the cigars.' So that meant go to Florida and keep smoking the fucking cigars. He wouldn't quit. I took him up to Sloan-Kettering and they cut him up to try and get it, but it was too late. Half his neck was gone from operations by the time he went."

The whole family grieved. Ralph was godfather to Tara at her baptism. He was Joseph's godfather too for his confirmation in 1966. Alone of Al's many gangland pals, Ralph had been a regular visitor to the D'Arco home and dinner table. Al's daughters doted on him, as did his younger son, John. Al tried not to show a lot of emotion. But he was quietly devastated. "Me and him did a lot of things together, traveled the whole world. We got along good."

He still had the burger stand going, but without the printing company he was now back to hustling, ever in search of daily scores to pay the rent.

He became friendly with an old-timer off the Brooklyn waterfront named Frank Gagliardi who had been part of Anastasia's mob. Gagliardi had been a major hijacker in his day. In 1947, he'd been nabbed by the FBI as the ringleader in $500,000 worth of heists that had plagued truck freight operators. "Frank had a nephew who was pulling jobs and he asked me to help him out. I didn't much care for the kid, but I liked Frank so I went along."

The hijacking jobs with Gagliardi's nephew made money, but each was a headache in its own way. "We had a load of dresses we'd snatched and were taking them out to Hackensack, New Jersey, to someone who had a dress plant and was going to take them off us. I'm in a Cadillac with Frank following the truck. The truck was this old Bulldog Mack and I could tell it was on its last legs. I can hear the engine whining from back where we are. The driver is wobbling all over the road. We get over by the World Trade Center and he pulls over and says he can't drive the thing."

Al volunteered to take over. "I get behind the wheel and I see why the other guy quit. It will barely turn. I'm swinging the wheel twice around just to take a corner. We had to go through the Holland Tunnel and I'm hitting the sides of the tunnel as we're going through. It was a miracle I didn't get pulled over, but we made it."

Another hijacking job involved dropping through the skylight of a Brooklyn garage guarded by a large watchdog, a German shepherd. "Frank's nephew said he had a plan to take the dog out without making any noise. He was going to use a crossbow once we opened the skylight. I figured he knew how to use it, but we get up on the roof and he can't even crank it back. So I took it, aimed, and hit the dog. One shot."

Al felt bad about killing the shepherd. "I thought about that for years. I was sorry about that dog."

Out on Flatlands Avenue, another mob associate with a penchant for fouling things up was wreaking havoc on Paul Vario and his crew. Henry Hill, a member of Jimmy Burke's hijacking team, had been busted on federal drug charges. Facing serious prison time and his own drug-addiction-fueled suspicions, Hill decided to cooperate. Al never had anything to do with Hill but he knew that Vario was fond of him, despite his many problems. "I remember one time he got in trouble on something out on Rockaway Parkway on some heist gone bad. Paulie had to send a rescue crew out to help him."

Hill wasn't a made member of the mob, but his decision to flip was a considerable coup for law enforcement. Before the half-Irish, half-Italian Hill started talking, the only significant mobsters to cooperate were Joe Valachi in 1963, followed by a West Coast–based Mafioso named Jimmy Fratianno in 1977.

Hill told the feds about the Lufthansa job, and how Paul Vario, who had taken Hill under his wing as a boy in Brownsville, had gotten a huge share of the loot. But his knowledge was mostly secondhand, and he had no solid evidence to offer. He did help prosecutors nail Burke on a point-shaving scandal involving players for the Boston College basketball team. They also got Vario on a separate charge for lying to federal parole officers to get Hill a job with a mob-tied nightclub operator.

The perjury rap wasn't much of a case to bring down a man dubbed as the criminal mastermind of south Brooklyn. But prosecutors made good use of what they had. And Henry Hill proved an effective witness on the limited scams he knew about.

The parole-scam trial also raised a curtain on a previously hidden part of Long Island politics. During the trial, U.S. senator Alfonse D'Amato appeared as a character witness for Phil Basile, the mobbed-up nightclub owner who gave Hill the job as a favor to his close friend Paul Vario. D'Amato was from Island Park, the Long Island South Shore town where Vario had lived and where Basile ran big, brassy nightclubs including one that hosted a D'Amato victory party. In the courtroom, the senator gave Basile a peck on the cheek, then took the stand to call him "honest, truthful, hardworking. A man of integrity." The jury didn't agree, convicting Basile of perjury.

Al heard D'Amato's name mentioned occasionally by Vario and his son Peter. "They called him 'Cappy.' Paulie knew him for a long time and D'Amato and Philly Basile were very tight."

As for Henry Hill's treachery, there was little energy for doing anything about it. "There was talk about trying to find him and hurt him. But no one pursued it. They had him too well protected. Only way Henry Hill had something to worry about was if he ended up driving a cab and Petey Vario got in the back. Then he'd have something to worry about."

Part of what drove Henry Hill to change sides, as he often admitted later, was his fear that Vario might kill him for having steadily ignored his orders not to deal narcotics. Vario may well have run out of patience with the incorrigible Hill. But Al had seen the mob's alleged sanction against drug dealing steadily ignored. "Half the crews were dealing. You didn't talk about it, but the bosses were happy to take their cut of the money." He'd watched as top figures in the Genovese crime family, including Vincent Gigante, were convicted in major narcotics cases with no penalty exacted. Vario's own Luchese family boasted many of the city's leading narcotics dealers.

Al had reached his own conclusions. "The rules were made for the peons. The guys making the big bucks? The rules weren't made for them."

Which didn't mean that he might not face difficulties if he dealt narcotics as a made member. But until he got his button he was still a free agent. He had long nibbled around the edges of the drug trade. There had been his failed effort with Ralph Masucci to sell Davie Petillo's Afghani heroin. Then, more successfully, the sale of the cutting agent, quinine, out of the stolen drums from the box company in Red Hook.

Not long after that, he also took a kilo of heroin "on consignment" from a crew of Luchese family members who operated out of a social club on Prince Street and who were actively dealing drugs. He took the kilo to a friend of his named Jakie Bove, a mob-tied drug dealer based in East Harlem. He did well at first, earning $70,000 on the sale. Then the deal quickly went sour. It turned out the heroin was laced with caffeine, a trick to make the drug give a false reading of purity when tested. He was forced to return both the cash and the drugs.

Equally frustrating were two failed efforts to do drug deals with Vic Amuso, the young gangster Al had first met at the bust-out on Washington Avenue and had later helped out at Sing Sing. Amuso was teamed up with a partner named Anthony Casso, a wisecracking mobster from the Gowanus neighborhood of Brooklyn. Casso's nickname was "Gaspipe." When asked about it, he would laugh and say friends called him that because of his proficiency with a heavy length of metal pipe as a weapon. Al had a different theory. "I remember Anthony's father on Kent Avenue coming around to check the gas because he worked for the gas company. I figured that's where the name came from."

Amuso and Casso told Al that they had a kilo of heroin they would sell him for $150,000. Al didn't have the money, but he was sure Jakie Bove would be eager to advance the cash if the heroin proved potent. Bove agreed to back the deal. Retrieving the drugs from Amuso and Casso, he eagerly waited to see the results of the tests. "Jakie comes back to me and said the same thing. The heroin didn't stand up. It was no good."

Al went to see Amuso to return the drugs and get Bove's money back. "Vic told me there was a delay, and I'd get it, but it would take a little while." Al was annoyed but didn't complain. Amuso and Casso were both made members of the Luchese family, and unless he wanted to lodge a complaint against them, there wasn't much he could do but wait.

"A few days later I get a call to come out to Brooklyn and get the money from Anthony." Casso told Al to meet him at the parking lot of a Chinese restaurant called the Golden Ox, on Avenue N in south Brooklyn. "He had the money but it was all in fives, tens, and twenties. It was $150,000 in small bills."

Despite those experiences, he was still eager to make the huge profits he saw others hauling in from drug deals. So when a hustler he knew named Francisco Solimene approached him in the spring of 1982 about participating in a heroin deal, Al, ever eager for a score, listened.

"I met Solimene around the neighborhood. His name was Frank, so of course everyone called him Cheech. I knew he was a big gambler, but so were a lot of guys, so that didn't seem a problem."

Cheech Solimene had a straightforward pitch: He had a willing buyer with deep pockets for high-grade heroin. What he needed was a supplier. "I figured he knew people I knew, and as long as the quality was acceptable, we could make some money. I said I was in."

Solimene's own luck in the drug business hadn't been great. He was just getting back on the streets after serving seven years for his last heroin deal. That conviction followed the discovery in 1971 by airport customs agents of 155 pounds of the narcotic in four suitcases. The trail led them to Cheech's Queens apartment, where agents found a key to a safety-deposit box in his wife's name containing $87,000, and the number of a Swiss bank account that held $105,000. Solimene didn't have a job at the time, so he had a hard time explaining the money. He was convicted of conspiracy to import heroin.

Al didn't press Solimene for details about his buyer. But after obtaining heroin for the deal from the same group of Luchese-tied operators on Prince Street, he began to wonder.

Late on the night of July 7, 1982, Solimene met Al outside his apartment at 32 Spring Street after making his sale to his buyer uptown. Al and Solimene climbed into a tan 1978 Lincoln Continental for a drive to meet another dealer. The car was Al's, but he kept it registered in Pete Del Cioppo's name, as one more way to keep a low profile.

The meeting was at Sarge's Delicatessen, a late-night restaurant on Third Avenue and Thirty-Seventh Street. Al and Solimene stayed only a few minutes and then headed back downtown. On the way, Al got suspicious of a car behind them.

"I thought this guy was following us, but I couldn't be sure, so I started driving around, squaring the blocks." He turned right, right, and right again in an effort to spot any surveillance. He headed down Second Avenue, then suddenly lurched across several lanes of traffic and made a fast left turn toward the FDR Drive. He sped down the highway, exiting at Houston Street.

On the service road paralleling the drive, he pulled over.

The car that he thought was following him cruised past. Al followed behind. At a stop light on Grand Street Al pulled abreast of the suspicious car. He gave a long hard look at the driver. Then he made a U-turn, heading back in the direction they had come. The car stopped following.

Solimene wanted to make another deal. Al was hesitant. He said he wanted to get a look at this deep-pocketed buyer. "I told him to bring him down to our territory so I could see him." Solimene told his buyer to meet him at Caffe Roma, the pastry and espresso place on the corner of Mulberry Street, at 9 p.m. on July 15. Shortly after Solimene and his buyer sat down at a table, Al came up the block. He peered in the window, trying to see if he recognized the man talking to Solimene. He didn't know him.

As a business deal, the heroin sale was a modest success. Solimene's buyer paid $31,000. Al made a decent profit after paying off his Prince Street connection. Solimene pushed Al to keep going. His buyer was hungry for more, he said. But Al had had enough. "I didn't get a good feeling. I made out okay. Nothing went wrong. But it wasn't worth a pinch. I told him no thanks."

In the ensuing weeks, Al noticed Solimene often on the streets of Little Italy, hanging out around a Genovese family club at the corner of Broome and Mott Streets, the Latineers Social Club.

Al didn't pay him much attention. Part of his distraction was that Joe Schiavo had revived the push to finally get Al his button. "Joe said he was fed up with Paulie's delaying."

The elder Luchese family statesman went on a lobbying campaign. First he took Al to a bar in Bensonhurst, Brooklyn, that was the headquarters for the family's consigliere, Christopher "Christy Tick" Furnari. The 19th Hole was a one-story tavern at the corner of Eighty-Sixth Street and Fourteenth Avenue, across from the Dyker Beach Golf Course. Furnari did much of his business in a back room there. One of those listening to Schiavo make Al's case was Vic Amuso. Amuso greeted Al warmly and promised to do what he could.

Another campaign stop was northern New Jersey, where Schiavo brought Al to meet an old-time power in the family. Joe Rosato was Tommy Luchese's brother-in-law. Known as "Joe Palisades," he had become a wealthy man helping to run the family's lucrative racket in garment trucking operations. Aside from a homicide arrest that didn't result in a conviction, Rosato kept a low profile. His chief brush with notoriety came when he was one of those arrested at the 1957 Apalachin conclave. Rosato was briefly jailed on contempt charges after he refused to tell the New York State Commission of Investigation why he was present at the underworld gathering.

Al was introduced, and then the two older men stepped aside to talk. Whatever Schiavo said, it apparently did the trick.

"Joe Palisades reached out to Tony Ducks Corallo, who was running the family then, and asked why they were keeping me out." There was no good answer, except for Frank Manzo's unspecified objections. And if it was possible to have dismissed Al as an "ice-cream vendor" back in 1974 when he was first proposed for membership, the description no longer held.

On August 23, 1982, Vario contacted Al. "Get dressed," he told him. "I knew what he meant."

Al put on a gray suit that Dolores had bought him, a white shirt, and a tie, and went to the Prince Street clubhouse that was headquarters for the DiPalermo brothers and their friends, the same place where he'd scored a kilo of heroin a few months earlier. Two of the brothers, Charles and Peter, were waiting for him there. "We got in Petey Beck DiPalermo's Cadillac, and drove up to the Bronx. I didn't know where we were, but we parked beside a brick wall and sat awhile." After a few minutes, a four-door Fleetwood Cadillac pulled up. In it was another Luchese member, Salvatore "Sally Bo" DeSimone. Beside him was an associate from the Canarsie crew Al had met, Louie Daidone. Also in the car was Frank Manzo. Al acted like nothing had happened between them. "I just said 'How ya doin', Frank? Good to see you.'"

The entire group piled into the Fleetwood and drove around. "They were looking for any kind of surveillance. It was the worst thing that could happen, if the cops spotted an induction ceremony. So we squared the blocks for a while." On Westchester Avenue, in the northwest Bronx, the car stopped in front of a row of small houses. "They said we should make straight for the door. We ran inside."

Al was just one of the inductees. Daidone was another. There were four other men, most of whom he didn't know. The recruits sat quietly in a small parlor. The room was made smaller by a sheet that was hanging over an entrance to a kitchen. Al couldn't see who was back there but he heard men talking and moving around.

"We got told to just wait there. We all knew what was going on, but no one said anything. We just sat."

Al's was the first name called. He was beckoned past the sheet into the kitchen area. A dozen men were crowded around a table. Al spotted Paul Vario, Corallo, Vic Amuso, the DiPalermo brothers, and Frank Manzo. He also recognized Salvatore Santoro, the family's underboss from the Bronx, known on the street as "Tom Mix." On the table a towel was covering a lumpy object.

Corallo spoke first. "Do you know why you are here?" he asked.

Al knew the correct answer. "No," he said.

"Well, you're here to be one of us," Corallo told him. "Do you have any objections to that?"

"No, I got no objections," Al answered.

Santoro spoke next. He lifted the towel. A gun and a knife were underneath. "If you were asked to kill somebody, would you do it?"

Al shrugged his shoulders. It was a gangster gesture that signaled he would do what he had to do.

Santoro asked Vario if he had a pin. Vario pulled out a safety pin and reached out for Al's right hand. He held his index finger, the one that Al would use to pull a trigger, something he hadn't had to do so far. "Paulie gives me a sharp jab. Then he lets the blood drip onto a tissue of paper he's got."

Vario told Al to cup his hands and dropped the bloody tissue onto them. Then he took a match and lit it. "I shuffled this burning paper back and forth between my hands."

As the tissue burned, Santoro gave the incantation of the Cosa Nostra and told Al to repeat it after him. "You live by the gun and the knife, and you die by the gun and the knife. And if I betray anyone in this room, or any friends of ours, may my soul burn in hell like this paper."

He dropped the paper into an ashtray. Santoro leaned forward and gave Al a kiss on both cheeks. "He says, 'This is your boss, Antonio Corallo. And I am your underboss, Salvatore Santoro, and this is your *caporegime*, Paul Vario." He then filled Al in on the names of the heads of New York's other crime families. "At the time, it was Rusty Rastelli for the Bonannos, Junior Persico for the Colombo family, Chin Gigante for the Genovese, and Paul Castellano for the Gambinos."

The induction ended with Al's own formal introduction as a member of the crime family to everyone in the room. "Then they told me to take a seat and went through it with the rest of the guys who'd been waiting outside in the living room with me."

After all the inductions and speeches were over, the men in the room stood and held hands. "It's an old-world thing. It means to 'tack up.' The Italian for it is *attacatta*. It basically means we're all in this together."

Tony Corallo then spoke in Italian. "He said, '*La fata di questa famiglia sono aperti*.' It meant 'The affairs of the family are now open.' And then he starts to lay down the rules."

The boss went over a list of prohibitions. "He said no narcotics, no counterfeit money, no stolen bonds and stocks. No fooling around with other members' wives and daughters. Then he tells us that when your captain calls you, no matter what time of day or night, you must respond. He says, 'This family comes before your family.'"

When he was done, Corallo instructed the men in the room that they were never to speak of what they'd seen and heard. Speaking again in Italian, he told them that the family's affairs were now closed. "Then we tacked up again, and that was it."

The men went back into the living room, where there was a snack of pastries and coffee. They had just pledged to kill on demand in a secret society but they stood around chatting like a church social. It didn't last long. "Everybody was anxious to get out of there. It was crowded and the bosses were worried about law enforcement. We went out a few at a time."

The next day, Al went out to Geffken's to see Paul Vario and the crew. Vario reintroduced him to men he'd known for years, this time as a member of the family. Among them was Bruno Facciola, the owner of the pizza parlor where Al had last seen Tommy DeSimone alive on the eve of what was supposed to be his own induction into Vario's crew. Facciola told Al he was going to have a big party in his honor at his club on Avenue D.

"The party was a few days later. It was made guys only, but there were more than fifteen guys there. Paulie opened it like a formal meeting. He says, 'I want to introduce you to our friend, Al D'Arco.' Then he goes over some of the rules that didn't get mentioned the first time. He says to make sure no business is discussed with wives in the room. And for everyone to concern themselves with the families of other members when they're in need. Then we had a feast. Bruno had a real spread for us, lobster, pasta. Everyone was congratulating me and making toasts."

After the dinner was over, Vario had the men ceremonially join hands again. Then he announced the meeting closed.

Al enjoyed the attention. But he was fairly clear about the bottom-line benefits of the club he had just joined. "What it meant, most of all, was that this thing is mine. Once you're straightened out, no one can take it off you. Not my boss, not anyone. No one can tell you what to do. You got all the privileges, and you can't get abused. You're not a second-class citizen anymore."

9

RAY BROOK

After all the speeches about steering clear of drugs, Al was a little thrown off guard when Paul Vario asked him a few months after his induction to help out on a cocaine deal.

The request came in November 1982, while Al was in Florida with his family at Dolores's parents' condo. Vario was in Miami as well and the two of them got together. "Paulie said that a couple of his guys were going to move a large quantity of coke and he wanted to know if I could help out."

Al thought at first that this was another test, like the time Paulie had handed him the knife in Geffken's to kill Red Gilmore. But it wasn't. "He wanted me to do it."

Al didn't want anything to do with it. He had several reasons, starting with his mob vows. "I swore I wasn't going to sell drugs when I got made. So I wasn't going to do it." Even if he wanted to, he didn't want to risk another close call like he'd had with Frank Solimene and his heroin buyer. There was one more good reason: the gangster handling the coke deal was one of the most ruthless members of the Canarsie crew, a twenty-seven-year-old armored-car hijacker named Ray Argentina.

He first met Argentina at Geffken's Bar. After the introduction, Paulie nudged Al. "He did three for me," whispered Vario. Al knew what he meant. Three murders.

Argentina was one of nine brothers. He and a younger brother, Peter, worked as strong-arm enforcers for Frank Manzo, helping to shake down businesses at the airport.

Even in a mob that valued brazen musclemen, Ray Argentina was considered dangerously impulsive. "He was a mad kid. He did everything hyper. He drove really fast, moved really fast. And killed a lot of people."

A few months before he was made, Al got a taste of Argentina's frenzied style. The opportunity came when he was asked to pick up an Ingram machine gun equipped with a silencer at a Luchese family social club in Little Italy and deliver it to Argentina in Canarsie. The weapon was a large, military-style machine pistol, the kind favored by drug dealers for impact, not accuracy. After he handed over the gun, Argentina thanked Al profusely. "Then he tells me this story how he once walked up behind someone on the street in the middle of the day and shot him. He said he used a 9 mm pistol in that one. I'm thinking, The guy hardly knows me and he's telling me this?"

Al didn't say no to Vario, but he didn't pursue it either. His new *caporegime* let it drop. He didn't hear any more about it.

The episode was one more reminder of the mob's empty rhetoric about drugs, at least when it came to established Mafia members doing the dealing.

The Luchese family's lead exhibit for that double standard was just a couple of blocks from Al's Spring Street home. At their headquarters on Prince Street around the corner from Old St. Patrick's Church, the fabled DiPalermo brothers had been running narcotics for decades without suffering any noticeable mob consequences.

The family had five brothers, each one with a long criminal résumé, with a major in drugs. The oldest of the brood was Joseph DiPalermo. Known on the street as Joe Beck, he was born in 1907 at 246 Elizabeth Street between Prince and Houston. He was still going strong in his seventies, working the same block, when Al knew him.

In the tabloids, Joe Beck was dubbed "the dean of dope dealers," though you wouldn't know it to look at him. He was reed-thin, balding, stood five foot six, and wore thick glasses. At one of his arraignments, the *Daily News* described him as "a wispy gnome-like creature with outsized horn rims." At another, he was a "skinny, tubercular little crook." The tuberculosis was the one thing you couldn't blame on him. He had picked it up sleeping in damp prison cells after being convicted of bootlegging in the 1930s.

DiPalermo's greatest claim to mob fame was for a murder he didn't carry out. His mission from Vito Genovese was to kill Joe Valachi in the yard at the Atlanta federal prison. Or at least Valachi believed it. He crushed the skull of a prisoner who looked just like Joe Beck from the back, the crime that caused him to seek refuge with the FBI.

DiPalermo's other brush with notoriety was a murder for which he was never charged. He was a prime suspect, along with his partner, Carmine Galante, in the slaying of Italian anarchist and Mussolini foe Carlo Tresca, gunned down on lower Fifth Avenue in 1943. It was a rare mob murder of a victim who was not one of their own. Tresca had offended pro-Fascist sympathizers, who licensed his assassination to the Mafia. A halfhearted investigation by the Manhattan DA never produced indictments.

Joe Beck and one of his younger brothers, Charles, dodged charges on another infamous murder, Al learned. That was the elimination of the young Jewish hoodlum who blinded *Daily Mirror* labor columnist Victor Riesel.

At 2:40 a.m. on April 5, 1956, Abe Telvi, twenty-two, tossed a vial of acid in Riesel's face as the writer was leaving Lindy's Restaurant at Broadway and West Fifty-First Street. Telvi was paid $1,000 for the attack, allegedly commissioned by labor racketeer Johnny Dio, who wanted to teach Riesel a lesson for his tough columns about Dio's corrupt union tactics. After learning that his target was a big-shot journalist, Telvi naively demanded more money. The DiPalermo brothers took on the task of giving Telvi his own lesson. "They shot him in the head and dumped his body in Jersey Street, the little alley off Mulberry Street."

That killing was also never solved. Meanwhile, the DiPalermo boys went on to notch repeated drug convictions: Joe Beck got fifteen years in the same 1959 narcotics case in which Genovese and Vincent Gigante were convicted. Charlie Brody, as the little brother was called, was nailed in the same case and sentenced to twelve years.

Decades later, they were still at it. In 1975, the feds picked up Charlie Brody with twenty-five pounds of heroin as he stood on the beach in Point Lookout, Long Island, waiting for his connection to show up with the buy money. Big brother Joe went him one better. He was convicted in 1978 of heading a ring that peddled the new drug of choice in those years, quaaludes, or methaqualone.

Then there was Peter DiPalermo, or Petey Beck, a paunchier but even shorter version of his older brothers. "Pete was the captain of the Prince Street crew. He was directing the traffic."

The crew's headquarters was a social club at 27 Prince Street, spread across a pair of storefronts. Charlie Brody fell in love with and married a girl named Marion Cuomo, whose family lived in an apartment above the club. The Cuomos and DiPalermos were close. Marion's teenaged brother, Ralph, began running around with Joe Beck's son, John Joseph. The two formed a gang that robbed restaurants in midtown, late-night jobs aimed at getting the night's receipts. Al steered clear of both. "Raffie was a stick up artist back then. Him and Joe Becky's kid were taking chances, armed robberies."

On August 19, 1956, the gang tried to rob a posh restaurant on Park Avenue and East Forty-Ninth Street. A gunfight broke out after a patrolman spotted them. The cop was wounded. John Joseph was shot dead.

Ralph Cuomo was captured at the scene. Back at the station house, police posed him for the cameras, mockingly pointing his own gun in his bleeding face. But he didn't do much time. He was out of prison by 1959, just as his brother-in-law, Charlie, and John Joseph's father, Joe Beck, were be-

ginning their own sentences for their narcotics bust with Vito
Genovese.

That year, Cuomo opened the pizza parlor in one of the
Prince Street club's storefronts. He called it Ray's Pizza. The
pies became popular, and the name famous. But the shop's
real trade was always drugs. "Raffie went into business with
Charlie and the rest of the Becks moving heroin. He became
a big narcotics guy."

In 1969, Cuomo earned his own heroin arrest when Bureau of Narcotics agents caught him with two kilograms of
heroin in his car trunk. He served a few years, then went back
to the pizzeria and started dealing all over again.

None of the members of the Prince Street crew were users
of drugs. But they had another addiction that drove them to
ever-larger heroin deals. "They were all degenerate gamblers.
Each one of them. They would gamble a hundred thousand
dollars, lose it, and then have to do another dope deal."

Their heroin business generated huge quantities of cash.
"They had one of the Becky's kids, Anthony, going over to
the East River Savings Bank at Lafayette and Spring Street
with bags of bills. They had a guy in the bank on their payroll who handled the money for them. They made millions
in *babania*, heroin. All the brothers and Raffie did. That's
what they were all about. They never stopped dealing. They
were at it night and day."

They also tutored Al in the trade. The kilo of poor-quality
heroin he took on consignment and tried to sell to his friend
Jakie Bove, came from Cuomo and the Becky boys. And when
he'd gone looking for heroin to sell to Frank Solimene's mysterious but deep-pocketed connection, he'd headed straight
to Prince Street to score.

Al's involvement with Solimene was increasingly looking like a devastating mistake. In the fall of 1982, the FBI
rounded up thirteen men, several of them Luchese family
mobsters, on charges of dealing $25 million in narcotics.
FBI director William Webster announced the case. An undercover agent of the Drug Enforcement Administration

named Gerald Franciosa, he said, had successfully manipu-
lated a chronically addicted gambler with mob ties. The
gambler's name was Francisco Solimene.

Al didn't know most of those arrested, but the neighborhood buzzed with the news. He didn't tell anyone, but he was
pretty certain that Franciosa was the buyer he'd seen with
Solimene at Caffe Roma. Solimene's name was also listed
on the indictment. But he was nowhere to be found. Investigators told the press they believed he was dead.

He probably would have been if anyone had been able to
find him. But the gambler had vanished. Al was beginning
to think he'd been set up. If so, there wasn't much he could
do about it at this point. He warily went about his mob business, looking over his shoulder for the arrest he knew might
happen any time.

The drug enforcement agents waited until St. Patrick's Day,
March 17, 1983. Al was driving uptown to a wake in the Bronx
when he noticed a car on his tail. He pulled over on Prince
Street. "They pinched me right there. I was standing on the
sidewalk and a squad car jumps the curb next to me. This
agent in a leather jacket jumps out, runs up, and puts a gun
right next to my head." Al grabbed the agent's arm. "You
don't need that," he said. "Put the fucking thing away." The
agent cuffed him.

"There's a crowd on the street watching. I saw Raffie come
out of the restaurant. Then he sees me and turns around, goes
back inside."

He was arraigned in federal court in Foley Square the next
morning. Representing him was George Spitz, an attorney Al
had come to know. Spitz had a reputation as a courtroom battler who had represented both mobsters and black militants.
The lawyer won Al's release on a $1,000 cash bond, plus a
pledge of $9,000.

In the days after the arrest, he decided he would fight the
indictment. "I wouldn't cop to it. I couldn't really." Maybe,
he hoped, a jury could be persuaded not to buy the prosecution's claims.

One thing in his favor was that there was no evidence of cash or drugs actually changing hands between him and Solimene. For another, Solimene wasn't around. He was listed as a co-defendant, not a witness.

He drew more hope when prosecutors released the original arrest complaint. It had been issued in November, at the same time the thirteen other mobsters who had dealt with Solimene were arrested. It hadn't been executed because the agents didn't even know who Al was. The original names on the warrant were Solimene and Peter Del Cioppo. To cover their legal bases, prosecutors had added a John Doe. Al understood immediately what had happened. The car he and Solimene had been driving the night they'd been tailed after making the drug sale was the tan Lincoln registered in Petey Del's name. It had taken them months to realize Solimene's partner in the deal was Al D'Arco.

The more Al thought it over, the more it sounded like reasonable doubt to him. A jury might well decide there wasn't enough evidence to convict a hardworking family man and ex-GI trying to scrape a living out of a tiny hamburger stand.

Paul Vario recommended his own lawyer, a savvy criminal defense attorney from Long Island named Joel Winograd. In 1974, Winograd had won a big acquittal for the mob captain's son Peter and crew member Bruno Facciola after they were charged with helping to fix harness races at Yonkers Raceway. Spitz, with whom Al remained friendly, stepped aside.

As far as the mob's rule against drug dealing went, Paul Vario didn't make a fuss. Whatever he'd done, Vario told Al, it was before he was made. So it didn't count. Others weren't so understanding.

His old antagonist, Frank Manzo, sought out the family's underboss, Salvatore Santoro, to once more make his case against Al's mob bona fides. "Frank the Wop goes to Tom Mix with my indictment papers. He tells him, 'Look at this, Al D'Arco got busted for drugs.' You know what Tom Mix did? He got up and threw the papers in his face. He said, 'Get the fuck outta here, you stool pigeon.'"

Or at least that's how the story came back to Al. Whatever the reaction of top Luchese family leaders to his legal problems, he never heard a direct criticism. It would've been a tough violation for the bosses to make stick. Several other Luchese members had already been convicted from the earlier indictments in the drug case.

His case went to trial on June 20, 1983. It was a Monday, and over the next three days, assistant U.S. attorney James B. Rather III called to the stand a string of drug enforcement agents who had taken part in the sting operation. Their testimony about Solimene was ironclad. The drug dealer had virtually lived with the undercover agent, Franciosa, for months while using tens of thousands of dollars of the agent's money to buy heroin from various mobsters. He'd even taken Franciosa with him to Atlantic City, where he'd gambled away $350,000 in a three-day binge. All told, Solimene told the agent, he'd lost more than $1.5 million that year in casinos. "When this is gone," Solimene said of his last $11,000, "I'll kill myself." He was a man on the edge, a condition that played to the agents' advantage.

The agents had also duly recorded the serial numbers on the $31,000 paid for the heroin purchased from Al. But that money was handed to Frank Solimene. And Solimene wasn't on trial.

The testimony putting Al D'Arco in the conspiracy was considerably less certain. The undercover agent testified that after paying the cash, Solimene had told him that he was "going to go and see the guy and give him the good news." Agents had then tailed him downtown to Al's building on Spring Street. From there they'd followed the pair to Sarge's Delicatessen on Third Avenue, then on their circuitous route to the Lower East Side as the driver of the Lincoln tried to shake them.

But Winograd pointed out to the jury that the bag containing the heroin had never been submitted for analysis to see if Al's fingerprints were present. There were also major discrepancies. The agent who had tailed Al that night described the

Lincoln's driver as being six foot two and weighing 210 pounds. Winograd had Al, all five feet seven inches and 175 pounds of him, stand up for the jury.

The same agent had snapped photos of Al the night he went to check out Solimene's buyer at the Caffe Roma. But the photos never came out, the agent testified. It was too dark.

What became of the negatives? Destroyed, the agent stated.

"What is this? A game?" asked Winograd in his summation.

The defense didn't get much help from federal district judge Richard Owen, who was hearing the case. An appointee of President Richard Nixon, Owen had been on the federal bench for ten years by the time of the trial. An amateur musician, Owen once wrote an opera about Abigail Adams, wife of the second president.

After Winograd got the surveillance agent to admit his gaffe about misjudging Al's height by seven inches, the judge put his own question to the witness. "When you saw the defendant, he was riding in a car, right?" asked the judge. "He was sitting down?"

The agent quickly agreed that, yes, the driver of the auto had been seated while driving.

The jury began deliberations on Thursday morning. They kicked the evidence around for a day and a half, waiting until Friday afternoon to announce a verdict of guilty on both counts.

Al was stunned. "I thought we won the case. Then the sons of bitches came back and found me guilty."

After the verdict, Al was immediately remanded to prison to await sentencing. He spent a month in the redbrick Metropolitan Correctional Center on Pearl Street, the main detention site for federal prisoners behind the federal courthouse.

He went before Judge Owen for sentencing on July 29. After a reminder that this was his second conviction, the judge gave Al six years. The sentence was to run concurrently on the two counts of possession of heroin with intent to distribute, and conspiracy to distribute the drug. Under a 1977 law, the federal Drug Abuse Prevention and Control Act, a mandatory special parole period was tacked onto the end of his sentence. It meant that any violations committed by Al during that period, such as associating with other felons, would put him back in prison. And he would have to serve an additional sentence of the entire term of his special parole. The law required a minimum parole period of three years. Judge Owen gave Al ten.

"That judge, Owen, was a vampire. He enjoyed putting people away as long as he could."

Cursing the judge didn't help Al's family much, though. He had told them he was going to beat the case. "They took it hard. Of course they did. Joseph had been through it once, but for John and the girls, it was tough."

This time there was no pretending that daddy had to go to work. The youngest, Dawn, was thirteen years old and already wise to the ways of her father's world. The rest of the children were already adults, or close to it. Tara was eighteen; John, nineteen. Ava, twenty-five, was already out of the house, as was Joseph, who was twenty-seven and living in Knickerbocker Village. Dolores was as stoic as ever. "My mother would follow my father into the gates of hell," said Joseph.

His first stop was a plum location, at least for those who had to be incarcerated. Allenwood Federal Prison Camp was in the Allegheny Mountains of central Pennsylvania. It was roughly a four-and-a-half-hour drive from New York City, farther than some facilities, but closer than most. Its relative proximity to the city made it a sought-after placement for convicted offenders from the metropolitan area.

Its other advantage was that it was an "honor camp," reserved for those convicted of nonviolent crimes. There were no walls or barbed wire to keep inmates from simply wandering off. Prisoners slept in camp-style dorms, not individual cells. Al's drug conviction made him eligible for the facility in the eyes of the federal Bureau of Prisons, which didn't view him as an escape hazard despite his criminal past. But Al wasn't going anywhere.

"Where the fuck are you going to go? They got a state police barracks right in back. You going to walk through the woods?"

Most Allenwood inmates were white-collar felons. A handful were politicians, nabbed at various schemes. Former New Jersey senator Harrison Williams, convicted for taking bribes in the Abscam sting operation mounted by prosecutors in Brooklyn's Organized Crime Strike Force, was already there when Al got to Allenwood.

"He gets next to me and gives me a wink and a thumbs-up. I guess he wanted to fit in. 'How ya doin', kid,' he says to me. I said, 'Who the fuck are you? I'll knock your ass off.' "

Another bunkmate in the dormitory was Joseph Margiotta, the former Republican boss of Nassau County convicted of taking kickbacks on insurance contracts. Margiotta also tried to make friends. "I told him, 'Get the fuck outta here.' "

The snarl was Al's basic approach to the world as he began his second sentence behind bars. He deeply believed he'd been wrongly convicted. Not that he hadn't done the crime. But that the evidence presented against him at trial shouldn't have been enough to find him guilty.

Part of it was his lawyer's fault, he decided. Winograd hadn't fought hard enough to keep the government from using what the agents claimed Solimene had said about him. "Don't I get to confront my accuser?" he asked over and over.

This time around, he wasn't a young rookie prisoner soaking up the stories and gangland wisdom of veteran convicts. He was an often hostile, two-fisted enforcer of the basic criminal code.

One of the first to offend that code was a fellow wiseguy named Sal Miciotta. A member of the Colombo crime family, Big Sal Miciotta was at Allenwood for his own nonviolent offense, dealing in untaxed cigarettes.

It was the least of his sins. A burly man of six feet plus weighing over three hundred pounds, Miciotta had taken part in a gangland murder just eighteen months earlier. The targets were a father-and-son duo who had failed to share their immense earnings from having produced *Deep Throat*, the

most profitable pornographic movie ever made at the time.
The hit took place on a street in the south Brooklyn neighborhood of Gravesend. As the victims tried to flee, an errant
shotgun blast killed a former nun as she stood in a hallway
inside her home. By comparison, the cigarettes rap was a tri-
fle. Miciotta was doing a relaxed stretch at the prison camp
when Al arrived.

"Big Sal was like a rhino. We played racquetball together
inside. When he hit it, he'd bust the ball. He was 350 pounds
of muscle."

At Allenwood, Miciotta was using his jumbo size and
street savvy to serve as protector for a wealthy financial con-
sultant from Morristown, New Jersey. Alex Feinman had been
convicted of issuing millions of dollars in bogus bonds for
construction projects. A millionaire himself, Feinman flaunted
his wealth. When his wife came to see him, she arrived by
limousine, loaded with expensive food. Dolores had taken the
bus already once to see Al. The trip took her six hours.

Feinman's more grievous conduct, however, was that he
was a spy. After his conviction, the financier had sought to
reduce his sentence by helping prosecutors make other financial cases, serving as both adviser and informant. His cooperation was no secret inside the camp, and Al scolded Miciotta
for protecting him.

"I said, 'Sally, you're hanging out with a stool pigeon. That
gets out on the street, you're going to be embarrassed.' "

Miciotta tried to allay Al's concerns. "Of course he's a rat,"
he told Al. "These guys are all rats in here. What do you want
to do? Go to the penitentiary and do real time?"

The way Miciotta saw it, mobsters like him and Al were
sharks, swimming in a sea of guppies at Allenwood. A wiseguy could gobble them up, or see about getting a chunk of
their money for themselves. Feinman was paying handsomely
for protection that he didn't really need. In Miciotta's view,
that con job canceled out any possible taint from associating
with an informant.

"I told Al he should be more forgiving," Miciotta recalled.
Al's gangster standards didn't permit the compromise. And

he didn't hesitate to use his hands to make his point with in-mates he didn't like.

"Al was being a bully, smacking all these guys around. He fancied himself a tough guy," said Miciotta.

There was no question Al knew how to use his hands. Miciotta heard the thuds echoing down the gym hall at night after they'd played racquetball. "You could hear him with the gloves hitting that heavy bag every night. He would get some workout."

Miciotta did his best to placate him. "I know you're a tough guy, Al," Sal told him.

"You're wrong," Al responded. "I'm not a tough guy. I do what I have to do."

Miciotta wasn't the only wiseguy inmate at Allenwood who resented Al's lectures about what they should or shouldn't do. Also in the camp was Anthony DiLapi, a member of the Bronx branch of Al's own Luchese crime family. The Bronx crew was headed by Salvatore Santoro, the Luchese under-boss known as Tom Mix who had performed the induction rites at Al's initiation into the family. Santoro was also DiLapi's cousin, a relationship he steadily reminded Al about.

"DiLapi was doing the same thing as Big Sal, feeding off this stool pigeon. They were getting money and food his wife's bringing in."

Unlike Miciotta, who tried to calm Al down, the dispute with DiLapi quickly escalated. "He started threatening me, saying he was going to tell his cousin Tom Mix about my getting arrested for drugs. That he was going to have me killed."

The argument got heated. Wisely, no one threw a punch.

Feinman wasn't as sensible. The financial crook was thirty-four years old and several inches taller than Al, who was fifty-one at the time. But Miciotta, who dwarfed both men, said the Jewish inmate was still no match for the Ital-ian gangster from Spring Street. "He couldn't fight his way out of a paper bag," said Miciotta.

Feinman apparently didn't know that. One morning while Al and Feinman were both working in the mess hall clean-ing up after breakfast, a loud argument erupted between the two. According to an incident report compiled by correction officers, Feinman got physical, giving Al a shove. What happened next was predictable: "At this time, D'Arco came at Feinman, swinging his fists and kicking." The battle took place in front of several other inmates, but guards quickly broke it up.

A few days later, Al was shipped twenty miles down the road to the federal penitentiary at Lewisburg, Pennsylvania, a high-security facility. In prison parlance, it was a "disciplinary transfer." Al saw himself as the victim. Describing the incident in a letter he sent to authorities, he said he had merely defended himself after being attacked. "I did not know or intend to find out if the other inmate, who was much larger and much younger and stronger than I, had a weapon (knife, spoon, or fork) that was readily available in the dining area."

To others, he gave a more compact version of the encounter. "I knocked a guy in the head in the mess hall. It was the worst thing you could do in there. You start a riot."

Lewisburg was a far tougher place to do time. But in many ways, it was a more comfortable fit for Al. There were still plenty of gangsters like himself, and no rich convicts to turn their heads from the proper path of Cosa Nostra. "They put me in the hole when I got there, and when I came out, right next to me is Johnny Gammarano, a Gambino gangster I know."

Gammarano was actively involved in his family's rackets in the construction industry. He was in Lewisburg for a tax-evasion charge, compounded by a conviction for extortion while he was on probation.

There were other familiar faces. Jimmy Burke had beaten the Lufthansa case, but he was doing twelve years for the basketball point-shaving scheme. The two convicts exchanged news about the Vario crew. Shortly after Al arrived at the prison, Sal Miciotta was sent there as well after his own fight with another inmate.

Miciotta wasn't happy to be back with Al. "I said, 'God is punishing me again.' This is the guy I wanted most to get away from." But Gammarano and Miciotta also didn't get along. This time, Gammarano brought his gripes to Al.

"He used to come to me every day, saying, 'Al, Big Sal is bothering me.' I said, 'Why are you coming to me? You're a wiseguy. You're a made guy in the Gambino family. Go make a complaint, or tell him yourself.' We were friends, but every day he's complaining to me."

The wiseguy bickering didn't last long. Miciotta was shipped off to Danbury prison in Connecticut after a month. Al was sent to the far reaches of northern New York.

Al's new home was the federal correctional institution at Ray Brook, located in the Adirondack Mountains near Lake Placid. It was just forty miles south of Dannemora, the Siberia of state prisons, where Charlie Luciano and Davie Petillo had suffered through the winters almost fifty years earlier.

Unlike Lewisburg, Ray Brook at least was a medium-security prison. Inmates often worked outside the gates on public roads. But it was a solid six-hour drive from the city, making visits tough on families. It was also bitterly cold much of the time.

"It was a freezing-ass place. Inside or outside. They said you had two seasons up there. Winter and August. Most of the time you froze in those cells."

The trip north had one beneficial effect. On the bus there he decided to quit smoking. "I'd never smoked that heavy. Only at nighttime. But all you could get in prison was that Bull Durham roll-your-own stuff. And I'm on the bus on the way from Lewisburg to Ray Brook and I am wrapping the papers and I look at my hands and they're orange from the cigarettes. I said, 'I'm gonna quit smoking.' After I quit, my face broke out in blisters. Shows what those cigarettes do to you."

Ray Brook was also old-home week. Paul Vario had been free on appeal from his perjury conviction concerning the no-show job he'd arranged for Henry Hill. In 1984, at age seventy, he was sent to prison for the last time. "Paulie was at

Ray Brook for a while. We got a chance to talk. It was good to see him."

He was less sure how good it was to see another old pal who was also at Ray Brook. Anthony DiLorenzo was the veteran Genovese family captain who had given Al's box company a nice boost with his order to make blue and red containers for his sausage firm.

"Hickey DiLorenzo and me were good friends. I first met him through Ralphie hanging out at Angelo Ponte's place." DiLorenzo had his own storied mob career. At one point, law enforcers had viewed him as Vito Genovese's likely heir apparent. He was well-spoken, well-read, and adept at business. Through the creative application of threats and sabotage, he and Johnny Dio had created an association of air-freight trucking firms that allowed them to dominate the airport's trade. Self-taught, he'd become a proficient jailhouse lawyer during an earlier prison term for assault.

Part of Hickey's legend was the story of how, while serving another sentence for transporting stolen stocks in 1972, he'd escaped from custody while visiting the dentist. The escape itself wasn't hard to pull off. A model prisoner at the Allenwood camp, DiLorenzo had been shifted to the old Federal House of Detention on West Street, where he was given permission to make an unescorted trip to see his own dentist on Long Island. DiLorenzo knew he was facing new charges stemming from the airport scams. So he just didn't return.

What was impressive was that Hickey stayed on the lam for five years until federal Drug Enforcement Administration agents located him in Venezuela in 1977. With no legal ability to arrest him there, agents tricked him into boarding a plane to Panama. There, he was snatched up at the airport by local police and taken to a Panamanian jail, where he was beaten and tortured. It was an early version of rendition by American officials, using a foreign country to do otherwise-prohibited dirty work.

Whatever the thugs in Panama did to him, DiLorenzo was not the same person by the time he left. The Panamanians put him on a Braniff airliner bound for Miami in DEA custody.

Aboard the plane, he went berserk and had to be subdued. Back at the Metropolitan Correctional Center in Manhattan, he required repeated medical treatment.

He wasn't so far gone, however, that he couldn't put his jailhouse lawyer skills to work. He sued the Justice Department in 1979 for damages and violating his civil rights. A federal judge scolded the DEA for abducting him and allowing their Panamanian surrogates to abuse him. But the judge ruled that Hickey's constitutional rights had not been violated, since there was no indication that the feds took part in the torture. Even his forcible abduction from Panama by the agents fell short of a civil rights violation. As for a lack of medical treatment, Hickey had failed to prove "callous indifference" to his well-being, the judge held.

The experience was enough to damage anyone's mental health, and by the time Al ran into DiLorenzo at Ray Brook, he was showing signs of being seriously troubled.

Al was proud to be reintroduced to his old friend, this time as *amico nostra*, friend of ours, the mob terminology for a fellow member. But DiLorenzo's behavior was otherwise odd.

"Hickey was always so sharp. He noticed everything. But now he was acting strange. He starts talking about drugs, about liquid cocaine, stuff he never talked about. He said he would go back on the lam to South America. He was talking wild."

DiLorenzo's other disturbing activity was an echo of what Al had objected to in Allenwood. "He was playing cards with this guy who was known to be a stoolie." Al talked to Hickey about it. "I said, 'You may not know it, but that guy you're playing cards with is a federal informant.' He said, 'You're right. I better not.'"

The following day, DiLorenzo was back playing cards with the same inmate. "So I pulled him up again. He said, 'Al, I am just playing cards with him.'"

Al raised DiLorenzo's behavior with two other Genovese crime family stalwarts who were also residents of Ray Brook. One of them was James Napoli, a dapper capo in the family serving a sentence for running a $35 million betting ring.

Jimmy Nap, as everyone called him, had briefly run the Genovese family after Al's old admirer, Tommy Ryan Eboli, was killed. Napoli was cut from somewhat different Mafia cloth. He had lived in an East Side town house with his wife, Jeanne, a songwriter and theatrical producer. While he was in prison, a musical about Marilyn Monroe, written by Jeanne Napoli and financed by her husband, was playing Broadway.

The other opinion Al solicited was that of Carlo Mastrototaro, who ran the Genovese family's satellite operation in Worcester, Massachusetts. Mastrototaro was yet another genuine war hero in the Genovese ranks. He won the Silver Star and a Purple Heart for having saved his platoon from a Japanese attack during the Battle of Saipan. Mastrototaro was doing a nine-year term for stolen bonds.

"I told Jimmy Nap and Carlo Mastrototaro about being worried about Hickey and the way he was talking and acting. They went and checked it out and agreed with me. They told Hickey the same thing. He ignored them, too."

After rejecting their advice, Hickey suddenly lurched back into the role of senior mobster, demanding to handle a sitdown to settle a dispute between Mastrototaro and a Philadelphia Mafioso also at Ray Brook. "You're not my captain," Mastrototaro told him, walking away.

Al cringed for his friend. "Hickey was way out of line. He didn't know what he was doing."

Napoli and others now confided stories they'd heard. How Hickey had run naked on a balcony in New Jersey while firing a pistol at police. Mastrototaro offered an ominous solution to the situation. "We will straighten it out in the street," he said.

Al's own conviction still gnawed at him. At each prison, he made his way to the library, thumbing through law books. His initial appeal denied, he wrote his own writ of certiorari to the U.S. Supreme Court asking for permission to appeal again. Rejected twice, he sent a third plea.

He composed his briefs on lined paper in the formal, slanting script he'd been taught by the Christian Brothers at St.

Patrick's. He lifted phrases that impressed him from cases he read. "I hope I have not burdened your Honor with lurid characterizations or detail," he wrote to Judge Owen in a petition for bail pending appeal.

At the same time, he invoked his limited learning as cause for any shortcomings in his filings, misspellings and all. "The Honorable Court should be aware that the Petitioner/Appellant has only a ninth grade formal education," he wrote in each appeal.

He even tried sweet talk to the vampire judge. "Thank you for any consideration shown for this petition," he wrote on Christmas Eve 1984. "I extend a Happy Holiday to Your Honor and his loved one's."

The appeals went nowhere.

That fall of 1984 while at Ray Brook, Al began to feel seriously ill for the first time in his life. He'd always been in good health. He still prided himself on his workouts on the heavy bag and his prison calisthenics. But his blood pressure now soared, his legs ached, and he had trouble standing. The doctors who visited Ray Brook recommended he be sent to the Bureau of Prisons hospital in Springfield, Missouri.

In Springfield he was put through a battery of tests that reminded him of his Army physicals. "It's like a military examination. They say, 'Put your leg up.' 'Put your arm up.' Then they take your blood about twenty times." The tests yielded an explanation: thrombophlebitis of the left leg. Blood clots in the veins complicated by elevated sugar in the blood. They were less clear about the cure. Al noticed that few of the other patients around him seemed to be faring too well. "I started thinking it might be healthier if I could get out of there."

He was scheming about how to do that when a visiting doctor came through the ward. "He looked at my charts and checked my blood pressure one more time. Then he said, 'If I were you, son, I'd become a vegetarian.' I'm thinking, How do you become a vegetarian in prison? You'd have nothing to eat."

But he took the advice to heart. Shipped back up to Ray
Brook a few days before Christmas, he swore off meat and
heavy foods. He did have less to eat. He stuck to the prison's
watery vegetables. But he felt better.

"I figured I would just as soon as have fish, pasta, and sal-
ads as anything else. So that's what I decided I'd have. If I
could ever get it again."

The Bureau of Prisons moved him once more, this time down
to the city, to the Metropolitan Correctional Center in the late
summer of 1985. Usually that was a last stop, shortly before
a prisoner's release. Al still had a year to go on his minimum
sentence, which was two-thirds of the original six years he'd
been given, assuming he didn't get into any more trouble behind bars.

But he didn't argue. It was good to be back in the city. His
Spring Street apartment building was less than a mile from
the prison, almost visible from the roof where he played ball
under the high metal grille.

Best of all, it was easy on Dolores, who didn't have to make
the long trips to visit.

It was also a remarkable time to be at the Manhattan federal lockup. In February of that year, Rudolph Giuliani, U.S.
attorney for the Southern District of New York, obtained a
racketeering indictment of the men he believed led New York's
crime families in what he dubbed "the Commission case."
They were charged with running a conspiracy enterprise, the
Mafia.

Among those facing lifetimes in prison were Al's boss
"Tony Ducks" Corallo, and his two top lieutenants, "Christy
Tick" Furnari and "Tom Mix" Santoro. The evidence included
Corallo's own words, captured by a secret bug planted in a
Jaguar he rode in.

It was one of a series of major mob cases filed by the prosecutor's office. The press declared Giuliani the biggest gang-
buster since Thomas E. Dewey, who had used perjured
testimony to convict Lucky Luciano of running the city's prostitution business. Actually, Giuliani's cases were built on the

work of a half dozen different law enforcement agencies and prosecutors before him who had been plugging away at the Mafia for years. Regardless, it was still a disaster for the mob.

It also gave Al a lot of wiseguys to talk to. Charlie Brody DiPalermo showed up after his latest narcotics arrest. He and his big brother Joe Beck were still at it, charged with running a $2 billion drug operation. The brothers were responsible for "a majority of the heroin sold on the Lower East Side," claimed prosecutors.

Charlie Brody introduced Al to Vincent DiNapoli, a jowly captain in the Genovese family from the Bronx. DiNapoli was part of another clutch of mobbed-up brothers, but unlike the DiPalermo boys, they were bipartisan in their affiliation. Louis and Vincent DiNapoli were with the Genovese crew, while Joseph was in Al's Luchese clan.

Vinny DiNapoli had a reputation for business brilliance. He ran several construction firms and had managed to control a large swath of the city's affordable-housing development activity. He was charged in another sweeping Giuliani indictment. Dubbed "the Concrete case," it claimed the mob controlled most of the city's concrete suppliers, making New York construction projects more expensive than anywhere else in the country.

The leaders of the the Colombo crew also passed through the MCC. Boss Carmine "Junior" Persico and underboss Gennaro Langella, known as Jerry Lang, had been the target of the first big mob racketeering case by the ambitious Manhattan prosecutor. They were defendants in the big Commission case as well.

Al was chatting with Jerry Lang in the recreation room one day when a Genovese member named Vincent Cafaro, a slim balding man from East Harlem, came up to join the conversation. Al had met "Fish" Cafaro before, but they hadn't had their *amico nostra* introduction as fellow made men. It didn't matter. Lang ignored him. "It was funny. He just butted right into our conversation, started asking questions. I said, 'What, are you writing a book?'"

Cafaro walked away. "We don't like him," Lang said.

"I don't like him either," said Al.

A few months later, Cafaro became a government informant. He was a close associate of Anthony "Fat Tony" Salerno, the cigar-chomping mobster who presented himself to the mob world as boss of the Genovese family while crafty Vincent Gigante held the true reins in his Sullivan Street clubhouse. Cafaro had been at Fat Tony's elbow for years, witnessing the comings and goings of mobsters, businessmen, and union chieftains at Salerno's Palma Boys Social Club on East 115th Street between First and Pleasant Avenues. The Fish was the biggest catch for law enforcement in a long time.

Al was present in the MCC for another Mafia upheaval, this one of the mob's own making, with no help from the government. On the evening of December 16, 1985, the boss of the Gambino family, Paul Castellano, was gunned down outside Sparks Steak House on East Forty-Sixth Street. Castellano's right-hand man and newly named underboss, Thomas Bilotti, was killed alongside him. The hit took place on a midtown street as pre-Christmas shoppers rushed past. Witnesses saw at least four gunmen. All got away.

The quick consensus among the MCC's residents was that John Gotti, a headstrong Gambino captain from Queens, was behind the hit. Among those agreeing to the thesis was Virgil Alessi, a drug dealer from New Jersey, whose DeCavalcante crime faction was allied with the Gambino family. Even Leonard DiMaria, a Gambino mobster from Brooklyn, said the same thing.

"The thing they were all saying was that you weren't allowed to kill a boss without the okay from the Commission. Nobody thought this had been approved."

DiMaria knew something about such matters. He had been hauled before a grand jury probing the last assassination of a mob boss, the shotgun killing of Joe Beck's old partner, Bonanno chieftain Carmine Galante, on a restaurant patio in Bushwick, Brooklyn. In that case, it was widely accepted in gangland, the murder had been fully sanctioned by the proper authorities.

* * *

Another veteran gangster shaking his head in astonishment at Castellano's assassination was Paul Vario, who was also shipped down to the MCC for a brief stay. It was his last hurrah in New York, before being shipped off to a federal prison in Texas. Al did his best to make his aging captain's stay pleasant.

"Paulie talked about wanting two things: cigarettes and *soppressata* sausage. He'd say, 'We gotta get some cigarettes.' The fucking things were killing him but he couldn't stop."

Al got help from a clever fellow inmate named Nicky Lanzieri who was assigned as a porter at the prison and had relative freedom to roam within the correctional center. Lanzieri was doing time for an innovative theft. An executive of an air freight company, he'd stolen almost $700,000 worth of silver sludge, the material used to process photographs. The silver was being shipped in three dozen barrels from London to Eastman Kodak headquarters in Rochester when it disappeared. Lanzieri got away with the silver, but customs agents later came knocking and arrested him.

"Nicky could move around in there—they even let him clean the warden's office. One time he snatched a whole list of visitors to the place, though we didn't do anything with it."

The more important goal was to get the thick Italian sausage and smokes for Vario. Al's own work assignment had him helping to haul the MCC's garbage outside for pickup. "Nicky knew guys who had the trash-collection contract, and he had them wrap up packages of cigarettes and *soppressata*, provolone, whatever we could get, in plastic wrap and dump them in the containers after they were empty."

One of Al's tasks was to wash down the trash site with bleach. "I'd pour it all over, then take a broom and scrub it. I was in the alleyway there at St. Andrew's Plaza. I'd see Giuliani come walking through all the time."

After the garbage truck pulled away, Al retrieved the packages from the trash containers and stuck them under his shirt. He had no way of hiding them, however, if he was searched, which he often was on his way back into the prison.

"But we had this one old hack, a black guy had been on the job for years. He knew every wiseguy who had come through the joint. He'd search me, feel the sausage and cigarette cartons, but he still let me take them in. I couldn't figure it out. Then Paulie tells me the guard used to be on West Street at the old detention center. He helped them out there, too."

One day while cleaning up in the alley, Al spotted a small doll. It was a Madonna figure, with a black face. "Somebody threw it away and I picked it up. I showed it to a Spanish guy inside and he says, 'That's a Shango, the god of fire. It's for black magic.' I said, 'Oh, I'm keeping this. I can use it.' I still got it."

Al was released to a halfway house on October 22, 1986. The facility was run by the Salvation Army and located on the Bowery at East Third Street. "They let you out early, six in the morning. They dropped me off at the Bowery. It was raining but I walked straight downtown to the burger stand on Laight Street."

It was about a two-mile hike in the rain. He was looking for Petey Del Cioppo and another helper, Joe Fiore, known as "Joe Cuz," whom he had told to run the stand while he was away. They were supposed to bring Dolores at least $150 every week from the receipts. They had missed a few weeks.

Before he was released from the MCC, he'd been reminded of all the special parole requirements that would govern his activities for the next decade. One of the trickiest was that he was not allowed to associate with known felons. He violated parole his first morning.

"I got to the stand and Vic Amuso is there waiting for me."

Al was surprised to see Amuso. But he was also glad. "It was good to see him. I liked Vic."

Amuso had prospered since Al had last seen him. The kid he'd met pushing a hand truck on Flushing Avenue was now a leader of the Luchese family. In fact, he was *the* leader.

"We had a cup of coffee, and then Vic says, 'Let's take a

walk.' And we start walking. First thing he tells me is that he's the new boss."

Al noted that Amuso was violating a rule by sharing the news. Mob protocol held that promotions were to be revealed only by way of formal introduction by another member in the know.

"But we go back a ways, so he was telling me like as a friend." Al was less surprised by the news than by Amuso's demeanor. "He seemed timid about it. Like he wasn't sure he could do it."

Al congratulated him. And then offered a small pep talk.

"I said, 'Let me tell you something, Vic. Tony Ducks was the boss and now he's looking at one hundred years. But he was the boss. Now you're the boss. They nail you and *you're* gonna get a hundred years too. So *be* the boss."

Amuso seemed grateful. "He says, 'You're like my brother, you know.'" The new boss told Al that he had promoted his close friend, Anthony "Gaspipe" Casso, to run Christy Tick's old crew at the 19th Hole.

The two men kept walking through the lower Manhattan streets in the rain. Al had the feeling there was something else Amuso wanted to tell him. He offered more encouragement. "I said, 'Vic, if I can help you with anything, just let me know.'"

Amuso sighed. "I don't like to bring this up," he began, "but Anthony—Gaspipe—he's involved in a deal with Joseph and he owes Anthony $80,000. And Anthony wants to get paid soon." Amuso stumbled about a bit, then added that the deal was for heroin. The reason Anthony was concerned, he said, was because Joseph seemed to be using drugs quite a bit himself these days.

Al didn't say anything for a moment. He didn't know about his son dealing drugs. He didn't know about him using drugs. What took his breath away was that the new leaders of the Luchese family were doing the drug deals with him, without apology or explanation.

"I was hot as a pistol. I tried not to show it. I said, 'He owes

Anthony $80,000? Anthony will get his money.' Vic says,
'Okay, good. I'll tell him.' "

They walked back to the burger stand and said good-bye.
Al watched his new boss drive away.

He tried to make sense of what he'd learned. "I'm in the
can for drugs? And they get my own son involved? While he's
using dope?" He started heading back to the halfway house.
He had no idea where he was going to get $80,000. Welcome
home, he told himself.

10

21 SPRING STREET

While Al was still at Ray Brook, a veteran gangster named Vincent Beltempo asked him if he wanted to go in on a heroin deal.

Beltempo grew up across from the DiPalermo brothers on Elizabeth Street. He was also a lifelong friend of Ralph Cuomo, whose name he invoked when introducing himself to Al. Beltempo's nickname was "Jimmy Balls" and he was associated with the Gambino family. He was already a two-time loser on heroin convictions. He was arrested with Cuomo back in 1969 when they were caught with twenty-five pounds of drugs. After his release, Beltempo had engineered an even bigger *babania* deal, smuggling forty pounds of heroin into the city from Palermo, Sicily, in false-bottomed suitcases. Nabbed again, Beltempo was given fifteen years and a lifetime special parole.

That's the sentence he was serving when he whispered to Al one day in the prison yard that he could move fifty kilos of "French goods" with the right help. Did he want in?

"I chased him. I said to get away from me. I had enough trouble with drugs."

That was one reason. There was also the putative ban against narcotics he had sworn to uphold when he'd been inducted as a soldier of the Cosa Nostra. Violation of the rule was a death penalty, Tony Ducks Corallo had said.

That was mostly mob make-believe, he knew. But a rule was a rule, and his old-school sensibility, ingrained in him by Jimmy Alto and again by Joe Schiavo, told him it was worth upholding, even if few others in the Mafia felt the same.

What he'd never really thought about before was what drugs might do to families. In fact, he'd given no thought at all to where the drugs he sold or, more often than not, tried to sell wound up. A few old-timers, like crazy Chalootz, had abused heroin and opium. But they were holdovers from another era. There were also neighborhood kids who had come back from the Vietnam War with serious habits. The son of a local drug dealer, who was involved in the original French Connection crew, returned from combat addicted to junk. What goes around, comes around, Al remembered thinking at the time.

But he hadn't seen needles going into the arms of friends, or rent and food money going to feed the addictions of parents instead of their children. He'd been spared the robberies and break-ins afflicting many neighborhoods where desperate junkies did anything for a fix.

Whatever he heard or read about it, that was someone else's world. Not his own.

But now it was in his own family, flowing into the veins of his firstborn son. And as he walked the streets of the neighborhood he had been away from for four years, he saw that his son wasn't alone.

"The neighborhood was saturated. Saturated. There were kids all over the place doing drugs. I couldn't believe it. The way it was before was that if you ever sold drugs in Little Italy, you got killed in a minute."

Joseph insisted his problem wasn't that bad. He told his father he'd take care of it, and not to worry. But the problem wasn't just Joseph. His wife was also a junkie.

Louise Musillo's family came from Elizabeth Street, the same block as the DiPalermo brothers. Her uncle was Charlie Musillo, a captain in the Bonanno crime family who ran bus junkets to Atlantic City casinos.

She and Joseph had met on the night of July 13, 1977, in the midst of the power blackout that darkened the city. Their romance was fast and furious. A few weeks later, they were married. Joseph had $10 in his pocket the day they wed at the city clerk's office. "I bought us each a drink and then I was broke," he said. His solution was to rob a drug dealer. He was soon dealing drugs himself. Eventually, curiosity got the better of him.

"I believed I was invincible. All these people got hooked. I said, 'It won't happen to me,'" he said of those days. He was soon an addict, his wife along with him. While his father was doing prison time for heroin sales, both Joseph and his wife were doing their own drugs, supporting themselves by dealing and robberies.

At the same time, Joseph saw himself as the protector of his fatherless family. He carried a gun with him wherever he went. On Mother's Day weekend of 1985, Joseph was enraged to learn that his fourteen-year-old sister, Dawn, had stayed out all night with a nineteen-year-old, a Puerto Rican. Spotting the youth on Mott Street with two other young girls, he threw him against a wall. "I pistol-whipped him. One thing led to another, and I lost my temper. I shot him." One bullet grazed the teenager's head. The other struck him in the chest. Badly wounded, the victim staggered into traffic. Joseph fled, tossing the gun down a sewer grating.

Detectives later came looking for him. Dolores told them her son didn't live there anymore. That part was true. He was on the Lower East Side, robbing drug dealers. A couple of weeks after the shooting, he was arrested while banging on a dealer's door in a housing project. He was packing a new weapon and police charged him with gun possession.

He wasn't so far gone that he couldn't see where he was headed. Not long before his father's release from prison, he decided he needed to get off of heroin. "I said enough of this nonsense. I got to get off of this shit." He and Louise both entered a methadone maintenance program. They were still addicts, but at least their habits were manageable. He won a favorable plea disposition to the gun arrest: five years probation and a promise that his criminal record would be expunged if he stayed out of trouble.

When Al got home, he was furious that the drug scourge had hit his own family. Even Dawn, his youngest, was using. He looked around for someone to blame. He didn't have to look far. "I blamed the Prince Street crew, Petey Beck, his brothers, and all of them."

He wasn't the only one. Drugs had been sold out of a small Puerto Rican–owned bodega down the street from St. Patrick's Old Cathedral School, the Catholic grade school on Prince and Mott Streets. "They were selling drugs out of that store and their own grandchildren were going to the school on the corner. This nun from the school went out and screamed at them, right in front of their club there on Prince Street."

He wasn't about to become a crusader. He was a gangster. Drugs sold and consumed elsewhere, he rationalized, had nothing to do with him. But the line had been crossed when his gangland pals had let them be peddled on their own streets.

"When I found out what was happening in the neighborhood, the first guy I grabbed was Petey Beck. And I took him to a luncheonette on the corner of Mott and Spring. I told him, broadly like, 'You know, if I ever get the fucking cocksuckers pushing drugs through these Puerto Ricans in this neighborhood, I am going to kill every fucking one of them.'"

DiPalermo knew who Al was talking about. "But he was a made guy. A captain. I wasn't going to say nothing direct at him. Him and his brothers and Raffie, because of all their gambling and need for money, were pushing it to the kids. How could you do that?"

The warning had little effect. A few weeks later, Ralph Cuomo called Al into the club next to the pizza parlor. "Raffie tells me he has four kilos of heroin to sell. I didn't scream at him. He was a made guy too, just like me. I just looked at him and said I wasn't interested. That I was on the special parole and couldn't take the chance."

Al left the club feeling like he was surrounded by addicts. Raffie Cuomo was addicted to gambling, so he pushed dope to support his own habit. In turn, his son and daughter-in-law had both gotten hooked. Al walked home wondering where this was headed.

Drugs weren't the only neighborhood ailment. Little Italy had been down at the heels for years, with most of its housing ailing, century-old walk-up tenements like the one where Al's family lived at 32 Spring Street. "We had rats running around there. Dolores was terrified of them."

In the 1970s, residents protested when the city sought to replace the old Public School 21 that had sat for more than a hundred years on the north side of Spring Street between Mott and Elizabeth with a new school. What the neighborhood really needed, they said, was new housing. Chinatown, they pointed out, which was steadily taking over the old Italian district, had gotten its own new housing, the soaring Confucius Plaza next to the Manhattan Bridge. Italians deserved as much.

It took the better part of a decade to get it, but in 1983, a brand-new seven-story brick building stretching the entire length of the block opened its doors to new tenants. Even better, the 152 apartments at 21 Spring Street were all subsidized by the federal government's Section 8 program, which held rents to no more than 30 percent of a tenant's income. The government covered the difference between what tenants could afford and the market rent. The complex included a center courtyard with a sitting area, a bocce court, and community space.

Tenants were supposed to be carefully screened, with entry limited to displaced former residents of the block, needy senior citizens, and families with low income.

But given its location in what was still the Mafia's central business district, wiseguys went to the front of the line. Al D'Arco's family was one of the lucky group that made it inside.

"The mob started it and the mob built it. So naturally we

got some of the apartments. Petey Beck got one, so did Joe Beck. He was upstairs with his girlfriend." Overseeing the project, Al said, was Pete DeFeo, the Genovese family power who had a strong hand in most things in Little Italy, especially its most famous event, the annual Feast of San Gennaro on Mulberry Street. Alex Morelli, one of DeFeo's top lieutenants and a heavy gambler, had an apartment above Al and Dolores.

The building project was sponsored by a local nonprofit group called the Little Italy Restoration Association. The group was known by its acronym, LIRA. Top officials of the organization included Oscar Ianniello, one of the brothers of Genovese family captain Matty the Horse.

The group selected the DeMatteis Development Corporation, one of the city's largest developers, to build the project. Called to the stand in the Mafia Commission case to talk about his dealing with defendant Vincent DiNapoli and other mobsters, company executive Frederick DeMatteis took the Fifth Amendment rather than discuss the matter.

Tenants were chosen in "consultation with the community," according to building records. Handling management and tenant selection was a firm headed by a former attorney for Frank Kissel's butchers union that had pressured meat companies to have their containers printed at Al's box company. Raffie Cuomo, who was making tens of thousands of dollars each month in drug deals and loan-sharking, was one of several mobbed-up local residents who finagled apartments in the much larger Independence Plaza North, another subsidized project on the far West Side along Greenwich Street. Federal prosecutors probed alleged application fraud there in 1975, but no charges resulted.

To Al, it was much ado about nothing. "We all had a hook. But at least I wasn't trying to get fancy by moving out of the neighborhood like some guys. I wanted to stay right there."

He still had to qualify on paper, however. The details were worked out after Al went to prison. In a notarized statement prepared by George Spitz, the attorney who briefly represented Al on his drug arrest, Dolores declared that she and

Al were separated. Her income was $185 a week from him in child support. Based on her declaration, she and her children qualified for a two-bedroom, two-bath apartment on the sixth floor at a monthly rent of $195. That was about $750 less than the full cost. The government picked up the rest.

It was partly true. They were separated, since Al was in federal prison. And Dolores's income was meager. All that was supporting the family was the earnings from the burger stand being run by Pete Del Cioppo and whatever other money Al could direct her way from behind bars.

But after he was released and reunited with his wife and family, Al went right back to making money in the street, as much as he could. He wasn't about to give up the apartment. The leases were regularly renewed every two years, accompanied by the same declaration that he and Dolores were separated. He was also careful not to give up the old apartment up the street at 32 Spring. "I used it for business when I needed it."

Both scams barely registered on Al's crime scales. "I was in that life. It didn't matter to me if I was cheating the government."

He used another bit of deception to satisfy parole regulations calling for regular and acceptable employment. He could have listed the burger stand, which he still operated, even though most daily chores were handled by others. But he didn't want his parole officer, a careful man named Joseph Veltre, dropping by and sniffing around.

Again his friend George Spitz helped out. Spitz agreed to carry Al on his books as a legal assistant and occasional investigator at a weekly salary of $250. Aside from a couple of occasions when Al snapped photographs of a sidewalk for a slip-and-fall case, he did no work. Each time he picked up his check, he would hand the cash back to Spitz.

Meanwhile, he showed the checks to Veltre as proof that he was gainfully employed and staying out of trouble. Every month he stopped by the office to fill out a form listing his earnings and employment and sign on the bottom attesting to the truth of its contents under penalty of law.

He and Veltre got along. They would chat about history and the city. Al encouraged the parole officer to quit smoking. To Al, the bogus work records were just one more petty crime. The important thing was not to get violated and sent back to prison. Having a lawyer as his employer was an added bit of insurance.

"George did it for me as a friend. I helped him out in some other things."

One of those things was a law client of Spitz's in need of some extralegal muscle. "George had this guy who was the CEO of a big chemical company. He'd been cheating on his wife, and one of his ex-girlfriends was trying to shake him down for dough. George asked if I could get the girlfriend off his client's back."

Al met with the executive, learned the girlfriend's whereabouts, and went to work. "It was simple. The girlfriend was living in Chelsea, and I had Petey Del call her up and talk real rough, making threats that if she didn't knock it off he knew where she lived and she would get hurt. She got scared and took off."

The executive was immensely pleased. "He gives us $12,000 in $100 bills. The money was all paper-clipped together. I don't think he ever handled cash like that."

Al's original arrangement was that he and Spitz would split whatever payment resulted. "But George had been complaining that his two sons, Dan and Dave, were music nuts and they wanted these fancy instruments that he said he couldn't afford. So instead of splitting it, I gave him $8,000 and told him to go buy his kids their instruments."

The lawyer's sons did well with their guitars. Dan Spitz went on to found the heavy-metal band Anthrax. His older brother, Dave, played for Black Sabbath. The music wasn't Al's style but he was glad later to attend the wedding of one of the two sons where he heard them perform. "It was a Jewish wedding. We had a good time. I kept the yarmulke."

* * *

He made sure to keep a low profile his first months back. Memories of prison were too fresh to risk an added ten years behind bars. The quickest way to get violated was to be spotted hanging around with other mobsters with records.

He spent a lot of time working the burger stand with Petey Del. "Joseph was working there, trying to get himself straight. And my son John started coming by a lot to help also. John loved to cook." They decided the place needed a grander name. The Burger Palace, they named it. A new sign was hung over the stand. A TV camera crew pulled up one day. The reporter said she was doing a feature on good, cheap places to eat. "They were from WPIX. She said she heard we had the best 75-cent hamburger around." They filmed Joseph working the counter. Al was careful to stay out of camera range.

He was at the Burger Palace one evening when a long black Mercedes parked in front of the stand. Vic Amuso stepped out from the passenger side. Anthony Casso got out from behind the wheel. Al was paying off the $80,000 debt that Joseph had racked up with Gaspipe Casso. But he hadn't forgiven him for doing a drug deal with his son while he was in prison.

Casso had soared in the Luchese ranks. He was made captain of Christy Tick Furnari's crew when Amuso became boss. When a veteran mobster from the Harlem crew named Aniello "Neil" Migliore went to prison, Casso replaced him as consigliere. A few months later, Amuso named him as underboss.

It was Casso's first visit to the stand, and Al invited them to have a cup of coffee. "They were both all dressed up, wearing suits. Anthony makes one of his little jokes. He says, 'Is it safe for me to come in there?' Like he was going to get dirty or poisoned just by walking inside."

Cracking wise was one of Gaspipe's trademarks. Often, he was genuinely funny. Sometimes he was just nasty. It was another thing Al didn't like. "I said, 'Cut it out, Anthony. You want a cup of coffee? Have some coffee.'"

As they were having their coffee, Amuso motioned Al outside onto Laight Street. On the sidewalk, Amuso spoke in a low, excited voice. "He says, 'We're going to a meeting with 'the Robe.'" As he said it, Amuso held out a curled index finger and thumb, forming a C with his hand.

Al didn't ask for details, but he knew what Vic meant. Vincent Gigante sometimes wore a dressing robe, like the ones he'd worn before his prizefights in days past. Amuso's old captain at the 19th Hole, Christy Tick Furnari, had coined the term. It was derogatory shorthand for Gigante's ongoing act of seeming mentally unbalanced. The C stood for Commission, a meeting of all the top bosses. It was one of those words never to be said aloud. But it explained their suits and why both men seemed giddy and keyed up.

"Vic keeps talking, telling me it's at a wholesale candy place up on the West Side. I couldn't figure out why he was telling me any of this, but I didn't say a thing. I just nodded."

Amuso and Casso finished their coffee, got back in the Mercedes, and continued uptown on West Street.

Al was often surprised that Amuso confided in him, telling him things he didn't need to know. His best guess was that Vic still wasn't comfortable in his role as boss and needed someone to talk to that he could trust. He'd picked Al. One of the things he eventually told Al was what the Commission meeting that evening had been about. When he heard, Al was impressed.

Together with top members of the Genovese, Colombo, and Gambino families, Amuso told him, he and Casso were part of a multimillion-dollar caper, with the city and federal governments paying the tab. With the help of corrupt contractors and union officials, they had rigged the bids on a massive federal effort to replace all the windows in the city's public housing projects. The New York City Housing Authority had 180,000 apartments in 334 projects. It was landlord to more residents than lived in the city of Atlanta. New double-glazed windows, officials had decided, would sharply reduce fuel costs, paying back the replacement cost over time.

There were almost 1 million windows to replace, but on paper at least, it made eminent sense. Like the Little Italy restoration project where Al lived, it was another publicly beneficial initiative. And like 21 Spring Street, the mob had seen its opportunity and seized it.

The scam had been going on since 1978 and had reaped millions for leaders of all four crime families. A key player in the scheme was a part-time drug dealer and hit man named Pete Savino, who had had the foresight to buy an ownership position in an aluminum window company when he saw demand rising. A close associate of several Genovese officials, Savino was also well liked by the boss himself. And Vincent Gigante didn't like many people.

Amuso and Casso, however, were not fans. As a fellow drug dealer, they'd gotten along fine with Savino, selling loads of marijuana and cocaine with him. But they'd had a falling-out over the lucrative windows business. Casso claimed Savino owed him $1 million for having edged him out of one windows company. On Gigante's orders, Savino had paid Casso the million. It was a good indication of the huge sums flowing from the scheme.

But in 1987, one of Savino's former drug-dealing partners had been arrested. The ex-partner had pointed the Brooklyn district attorney's office to a pair of bodies buried beneath a warehouse Savino owned in Williamsburg, Brooklyn. He and Savino had put them there, he admitted. In a joint investigation, the DA and federal prosecutors used the information to pressure Savino, telling him he faced a choice. He could be arrested for at least two murders, or he could cooperate. Savino was soon going to meetings about the windows scam wearing a secret wire for the FBI.

The purpose of meeting with Gigante the night they came by the burger stand, Amuso told Al, was to alert him that Savino had turned. "Vic told me he was trying to tell the Robe that Petey Savino was a rat. That he should kill him. But he said Gigante wouldn't hear it. He defended the guy to them."

Amuso and Casso were both frustrated with the obstinate Gigante. Two years later, when Savino's informant role became public, they were enraged. "Vic said, 'That asshole should shoot himself now.'"

Amuso didn't offer any clues about how he and Casso came

to know about a top-secret federal informant. But crucial tips
from an unknown source soon became a trend with the duo,
Al noticed. Casso sometimes had a name for his tipster. "My
crystal ball," he'd say with a laugh. He enjoyed the gag.

Paul Vario died in a Texas prison cell on May 3, 1988. He
was seventy-three. The cause was a heart attack, brought on
by a chronic lung disorder he owed to the nicotine habit he
could never kick. Prison officials found him dead during a
routine head count. "A cigarette was still burning in his ashtray," an assistant to the warden told the *Daily News*.

By the time he died, Vario was a lot better known than
your average mob captain, thanks to the best-selling book
about his protégé turned government informant, Henry Hill.
Wiseguy, by veteran crime journalist Nicholas Pileggi, depicted Vario as a brilliant crime manager prone to soft-headed
decisions when it came to friends, like the drug-addled Hill.
A couple of years later, Big Paul became even more famous
when actor Paul Sorvino played his character in the movie
version, *Goodfellas*, by Martin Scorsese.

Al mourned the loss of another mentor. They were all gone
now. Joe Schiavo, who had retired to Florida just weeks after the party celebrating Al's getting his button, died in the
fall of 1987. He was seventy-six. "Cancer. Fucking cigarettes
got him, too." Amuso had already told Al that he wanted him
to take Paul's place as head of the Canarsie crew when he
went. The conversation took place during another walk, this
one outside the Walnut Bar, a tavern just a couple of blocks
from Geffken's on Flatlands Avenue that Vic used as a headquarters. The bar was owned by Vic's brother, Bobby Amuso,
a Luchese soldier who impressed Al by ignoring the mob politics always swirling around his brother.

Outside the bar, Vic told Al that he'd heard that Paul was
not likely to last much longer. "When he goes, I want you to
be the captain," he said.

Al protested that he was still on special parole. He was
also worried that his drug conviction hung over him as a stain

against his wiseguy honor. "I want to give you my word of honor," he told Amuso. "I will never deal in drugs."

Amuso, still doing his own drug deals, looked at him oddly. "Okay, but that's not what I'm talking about," the boss said. "I just want you to be captain."

A couple of weeks after Vario's death, Al was summoned to Canarsie to see the boss. The summons was relayed by Jimmy McCann, an Irish construction worker and one of Amuso's closest associates. Al immediately drove out to the address McCann had given him, a small house on a Canarsie side street.

McCann met him at the door and directed him to the basement stairs. Waiting for him in the small furnished basement were Amuso and Casso. "Vic tells me right away they are making me skipper of Paulie's crew." Amuso began laying out his instructions as captain when the basement stairs groaned. "I look up and there's a guy the size of a whale coming down."

The human whale wearing glasses under a mop of black hair, was Brooklyn gangster Pete Chiodo, who often tipped the scales at four hundred pounds. Despite his enormous girth, Chiodo had a reputation as a shrewd businessman. From what Al had heard, he had made both himself and his friend Gaspipe Casso wealthy with his construction companies.

Amuso announced that Chiodo was also being bumped up to captain, running the crew once headed by Christy Tick and later by Casso. "Vic tells us both that we should get our crews together, then get them one at a time and ask each one what they're doing." The important thing, Amuso stressed, was to make sure that all their activities, both legal and illegal, were "on the record" with the family. It was an important mob distinction. If a dispute arose with another family, they would lose if the person or venture wasn't already on record.

As they were talking, other Luchese captains and members joined them in the crowded basement. "Sally Avellino, the captain from Long Island who ran all the trash companies out there, came down. Then Petey Beck and Raffie

Cuomo came together. Vic's brother Bobby showed up and Petey Vario, Paulie's son. Vic tells everybody when they're all there that me and Fat Pete are both captains." No formal induction ceremony was required, but everyone present shook Al's hand and congratulated him.

Al thought he knew all the members of the Vario crew. There were a few old-timers who were semiretired, trying to keep their hand in the game while aging into Mafia senior citizens. One of them was Alfonso Curiale, who was in his late seventies. "Foo," as he was called, was the son of the crew's original founding father, Don Turrido, another immigrant from Agrigento, Sicily, who had given Joe Schiavo his button. Foo Curiale had somehow managed to practice his father's trade as a Mafioso while a full-time employee of the United States Post Office. "He was proud that he got his pension there. He was going back and forth to Florida, but he had a bunch of stores where he ran scams, and a piece of a factory that produced porn tapes."

Al was already friendly with another veteran, Peter Abinanti, known as "Pete the Killer." The nickname was for the sharp way he always dressed, not his weaponry. Abinanti had been one of Paul Vario's closest associates. Now in his seventies and ailing, he still ran a small loan-sharking operation from his home in Howard Beach, Queens.

Pete Abinanti told him there was one veteran member of the crew who was too aged to leave his home. But protocol demanded that he be introduced to his new captain.

"So Pete the Killer drives me out to a little house on East 102nd Street in Canarsie. We go inside and there's this little old guy. He gets up when we come in and he wasn't more than four feet ten inches tall standing with a cane. Pete said his name was Paul D'Anna, but everyone called him Zu'Paolo, for Uncle Paul. He was one of the oldest mobsters alive."

With his cane, Zu'Paolo pointed Al and Vario to the dining room where his wife, Annunziata, served them espresso and strega, the strong Italian liqueur made with herbs.

"I am glad you are my captain," D'Anna said to Al in a

Al D'Arco as a baby. Brooklyn, 1933. Everyone called him Sonny. *Alfonso D'Arco*

D'Arco's teenaged Navy Yard gang, Brooklyn, 1949. "Back then, I was always in trouble." *Alfonso D'Arco*

Volunteer GI: At Fort Jackson, South Carolina, 1952. "I told them straight up: I want to go to Korea." *Alfonso D'Arco*

MP: D'Arco, left, in Alaska, in military police uniform, guarding nuclear-armed Strategic Air Command bombers. "They'd tell us every day: 'One word about this and it's straight to Leavenworth.'" *Alfonso D'Arco*

Hitting the bag at army base in Alaska. "We did everything we could to keep from thinking about being a million fucking miles from nowhere, with a giant target on our backs, waiting for the Russians to hit us." *Alfonso D'Arco*

Army pals: Tony Verni, Oscar Luciano Feal, and D'Arco at Ladd Army Airfield, Alaska. "We were either the Three Amigos or the Three Amici, depending on who was talking." *Alfonso D'Arco*

Back from the Army, 1954. "I picked up where I left off, shooting craps and looking for scores."*Alfonso D'Arco*

With Dolores in Dave's Corner Luncheonette on Canal Street. "Nobody was there but me and her."
Alfonso D'Arco

Al and Dolores at Oyster Bay, Long Island. "I was never interested in anyone before Dolores, and never since. I didn't need a *goomada*."*Alfonso D'Arco*

The Italian Riviera: Up on Dolores's roof, Mulberry Street, 1955. "She'd walk right to the edge, look straight down. Nerves of steel." *Alfonso D'Arco*

Honeymoon suite. *Alfonso D'Arco*

D'Arco's furniture company after Sing Sing. "I liked making a business. No sitting around." *Alfonso D'Arco*

INVOICE

Siano & Company

FURNITURE SHOWROOMS
851 KENT AVENUE
BROOKLYN, N. Y. 11205

Telephone: 622-5293

David "Little Davie" Petillo, 1936 arrest in Lucky Luciano prostitution case. "We did any crimes he could come up with. He'd say, 'We're going out to shake the trees.'" *Government Photo*

N.Y.C. POLICE
65556
2   6   36

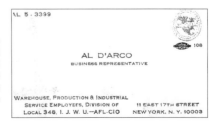

Partner in crime Ralph Masucci, 1968. Al's son John is on his lap. Joseph D'Arco, 12, standing. "Me and him did a lot of things together. Traveled the whole world." *Alfonso D'Arco*

Business card from rogue union Local 348. "I would go up to the shop and show the guy my business card. My end was to scare guys." *Alfonso D'Arco*

AL 5 - 3399

108

AL D'ARCO
BUSINESS REPRESENTATIVE

WAREHOUSE, PRODUCTION & INDUSTRIAL
SERVICE EMPLOYEES, DIVISION OF
LOCAL 348, I. J. W. U.—AFL-CIO

11 EAST 17TH STREET
NEW YORK, N. Y. 10003

Waiting: Dolores, in the backyard of 847 Kent Avenue, went on welfare while Al was in Sing Sing. "No one had any money." *Alfonso D'Arco*

A dapper Al D'Arco, shortly after release from his second prison term. He didn't gamble, smoke, or drink heavily. His only goal: "Respect. From whoever I had to deal with." *Alfonso D'Arco*

La Donna Rosa

RISTORANTE

SICILIANA

19 CLEVELAND PLACE
(Bet. Kenmare & Spring St.)
NEW YORK, NEW YORK, 10013   TEL: (212) 941-8160

We feature Sicilian cuisine from the various provinces of this enchanting island. All of our specialties are authentic to ancient tradition and include the various vegetable, fish, almond and Marsala essences, spices and meats of this rich cuisine.

Sicilian cuisine, a la Cosa Nostra. JFK Jr. came for lunch. Robert De Niro came to study the wiseguys. Mayor Koch was turned away. "I had some guys from the Gambino family here. I told him it was a private party." *Alfonso D'Arco*

"La vera cuccina di la Mediterraneo e la cucina Siciliana."

"The true kitchen of the Mediteranian is the kitchen of Sicily."

Chef D'Arco: "We got the best vegetables and fruits from our contacts in the produce markets. The guys in the butchers union got us top-grade meats." *Alfonso D'Arco*

Al and Dolores, corner table at La Donna Rosa. "It's a restaurant you want to hug," wrote *Newsday*'s food critic. *Alfonso D'Arco*

Law enforcement surveillance photo of a meeting between Gaspipe Casso relaying instructions to D'Arco outside La Donna Rosa. "These guys were always looking to kill the whole world." *Government Photo*

June 1990: Luchese capo Mike Salerno's Jaguar abandoned on a Bronx street. Note blood stain leaking from trunk where Salerno's body was found. Death came with the territory. "It's blood in, blood out." *Government Photo*

D'Arco's Italian-Chinese restaurant, host to members-only Luchese crime family Christmas party, 1990. "Soon as guys would pull up in their cars, we'd drive them a few blocks away so no one could spot all the plate numbers." *Alfonso D'Arco*

"Deads": At Gaspipe Casso's request, D'Arco compiled a list of deceased Luchese crime family members with their year of death. FBI agents found the list at Casso's Pennsylvania hideout after he was captured. *Government Photo*

FBI

DEADS
PAOLO D'ANNA_____ "PAUL" ZUPOLO 1985
ANTHONY STABILE___ "BLUE EYES" 1982
LUIGI SACCO_____ "SCANELLO" '83
LUIGI SACCO_____ "SCRATCHY" 1984
PIETRO BARBERA_____ "PLUMBER" 1982
SALVATORE PELLEGRINO "SAL THE BARBER" 1982
Joe FALZONE_____ 1983
Joe SPATARA_____ 1983
GIACINO LoPINTO___ "JACK" 1986
ZAZA GIAMBALVO_____ 1986
PAUL VARIO_____ "PAULIE" 1987
NUNZIO ARRA_____ 1990
PETER DePALERMO___ "Petey Beck" 1989
LEONARD PIZZOLATO now "LENNY" 1990
Joseph SCIAVO_____ "Joe Reese" 1988
MICHAEL LAROSA____ "MIKE" 1989
VINCENZO RAO_____ "VINCE" 1987
THOMAS DioGUARDIA_ "Tommy Dio" 1985
WILLIAM LoCASIO___ "WILLIE BROWN" 1984
GUISEPPI PECCORARA "Joe Peck" 1982
FRANCESCO PECCORARA "FRANK PECK" 1983
STEPHANO PECCORARA "STEVE PECK" 1985
DONT HAVE SPELLING "TONY HIGGINS"
SAM CAVELLERI_____ "BIG SAM" 1988
VINCENT FOCCARI___ "VINNY BEANS" 1983

043

Mob scene: John D'Arco wedding celebration, June 1991. Al didn't attend out of fear of being nabbed on a parole violation for consorting with convicted felons. "I figured, what's the sense of getting violated?" *Government Photo*

The cooperator: "Vouch" photo snapped by FBI agents in the hotel room where D'Arco was first hidden. As proof that D'Arco had turned, agents showed it to Luchese mobsters they hoped to persuade to cooperate. *Author's Private Collection*

shaky voice. The aged mobster then pointed to an oval framed picture on the wall. It was a portrait of a nineteenth-century figure with a large mustache. *"Il Mio capitano in Sicilia,"* he said. Al looked at the picture and realized the portrait hanging on the dining room wall was of D'Anna's first Mafia captain.

"I am at your service," D'Anna said. "I am a little old, but I still got a good eye, and I can still do this." He held up his hands as though shooting a rifle.

Al asked him when he was born. "I was born eighteen hundred and eighty-five in 'Grigento, Sicily," the old man told him. He was 103. His first assignment in America, he said, had been to defend Sicilian sheepherders fighting against the cattle ranchers in Colorado. He had later settled in Brooklyn with Don Turrido.

In Italian, Al told the elderly soldier that he would certainly call on him should he need him.

The new skipper summoned his more active troops to a gathering in another Canarsie home. Some of his crew had excusable absences. Frank Manzo was doing prison time for the same airport racketeering scheme in which Paul Vario had been convicted. Al wasn't sorry to miss him.

Al repeated Amuso's warning that they all had to put everything they were doing on record. He also added a warning of his own. He reminded them that they were not to deal narcotics. If they were caught or caused a problem, they would be killed, he said. The crew nodded knowingly, although he suspected they heard his words as just more empty rhetoric. He then met with each member individually to take the measure of his worth and his activity.

After the wealthy Manzo, Bruno Facciola was probably the most successful. He had a large loan shark operation, lending cash to businesses in south Brooklyn and Queens. He also ran gambling and card games where tens of thousands of dollars changed hands at his club on Avenue D, where he'd hosted Al's induction party. His own businesses included the pizzeria where Al had last seen Tommy DeSimone alive, and partnerships in an auto-wrecking yard and even a Brooklyn horse-riding stable. In addition, Facciola had a jewelry shop where Al suspected heroin was also an item for sale.

Ray Argentina, who had been so thrilled at the sight of the automatic machine gun Al had brought him, wasn't a businessman. But he was so adept at terror and strong-arming that his services were often in demand from other crews.

Louie Daidone had been one of the men sitting nervously in the small Bronx parlor on Westchester Avenue next to Al just two years earlier as they waited to be called behind the curtain for their inductions. Daidone had a couple of businesses going. There was a bagel shop on Cross Bay Boulevard in Queens called Bagels by the Bay, as well as a nearby car service. He was also active in hijackings, heisting loads of cigarettes and tires with younger hoods he kept gainfully employed.

Peter Vario was the likely heir apparent to his father's realm. A made member in good standing, he had forged his own mob assets, with interests in gambling and labor rackets. But "Rugsy," as most called him, expressed no direct interest in the captain's job. The trickier part was figuring out the son's inheritance.

Under mob rules, there wasn't any. The Mafia imposed a 100 percent estate tax on its fallen captains. The operating theory was that everything acquired was due to Cosa Nostra clout, so the spoils went not to the next generation but to the succeeding capo.

Al was instructed by Amuso to collect everything Paul Vario had acquired. "Vic wanted me to take the house in Island Park, Geffken's, even a condo down in Boca West in Florida. I didn't take any of it. It's a creepy thing to do. He has sons, the sons have families. Think I'm going to be a ghoul and take Rugsy's house away from him? No. Let them keep it."

He had no problem, however, with taking Vario's extensive loan shark accounts and the thousands of dollars that rolled in weekly as interest. He also wanted to see whether any of the Lufthansa money was still around. Al's understanding was that Vario had taken a modest 10 percent of the $5.8 million haul, although most of that money disappeared.

"I went over Paulie's shylock book with Rugsy and we agreed I would take half." It came to about $318,000. A few days later, Peter Vario brought Al a large black plastic garbage bag. It held $159,000 in cash.

There was more. Paulie Vario had left additional loan shark accounts with Danny Cutaia, an active crew member and one of Vario's chauffeurs. In addition to handling Vario's book, Cutaia ran his own loan shark and gambling operations and held sway over a carpenters union local in Brooklyn.

Al arranged to let Cutaia continue handling the accounts that Paulie had left with him. They agreed that Cutaia would bring Al $4,800 a week from his collections, about half of the interest earned.

For the first time in his gangster life, he was making the kind of money that gangsters go into the business to make. The first thing he did was to take a fistful of the money and bring it to Anthony Casso to repay what remained of the $80,000 debt that Joseph had run up in the drug deal. But there was a lot left over. He was suddenly a wealthy man.

Joseph told his father that he had his drug demons beaten. What he wanted now in life, he told him, was to follow in his footsteps and become a wiseguy.

"I was going to go that way no matter what," Joseph said. He was thirty-two years old and wanted to get ahead in his chosen career. "I had ambition. My ambition was that I wanted to be the best criminal I could be. I wanted to be in business with my father."

Al heard his son's plea with a mix of pride and regret. "I had mixed feelings. I'm his father and I didn't want anyone else to tell my son what to do. But if I didn't think he was capable, I would've stopped it."

Al had another little poetic saying he'd picked up along the way that explained the best course of action in these situations. "What I was taught is that if a tree is bent, you try to straighten it up. But if it keeps bending that way, it is going to break if you try to bend it back. So you let it grow the way it wants."

Amuso and Casso were preparing to add to the ranks of the family's membership. "Vic proposed that we make Joseph. I said fine."

His son's name was added to a list of a half dozen proposed new Luchese family members. The list was circulated and returned with no opposition. An induction ceremony was organized in the basement of another Canarsie home.

Most of the other men being inducted that evening were Joseph's age. Three of them, George Conte, Anthony Senter, and Joseph Testa, were good friends. Joseph was thrilled to be joining the family with his pals.

The initiates waited upstairs to be called into the basement, where Amuso, Casso, and Al presided at a table.

Bobby Amuso had brought a large safety pin to do the honors. Al looked at it and shuddered. "It was this big, nasty-looking thing. He was using it to prick their fingers, but he was jabbing it in hard. He almost punched it right through. There was blood all over."

As part of the formal mob liturgy, once Joseph's induction was complete, Vic Amuso introduced him to his father. "This is your captain, Alfonso D'Arco. You will be with him."

The father kissed the son on both cheeks. They were now together in two families.

A few days after the induction ceremony, Al had dinner with Amuso and Casso. They dined at Gargiulo's, the big, rambling seafood restaurant on West Fifteenth Street in Coney Island, a block from the boardwalk and around the corner from where Al and Dolores had held their wedding party.

They were seated in a corner, back by the fish tanks so they could talk. Gaspipe congratulated Al on his son's induction. Al shrugged his thanks but didn't say anything.

"Now your son belongs to us," added Casso with a grin.

Al felt his face flush with anger. He nodded. "Yeah," he said. "Now he belongs to you."

* * *

Later that fall, Al ran into Hickey DiLorenzo on Prince Street. It was the first time he'd seen his friend since the troubling episodes at Ray Brook prison when he started wondering if the veteran Genovese gangster was coming unhinged. Al was glad to see Hickey. But he could tell right away he wasn't doing any better.

When he saw him, Hickey was sitting in the club next door to Ray's Pizza on Prince Street. "Hickey was there with Raffie Cuomo and Big Pete Chiodo. I'd never seen Hickey with those guys before and I suspected he might be doing a drug deal with them."

His suspicions were confirmed a week later when he ran into DiLorenzo again, this time at a nearby restaurant.

"Hickey says, 'Hey, I gotta ask you something,' and he starts to talk to me right there in the restaurant." Al pulled him outside to the street. DiLorenzo told Al he wanted an introduction to someone connected to the Canarsie crew who had just gone into hiding after being charged in a drug case.

Al asked DiLorenzo what he wanted with him. "Hickey says, 'We can make money,' and then he makes like he's shooting dope in his arm."

Al shook his head. "Anthony, I don't know what you're talking about," he said. "But I'm not interested." Al walked away without saying good night.

After the encounter, Al warned Pete Chiodo and Raffie Cuomo to stay away from Hickey. "The way he was acting, I couldn't tell if he was nuts or wearing a wire."

The warning didn't have much effect. The next time Al saw DiLorenzo he was with the Dean of Dope himself. At the age of eighty-one, Joe Beck DiPalermo was still busily trafficking in narcotics. Al warned DiPalermo as well to stay away from DiLorenzo. The little man insisted he was long finished with the dope trade. "He said he was too old for that stuff anymore."

A few days later, Al walked into a café on Mulberry Street that doubled as a gambling parlor. Called Tazza di Caffe, it was owned by Jimmy Ida, a captain in the Genovese family. Al and Ida were friendly.

Al was with Dom Truscello, a fellow Luchese soldier. Jimmy Ida was sitting at a table with DiLorenzo. Al and Truscello sat down across from them. DiLorenzo pointed at Al and began shouting. "I know this kid," he said. "I go back with the kid. I used to hijack trucks with him."

DiLorenzo kept up the rant for several minutes. Al looked at Ida for his reaction. "Jimmy was sitting there with this tight little smile on his face. You could see he was livid. I was mad myself, this guy shooting his mouth off like that." DiLorenzo's speech was interrupted when Joe Beck and Raffie Cuomo walked into the café. They greeted DiLorenzo. It was clear to Al that, despite his warning, they were still hanging around with him. A few minutes later, DiLorenzo walked out with Cuomo and DiPalermo.

After the other men had left, Ida motioned to Al. They stepped outside. "Jimmy starts to talk on the sidewalk, but I stopped him. I thought there might be a bug near that club. It was a pretty busy place." They walked down the block a few yards and paused in front of a small parking lot behind a chain-link fence.

"Jimmy had a way of talking real low, so he couldn't be heard. He'd mumble things." Now, Ida was seething. "He says, 'Why do these guys stay around him? Why do they give him confidence like that? Don't they know to stay away from him?'"

Al started to ask Ida why the Genovese crew didn't just tell Hickey to stop. After all, he was their soldier. But Ida interrupted him. In a low murmur, Ida said, "You know what we're going to do, right?"

Al didn't answer. Ida continued. "We're going to whack him," he said.

Al was astonished to hear Ida say it aloud. "Jimmy was a very cautious guy. He never blurted things out. But he was steaming." Al just looked at Ida. Then they said good night and parted on the sidewalk.

A few nights later Al was walking past Ray's Pizza on Prince Street. The store was closed but the lights in the back were on, the way Raffie often left them after he'd closed up for the night. Al had just returned from Brooklyn. He looked in the window of the pizza parlor and saw Hickey DiLorenzo. "He had his back to the window and Joe DiPalermo was there with Raffie. Dom Truscello was inside as well."

Al had been looking for Truscello. "I walked in and everyone immediately stopped talking, like they didn't want me to hear them." Drugs, he figured. But he didn't say anything.

Al told Truscello he needed to talk to him. The others made for the door as well. DiLorenzo stepped over to a brand-new red sports car parked at the curb. Al couldn't tell what make it was, but it was clearly expensive. "Hickey says to me, 'How do you like it? I just got these wheels.' I said, 'That's a nice car, Hickey.'" The gangster drove away. Al never saw him again.

On November 25, 1988, a few nights after Al saw the sports car disappear down Prince Street, a jogger trotted past DiLorenzo's home in West New York, New Jersey. The runner glanced at the house and was amazed to see someone shooting into the door. A car with New York plates was double-parked on the street, with someone sitting behind the wheel. The runner raced to call the police. By the time they arrived, the car was gone. Hickey DiLorenzo was lying in his backyard patio, having been shot to death. The gun used to kill him was found on the other side of the fence where the shooter had tossed it.

The FBI ran a check on long-distance calls from local phone booths near DiLorenzo's house. Someone had made four collect calls from one of the booths, each one for a minute or less, to Jimmy Ida's home in Staten Island within three hours after the murder. Unfortunately for Ida, they were the only collect calls to his number from West New York that month.

The Genovese family, headed by a mobster who pretended to be mentally ill, had decided to kill one of its own. Hickey DiLorenzo had violated mob rules by actually being crazy.

11

CLEVELAND PLACE

It was never about the money. Some weeks, thanks to the loan shark interest collected by Danny Cutaia and other scores that now drifted his way as the new captain, he was taking in as much $10,000. He was glad to have it. He wasn't about to give it back. But it had never been about the money.

He was satisfied to live in the two-bedroom apartment in the neighborhood where his wife had grown up, walking the same streets where he'd learned most of what he knew about being a gangster. If the family traveled, which they did on occasion, they went to the Miami Beach condo Dolores's parents had left her. It was a small place, not far from the water, but it was fine with him.

He didn't lust for expensive cars, big or small, like the sporty little job that Hickey DiLorenzo had been driving the last time he had seen him alive. In fact, he didn't even own a car. Other men drove him around these days, Pete Del Cioppo or Dom Truscello. If his men needed an auto, he bought them one. "Nothing cheap, I didn't want them in old heaps. But nothing flashy either."

He didn't gamble anymore. He'd once enjoyed the toss of dice in a crap game, but that pleasure had ebbed. He'd never cared much about the horses, a passion of many of his pals.

He'd given up smoking. At dinnertime, he still enjoyed a

single glass of wine or cognac, but that was it. And there were
no girlfriends tucked away in their own apartments. He still
had eyes only for the woman who had swept him off his feet
that night at the Town & Country Inn out on Flatbush Avenue in 1953, the mother of his five children.

In many ways, Al D'Arco wasn't much of a mobster. At
least he didn't aspire to be the new neon-light-flashing model
that John Gotti was then putting on display to the world as
he swaggered through the city's nightclubs in designer suits.

So what was the point? His special parole status guaran-
teed him another prison stretch if he was found to have violated the rules, as he did every waking day. A third conviction
on any one of the crimes he actively pursued would be likely
to send him to prison for most of the good years that, at the
age of fifty-six, he could rightfully expect.

Not that he thought much about it, but when pressed Al
D'Arco's answer was that status in the gangster life was
every bit as important to him as the family he loved. And
respect from those around him was probably even a little bit
more so. Money was one key measure of that respect. And at
the end of the day, he said, that was probably the one thing
that mattered to him most in his life and his chosen line of
work. "Yeah, respect. From whoever I had to deal with."

He still needed to do something with the money. He had one
idea, a notion that the more he tossed it around, the more he
liked it. He would open an Italian restaurant. He would do it
for his younger son, John, who liked to cook and who wasn't
cut out for the gangster life like his older brother. He would
do it as well to have a place to gather his troops, fete his
friends, and celebrate the food of his ancestral homeland. He
wasn't sure where or what it would be, but he kept his eyes
open for possibilities.

He was inspired by the example of Dom Truscello, another
jack-of-all-trades like Petey Del who had helped out with the
burger stand and acted as an occasional mob messenger. Truscello was partners with a neighborhood landlord named Joe
Zaza in a pair of buildings on a one-block strip of Little Italy

called Cleveland Place. On the ground floor of one of the buildings, they'd opened a small café for pastry and coffee.

Called Il Giardino, it aimed at the tourist trade and was doing a good business. Truscello and Zaza had purchased the property with three other partners from Joe LaForte, a wealthy Gambino captain whose real estate holdings included the tenement around the corner at 247 Mulberry Street that Gotti had adopted as his local base, the Ravenite Social Club.

The four-story building where the café was located had its own history. It had played a bit role in the 1984 presidential election when it was revealed that the broker who helped mob real estate mogul LaForte turn a healthy profit on the sale was John Zaccaro, the husband of Democratic vice presidential candidate Geraldine Ferraro.

Zaccaro's brokerage business operated out of a second-floor office on Lafayette Street across from the café on the other side of a small wedge of park. The park had a history as well. In 1987, the local city councilwoman, Miriam Friedlander, had persuaded the city to name the little spot after a much-neglected hero. City police lieutenant Joseph Petrosino had grown up on the block. Handpicked by then police commissioner Theodore Roosevelt, Petrosino had been one of the first Italian American detectives. Wearing an ever-present derby, Petrosino had made it his mission to combat the gangsters who preyed on neighbors and local businesses. In 1909, he traveled to Sicily in an effort to identify New York's most powerful Mafiosi. Tracked by the mob, he was assassinated. A crowd of twenty thousand lined the streets for his funeral at St. Patrick's Old Cathedral.

Al the history buff got a kick out of it all. "I saw the movie where Ernest Borgnine plays the cop Petrosino, *Pay or Die*. He's looking for the boss of the mob in Palermo and the boss comes up to him and says, 'It's me!' "

He was bothered, however, that next door to Truscello's café a member of the Bonanno crime family had opened a sandwich shop called Big Mike's Heros. Al viewed it as an intrusion on his turf. "This was our area—they were supposed to talk to me first." Adding to the insult, the Bonanno operators were running a gambling den in the back catering to local Chinese gangsters, many of them drug dealers.

Al initially decided to let things be. "I figured, all right, we can make money here too. My cut would be to put a couple of slot machines back there." He had Joseph and his friends install a pair of Joker Poker machines in the back. The Chinese gangsters unplugged them. After Al sent his team back into the shop to reinstall the machines, they were again disabled.

That was enough for Al. "I go in and tell them that's it, everyone clear out. Mike and his hero shop, the whole bunch of them. I told them this is our place now."

Aside from occasional scrapes over gambling dens, the Italian American mob and their Chinese counterparts got along pretty well in lower Manhattan. "Normally they dealt with fireworks, and they had their own gambling, the mah-jongg, and drugs. There was no tension unless you started tension."

The sharpest local exchanges were over real estate. When reporters went knocking on doors to find out more about John Zaccaro's mob dealings during the 1984 campaign, residents defended the broker. "Leave him alone, he kept the Chinks out!" shouted one woman from an upstairs window.

But the Chinese expansion into Little Italy was also assisted by some Italian American dealers looking for fast profits. "There was a guy, Joe Cap, they called him. His name was Joe Caputo. He was going around to the Italians in the neighborhood trying to get them to sell their houses to him so he could sell them to the Chinese who were buying with big bags of cash. He'd come with these gifts for the ladies, a little bottle of olive oil with a sprig of *basilico*, basil, inside. He'd say, '*Signora*, you want to sell your house? The Chinese are moving in next door but you can get away from them right now, I'll give you all cash money.'"

Joe Cap's block-busting had been interrupted by Al's old friend from 121 Mulberry Street, the broad-shouldered Genovese mobster Georgie Argento Filippone. "One day Georgie Argento grabs Joe Cap and tells him to cut it out. Joe Cap tries to argue and Georgie belts him. *Bang!* He smacked that guy, drew blood with one punch."

The Chinese gang that had adopted the gambling parlor in the back of the hero shop as its hangout also put up a brief argument. The gang was the Flying Dragons, one of the largest in Chinatown. After their eviction, the gang members returned in force. "They came walking in one behind the other, about twenty guys, like in military formation, all of them trying to look fierce."

The leader of the group was John Eng, known as "Onion-head." Eng was already facing charges of smuggling thirty-two kilos of heroin from Hong Kong in boxes of tea. He was soon to flee the country after being indicted in an even bigger dope deal, hiding three hundred pounds of heroin in stuffed animals and machines for washing bean sprouts.

Al was diplomatic. "We had a sit-down, me and this Onionhead. I told him he shouldn't get involved. I said, 'You don't want to cause a problem over this. It's not worth it.'" It was the last complaint he heard about the building from the gang.

He already had a name in mind for the restaurant. "I called it La Donna Rosa, a woman like a rose. First thing, I had a girl draw a picture of a nice red rose we could use on the menu. Our slogan was 'Authentic Sicilian cooking by authentic Sicilian chefs.'"

The storefront at 19 Cleveland Place had been a plumbing supply house for years, and he set about remodeling the dining room and kitchen, and remaking the basement into a bar. "I spent a lot of money there. I put in new floors, we laid in brickwork downstairs to make these grottolike alcoves. There were these old beams supporting the floor, and I got a guy to come in and sand and polish them. It looked like *Casablanca* when we were done."

He found a Sicilian chef to fit the bill as advertised, although his son John often did the cooking. Al also sometimes pitched in, donning a chef's apron and hat in the kitchen.

"We got the best vegetables and fruits from our contacts in the produce markets where we had the Teamsters union.

The guys in Frank Kissel's butchers union got us top-grade meats. Richie Tortorello, Anthony's brother, was in the fish market and he got us the best fish. Fat Mikey Flowers, who had the stall in the Brooklyn market, got us fresh flowers every day for the tables. Everyone who sat down got a bowl of fruit after their meal, on the house. It cut into your desserts, but people were still asking for the Tiramisu and the Sicilian cheesecake."

He enjoyed describing his menu. "I had them make *disco volante*, the big ravioli stuffed with *mousse di coniglio*, wild rabbit mousse, with the wild mushroom sauce on top. That was a big favorite. Then we had the basics, *sarde ripieni palermitana*, stuffed sardines, and stuffed calamari. We had *spaghetti carretiera*, the pasta with mushrooms that all the truckers eat. I gave them *vitello scaloppine carpene di grappa*, *salsiccio al forno con broccoli rabe*. For fish we had *tonnino agro dolce*, the sweet-and-sour tuna. Everyone asked for that."

On his wine list, he offered *Moscato di Noto*. "It comes from an island off of Sicily. It's pretty strong, but Sicilians love it."

To lend an air of elegance, he had his men dress up to greet diners. "Pete Del Cioppo and another guy we had with us, Tommy Christopher, were both tall, so we put them in tuxedos. They looked good. I had Shorty DiPalo, who lived down the street, out front by the door. It was a dark block, so you wanted someone there to give people confidence. We had a signal. If he saw cops or heat, he'd stamp his feet."

To draw the tourists, he set up a line of tables outside. "On the side of the building there was this little passageway under the fire escapes. I called it Cappuccino Alley. We served coffee and dessert out there."

The liquor license was in the name of John D'Arco and Joe Zaza. For anyone who had to ask, that's who owned the restaurant. But a steady flow of money from his newfound criminal riches funded both renovations and operations. The funding flowed mainly in one direction. The restaurant eventually made a modest profit, but free meals cut sharply into the earnings.

"I invited all the old ladies in the neighborhood, some of them had never been to restaurants, to eat for nothing. Father Vinci from Old St. Patricks was in there a lot. Never got a bill. Guys I knew from the crew, they came in to celebrate something, I comped them."

When the brother-in-law of Anthony "Curly" Russo, a member of Al's Luchese *borgata* and a neighbor at 21 Spring Street, died, Al hosted the family after the wake at the restaurant. "I told them, 'Bring everyone.' I closed the place down so they could have it to themselves."

Joseph walked the dining room some nights looking at the tables. "The place was full, but three-quarters of them were eating for free. And they would've paid, but my father didn't take their money."

The new restaurant attracted attention. Burt Young, the actor who enjoyed hanging around with gangsters, came and signed a poster of *Rocky*. Robert De Niro came by to dine and signed his own movie poster for *Raging Bull*. De Niro lingered over his meals, watching Al and his friends. "He was studying us, how we talked and moved, trying to model himself after us. I didn't care for it."

Close on De Niro's heels was the fallen prizefighter De Niro had portrayed in the movie. "Jake LaMotta comes in and after a couple drinks he stands up to do his act, the Shakespeare bit. I said, 'That's okay, Jake, everyone's heard it.'"

The food and ambience won raves from critics. "It's a restaurant you want to hug," wrote Cara De Silva of *Newsday*. "Totally authentic, warm and unpretentious."

He had the name painted in gold leaf on the window: La Donna Rosa, Ristorante Siciliana. It served lunch and dinner, its doors open to customers as late as 1 a.m. The lunch trade drew businessmen and -women from lower Manhattan. One afternoon Al was standing in front when a well-built young man in a suit walked up to the window. Al's law enforcement radar sounded. He took a closer look. The young man looked familiar. He seemed to be trying to make up his mind. When he walked inside the restaurant, Al followed. "I look and it's John Kennedy Jr."

Al was right about the law enforcement part. Kennedy was then working for the Manhattan district attorney a few blocks away on Centre Street. But he was clearly there for the food. "I told the waiters, 'Don't treat him any different from a regular customer. Make sure you give him a bill. You'll embarrass him and he won't come back.'"

The son of the slain president appreciated the anonymity. Kennedy returned for several more lunches, sitting quietly by himself enjoying pasta and a salad. Al also put the restaurant to work as a meeting place. "All the other Italian restaurants in the neighborhood would close on Mondays, so we closed on Tuesdays. And then we'd have get-togethers there on Tuesday nights."

One Tuesday evening, Al was meeting with a dozen organized-crime members and their bodyguards in the restaurant when someone knocked on the door. "I had some guys from the Gambino family there and some from our family, working some things out. Everyone stops talking and looks up. There was supposed to be guards out front, but they were nowhere around."

Al went to the door. "We had these double doors and the outside entryway is crowded with people. I open it and it's Mayor Koch, and he's got this whole entourage with him, about a dozen guys, including the police detectives who stay around him all the time. Koch says, 'Hi, we heard about your restaurant and we'd like a table.' He's looking past me through the inside door at all the guys sitting in there. I had food on the tables and everything so it looks like we're serving. I said, 'I'm very sorry, Mr. Mayor, but we're closed.' And he gets this look on his face because he can see we're open to somebody. So I say, 'No really, we're closed. It's a private party.' He smiles and says, 'Okay, well, I'll be back.'"

Al returned to his guests. "I said, 'It was the mayor. I told him he wasn't invited.'"

Others took note that La Donna Rosa seemed geared to the tastes of godfathers and their lieutenants. One restaurant critic praised the cuisine, writing that the air of authentic Cosa

Nostra only added to the atmosphere. "The guy writes that 'a certain plumbing salesman dines in the back room.' That was supposed to be Gotti, since his cover job was salesman for Arc Plumbing. But he was never in there. We had almost every other gangster in New York, but he wasn't welcome."

Around the corner from the restaurant, John Gotti was reigning supreme at his Ravenite Social Club. Acquitted in two cases, Gotti was in his heyday, hailed in the tabloids as "the Teflon Don." When he held court, everyone showed up: mobsters, reporters, TV cameras, plus squads of law enforcement agents taking it all in.

"Every wiseguy in the city was aggravated with him. Wherever he went, the agents were all over the place."

Gotti's "walk-talks" through the neighborhood with his retinue following in his trail created a small local circus. Agents tailed the mobsters leaving his clubhouse to see what other interests they had in the neighborhood.

Vic Orena, acting boss of the Colombo crime family, came into the restaurant one night. Al challenged him. "I said, 'Vic, where'd you just come from? Around the corner with that bum? And then you walk in here, bringing all that heat on you?'"

Actually, La Donna Rosa was doing a pretty good job on its own at drawing law enforcement attention. Not long after it opened, in 1988, investigators from the Manhattan district attorney's office started noticing the steady flow of wiseguys into the new restaurant at 19 Cleveland Place. The investigators didn't start out looking at Al D'Arco and his friends. Their original target was Joe Beck DiPalermo and the nonstop heroin plague he brought to the city. But when they saw Joe Beck and Ralph Cuomo coming to the restaurant, they decided to take a closer look.

Al never spotted that surveillance. He did have a friend from Pittsburgh come in and sweep the place for bugs. "He didn't find anything, but he did say he thought there was a chance the rear windows in the place, back by the kitchen, might have been targeted by some parabolic microphones or something. So we just stopped talking in that part of the restaurant."

The underboss of Al's own family wasn't worried about drawing attention. Gaspipe Casso was so taken with the restaurant that he asked to buy in as a partner. "Gas says he wants to come in with us. He wanted to put a sign up on the roof, a big one in bulbs with Italian colors, red, white, and green, spelling out 'La Donna Rosa.' He also wanted to make a penthouse on the top floor. He says, 'We'll make it our hang-out.' I said, 'Anthony, they got tenants up there.' He says, 'So we'll pay them to get out.' I said no, we were doing just fine as we are."

It wasn't all *tonnino agro dolce* and moscato wine. In late 1988, for the second time in his gangster life, Al was summoned to a bar where he was given an order to kill someone. The first time had been Paul Vario's test in Geffken's when he'd handed him the knife and told him to go out and stab Red Gilmore. The second time, there was no knife, but the order and the target were the same: Red Gilmore was still walking around, and Vic Amuso wanted Al to find him and kill him. And it wasn't a test.

The order was given at the London Squire Restaurant, a small tavern located on a commercial strip on Cross Bay Boulevard in Howard Beach, Queens. The neighborhood was a mostly Italian American pocket of single-family homes near Kennedy Airport. Its residents included John Gotti and other gangsters who had found a modest piece of suburban comfort within the city limits. Amuso lived just five blocks from Gotti in a large two-story brick home near Shore Parkway. He had a spacious side yard, a large swimming pool, and a tennis court. For protection and companionship, he had a massive Rottweiler named Bear. Whenever he could, he walked the dog to a nearby park where Amuso played handball.

The London Squire was about a mile from Amuso's home, and Al had Pete Del Cioppo drive him out there. Del Cioppo waited on the sidewalk outside while Al went into the dark bar to talk to Amuso. They sat at a table in a corner in the back. "Vic leans real close. He tells me that he wants us to clip Red Gilmore. He says, 'I think he's trying to set me up. He keeps trying to make appointments with me. I think he's a rat.'" As boss of the family, Amuso didn't need any justification for deciding to kill one of his associates. But he added that he had another reason for wanting Gilmore dead. "He said Red had robbed his brother Bobby's apartment."

Al wasn't convinced by either explanation. He knew Gilmore was a burglar, but he doubted he'd be foolish enough to have robbed the home of a made member of the mob, the brother of the boss of the family no less. And while it was possible that police had jammed Gilmore up and made him an informant, the more likely reason was the same one that had long hovered over Tommy Gilmore like a dark cloud. Some people just didn't like or trust him.

Gilmore's chief value to the Canarsie crew had always been as a driver and his handiness with cars. He had often chauffeured Paul Vario around, and he was one of those picked up on the Brooklyn DA's Gold Bug wire back in 1973. He was fifty-seven years old now, and he had spent his career assisting friends from his east Brooklyn neighborhood in crimes large and petty.

For someone who had been relegated to the mob's fringes, he'd done all right for himself. He had a limousine service, plus a used-car lot that doubled as a chop shop for stolen autos. His specialty was making cars disappear. His customers were those who didn't want to make their lease payments, or who needed to make their auto vanish for other reasons. "He'd steal the car, smash it into a block. Then help them collect the insurance."

Al had once bought a car off of Gilmore, an Oldsmobile 88 that he'd passed on to Shorty DiPalo. He'd later argued with Red when he'd found a stack of unpaid parking tickets in the glove compartment.

As far as Al was concerned, that was Tommy Red Gilmore for you. Always trying to sneak one past. But he didn't wish him dead now any more than he had the first time he'd been told to kill him. Like the first time, however, he didn't hesitate to do what he was told.

At the table, Amuso told Al to pick someone to help him do it. Al's first suggestion was a family associate named Frank Trapani. Known as "Harpo," Trapani was another veteran of the Canarsie crew who had also served as a Vario driver in the past and was now driving Al on occasion. "I knew Harpo was close to Red Gilmore and he was dying to get made. So I said, 'How about I use him?'" Amuso rejected the idea without saying why. "Just get it done," he said.

Al decided to try to carry out the assignment immediately. He knew Petey Del had a pistol with him in the car. "I said I had an idea we might find Red Gilmore at a bar where he hung out on Jamaica Avenue." They drove straight north on Cross Bay Boulevard for about a mile where it turned into Woodhaven Boulevard. At Jamaica, they turned right under the elevated train tracks.

As if he were waiting for them, Red Gilmore was sitting behind the wheel of one of his white limousines, double-parked in front of the bar. Al was amazed at their good luck. "There he is, Pete," he said as they pulled up. Del Cioppo started to slow down. Al told him not to stop. "He'll see me. Keep going," he said.

They drove down the avenue and made a U-turn, approaching the bar from the far side of the street. There was a short block that dead-ended at the elevated tracks. Al told Pete to pull in and park. They couldn't see Gilmore's car from where they sat, but they could spot him if he started to drive away. Al figured Gilmore would spook and run if he saw him. But Red didn't know Del Cioppo that well. He told him to get the pistol. It was a small weapon, a .22-caliber that Pete had gotten from the crew's gunsmith, Ray Argentina.

"Take the gun," Al told him. It was cold outside and Del Cioppo was wearing a heavy peacoat and a knitted cap. "Go walk back by Red's car. See if he's still sitting there. If he is, pull the cap down low on your face, wait for the train to go by, and then lean in and shoot him in the ear. Then walk back on this side of the street. I'll swing out and pick you up."

Al got in the driver's seat and watched Pete walk back down the avenue toward the bar. He sat there waiting for his first murder to take place.

After a minute he saw Del Cioppo walking rapidly back toward the car. He opened the passenger door and climbed inside. "What happened?" asked Al. Del Cioppo's chest was heaving. His face was tight.

"He's still up there," Pete said. "But he's across the street in the White Castle parking lot." Gilmore was sitting in the back of a white Chevy, Del Cioppo said. There were two men he described as "Irish-looking" in the front seat. "They look like cops to me," he said. The car also resembled the type used by police for surveillance, he added. "And they had these coffee cups on the dashboard. Like they're sitting there awhile." He had one more damning fact. The men seemed to be showing Gilmore some papers that he was flipping through.

It was the most detailed description Al had ever heard out of Pete Del Cioppo, who normally wasn't particularly observant. He wondered if he had gotten cold feet and made it all up. Alternatively, Gilmore might be negotiating prices for a chop shop deal. Either way, Al didn't want to stick around. "We got out of there fast."

A couple of days later, Al met Amuso back on Cross Bay Boulevard. The Luchese boss was coming from the law office of Richard Oddo, the labor attorney who was Paul Vario's cousin. Vic and Al walked along a side street until they got to a short one-block lane. The street sign said "Rico Place." It was an appropriate spot for a mob murder discussion.

Al explained that they'd had to abandon their first attempt to kill Red Gilmore. He said they were going to keep trying. But Amuso had new instructions.

"I want you to give it to Louie Daidone," he said. "Tell Louie to do it. Tell him to get it done right away."

Al didn't ask why. The boss had the right to choose both killers and method as he saw fit. It was a lesson Al was to learn painfully clearly over the coming months. Both Amuso and his underboss, Gaspipe Casso, took special interest in the architecture of the deaths they ordered.

After leaving Amuso, Al went looking for Louie Daidone. He started with his car service. It was also in Howard Beach, on the boulevard across from a long narrow finger of water called Shellbank Basin. Pleasure boats cruised up the basin from Jamaica Bay, docking at marinas and restaurants along the mile-long stretch. The car service was next door to the neighborhood's biggest dining hall, the looming Russo's on the Bay, a popular catering facility associated with the Gambino crime family. Directly across the street was Daidone's other operation, Bagels by the Bay. It was what gave Daidone his nickname. He was often called "Louie Bagels."

Al found Daidone inside the trailer that served as offices for his car service. He gave him the rundown. "Red is looking to set Vic up, and he wants you to kill him," he said. Daidone shrugged. Like Al, he had no choice. He'd known Gilmore longer and better than Al had, but it didn't matter. "Louie said he would take care of it."

But it was tougher than he'd thought. "Louie comes to see me a week later apologizing that it is taking so long." His first effort, he explained, had been a near disaster. Along with a partner in his bagel business named Patty Dellorusso, Daidone had driven to the same bar on Jamaica Avenue. There, they spotted one of Gilmore's limousines. The plan was for Daidone to crawl into the back of the limo and hide. He'd jump up and shoot Gilmore once he pulled over. Dellorusso was to follow behind and pick him up after the hit.

Daidone broke into the limo easily enough. He was lying on the floor, hiding behind the car's front seat, when Gilmore emerged from the tavern. He had a woman with him.

"Louie doesn't want to kill the girl, too, so he doesn't do anything. Red drives off and Louie is stuck in the back." Daidone spent a half hour trapped in the back of the limousine, trying not to breathe, listening to the chatter of Gilmore and the woman. Finally, the couple got out. Daidone waited until they left, then slipped out the side door.

"Louie kept apologizing, saying he would get him the next time." Amuso was pressuring Al, and he passed the message along. "Vic wants it done soon," he reminded him.

It isn't so easy to kill someone, Al thought after one of his frustrating talks with Daidone. Even a small-time crook like Tommy Gilmore.

A few weeks after Daidone had been given the assignment for murder, he showed up at the restaurant on Cleveland Place. "He said it was taken care of." The night before, Daidone told him, he, Dellorusso, and another associate had caught Gilmore returning to his home in Richmond Hill.

They had shot him in an alleyway behind where he lived, in a basement apartment of a two-family house. It was just three blocks from his favorite bar.

The job had gone smoothly, Daidone insisted. There was one small hitch. "He said a woman on the second floor of the house next door might have seen something."

Proof of the hit was in the next day's *Daily News* and *New York Post*. Gilmore's body had been found at 9 p.m. on February 6, 1989, by police responding to reports of gunshots. The victim was lying faceup in the alley with three bullets in his head and neck. He was declared dead at the scene. If anyone saw anything, they weren't talking about it. "All we heard was one big bang," a neighbor told the *Post*. Another said he wasn't surprised. "Everyone knew what kind of business he was in. He didn't have a job, but he had a big white limo."

The only importance both newspapers attached to the rubout was Gilmore's past connections to Paul Vario. "A low-level hood," the *News* called him.

Al went to the Walnut Bar to see Amuso to report that the mission was accomplished. When he got there, Gaspipe Casso was with Vic. Al told them what Daidone had said about a possible witness, but that it didn't look like they had anything to worry about.

The boss expressed satisfaction. But he still wasn't finished with Tommy Gilmore. He instructed Al to pass the word that no one was to go to Gilmore's wake. "He said if no one went, it will show that Red was a rat."

Al rarely attended wakes and funerals, or weddings, either. The easiest way to get violated on his special parole was to be spotted with one of his ex-con friends at a public gathering where FBI agents were snapping pictures. But he still wasn't sure of the wisdom behind Amuso's order. Many of the Canarsie crew had known Gilmore most of their lives. If none of them attended his services, the clear implication was that Red's pals had something to do with his death. But he said he'd pass the word along.

It wasn't the most emphatic command Al ever gave. Two of Gilmore's oldest friends in the crew showed up at his wake anyway. Pete the Killer Abinanti went, as did Rugsy Vario. Neither one of them knew that Amuso had ordered Gilmore's execution.

Amuso was irate when he found out his order had been disobeyed. He summoned Al to find out what had happened. "Go ask them why they went," Vic said. "Tell them if they like wakes so much we can have one for them."

12

ROCKAWAY
BOULEVARD

It was his first murder. He hadn't fired the gun that killed Tommy Gilmore. He wasn't even anywhere nearby. When the hard-luck burglar and chop-shop operator was fatally way-laid outside his Queens apartment, Al was across the river, busy with his Little Italy restaurant. But in the eyes of the law, Al D'Arco was just as guilty as those who pulled the trigger. He had passed on the order that had been passed on to him, and the words he spoke resulted in a man's death.

Not that he had anything to worry about. The eyes of the law weren't on Al. They weren't on anyone else for that matter. Law enforcement authorities never had any solid suspects in the shooting death of Thomas Gilmore until Al told them about it more than two and a half years later.

But during that thirty-one-month stretch Al was to pass on orders that resulted in the killings of a dozen men. More than a dozen others were marked for death, but fate inter-vened: In a couple of cases, guns jammed. Other targets simply got away.

No one realized it at the time—not Vic Amuso, not An-thony Casso, not Al D'Arco, or any of the others assembled under the Luchese crime family banner—but the murder of Red Gilmore was the start of a massacre. The family's top leadership was about to embark on a vicious bloodletting in which it would turn on itself, devouring young and old alike among its members and allies. They would even violate century-old Mafia prohibitions against killing the innocent, including family members of those who crossed them.

In many of those killings, Al D'Arco was the messenger, relaying orders to others to carry out executions. But in one of them he was an executioner as well. For all his brash talk over the years about wanting or trying to kill people who angered him, he'd never actually done it. He'd never had blood directly on his hands. In the spring of 1989, however, the blood got not only on his hands. It got all over his body.

The blood was that of a veteran Luchese crime family member named Michael Pappadio. He was sixty-six years old and walked with a limp thanks to a partially disabling stroke he suffered in 1982. He wasn't much of a match for a vigorous tough guy like Al, who still pounded the heavy bag whenever he found time.

Mike Pappadio was a holdover from the days of the old Luchese regimes. Along with his brothers, Pappadio had been helping manage the crime family's vast interests in the city's garment business since the 1950s. The rag trade, as it was known both on and off Seventh Avenue, where the biggest firms were based, was always crucial to the family's leadership. It supplied both huge profits and acceptable entrée into New York's political and business establishments.

Thanks to their positions as owners of legitimate garment shops, family leaders could count on influential friends in places both high and low. When family boss Thomas Luchese was summoned before a state crime commission in 1951, he could honestly say he was just the moderately prosperous coproprietor of a ladies' coat manufacturer called Braunell Ltd. with showrooms on West Thirty-Eighth Street.

New York City's police commissioner Thomas F. Murphy described Luchese the same way that year when, nominated for a federal judgeship, he was asked about his long-term friendship with a mobster whose street name was "Three Finger Brown" or, more simply, "Tommy Brown." Murphy, a big man with a walrus mustache, made his mark as a dogged federal prosecutor, famously winning the perjury conviction of Alger Hiss, the former State Department official accused of aiding Soviet agents. But Murphy noticed nothing amiss about the mob kingpin. The police chief said he knew Mr. Luchese only as "a reputable garment manufacturer" when he had invited him to dinners at his home.

Mayor Vincent Impellitteri offered the same excuse when asked why he dined with Luchese at the gangster's favored restaurant, Bentivegna's on East Houston Street. Manhattan U.S. attorney Myles Lane said he too was unaware of Luchese's alleged criminal ties when he stayed at the garment manufacturer's hotel suite in Washington, D.C., and accepted his invitation to attend a football game at West Point, where Luchese's son Robert was a cadet.

Congressman Vito Marcantonio, who sponsored Robert Luchese's application to the U.S. Military Academy, said he knew the father only as a supportive businessman from his East Harlem district.

That's where Luchese had started out, on East 107th Street. His crew had moved downtown from there, elbowing its way into the garment center, then the city's biggest jobs generator and chief industrial hub.

Most of the garment rackets had been run by Jewish gangsters, led by Louis "Lepke" Buchalter, whose thugs worked both sides of the industry's many labor battles. But Luchese worked out an accommodation, cutting Lepke into the family's small but growing narcotics trade in exchange for room at the table on Seventh Avenue.

After Lepke was convicted of his Murder Inc. slayings and died in the electric chair in 1944, Luchese's men had things mostly to themselves. The crime family's principal role in the garment district was officially confirmed by a Mafia Commission ruling in the 1950s. The other families were allowed to have pieces of the trade, but the Luchese crew ruled. Carlo Gambino's sons Tommy and Joey ran several large garment trucking companies. But their position and influence there stemmed partly from a wedding gift Thomas

Luchese had made when Tommy Gambino married his daughter.

In a bid to avoid notoriety, the father juggled the spelling of the family name. Police and newspapers spelled it as "Luchese." Joe Valachi gave him an extra "c" when he began singing to prosecutors. His own preference was "Luckese." Jokesters had teased him with rhymes of "cheese," he explained. That's how the name was carved on his tombstone when he died in 1967.

Over the years, garment manufacturing steadily slipped out of the city, headed to cheaper labor ports in the South and overseas. The mob's tax on every piece of clothing, estimated at $3 per garment at one point, didn't help make clothing jobbers want to stick around. But even as the industry declined, the Luchese crew retained its dominant position and zealously defended its turf. By the late 1980s, when Al got his first good look at the family's operation, he was impressed.

"It was bigger than anything we had, the biggest money-maker of all. It was a time business. The contractors have to get their work out on time. Because if you're making the fall line you got to get it out before fall. You can't be late. And if you're a contractor making dresses, you got to buy your buttons in a certain place. You got to buy cotton in a certain place. And each garment is on a hanger and has plastic on it. You have to get it all where you're told. It's a huge business. You've got not one contractor, you got hundreds of contractors. Thousands. And they're making garments for all the stores in the whole country."

Michael Pappadio mastered all those loose threads of the industry as he spent more than forty years in the business. He started out working alongside his older brother, Andimo, one of Tommy Brown Luchese's closest associates. Known as "Tommy Noto," the older brother had a dozen garment companies in his name when the FBI took a close look at his holdings in 1959. That was after Tommy Pappadio was one of those charged in the multimillion-dollar federal narcotics case that included Vito Genovese, Vincent Gigante, and Joe Beck DiPalermo.

When federal prosecutors convened a grand jury in 1965 to dig into Luchese's operations, Tommy Pappadio took a one-year contempt charge rather than testify. After Luchese died of a brain tumor, Tommy Pappadio helped run the family for a few years. But either jealousy or greed disrupted what had been a smoothly functioning operation.

Al heard the story from both Paul Vario and Joe Schiavo. "They said that Tommy Pappadio wasn't sharing. That he was hiding some of his garment shops and keeping the money."

Family warnings to cease and desist were allegedly ignored. On the night of September 24, 1976, Pappadio and his wife had just returned to their comfortable two-story home in Lido Beach, Long Island, just a few blocks from where Tommy Brown Luchese had lived. As they pulled into the driveway, they noticed a red car parked across the street. Pappadio went to investigate. As his wife put their Cadillac in the garage, she heard shots. A medical examiner later determined that twelve rounds were fired with eleven bullet slugs reaching their target.

The murder of Andimo "Tommy Noto" Pappadio was never solved. The killer had been dispatched after warnings were ignored. "They gave him a message. They said, 'You're one of the guys, but the garment center don't belong to you.'"

By the time his big brother was murdered, Michael Pappadio was fending off his own criminal charges. In April 1975, Michael was arrested in a tax-fraud scheme for keeping two mob captains on the payroll at his garment shops even though they did no work. His lawyers protested that he was a legitimate businessman, making $150,000 a year. Pappadio went to trial in Brooklyn federal court and lost. Before he was sentenced, he was hit with new charges in a separate tax-fraud case in Manhattan. He then proceeded to give judges in several courts a lesson in garment center haggling.

He told the judge in Manhattan he was not only too ill to go to trial, he couldn't even make it to arraignment. He had a "severe, degenerative arthritic condition" that made it impossible for him to drive to court, let alone sit in a courtroom for seven hours a day.

Independent doctors determined that that was somewhat of an exaggeration. At that point, Pappadio, then fifty-six, pled guilty, agreeing to serve a one-year sentence.

But he didn't really mean that, either. After his plea, Pappadio pursued repeated appeals, claiming that his health was too poor to survive prison. After two full days of hearings, that claim was also rejected. By the time his last appeal was heard by an appellate panel, the judges had clearly lost patience. The defendant, they wrote, was "a scheming, manipulative, financial operator" who had repeatedly conned banks and accountants. They quoted the similarly exasperated U.S. probation officer. Pappadio, the officer wrote, was "a shrewd, superficially ingratiating individual." His poor health, the judges noted, hadn't prevented him from putting $1,095,000 in the bank and buying a posh $150,000 home for cash in Bayside, Queens, while ducking taxes on more than $500,000.

Prison turned out to be not that bad. Pappadio served weekends at the MCC and a few months in a halfway house. He went back to the garment center and began hustling all over again as the Luchese family's point person. He was close to Tony Ducks Corallo and Tom Mix Santoro before those two top Luchese bosses got their one-hundred-year sentences in the Commission case. He handled garment shipping through his firm, Ideal Trucking, and had a "cutting room" company called Candy Joe Limited, a textile firm called Prints George, and a half dozen more companies.

It kept him busy. Most mornings he could be found in a lower-level dining room at Pickles Restaurant, a delicatessen on Seventh Avenue across the street from Macy's, talking business with fellow garment center racketeers. A close chum was Joseph "Joe Stretch" Stracci, a veteran Genovese family stalwart from his old East Harlem neighborhood.

He had won some notoriety in 1982 when a crusading state legislator from Manhattan's West Side named Franz Leichter cited Pappadio as the poster child for corrupt practices in the garment center. In a report on mob-tied sweatshops, Leichter detailed how Pappadio had helped bust out a garment firm called Fashion Page, which then suffered two fires. Pappadio had to sue to collect, but he eventually recouped $300,000 in insurance proceeds.

But that same year, he experienced real health problems when the stroke hit him. He stayed in the business but his younger brother, Fred, now pitched in to handle much of the daily chores. Mike Pappadio should have retired to Fort Lauderdale, where he and his wife had a comfortable condo. But he wouldn't, or couldn't, quit.

His fall from grace began when the power center shifted in the Luchese family. Gone was the old East Harlem–Bronx axis represented by Corallo and the family's founding fathers. The new family chieftains in Brooklyn, Vic Amuso and Gaspipe Casso, had cut their criminal teeth on drug dealing. As bosses, they were learning about construction schemes like the lucrative window-replacement operation. But they knew little about the often byzantine world of the garment center.

What they did know was that it spun off immense amounts of cash. And when one of the family's crime associates started telling them that Mike Pappadio was holding back shops and earnings, just the way his sneaky older brother Tommy had, they listened closely.

The man doing the whispering was another wealthy garment center fixer named Sidney Lieberman. Lieberman had been nailed in the 1970s by a special prosecutor investigating kickback schemes between vendors and nursing homes. He had gone from there to the rag trade. He was an owner of the nation's largest garment trucking company, Interstate Dress Carriers.

Lieberman's expertise became helping corrupt union officials shake down employers as part of the overall garment center labor policy in which shops that didn't pay off were targeted for organizing campaigns. In 1981, he pled guilty to obstruction of justice for bribing a union official to leave most of his employees off the books. Despite the conviction, he was considered a crafty practitioner of the art. "Lieberman had a reputation as a tough guy, a strong arm. If you needed something in the garment center, he became the guy to see."

It helped that Lieberman was Jewish, like most of the businessmen in the trade. "Vic and Gaspipe thought he was better equipped to handle things. He was also cutting them into a lot of deals and companies."

Casso was impressed with Lieberman's racketeering know-how and his earning power. In addition to his garment district contacts, Lieberman was also close to major airport freight-trucking operations. "If he wasn't Jewish, I would have straightened him out already," Casso said one day, throwing his arm around the portly Lieberman.

Meanwhile, the garment center's ripe pickings were off-limits to everyone else in the family. Al had been told in no uncertain terms by Amuso and Casso that he should steer clear of any involvement there. "It was for the bosses only. It had always been that way. There was so much money being made, they wanted to keep it among themselves."

But even at a distance it was hard to miss Sidney Lieberman's campaign to replace Mike Pappadio as the Luchese family's chief instrument in handling that fortune. "You would see Sidney Lieberman whispering in Vic's ear. He was telling them that Pappadio was hiding fifty garment shops from them that he wasn't sharing. He kept telling them that Mike was making $15 million off our backs."

Some of it was true. Called on the carpet by the bosses, Pappadio and his brother, Fred, acknowledged that there was at least one shop, located just north of the Bronx in Yonkers, that they hadn't gotten around to reporting yet.

But otherwise, Pappadio denied Lieberman's claims. "He was telling Vic, 'What are you believing that Jew bastard for? He's not even a member. How come you don't back one of your own?'"

The unspoken answer was that Amuso and Casso felt a closer kinship to Lieberman and his greater profit potential than to a fellow member. Pappadio was edged toward the exits. First, they assigned him to Al's crew. The move obligated Pappadio to check in with Al prior to making any moves, and to let him know his whereabouts at all times. "That right there should have been a warning to him. They were putting him with me because they were going to have me take care of him."

Al didn't know all the specifics of the money aspect of the dispute, but he sympathized with Pappadio's plight. "He was from the old Harlem wing of the family and they were pushing him out. Mike was a rich guy. They wanted what he had."

The feud between the two garment center racketeers continued to escalate. Lieberman fed Amuso and Casso details of what he said were Pappadio's secret holdings. "Then I get told by Vic to bring Mike to a meeting. He says we're gonna settle this thing."

Al had Danny Cutaia, who was friendly with Pappadio, contact him. The meeting started at La Donna Rosa. Both Pappadio brothers, Mike and Fred, showed up, as did Lieberman. Amuso and Casso began the discussion at the restaurant, where Lieberman aired his charges. Pappadio refused to back down. He repeated his protest that they were taking Lieberman's word against that of a made member of the family.

"So we moved the discussion up to Shorty DiPalo's apartment next door above the pastry shop. Now it was only made guys in the room."

In the apartment, Amuso told Pappadio he'd made up his mind. He wanted Mike out of the garment district. "They barred him. They said, 'Don't come around the shops anymore. Stay out of it.' They told him to bring in all his books and records so Sidney Lieberman could go through them."

Pappadio didn't say anything at first. He hung his head and looked at the floor. Then he started to protest. "I'm a member of the family and I've done a lot for it over the years. I shouldn't have to take this abuse from a guy who isn't one of us."

Amuso shook his head. He pulled Al aside and whispered fiercely into his ear. "You go out there and talk to Mike and tell him that he keeps it up, he is going to be whacked. And tell him that you're the one who's going to have to do it."

Al nodded. He took Pappadio by the arm and led him into the hallway. "I said, 'Mike, you are near my age. Stop being stubborn. You can see what's happening here. Just back up.' "

Pappadio seemed to calm down somewhat. Al went back to the restaurant, where he gave the same message to Fred Pappadio. "I said, 'Speak to your brother. He's going to get whacked if he keeps this up.' Freddy got real scared when I told him. He grabs his brother and they left."

After the Pappadio brothers departed, Amuso and Casso sat down at the restaurant with Lieberman. "They told Sidney what they'd told Mike. That he was out and that Sidney should take over." Al noticed that all three men seemed pleased by developments.

It's not clear what was going through Michael Pappadio's mind. Maybe he thought the same obstruction and delay tactics that he had used with the judges to delay his prison sentence might work with his crime family superiors. But there was no mob appellate court willing to hear one more appeal.

Whatever his reasoning, he did little to help his cause. He brought some records to the restaurant for Al to pass on to Lieberman. But Lieberman looked at them and scoffed. He insisted that Pappadio was holding back the real books. "Then Mike starts ducking me. I can't get hold of him. And Sidney Lieberman keeps it up, telling Vic and Gas that he's still coming around the garment center."

Al made one more stab at trying to get Pappadio to see the light. He had Petey Del drive Danny Cutaia and himself out to the garment racketeer's home in Bayside. The house was impressive. It was a prosperous businessman's home in a gated community alongside a country club overlooking Little Neck Bay. The four-bedroom house was a wide two-story brick Colonial with four tall pillars supporting a center portico, with a long U-shaped driveway. It had been constructed to Pappadio's specifications.

His wife, Frances, met them at the door. She brought them into the living room to wait for Michael, who was upstairs. She served coffee while they waited. "I didn't want to touch anything. I was thinking what was going to happen might happen and I didn't want any fingerprints in the place."

When Pappadio appeared he went right into his rant, telling them that Lieberman was still lying and that he had obeyed Amuso's orders to stay away from the shops. As for the records, he promised to look around for more. Al pressed him. "We're running out of time here, Mike," he said.

On the way back to the city, Al told himself he'd done about all he could. "I'm thinking they're going to tell me to kill this guy any day now." But a few days later, Pappadio called him and said he wanted to meet. Thinking Michael had finally decided to save his own life, Al went back out to Bayside, this time meeting him at a diner on Bell Boulevard, a few blocks from his house. But when they sat down in a booth at the diner, Pappadio only repeated his complaints about Lieberman. He was being displaced by an outsider after all he'd done for the family. "He just didn't want to listen, no matter how many times I told him."

His last meeting with the veteran gangster brought a new level of anxiety. "One afternoon Mike just shows up at the restaurant. The place is empty but he walks in and starts talking real loud. He says, 'Al, Vic is my boss, Anthony is my underboss, and you are my captain.'" Al had been seated at a table having a cup of coffee when Pappadio came in. He bolted out of his chair, twirling his hand over his head to signal that the restaurant could be bugged. Al grabbed his arm and walked him outside to the corner of Kenmare Street.

He pulled him close. "I said, 'What the fuck are you doing talking that way? In the middle of my restaurant?'"

Pappadio said he just wanted to come by and talk, to let Al know he knew whom he worked for, who was in charge of things. Al poked his finger in Mike's chest. "I said, 'Listen, you dumb guinea, I told you, you're going to get killed. And you know who is going to have to kill you, Mike? Me. Wise up. You gotta follow orders.'" As he was saying it, Al noticed a sedan parked nearby with someone at the wheel. He thought the driver looked suspiciously like an Irish cop.

"Who's that?" he asked Mike. Pappadio said it was a neighbor who had driven him there from Queens. Al frowned at the man in the car, who sat there ignoring him. He turned back to Pappadio, offering to get him a ride home. "No, that's okay. I can get back with my friend," he said. Al shook his head and went back into the restaurant. He knew Mike Pappadio had already dug himself a deep hole. Now he wondered if he was trying a different rescue strategy by becoming an informant.

The garment kingpin's fate was decided a few weeks later at a club in Canarsie called Le Parc Night Club. Located on an otherwise drab block of one-family homes and warehouses at the corner of Rockaway Parkway and Avenue N, the bar had long been a popular hangout for the Canarsie crew. A few years back it had been called the Bamboo Lounge, where Jimmy Burke and Tommy DeSimone partied to celebrate the Lufthansa heist. The club was owned by a loan shark and close friend of Amuso's named Angelo McConnach, known as "Sonny Bamboo."

By the time Al got there, the decision had already been made. He sat down at a table alongside Vic Amuso and Gaspipe Casso. "Mike is going," Amuso told Al when he arrived.

Seated across from them were two of the family's leaders from Long Island. Al knew Salvatore Avellino mainly by reputation. Known as "the Golfer," he was the captain of the family's Long Island branch and headed a major private trash-collection firm and ran the island's association of carting companies. The business had made him a wealthy man. He lived in the leafy suburban enclave of Nissequogue on the North Shore.

Avellino had been Tony Ducks Corallo's driver in the ill-fated Jaguar that had been bugged by state organized-crime investigators. It was Avellino's steady line of curious questions that helped fill the tapes that were played at the Commission case trial, securing the conviction of Corallo and his fellow mob bosses. Al had a hard time seeing the dapper Golfer at a murder. His brother Carmine, a soldier and involved in construction trades and air freight schemes, seemed like a more solid bet.

Casso already had the murder all planned. The Avellino brothers were old and trusted friends of Pappadio. They'd tell him they needed to meet with him, he said. They'd pick him up and bring him to a bagel bakery on Rockaway Boulevard in the Queens neighborhood of South Ozone Park. Carmine Avellino was a part owner in the bakery and would arrange for the place to be deserted. Al was to meet them there. Waiting with him would be George Zappola, one of the family's younger recruits and a fiercely devoted Casso aide. Zappola's uncle was a partner in the bakery as well, and he knew the layout.

"After you kill him, go through his pockets," Casso instructed. "I want to see whatever he's got. Any piece of paper. I want to know if this guy's cooperating." Al nodded.

They'd have a body bag ready for the corpse, Casso said. They'd put the bag in a car trunk. George Zappolla would take care of the rest.

Body bags were as morbidly effective for mob removals as they were for armies and morticians. Their advantage was that they didn't leak, leaving potential evidence behind. But they weren't sold at hardware stores. Unless a purchaser was legitimately in the mortuary business or the armed services, dealers tended to look curiously at him. Al asked where they were getting the bag. "He's got one here, outside in his car," said Casso. He nodded his head toward a man at a corner table. Al looked over. He recognized Vic Orena Jr., son of the Colombo crime family acting boss. Al recalled that the Colombo family had a major funeral home operator in their *borgata*. Gaspipe came prepared, Al thought to himself.

He followed Orena out to the parking lot, where the mobster pulled his car next to Al's. He hauled a heavy white plastic vinyl bag with a zipper out of his trunk. Al opened his own trunk and Orena dropped it inside.

On Saturday morning, May 13, 1989, Michael Pappadio and his wife, Frances, rose early. They were planning a small party for the afternoon, a barbecue on their lawn overlooking the bay. The weather looked like it was going to cooperate. It was clear, the temperature in the mid-sixties. The party was to be a dual celebration. Michael's birthday was on Sunday. He'd be sixty-seven years old. Sunday was also Mother's Day. It was to be a family get-together. Guests were to include their four children, all of them Frances's by a previous marriage. The couple had wed late in life. Michael was forty-nine years old when they married in 1972. It was his first marriage, and he'd adopted all four of Frances's offspring, three daughters and a son. All were grown now, ranging in age from twenty-five to thirty-two.

Since his stroke, Michael had managed much of his operations from home. He never discussed his business with his wife, but he had four different phone lines going into a study. The phones rang constantly. In recent weeks his telephone conversations had grown increasingly agitated. As a housekeeper later told the FBI, Pappadio was heard yelling that he was "in hot water." The housekeeper, who had been working for the family for ten years, said she had advised him to calm down or he risked another stroke. Pappadio told her that "they" were driving him crazy. He confided that he couldn't get out of his garment businesses because he needed the money.

The family lived well. In addition to the home in Bayside and the Florida condo, they owned an apartment on lower Park Avenue in Manhattan, a home in the Hamptons, and commercial real estate in the garment center and the Bronx. They drove only Mercedes-Benzes. The lifestyle had been part of his past legal problems. He had paid for most of it with checks drawn on his various garment companies, never declaring the revenue as income. More dangerously, he had also never declared it to his more demanding auditors in the mob. It was one more reason why he couldn't walk away from the business.

That morning, he and Frances went out in the Mercedes to pick up some supplies for the party. They left the house at about 8:30 a.m. Michael told his wife to drop him off at the

diner on Bell Boulevard. He said he was going to get a cup
of coffee, then pick up some fruit and vegetables at the store
next door.

Frances went ahead in the car to run errands. They didn't
make an exact time to rendezvous back at the produce store,
but Frances expected her chores would take about an hour
and she'd pick him up on her way back. Michael didn't say
anything about meeting anyone or going anywhere else. She
didn't see how he could have. She knew he carried a wad of
cash with him, possibly several hundred dollars, as was his
habit. But he hadn't bothered to bring his wallet. He was
dressed for a casual Saturday around the house, like the semiretired businessman she believed him to be: he had on yel-
low pants, a windbreaker over a pullover shirt, and white
sneakers.

Al was up early that morning as well. He had arranged for
Pete Del Cioppo to pick him up outside his apartment on
Spring Street. Del Cioppo had the necessary tools for the day's
task in his car trunk. The white body bag was there, as well
as a .22-caliber pistol Al had gotten from Ray Argentina. That
was a backup weapon, however. He also had a heavy home-
made sap, an eighteen-inch length of thick copper cable
wrapped in blue rubber insulation. Al had kept it behind the
counter in the burger stand in case of problems. He'd never
had to use it before, but he figured it would quietly do the trick.

After Petey Del arrived, they drove out to Cross Bay Boulevard, to a parking lot behind the Chelsea House, a steak and
seafood restaurant favored by Amuso. George Zappola was
already there, at the wheel of a dark blue Lincoln Town Car.
Al had Petey transfer the bag and the weapons to the trunk
of the Lincoln and then told him to take off. Then he got in
beside Zappola as they drove the two and a half miles east to
the bakery on Rockaway Boulevard.

When they arrived, Carmine Avellino was waiting for
them. Zappola parked the Lincoln in a loading area, behind
a garage door and out of sight from the street. Then the three
of them went inside the bakery.

"I thought his brother Sally was supposed to be there with him, but Carmine says he is going to get his brother before they pick up Mike. So he gets in his car, he had a Mercedes, and takes off to go get them."

Al and Zappola went into a small office behind the bakery area to wait. Al positioned himself behind a set of blinds on the office window. "I closed the blinds but I could see through them, to spot them when they came in the door." They'd have plenty of time to see their victim coming. Pappadio, escorted by the Avellinos, would have to walk about thirty feet through the bakery to reach the office.

As they waited, Al and Zappola went over their plan of attack. The plan was for Al to slug him with the cable sap. Then Zappola would shoot him with the .22. They put the body bag in an open file cabinet drawer in the office and put the gun on top within easy reach.

Al had lost track of time when he heard Zappola speak. "Here they come!" he hissed. Zappola was standing directly behind Al, both of them shielded from view by the blinds. Al saw Carmine Avellino coming through the bakery's outer door with Mike Pappadio behind him. Sal Avellino wasn't there.

Carmine Avellino opened the office door. Pappadio stepped into the office, blinking at the sight of the two men. Avellino let out a shout. "Surprise!" he yelled. "Look who's here!"

As he shouted, Al smashed the sap on Mike Pappadio's head, swinging the heavy cable down as hard as he could. The businessman was solidly built, five foot eight, weighing about two hundred pounds. He didn't fall. "He's looking at me. He puts his hand up to his head and says, 'What'd you hit me for, Al?'"

Al hit him again. He still didn't go down.

"I don't know how the hell I didn't knock him down. I banged him hard, about four times. I guess the fear was holding him up." Zappola reached for the .22. He pointed the gun at Pappadio and pulled the trigger. The bullet ricocheted wildly off the victim's head, lodging in the office door.

"The guy had a head like a rock. Then Georgie pulls out a big snub-nosed gun, a .357. I didn't even know he had it. He puts it up to Mike's head and shoots. The guy was still standing. I couldn't believe it."

Mike Pappadio was stubborn to the end. But he was now finished. The three killers watched as he slumped against the wall, then slowly slipped to the floor.

He lay there, a gurgling noise coming from his throat. "We waited and then he stopped making the noise and we knew he was dead."

Blood from the savage attack was everywhere, splattered on the floor, the walls, and the ceiling. "It was on my clothes, my jacket, my hands."

Avellino was the first to recover. As per Casso's instructions, he bent over the body, rifling the pockets. Al watched as he pulled a thick wad of cash from one pocket. Another held a brown leather item. At first Al thought it was a wallet but it was an address book. Avellino passed them to Zappola for delivery to Casso.

They unfolded the body bag and began maneuvering Pappadio's corpse inside. As they tried to zip it shut, the zipper broke. So much for professional products, thought Al. The three of them gripped the sides of the bag and hoisted the body out of the office into the bakery. There, Zappola grabbed a large plastic sheet that had been covering a rack of baking trays. "I'm not getting blood in the back of my fucking car," he said.

Avellino, part owner of the bakery, spoke up. "I'm going to need that sheet back later," he said. Al and Zappola both looked at him in wonder.

Zappola went out to his Lincoln and laid the plastic down in the trunk. Then they carried the body bag out to the loading area and laid it on top.

"Georgie was supposed to drive. It was his car. But at the last minute, he says to me, 'I ain't got a license. We shouldn't take the chance in case we get stopped.'" Al shrugged and got behind the wheel. Avellino stayed behind to start cleaning up the carnage.

Al pulled out of the loading area, then made a right on Rockaway Boulevard. He went straight about a mile and a half, then turned right on Woodhaven Boulevard.

With the body in the trunk, they drove north for another couple of miles along one of Queens' busiest streets, now bustling on a late Saturday morning. They crossed Jamaica Avenue just a few blocks from where Red Gilmore was shot to death. Just past Union Turnpike, Al pulled over. Zappola got out to make a call from a phone booth.

Al sat in the car waiting. When Zappola returned he told him that his contact for delivery of the body bag wasn't ready yet. He directed Al a few blocks farther up the avenue until they came to a Roy Rogers restaurant. Al pulled in the back and parked. They agreed that Zappola would stay with the car, waiting for his contact. Al would go back to the bagel bakery to help Avellino clean up. That was fine with Al. He didn't need to know anything else about what was done with the body.

He went into the Roy Rogers to use the bathroom and wash his hands. As he washed off the bloodstains in the warm water he looked at himself in the mirror. A partially balding fifty-six-year-old man looked back at him. A man who had just finished participating in a ferocious murder. He saw something else as well.

"I'm looking in the mirror and I see I still have blood on my jacket." He had foolishly worn a new suede, bomber-style coat that his daughter Dawn had given him a few months earlier for a Christmas present.

He mopped up the stains as best he could with a wet paper towel. Then he went out to Woodhaven Boulevard, where he flagged down a passing gypsy cab that brought him back toward the bakery. "I had him drop me off by a lumber yard near the bagel place. I walk over to the bakery and Carmine's still there scrubbing. There was so much blood." Avellino was making do with a few towels. Al offered to go out and buy some more cleaning materials and plastic garbage bags.

He felt like he was in control and knew what he was doing. But his actions later that morning were those of a man in a daze. Once he got out on the street he walked a full two miles to the lawyer Richard Oddo's office on Cross Bay Boulevard. He told himself it was because he couldn't find a cab, and that it was the nearest spot where he could find what he needed. If Oddo was there, his plan was to ask to borrow his car. But his hike down Rockaway Boulevard took him past a half dozen stores selling cleaning supplies.

Vic Amuso owned a building near Oddo's office, and when Al got there he ran into Amuso's friend, Jimmy McCann, the construction worker. McCann was with two of his sons doing work on Amuso's property. Al told him what he needed, and McCann immediately sized up what was going on. "Jimmy says, 'Let me help you out.' He takes me to a C-Town supermarket and we buy some stuff, disinfectants, plastic bags, and whatnot. Then he took me over to the bakery."

When they got there, Al saw that the place was filling up. Several cars were parked outside, and the bagel delivery truck was there. Carmine Avellino was outside talking to a group of men Al didn't know.

"I told Jimmy to keep going past and then we pulled up and I made a call back to the bakery." When Avellino got on the phone, he told him he was nearby with the cleaning materials. "I said who the hell are those guys out there you're talking to?"

Avellino told him there was nothing to worry about, that he'd managed to clean everything up. Al hesitated, unsure of what to do next. Then he remembered the sap and the guns. He told Avellino to make sure he got the "baker's tools" they'd used that morning. Avellino said not to worry.

It was the last time he and Avellino ever discussed what they'd done that morning. "You don't talk about it when it's over. It's an old rule and a good one."

Jimmy McCann, still anxious over Al's condition, graciously offered to drive him home to Spring Street. Al, feeling exhausted for the first time, gladly accepted the lift.

Home in his apartment, he pulled off his shirt, pants, and shoes. He cut them all into pieces. Then he took them to the garbage chute in the building and tossed them inside. He hesitated at the jacket. He put it aside, thinking that Dawn would want to know what had happened to her gift. He thought maybe he could keep it, that a good dry cleaning just might eradicate any telltale bloodstains.

Then he went to take a long shower.

An hour or so later he went to a dry cleaner on the East Side. It was one he'd never been in before, and he left the jacket under a made-up name. On his walk back to the neighborhood he thought better of it. They have all these sophisticated methods for detecting blood on items, he thought. "I figured I'd just have to tell Dawn I lost it or something. It wasn't worth the chance." He never went back to get the coat.

At the corner of Kenmare and Mulberry Streets, he used a pay phone to call Amuso and report in. Amuso expressed his thanks. "*Grazie, hai fatto bene*," the boss told him. He'd done well.

Out in Bayside, Frances Pappadio was frantically calling around looking for her husband. When she hadn't found him back at the fruit store, she thought maybe he'd caught a ride with a neighbor. But no one knew where he was. She began thinking that if he'd collapsed and had another stroke, he had no identification on him. He could be lying in a hospital as an unidentified patient.

After her children began arriving at the house for the party, they started calling hospitals and police. There were no signs of him anywhere. Her son, Michael Jr., drove to the diner to ask if anyone had seen him. His adoptive father had never even come in the diner that morning, he was told.

She didn't reach her brother-in-law, Fred Pappadio, until later that evening. Fred told her that he had been out on Long Island attending a cousin's christening ceremony. He said he'd be right over.

An hour later, Fred showed up at the house. With him was Victor Panica, a veteran Luchese crime family member who had been close to Tommy Pappadio years back. He had once done time for heroin dealing. Panica's brother Butch was there as well. Frances knew them only as partners in some aspect of her husband's business. Other than that, she didn't know anything about them.

None of the men had any solid ideas to offer. Fred suggested she file a missing-persons report with the police. The next day, Sunday, Michael's sixty-seventh birthday, she went to the 111th Precinct near Bell Boulevard and did so. The police came up empty-handed as well.

Later, Frances Pappadio was to remember clearly how quiet and downcast her brother-in-law and the other two men were that night as they sat in her living room.

13

FORT HAMILTON PARKWAY

A few days after the murder, Anthony Casso came to see Al at La Donna Rosa. He had already heard the story of the bullet that bounced off Mike Pappadio's head and how the old man had stayed standing, despite the vicious beating.

They were outside the restaurant on Cleveland Place. Casso nudged him. "He says, 'Hey, Al, Mike had a really hard head after all, huh?' He thought it was funny. That was his kind of humor."

Al wasn't laughing, but he wasn't remorseful either. "Mike killed himself. He wouldn't do what he was told, and he was a stool pigeon. He was trying to set me up."

Actually, there was never any evidence that Michael Pappadio had become an informant in the weeks before his murder. None of the agents or prosecutors pursuing the Luchese family in those years ever wired him up. If they had, there would've been far greater law enforcement interest in his sudden disappearance.

As it was, the only one who came inquiring was his little brother. "Freddy Pappadio came around the restaurant a couple of times, talking about how his brother was missing and did we know anything about it?" On one of his visits, Amuso and Casso were there. They hustled Fred next door to Shorty DiPalo's apartment, the same place his brother had received his own warning. "I said, 'What are you asking me for? What the fuck do I know? Maybe he ran away with a girl?' That was the old thing you always said when someone was made to disappear. 'He probably ran away with some girl.'"

He justified the grisly murder that had left him covered in his victim's blood, the first by his own hands, as simply part of the business he had chosen. "You're stuck with it like anything else. You've got a job to do? You do it. It's like the Army. You go through basic training, they send you to war, you go out there and shoot who they tell you. You don't do it, they throw you in Leavenworth. It's the same thing in the Life. You're a soldier. You don't do what you're told to do, you're gonna get killed."

Contrary to popular wisdom, murder wasn't a required initiation rite for admission to the secret society. But when ordered, a member had to participate. "The press pushes all that stuff. They write how you've got to make your bones before you can get made. Nah. It doesn't hurt to have done it, but guys also get made because they earn, or because they're smart."

Wealth also opened Mafia doors. "We had a guy in our neighborhood, his father owned half the parking lots in downtown Brooklyn. They gave him his button. Who'd he ever kill? He was rich, so they wanted him."

But the order might come at any time. "You could be in the Life for twenty years, and you don't do anything. But you have to remember that there will come a day, the guy will say, 'Al, you gotta do this.' And you can't say, 'No, I quit.' You do or die. It's blood in, blood out. That's the way it works."

He did know one story about a mob recruit who had resigned rather than kill. He didn't know the name but he'd heard the tale. "It was a guy going back. He wasn't made, but he was close to being made. They were grooming him. They told him to help kill a guy and he wouldn't do it. He ran away because he couldn't take it. He couldn't take that life, being forced to kill someone you don't want to kill. He got labeled a rat for running. His family was shamed."

* * *

About his own victim, Al asked no further questions. He never inquired what became of the corpse that he'd last seen wrapped in the white body bag with the torn zipper in the trunk of George Zappola's Lincoln Town Car. "You don't need to know. The less, the better."

Years later, other informants filled in the tale. After Al went to find a bathroom at the Roy Rogers, three men met Zappola in the parking lot. Two of them were brothers, Benedetto and Vincent Aloi. A top official of the Colombo crime family, Benny Aloi had his own holdings in the garment center, where he'd had his own run-ins with Mike Pappadio. He was not unhappy to see him taken out of the picture. Aloi was also close to Casso, thanks to their joint involvement in the profitable replacement-windows scheme.

The third man was a professional undertaker named Jack Leale, a Colombo associate who had provided the body bag. Leale got behind the wheel of the Lincoln and drove it to a nearby crematorium. As he readied the body for cremation, he later told the Aloi brothers, he was surprised to see that it had been stripped of both jewelry and cash. Standard wiseguy practice was not to steal from fellow mobsters you kill.

In Little Italy, the John Gotti parade continued nightly, the peacock mobster strutting the streets, followed by his retinue. The spectacle caused Al and other old-school hard-liners continuing agita. Gotti was out on bail, charged in state court with ordering the wounding of a carpenters union boss who had trashed a Gambino-controlled restaurant. "I'll lay you three to one I beat it," the chronic gambler told the arresting detectives when they put the cuffs on him on the corner of Prince Street and Broadway in January that year.

But it was Gotti's younger brother, Gene, who was in the more serious legal jam. A long-delayed trial from his 1983 arrest on heroin trafficking with two fellow Gambino members had resulted in a fast jury verdict of guilty in May, a few days after the Pappadio execution. Gene Gotti was out on bail, awaiting sentencing. His chances hadn't been helped by a crack made by his co-defendant, John Carneglia, who told a reporter he'd be back from prison in time to "piss on the grave" of the eighty-nine-year-old judge who would be sentencing them.

Al genuinely liked Gene Gotti. "He was solid as a rock, a real *uomo di honore*. A man of honor." When he ran into him in early July in Canarsie, he sympathized with him.

"He was at a barbershop I went to, Pepe and Jerry's on Avenue L in Brooklyn. A lot of wiseguys went there. Jerry collected shylock payments for Danny Cutaia, and he had a phone extension in the back room he'd let guys use for business."

Al asked Gotti how he was doing. "Not so good," answered Gotti. "I got to go in for sentencing tomorrow."

Al thought he was lucky to be out on bail. Defendants convicted of drug charges are usually taken into custody to await sentencing. But he felt bad for his friend.

"Gene, you don't have to listen to me," he said, "but you want some advice? Go on the lam."

Gotti shook his head. "I can't. My brother, you know . . ."

"I knew what he meant. That his brother wouldn't want him to because of the problems it might cause him. But I said, 'Don't worry about your brother. Your brother can take the heat. He makes his own heat.' I said, 'Gene, they're gonna give you fifty years. You hear what I'm saying? Go on the fuckin' lam, and stay on the lam for four or five years. They'll be embarrassed. They'll make a deal. You'll come in, and maybe you'll get a few years, but at least you'll see some daylight. This way, you're getting fifty.'"

Gotti thanked him but repeated that flight wasn't an option. Al wished him luck and they parted in front of the barbershop. It was the last Al saw him. The next day the judge smacked Gene Gotti, then forty-two years old, with a fifty-year sentence. Al had hit the number on the head. "The guy was more loyal to his brother than himself. It was a shame."

For the Luchese bosses, the executions of Red Gilmore and Mike Pappadio were only the start. Murder was becoming the quickest prescription for every ailment they suffered. Hit contracts were the aspirin for the slightest headache.

To some extent, they were following Mafia tradition. As long as proper permissions were secured, and standard precautions taken, murder was considered an acceptable sanction for those who broke the rules, stole from the organization, or otherwise aggravated mob officials.

But the accepted practice was to keep such killings among themselves. The rules of the Commission set out by Lucky Luciano and his partners prohibited targeting those whose deaths were likely to bring more heat than help. The protected list included police officers, religious figures, and newspaper reporters. Men like Tommy Red Gilmore and Michael Pappadio could disappear or be left slaughtered in the street without sparking enormous investigations. Outsiders—civilians, as they were called by the soldiers of organized crime—were a different story. An occasional instructional beating? Yes. Murder? Not usually.

But for months, Luchese capo Sal Avellino had been itching to kill a pair of outsiders who had interfered in one of the mob's biggest moneymaking schemes. Robert Kubecka and Donald Barstow were brothers-in-law who ran a Long Island waste-hauling firm. They had not only blatantly ignored the rules of the mob's price-fixing monopoly that carved up the island's customers among favored firms; they had also talked about it to authorities. They had named Avellino and others as engaging in extortion in the private sanitation industry.

It was Kubecka who had first suggested to investigators from the state's Organized Crime Task Force that they figure out a way to hide a recording device in the black Jaguar in which Avellino squired former Luchese boss Tony Ducks Corallo around town. The agents had followed up on the suggestion, using Kubecka's knowledge to help secure a judge's approval for the bug. The resulting tapes had helped bring down not only Corallo, but the rest of the Luchese leadership including underboss Tom Mix Santoro and consigliere Christy Tick Furnari.

The rebel carters had begun cooperating with investigators in 1982. Kubecka hadn't hidden his opposition. He testified before both grand juries and state trials, resulting in a coercion conviction for Avellino. When a researcher for the RAND Corporation, a policy think tank, published a lengthy study on the racketeers and their carting monopoly, Kubecka was featured as the essay's star.

Robert Kubecka wasn't your average garbage hauler. He was an ardent environmentalist with a master's degree. He had taken over the carting company from his father, running it with his brother-in-law, Barstow. Kubecka and his wife had a boy and a girl, aged six and eight. Barstow, wed to Kubecka's sister, had a seven-year-old daughter.

Al first started hearing Avellino's complaints about the men in late 1988. "He said they shouldn't be walking around. That an example should be made of them." Avellino told him that the hit on the two carters had been authorized years ago by Tony Ducks, who shared Avellino's outrage over their cooperation. The hit had been put on hold in a bid to avoid antagonizing judges ruling on cases involving Luchese members.

What Avellino wanted from Al was permission to use Ray Argentina, the proficient killer who belonged to Al's Canarsie crew, as the shooter for the hit.

Al balked at the request. Not because he disagreed with the Golfer's proposed solution, but because he didn't see why the wealthy Long Island crime captain didn't use his own gunmen for the mission. "I said, 'Sal, it's okay with me. But you've got to check it out with Vic and Gas.'"

The Long Island mobster became more determined after federal attorneys in Brooklyn filed a sweeping new civil racketeering lawsuit in June 1989. It named Avellino and his Private Sanitation Industry Association of Nassau and Suffolk. Avellino saw the civil case as leverage for new criminal charges against him. And he viewed the rebels as responsible for that as well. Both Kubecka and Barstow were slated to be witnesses in the civil RICO case.

Avellino eventually confessed to Al another, more complicated motive for wanting the men dead. "Sal told me he felt like a rat. He was worried that people think he was the reason Tony Ducks got nailed in the Commission case, that it was his talk on those tapes that hurt everyone." Making things worse, Avellino had skated on the charges. He received community service. Corallo took a life sentence.

The go-ahead to have the carters killed was given in early August 1989. It was during a meeting at Sonny Bamboo's place, Le Parc Night Club, the same spot where Michael Pappadio's death warrant had been issued. The group was the same as well. Al was at the table with Amuso and Casso. Sal Avellino was there with his brother Carmine. They immediately started laying out everything they knew about the carters' habits. "They'd done a lot of homework on it. They knew when they arrived each morning in the office. They even had the layout of the place."

Casso listened to their plans and then waved his hand dismissively. "Do it any way you have to," he said. Al just listened. He was out of it. Avellino was told to get his own hit men.

The killers struck early on the morning of August 10 when Kubecka and Barstow arrived at their offices in East Northport, on Long Island's North Shore. Barstow, thirty-five, was shot to death. Kubecka, forty, grappled with one of the gunmen, scratching him badly enough to leave a trail of blood. The mortally wounded carter made it to the phone to dial 911. He tried to give a description of the assailants. He died in the ambulance on the way to the hospital.

Sal Avellino was ecstatic over the successful double hit. "Good, those rat cocksuckers are gone," he said when Al saw him after the murders. As he spoke, he chopped his hand down as though beheading his now deceased antagonists.

Casso seemed amused by the whole thing. At a dinner with Al and Amuso at Gargiulo's in Coney Island, he remarked how Avellino had a huge load off his shoulders. "The Golfer can breathe easier now. He can stick his chest out. Thanks to us, he doesn't have to go around thinking he's a rat anymore."

It was to be a summer of murder.

It was one thing to push the mob envelope by killing a pair of civilian businessmen who had stuck their necks out by complaining to law enforcement. It was another to actually kill a member of law enforcement itself.

A few months earlier, a twenty-eight-year-old drug dealer associated with the Bonanno crime family had done just that. Costabile "Gus" Farace shot a veteran Drug Enforcement Administration agent who had been working undercover to bust a cocaine ring. Farace shot the undercover agent four times in the head and chest after luring him to a dead-end street in a remote spot on Staten Island to discuss a drug sale. Everett Hatcher was wearing a radio transmitter, but his backup team from a DEA-FBI task force lost contact with him before he could radio the location of the meeting. They found him an hour later, slumped dead in his car.

The result was the kind of heat that Luciano's no-kill rules had been designed to avoid. The shooting deaths of Kubecka and Barstow were reported in a handful of news articles after their murders. Hatcher's killing brought hundreds of bulletins. A smiling photo of him ran in newspapers and magazines and on television around the world.

At age forty-six, Everett Hatcher was a twelve-year veteran agent. An African American, he had served in the Army and as a New York City high school physical education teacher. He was a big man with a warm smile and a wide mustache. He hadn't even brought a gun with him to the meeting with Farace.

He was the first agent killed since 1972 and the first drug agent ever slain in New York. The death sparked the largest manhunt in years. Five hundred DEA agents were assigned to find the killer. They already had Farace's name as the prime suspect. Anyone remotely connected with him had agents and cops pounding at the door.

Mobsters were rousted in their clubhouses and at home. Even the president of the United States got into the act. George H. W. Bush invited Hatcher's widow and two sons to the White House, declaring that "open season" on cops was over. United States attorney general Dick Thornburgh vowed that when caught, Farace would be the first to face the death penalty under a new federal law.

The Mafia had the same idea, under its own long-standing laws.

Al knew the rule without being reminded. "Gus Farace had to go. You kill an agent, or a cop, or a reporter, and you're dead." The Luchese leaders felt the pressure as well. Agents came to Amuso's home asking what he knew about Farace. Nothing, he told them. Detectives pulled him over on the street, asking the same questions all over again. After Amuso was grabbed a third time, the tactic began to have its effect.

Actually, Amuso knew quite a bit. Ralph Cuomo took a break from his own drug dealing at Ray's Pizza on Prince Street to whisper to his boss that one of Amuso's own men was hiding Farace. "Raffie was making points, ratting on a guy named Johnny Petrucelli, a member that Vic had made himself. Raffie was telling him that Johnny was hiding Farace."

Petrucelli was forty-seven years old. He had spent ten years on the run himself in the 1970s, hiding from a manslaughter conviction in which he'd helped kill two men in a Bronx bar. He later became friendly with both Vic Amuso and his brother, Bobby. Vic had given him his button and assigned him to Bobby's crew.

While doing time in prison, Petrucelli also got to know Gus Farace, a muscular young hood serving a sentence for his own manslaughter rap. In a brutal episode, Farace had beaten a teenage boy to death after the teen tried to pick him up in a Greenwich Village bar. In prison, Farace bulked up in the weight room with the help of smuggled steroids. When another inmate threatened to drop a set of weights on Petrucelli's head, Farace intervened, saving the older inmate's life. After he was paroled in 1988, Farace started dealing drugs with a gang in Staten Island. When he desperately needed to hide after shooting the undercover agent, he sought out his old pal from prison for help. Petrucelli dispatched him to an upstate hideaway, a cabin in the woods where he could safely hide.

Al rightly shouldn't have had any involvement in what came next. Petrucelli was in Bobby Amuso's crew, so if he was breaking the rules by hiding a cop killer whose execution had been ordered by the mob, it was the Amuso brothers' problem. But Bobby Amuso was in bad shape, suffering from lung cancer. And in the late summer, after months of law enforcement harassment, Vic Amuso turned to Al when he found out one of his own men was hiding Farace. Al's pager buzzed while he was at the restaurant. He returned the call from one of the nearby pay phones.

Amuso sounded rattled. The police were all over him, he said. And he was furious about what he'd been told about Petrucelli. "He said I should reach out to Johnny Petrucelli and call him down. He said I should tell him to either kill Farace right away or else shoot himself."

Al was surprised at the note of panic in the boss's voice. But he quickly went to work leaving messages for Petrucelli to call him. By the time the call came in he was already out of patience. "You know who this is?" Al demanded. Petrucelli said he did.

"You've got to get down here right now," Al told him. Petrucelli started offering excuses why he couldn't make it. He didn't have a choice in the matter, Al said.

Petrucelli showed up a couple of hours later. They spoke briefly on the street; then Al took him down to the basement of La Donna Rosa. He didn't give Petrucelli a chance to argue. "You're pinched," Al told him. "Everybody knows you're hiding this guy out." Petrucelli didn't deny it.

He relayed Amuso's message. "He said you either shoot Farace right away, or shoot yourself." The body should be left in a place law enforcement would find it, Al added.

Petrucelli began to protest but Al interrupted him. "Are you listening to what I'm telling you?"

Petrucelli visibly sagged. "All right, all right," he said.

"If you want me to help you, I will," Al offered. "But it's gotta get done."

"No. I got him upstate in the woods. He sees anyone else he'll start shooting."

"Okay," Al said. "Just go do it." He watched as Petrucelli bolted up the stairs.

But Petrucelli couldn't bring himself to kill his friend. A couple of his own crew members were delivering food to the fugitive in his upstate hideaway, and he delegated the task to them. Farace, however, was already on full alert. The crew members reported back that the fugitive was heavily armed and extremely nervous. They couldn't make a move without a fight, they said.

Petrucelli relayed the situation to D'Arco. "I said, 'That's not good enough. This is not me talking, Johnny. This is the boss. You got to shoot Farace.' "

On another run upstate, the crew members couldn't even find the cop killer. He was hiding out in the woods someplace, they believed. "He's gone Rambo," they reported back.

A frustrated Petrucelli called another friend, a Luchese associate named Frank Gioia, to meet him for a drink. They met at a bar in Yonkers. Petrucelli told Gioia about Amuso's directive.

"Gus is a good guy," he moaned. "He doesn't deserve to die for this." He wondered aloud why the mob would do the government's work. "We're our own government," he said. "We shouldn't be doing this." He added that he was ready to kill both Amuso and Casso over the jam they'd put him in. He was the only one who could probably get close enough to kill his friend, he said. But he couldn't do it. "We were in prison together," he said. "We're too close."

Gioia offered to accompany the crew members upstate on their next groceries delivery and try the hit himself. Petrucelli was grateful. "If you get him," he told Gioia, "you have to shave him before you ditch the body. He's got a big beard and they've got to be able to recognize him."

At a supermarket on the way upstate, Gioia and the crew members stopped to buy groceries. As they left, he thought he spotted police surveillance. Spooked, he called off the operation and headed back to the city. By then, Petrucelli had run out of time.

Al got the call from Anthony Casso. "Gas said Vic and him wanted me to go up to the Bronx to see Mike Salerno, the captain up there. He said I should tell Salerno he wanted him to kill Johnny Petrucelli for refusing the order." Casso had further instructions: he said to be sure and tell Salerno to have a young associate named Joe Cosentino carry out the hit. Known as "Joey Blue Eyes," Cosentino was related to Tom Mix Santoro, the jailed-for-life former underboss of the family.

Michael Salerno was a veteran captain in the family's Bronx branch. He had been close to Christy Tick Furnari and had grown wealthy with a hefty portfolio of loans on the street. He lived in an upscale town in Westchester County, wore expensive jewelry, and drove luxury cars, a Jaguar and a Cadillac. His base of operations was a triangular brick building at the corner of Williamsbridge Road and Allerton Avenue in the northeast Bronx, where he ruled from a storefront under a sign reading "Larry's Tobacco and Candy."

Shorty DiPalo drove Al up. He met Salerno at the tobacco shop and the two of them took a walk around the corner. Al relayed the orders in the most formal terms he could summon. He lapsed into Italian to avoid naming Amuso and Casso.

"I said, 'Mike, your *rappresentanti* have sent me with this message. The *rappresentanti* want you to kill Johnny Petrucelli and to use Joey Blue Eyes on it.'"

Salerno looked at Al in alarm. Petrucelli's close ties to the Amuso brothers were well known. "Do you know what you're talking about, Al?" he said. "That's Vic's guy."

Al held up a hand. "Mike, I'm telling you the way they relayed it to me. This is what they want, and they want it right away."

Salerno just nodded. He spun around, walking quickly back toward the tobacco shop. Al followed behind, headed to where DiPalo was waiting. He looked up when he heard a car roar past. It was Mike Salerno in his Cadillac racing away.

A few days later, Al heard that Petrucelli had been killed. The hit had been a mess, however. Both shooters, Joey Cosentino and another member of Salerno's crew, Anthony Magana, had been caught.

On September 13, 1989, the killers had knocked on the

door of the apartment of Petrucelli's girlfriend in White Plains. When the man they were looking for answered, the gunmen fired. Wounded, Petrucelli staggered back to a bedroom where he had a rifle hidden, an M16. The shooters fled. Petrucelli made it out to the street, only to collapse in front of the building.

Out on the street, the gunmen panicked. Cosentino took off in a car, leaving Magana behind. Magana tried to walk away but was grabbed by police responding to the report of shots fired. Cosentino was arrested later.

Al got the details from Mike Salerno, who came down to Cleveland Place to see him. They walked up to the bank building at the corner of Spring Street to talk. There had been at least five witnesses, Salerno told him.

"Mike had the names of the witnesses. He said he'd already laid out $27,000 in expenses for lawyers for Cosentino and Magana. He said the killing had brought real heat. The cops were all over him, agents were on him all the time. He was very worried."

Al relayed the Bronx captain's concerns to Casso. The underboss wasn't sympathetic. "Tell him to lay out the money himself," said Casso. "Go tell him that for me."

Al drove back up to the Bronx. He found Salerno at an auto shop on Boston Post Road run by Joey Giampa, a member of Salerno's crew. "I told Mike what Gas had said about paying the lawyers' expenses himself. Mike didn't say a word. He just listened."

A few weeks after Petrucelli's execution, Farace was rubbed out as well. It wasn't the Luchese crews that got him. A trio of would-be mobsters from Farace's own Bonanno crime family looking to make a name for themselves caught up to him as he cruised through Bensonhurst, Brooklyn, in a van. Police initially had a hard time recognizing the most wanted man in New York behind his thick beard.

Frank Gioia, who knew Petrucelli could have saved his own life by going up to the woods to kill his friend, heard a rumor that bounced around in the days after the murders. It put a different spin on the deadly events. Vic Amuso, the rumor went, was seeing John Petrucelli's wife, the widow of the man he'd ordered killed.

Just four days after Petrucelli was gunned down, another murder prescription was filled. The Petrucelli killing had been spurred by panic, but it was presented as a bid to uphold Mafia rules and honor. There was no disguising this one. It was sparked by blatant self-interest on the part of the Luchese bosses. It was also premised on another lie.

In late June, the mobsters in the four crime families who had been sharing the glorious profits of replacing windows in low-income apartments got confirmation of what Casso and Amuso had warned them about two years earlier: Pete Savino was indeed a rat. He had been wearing a wire for the FBI for over a year, recording conversations with many of the key players in the scheme.

It was too late to do anything about Savino, already rushed into the witness protection program. But Amuso and Casso decided that as a precaution they should get rid of the next possible weak link.

John Morrissey was a business agent for Local 580 of the ornamental ironworkers union, whose members had installed most of the replacement windows. Morrissey was an old friend of Amuso, who had helped bring his pal into the fold. Known as "Sonny Blue," the ironworkers' leader had been an enthusiastic participant. Legitimate outside bidders got his warning that every window they installed would be smashed.

Savino had dealt closely with the union official, passing him regular payoffs. Amuso's assumption, given Savino's cooperation, was that some bribes had been monitored by the FBI. He was right about that. Agents had observed more than a dozen hand-to-hand payments from Savino to Sonny Blue. But nothing suggested that Morrissey, a tough Irishman, was cooperating with investigators. Amuso still decided to have his friend taken out.

The contract was passed by Casso to Pete Chiodo, the whale-sized capo, who was active in the construction industry and had worked with Morrissey. "Sonny's talking," Casso told him. He was to kill him and bury the body where it wouldn't be found. Chiodo, aware of the friendship between Amuso and the union man, expressed surprise.

Casso nodded. "Sonny was Vic's friend," he said with a sharp look at the captain. "Imagine what he'd do to you."

Chiodo contacted Morrissey. He told him that Amuso needed to see him to talk about Savino's cooperation. To put Morrissey at his ease, Chiodo brought along another Luchese associate, Thomas Carew, known as "Tommy Irish." They picked him up in Chiodo's wife's maroon Chrysler convertible. Chiodo drove with Carew seated next to him upfront. Morrissey sat in back. He seemed relaxed and pleased to be going to see his pal Vic.

They chatted on the way out to Morris County, New Jersey, where Chiodo was helping build a new housing development called Hidden Hills in Jefferson Township. It was about a fifty-mile drive. At one point Morrissey asked how long it was going to take. "We're almost there," Chiodo told him.

When they got to the development—a series of half-constructed homes around a man-made lake—another Chiodo associate, Richard Pagliarulo, welcomed them at the little model house used as an office by the developers. Chiodo said he would go find Vic and headed out the back door. As Morrissey turned to watch him go, Pagliarulo reached under a folded newspaper and pulled out a pistol with a silencer. The ironworker saw the move and instantly understood what was happening. He whirled around. Just as Pagliarulo fired, Morrissey shouted his innocence. "I'm not a rat!" he yelled.

Pagliarulo fired again but his pistol jammed. Morrissey lay writhing on the floor of the little office. He was trying to prop himself up on one arm. "It hurts," he said. "Finish me."

Carew had a backup gun he hadn't planned to use, since it didn't have a silencer. It was a five-shot snub-nosed revolver.

Carew fired four times. He stopped when Pagliarulo signaled him he had cleared the jam in his own pistol. Morrissey was flat on his back, making a low, moaning sound. Pagliarulo stepped in close. He fired once into his head at close range. Sonny Blue stopped moving.

Out back, another member of Chiodo's crew, Michael DeSantis, used a backhoe to dig a hole. He wasn't very good at it. He slashed a gash in a trailer home with the backhoe's bucket. The hole he dug was uneven, four feet deep at one end, two feet at the other. They carried Morrissey's body over anyway and threw it in. They took his wallet first.

In the car on the way back, they tore Morrissey's license and papers into pieces and let them flutter out the top of the convertible. Chiodo asked Carew if he thought that Morrissey really was a rat. Tommy Irish told him what the union official had shouted just as he was shot. Probably not, they decided. Still, even if he wasn't cooperating, they consoled themselves, they'd done their jobs.

That same summer the Luchese bosses switched their orders from retail to wholesale murder. The family's entire New Jersey faction should be wiped out, Amuso and Casso declared. There were at least a dozen members and associates in the group. "Kill them all, they're outlaws," Amuso shouted during a meeting with Casso and Al.

The immediate cause of his fury was the refusal of the crew's wealthy captain, a gangster named Anthony "Tumac" Accetturo, to agree to pass along a larger share of his earnings. Accetturo was "a rat," the bosses said. Their anger was compounded when the rest of the crew, terrified that they were being set up for their own slaughter, refused to show up at meetings to which they'd been summoned.

Al did his best to mediate, making a late-night visit to the home of a top crew member, Michael Perna, to encourage him to settle the problem. "Mike, nobody's here to hurt you," he shouted through the basement window as Perna fearfully peered out at him. Despite his appeals, the faction refused to comply, convinced that the Luchese chieftains would kill them at the first opportunity. Only luck and poor hunting skills on the part of the mobsters assigned to carry out the contracts kept the body count from growing.

* * *

That fall, the Luchese family leaders marked their harvest by inducting new members. The ceremony took place in November, just before Thanksgiving.

"We did it in the basement of Petey Vario's nephew's house in Canarsie." Amuso and Casso presided. Most of the family's captains were present, including Al, Sal Avellino, Pete Chiodo, and Bobby Amuso, despite his ill health. Anthony Baratta, a wealthy capo based in East Harlem, was present as well. Frank Lastorino, who was making his own small fortune handling Gaspipe Casso's end of a massive scheme orchestrated by Russian mobsters to steal gasoline taxes, also showed up.

Five soldiers were inducted. Included were two of those who had helped carry out the messy execution of Sonny Morrissey a few weeks earlier. Richie Pagliarulo, whose nickname was "the Toupe" pronounced "toop" for the hairpiece he wore to make himself look years younger, got his reward. So did Mike DeSantis, the fumbling backhoe operator.

Another inductee, Al noted with interest, was a sixty-one-year-old heroin dealer from Pleasant Avenue in East Harlem. Frank Federico had been around the Luchese family for years. Al had run into him a few times, including in prison. Thanks to his steady drug dealing, dating back to the 1960s, Federico had never been viewed as soldier material. Everyone called him "Frankie Pearl." He'd gone gray waiting to be made.

Al had never asked for details, but his understanding from Sal Avellino was that Frankie Pearl had been one of the gunmen who killed the two rebel carters on Long Island that summer. It was Federico who had suffered the deep gashes from Robert Kubecka's nails as he fought for life. The mob didn't give Purple Hearts. But it did award buttons.

Amuso, who had seemed so unsure of himself when he first took the reins of the family, was clearly enjoying being the boss. His nickname, when it was used, had always been "Little Vic." At five foot six, he was about an inch shorter than Al, who had long been stuck with the moniker "Little Al." That winter, Vic decided he wanted a new name. "He told us all he wants to be known as 'Jesse' from now on. Like Jesse James."

On the street, however, the bosses instructed their troops, names were to be omitted altogether. From now on, the Luchese leaders would be referred to in furtive gestures, the same way that Genovese members pointed to their chins when indicating their own boss, Gigante. Two fingers pointed up, forming a V, meant Vic Amuso. Flipped down, the same two fingers stood for Anthony Casso. Vic and Anthony. Mob sign language.

They altered their costumes as well. Amuso and Casso began dressing like outlaws of old, wearing long black leather coats reaching down to their heels. Amuso added a wide black fedora to his attire. "He looked like Al Pacino in *The Godfather*. Then I notice he's walking like him too, long strides, like he'd been practicing."

Anthony Casso had never lacked for self-assurance. But now he reveled in the riches that flowed his way as the number two leader of the family. He filled his house in Brooklyn's Bergen Beach with wide-screen televisions. He developed a taste for expensive wine. Visitors to his home were shown the jeroboam of rare champagne he'd purchased. He kept the huge vessel prominently in his living room nestled in a wooden holder, carefully tilted toward the cork.

He delighted in showing how little he cared about the cost. He bragged to Al how how he and his garment center adviser, Sidney Lieberman, had given a sommelier at an expensive restaurant a minor heart attack. "They were at the Forge, a high-class steakhouse in Miami. A lot of wiseguys went there. He calls over the wine steward and asks for the most expensive bottle, it's like $10,000. The wine guy is thrilled. But he says, 'You sure you want it? Because once we open it . . .' And Gaspipe says, 'Yeah, bring it up.' So he goes through the whole thing, and pours a glass. And Gas tells him, 'Bring me a Coke.' The wine guy says, 'You want a Coca-Cola?' Gas says, 'Yeah.' When the soda arrived, he poured it into the wine. The wine steward almost faints. Gas would crack up telling that story."

He also tolerated no slights, real or imagined. "I'm at his house for dinner one night and we're in this shed he's got in his backyard. And he shows me how his neighbor's yard was elevated above his. It made him nuts. The neighbor is standing right there above him on the other side of the fence. He says, 'I want to kill the guy. We'll get him over here and we can kill him right here in the shed.' Gas's wife, Lillian, was in the house cooking dinner, and he wants to kill the guy. I said, 'Let's think about it, Anthony.' The nut was ready to do it."

The underboss voiced even darker fantasies. "He had this plan, we were going to buy a house in Canarsie. He had it picked out, it was going to cost $70,000. He says it's got a big basement with a dining room table down there. He said, 'We're going to invite ten guys I hate for dinner, get them down there and kill them right before they eat.' "

Al listened. He had no idea if he was serious.

Late that year, the crime bosses in their long black coats expanded their reach by ordering a murder on the other side of the country. Anthony DiLapi, a union racketeer who led a small Teamsters local in the Bronx, had long been on their hit list. DiLapi was the fellow wiseguy who had feuded with Al at the Allenwood prison camp when Al had chided him for hanging around with an informant. DiLapi had fired back, threatening to use his connections to his uncle, then underboss Tom Mix Santoro, to have Al reprimanded or worse for his drug-dealing conviction.

Al wasn't fond of DiLapi, but he'd long ago put the fight at Allenwood in his rearview mirror. "To me it was forgotten about."

Amuso and Casso were less forgiving. What they wouldn't forget was that DiLapi was an ally of both Santoro and another member of the Bronx faction named Buddy Luongo, who had briefly been a leading candidate for boss. Santoro had been grooming Luongo for years to take over his rackets. He was a regular at meetings at the Santoro Beverage Company on Morris Park Avenue in the Bronx, where Tom Mix often held court.

The way Amuso and Casso told it, Luongo and DiLapi had been part of a plot by Tom Mix to seize power in the family in 1986. The plot was hatching just as Santoro and Tony Ducks Corallo were being convicted in federal court. But as Vic and Gas repeatedly told the story to Al, only fast footwork on their part had saved the day.

They first took care of Luongo. Claiming they needed to consult with him about an intra-crime-family dispute, Luongo was lured to the 19th Hole, the Bensonhurst bar. From there, he was coaxed to a nearby house owned by one of Amuso's pals. Amuso sat with him in the kitchen for a few minutes, chatting. Then he excused himself and went into a bedroom, where he retrieved a pistol with a silencer hidden under a pillow. He walked back into the kitchen and killed Luongo, forty-seven, with three shots to the head.

The body was buried someplace in Canarsie. Luongo's car was driven to Kennedy Airport and abandoned. He was another guy who must have run away with a girl.

But that was only one offender in what Amuso and Casso viewed as foul rebellion in their ranks. Another Bronx veteran, Mariano Macaluso, had been a member of the family for fifty years, growing wealthy from his own garment center holdings and other businesses. Macaluso had briefly served as acting consigliere for the family. But after Amuso took over, Macaluso, at age seventy, was summarily evicted from his post. "They gave him a choice: retire or die. So he went."

Next up was Anthony DiLapi. The new bosses summoned him to Brooklyn to account for all his holdings and activities. Having witnessed Macaluso's forced retirement, and how well Buddy Luongo had fared on his own visit to Brooklyn, DiLapi never showed up. Word soon filtered back that he had fled to California, saying he wanted to sever his ties to the crime family. Nothing doing, said Amuso and Casso.

They had been trying to locate him for two years when, in late summer of 1989, Amuso called Al to tell him he had a job and an address for him. The job was to snuff out DiLapi. He didn't want Al to do it himself. He wanted Joseph and two of the other new recruits to handle it.

The details were provided at a meeting at a popular Chinese restaurant called Joy Tang in a shopping mall off of Rockaway Parkway. "Gaspipe told me he wanted to send 'the kids' out to California. That's what he called Joseph, George Zappola, and George Conte. He had an address for Anthony DiLapi he said he got from his source. I asked him about expenses, and he said to take $10,000 out and give it to the kids. He said Pete the Killer's son Joey Abinanti was out there and that he'd help them get around."

Casso gave Al a handwritten piece of paper with a Los Angeles address. He said he'd gotten it from the cops, as he sometimes referred to his tipster. Al assumed anything Casso said about his precious law enforcement source was disinformation. "I figured he said things to throw you off."

The address was written in code, and Casso had to show Al how to puzzle it out.

If Al had major reservations about sending his son to a state with the death penalty still on the books to commit murder, he didn't show it. One good reason to get Joseph off the hook would have been to argue that he was on probation for the 1986 gun-possession rap.

For Joseph, that wasn't an obstacle, though. He was eager. He wanted to finally show what he could do. He and the two Georges boarded a flight to Los Angeles in the late fall of 1989. Airport screening was lax enough that Joseph was able to smuggle aboard a knife in his luggage. He figured that would be all he'd need for the job.

They got to L.A. to find the address was a bust. It led them to a used-car lot where DiLapi had once worked. He was long gone. They had a picture of him, but he was nowhere to be seen. They had a gun, thanks to a delivery from a Luchese member who drove in from Las Vegas. But they had no one to shoot. They were three young men in a city of 3.5 million people. None of them had ever been there before. They had no idea where to even look.

Joey Abinanti helped them out as best he could, giving them a place to stay. Joseph grew his hair long and let his beard grow out. He wrapped a bandanna around his head, affecting a motorcycle gang look as cover. The two Georges seemed more interested in the local bar scene. They went out to the beach and got tattoos at one of the joints on the boardwalk.

With no good leads, and no prospects of getting any, the hit team returned to New York. They ended up making three coast-to-coast trips in the quest to find their target. In January 1990, Casso's source came up with a new address. This one was for a mob-owned gay club called La Cage Aux Folles where DiLapi was supposed to be working. Joseph, figuring he was now on the right scent, rounded up a Luchese associate who specialized in stealing cars and brought him back with him to L.A. "He needed a couple of work cars, cars you steal for a hit that can't be traced back to you."

The second address was on the money. After a couple of nights staking out the club, they spotted DiLapi and followed him to his home in Hollywood. He lived in an apartment house complex with an underground garage where he parked his car. It was the likely spot for the hit.

Shortly after dawn on February 4, 1990, Joseph hitched a ride in the back of Zappola's car into the garage. He slid out the back door and waited behind DiLapi's automobile. He sat there in the dark watching the elevator entrance, waiting for his target to arrive. He got anxious as other residents came and went. When DiLapi finally appeared, he was carrying suit bags over his shoulder. Joseph jumped up, pointing his weapon. "Oh my God!" shouted DiLapi. He began to run.

Joseph steadied himself and fired twice. DiLapi fell. He shot him four more times as he lay on the ground. The escape wasn't perfect. As he was stepping into the getaway car, a man stared at him. Joseph pointed his gun and the witness fled.

Photos of the fifty-three-year-old used-car salesman slain gangland-style in a Hollywood garage showed DiLapi, his shirt riding high over his stomach, spread-eagled on the concrete floor, blood pooled bedside his head. He had several rumpled pieces of clothing next to him. His daughter, Mary Ann, explained that he was on his way to the dry cleaners when he was killed. She had talked to her father the day before on the phone. He was looking forward to seeing his new six-week-old grandson for the first time.

After the shooting, the killers split up. Conte and Zappola traveled back to New York separately. Joey Abinanti drove Joseph to Phoenix, where he caught a flight home.

Al drove out to Paerdegat Basin, a shorefront area of Canarsie where Joseph was living, to see his son and hear the story of his first murder. Now they were both killers.

Al went from there to Howard Beach to report in to Vic Amuso. He stopped a couple of blocks away and walked to the big split-level house. Vic was waiting for him.

"We went upstairs. Vic had this little den in his place and we talked up there. I gave him the report. He was pleased. He said the kids had done a good job but they should just be quiet about it, that they should never talk about it to anyone."

In the early spring of 1990, the one menacing cloud on the Luchese bosses' horizon was Pete Savino and the windows scam. By the time the crime families had pulled back, the racket had expanded far beyond the city Housing Authority projects. Every hotel, college, hospital, and high-rise apartment house ordering replacement windows had been a target. The profits had been immense. Now so was the threat.

There was no question in their minds that they would eventually be charged. Months earlier, on October 1, 1989, the *Daily News* had identified Savino as a cooperating witness in the case. Amuso and Casso were targets. The federal probe was being led by a pair of determined Brooklyn prosecutors named Gregory O'Connell and Charles Rose, along with Mario DiNatale from the federal Organized Crime Strike Force.

The Luchese bosses spent a lot of time trying to figure out who else, aside from the late Sonny Blue Morrissey, might present a problem as a potential witness should the case go to trial. Going down the long list of players, Amuso's finger stopped at a contractor named Mike Realmuto who had figured in several of the windows deals.

Al was called out to Cross Bay Boulevard to meet Amuso

at the office of Richie Oddo, the lawyer. They walked around the corner to Rico Place, the same spot where Vic had given Al his instructions about Red Gilmore. "He told me to get a team to kill this Mike. To get it done right away. That's all I knew, the name and that he had something to do with the windows business."

As a favor to Bruno Facciola, who was in bad health, Al assigned one of Bruno's brothers, Louis, to the hit. "I had promised Bruno when he got sick I would try and help his brother get straightened out. I said I'd do the best I could, so I figured having him on the job would help his chances." He also ordered Danny Cutaia, the crafty loan shark who handled Paul Vario's book of debts, to help.

The contractor's office was in Canarsie, so Al figured Cutaia and Facciola would know the territory. A few days later, Cutaia reported back to Al that they had waited near Realmuto's business, armed and ready to shoot, but that each time they'd seen the contractor he was with a woman. Al told them to keep at it.

The bosses were impatient, demanding to know what was taking so long. Casso told Al to meet him out on Canarsie Pier, a popular fishing spot that juts into Jamaica Bay at the foot of Rockaway Parkway. It also held a restaurant, Abbracciamento on the Pier, a favored meeting spot for wiseguys. Al had one of his drivers, Frank "Harpo" Trapani, take him there.

When they arrived, Casso was irate. "Gaspipe was yelling that Louie Facciola and Danny Cutaia were dogging it. He wanted to know how long is this going to take." Al also suspected that his men were less than committed to the assignment. But he defended his crew members to his mob superior. His defense was undermined when Louie Facciola came walking up. "He's got a fishing rod on his shoulder. I couldn't believe it. He's supposed to be out trying to hit a guy and this boob is going fishing." Casso shook his head in disbelief. Al laughed at himself. "I said, 'See how hard he's working?'" He then grabbed Facciola, warning him that he had one more chance.

On the drive back to the city, Al thought about how nervous and agitated the usually well-controlled Casso was behaving. The windows investigation must be pretty hot, he thought.

Two days later, the bosses made a complete reversal. "Vic beeps me and when I call him back he says to forget about that thing. He was telling me that the hit was off." When he saw Amuso the following day, the boss explained that the four crime families involved in the windows racket had held a council about how to cope with the investigation. "He said they were putting any hits on the side for the time being. They were worried that it would hurt them at bail hearings."

Except that Amuso and Casso were planning to skip any possible bail hearings. In fact, they had decided to skip town altogether when the windows indictments came down.

On the Sunday of Memorial Day weekend, Casso called Al and told him he needed to see him immediately. He said he'd be waiting for him by "the cannon." It was their shorthand name for the small park at the foot of Fort Hamilton Parkway in Bay Ridge beneath the soaring Verazzano-Narrows span to Staten Island. It was a convenient and quiet spot for sharing mob secrets.

Trapani drove Al out to Brooklyn. Al had him park a couple of blocks away and wait. He found Casso sitting on a park bench near a large antique cannon, a monument from the War of 1812 aimed at the nearby bay.

They walked through the park. "Gaspipe said the arrests were coming down in a couple of days and he was going on the lam. He said Vic was already gone."

Al wasn't surprised the bosses were going underground. The strategy was to stay away for a while and wait to see what the evidence in the case was and let things cool down. It was a tried and true Mafia tactic. But he wondered why Amuso had fled without giving Al a heads-up. "I said, 'What do you mean he already went? We were just together a few days ago and he didn't say anything. He didn't say good-bye.'"

"No, he took off," said Casso.

"What are you doing still here?" asked Al. "You'd better get out of here too."

"I've got time," answered Casso. "I've got a few things to do at my house tomorrow."

Al didn't understand. "How do you know they're not waiting for you at the house? You're going to be pinched. What's the difference you leave today or tomorrow?"

Casso repeated that he knew the timetable. "I've got time," he said again. His information was solid. His law enforcement source, he said, had let him know exactly when the arrests were coming down.

They kept walking, circling through the park back past the cannon. "I'll contact you through Georgie Neck," Casso said, using George Zappola's nickname. He had another instruction as well.

"Me and Vic want you to kill Mike," he said.

Al wasn't sure who he was talking about. Mike the contractor? Mike the capo? "Mike?" he asked. "Mike who?"

"Mike Salerno," said Casso. "He's a rat. We want you to do it right away."

Al was still confused. He considered Salerno, the Luchese captain in the Bronx, an old-school gangster, a family veteran and one of the least likely ever to turn. "*Mike's* a rat? Are you sure?" he said.

Casso had been talking quietly and calmly up until that point. But the question made him snap. "*I said he's a rat,*" he exploded, jabbing his finger at Al. "Me and Vic found out. You've got to do it right away," he repeated.

They walked a few paces in silence. Then Casso asked Al who he would use for the murder. Al's head was spinning. For a moment he couldn't remember anyone's name. Who should kill Mike? There was a right answer he knew, he just had to remember it. "Joey," he finally said, referring to the Bronx soldier whose auto shop on Boston Post Road had become a part-time headquarters for Salerno. "Joey Giampa knows Mike good. I'll use him."

Casso lurched again. "No!" he barked. "Don't trust that guy."

Al was now thoroughly baffled. "Don't trust him?" he said. He looked at Gaspipe, who was glowering, staring at the ground.

Then the underboss visibly relaxed, regaining his composure. "Okay," Casso said. "Okay. Whoever you trust, use them. Just make sure you do it right away."

Al promised to take care of it. Casso walked on, mentioning some other items that would need Al's attention. He stopped back by the cannon. "We'll be in touch," he said. "Only do the important things, don't bother with the small things. We'll see you."

Al looked and was surprised to see tears in Casso's eyes. The underboss was crying. He embraced Al in a hug. Al felt himself tearing up as well.

This is something, he thought, as he hugged him goodbye. Two wiseguys hugging and crying in a park.

Casso turned and walked away toward Fort Hamilton Parkway. Al saw him get into a car. He thought he saw George Conte, one of the kids who had flown out to Los Angeles with Joseph to kill Anthony DiLapi, at the wheel. Al walked in the other direction.

It sounded like he left me in control of things, he thought as he headed toward Harpo Trapani waiting patiently in his car.

14

FOSTER AVENUE

Three days after Anthony Casso's tearful good-bye at the little park beside the soaring bridge in Brooklyn, the arrests in what came to be known as "the Windows case" came down exactly as he said they would.

On the morning of Wednesday, May 30, 1990, federal agents and New York City police detectives fanned out across the metropolitan area to pick up fifteen defendants named in the indictment. Agents found the boss of the Genovese crime family, Vincent Gigante, in his eighty-eight-year-old mother's walk-up apartment on Sullivan Street, just down the block from his social club. Gigante was sixty-two years old. It was his first arrest since his 1959 heroin bust with Vito Genovese. The crime boss was wearing a pair of striped pajamas when the FBI arrived. Agents gave him a chance to put on some clothes. He mumbled, then pulled on a tattered, hooded bathrobe. Photos of him in his sleepwear and robe, agents on both sides, ran the next day around the world.

Two of Gigante's top captains dressed for the occasion. War hero Benny Eggs Mangano was arrested a few blocks away at his apartment on Charlton Street. Also picked up was Dominic "Baldy Dom" Canterino. The pair had handled day-to-day matters of the windows scam for Gigante, meeting frequently with Pete Savino.

Agents also grabbed Benedetto Aloi, the Colombo family consigliere who had helped dispose of Mike Pappadio's body after last summer's murder. Peter Gotti, John and Gene's older brother, who had started out as a city sanitation worker, was the main Gambino family figure on the indictment roster.

But some of the arresting officers returned empty-handed. Prosecutors said ironworkers union official Sonny Morrissey had escaped their dragnet. No one yet knew his body had been lying for months in the uneven hole out in Morris County.

Also missing in action were the men who gave the order to put him there. Vittorio Amuso and Anthony Casso were officially declared fugitives. But prosecutors had no doubts about their role. The absentee defendants were described as the Luchese crime family's top officials and instrumental in making payoffs to Morrissey and others.

Left holding the bag was Big Pete Chiodo, arrested at his home in Staten Island. Amuso and Casso had slipped out of town without letting their captain know the ax was about to fall.

The case was international news. Dick Thornburgh, the U.S. attorney general who had lost his race with the mob to see who could be the first to execute cop killer Gus Farace, showed up in Brooklyn for the press conference. Thornburgh hailed it as the most significant blow against the mob since the 1986 Commission case.

It was a good catch for the feds. But it had been an audacious crime by the mob. The windows racket was proof that the Mafia still had the reach and the muscle to dig deeply into the public purse. The decade-long scheme had succeeded in rigging $142 million in the Housing Authority's window-replacement contracts. Greg O'Connell, one of the Brooklyn federal prosecutors handling the case, estimated that the mob had reaped tens of millions of dollars from the caper.

Pete Savino's name wasn't mentioned in the indictment, but law enforcement sources told reporters that he was the mob turncoat who had helped make the charges by wearing a wire for eighteen months.

Gigante was held without bail. But it wasn't much of a punishment. He was allowed to spend the night at St. Vincent's Hospital in Harrison, New York, where his doctors said he had been receiving psychiatric treatment for the past twenty-four years. A few days later, a judge allowed him to go home to his mother. In court, Gigante's attorneys began a years-long effort to prove that the oddball godfather was mentally incompetent. His real punishment was having to think about how he had waved off Anthony Casso's information two years earlier that his friend Savino was cooperating.

The indictments were proof of something else as well: whoever he was, Gaspipe Casso's source was clearly close to the law enforcement center. As hard as it was for Al to accept that Michael Salerno had "gone bad," just like Pete Savino, he now set aside his doubts.

He would have arranged the execution regardless. It was one more distasteful chore demanded by the life he had chosen, to follow the orders of his appointed leaders irrespective of his own beliefs or wishes. It was "blood in, blood out," as he was fond of saying.

Designated hit man Joey Giampa, who had known Salerno most of his life, made the same leap of faith when Al relayed the order.

"I beeped him and had him come downtown. We walked over to the Bowery. I said, 'Joe, I'm going to tell you a few things you won't like to hear. I don't like to hear it myself. You're going to be shocked. But Mike is no good. He's a rat.'"

Giampa seemed as stunned as Al had been. But he made no protest. Al went on talking. "They want him killed, and you have to do it. You can use anyone you want to help."

Unlike Al, Giampa had a quick answer. "I don't trust anybody," he said. "Only my own blood. I'll use my brother, Jay." Joey and his older brother, Santo, often worked together.

Al nodded. He added an incentive. "They'll probably make you the captain after this," he said.

Giampa seemed to brighten. He started thinking aloud.

"I've got Mike's car in my garage for repairs right now," he said.

"Just do it right away," coaxed Al.

Joey Giampa had been another of those sitting in the crowded parlor in the house in the north Bronx with Al in August 1982 as they waited to have their fingers pricked in the Luchese initiation ceremony. Al hadn't had a lot to do with him since then. In addition to his auto body shop, Al knew that Giampa and his brother did an active business as loan sharks in the huge Hunts Point Market, the teeming city-owned produce terminal off the Bruckner Expressway in the southeast Bronx. He also knew that, of the two brothers, Joey was considered the tougher and more aggressive.

Al hadn't had much to do with Mike Salerno, either, aside from the Petrucelli hit and one other notable occasion. That was when Gaspipe Casso, furious that Salerno had sole control of a lucrative construction dump site in Pennsylvania, had used Al as a kind of bad cop to badger the senior Luchese captain.

Even then, Al had watched with admiration as the wealthy mobster tried to talk his way out of trouble. In gangster lingo, Salerno had been "banging down" his earnings from the dump, meaning he was hiding it from the family's administration, a potentially serious violation of the rules.

"He's supposed to report everything he's got going. But he's got this big dump, out in someplace called Matamoras, where they've got trucks dumping construction debris. It was making a lot of money and Gas was saying they didn't know anything about it."

Casso had Al drive out and take a look to see what was going on. After Al reported back that the place was humming with activity, Casso instructed him to tell Salerno to join them at a meeting at La Donna Rosa.

"Gas told me he wanted me to lay into Mike, give him a really hard time. I said, 'Mike's been around a long time. You really want me to go after him?' Gas said, 'Yeah, lay into him.'" At the meeting, Salerno insisted that the dump had always been on the record with the family, and that he'd been sharing its proceeds right along. "Mike kept saying, 'Trust me, trust me.'"

Al thought he was bluffing, but Casso listened quietly, nodding his head. "So I was the one had to say, 'Hey, Mike, they never knew. Why should they trust you? What were you thinking?' Gas just lay back and let me be the tough guy."

Casso resolved the problem by seizing most of the dump revenue for himself and Amuso. Al was instructed to drive back out to Matamoras and toss the dump supervisor, Salerno's nephew, off the site. "So I did. I chased Frank Salerno out of there and put Shorty DiPalo and Harpo Trapani on the job." Salerno's nephew gave him a hard look when he ordered him off the site.

"Don't stare so hard," Al told him. "You'll be part of the dump. You'll be staying here."

When he got a look at the books, Al realized why Casso had been so eager to take over. Some weeks, the dump was taking in more than $100,000 in fees.

Mike Salerno escaped any further punishment. Al thought that might have been because he remained a popular captain. Wise in the ways of mob moneymaking, Salerno, sixty-seven, had largely stayed out of trouble with the law. His rap sheet consisted only of a teenaged robbery conviction in the 1940s, and a weapons charge in 1963. "He was a smart guy, very well respected among all the families. He had a lot of class."

But Casso and Amuso made clear they had little use for him. "They were always knocking Mike. They said he was disappointed because he thought he should have been made part of the administration after Tony Ducks went to prison, that he was jealous that Vic and guys from Brooklyn were put in charge. They'd say, 'Keep your eye on him.'"

Al chalked it up to the same Bronx-Brooklyn factional fight that had already resulted in the slayings of two other Bronx veterans, Buddy Luongo and Anthony DiLapi, and the ouster of Mariano Macaluso. Salerno had to know he was on thin ice as well, Al figured. He still wondered if that wasn't the real reason behind the order to have the capo killed. It certainly made sense. With Gas and Vic on the run, they had to be worried that someone might stage a coup while they were away. A respected leader like Mike Salerno might actually pull it off.

He tried not to think about it too much while he waited to hear back from Joey Giampa.

He didn't have to wait long.

A few days after receiving his instructions, Giampa and his brother drove to Little Italy to see Al.

"I met him on Broome Street. We took the same walk we had before, over to the Bowery." Al stepped behind a large van parked along the curb, trying to stay out of sight of passing traffic. "Joe said it was done. He told me he had called Mike to the auto shop to see about his car. When he got there, he shot him through the heart. He said they put him in the trunk of his car. Mike was still making noises, he told me, so they stabbed him in the throat."

They walked back to where Jay Giampa was parked. Al reached in and patted the brother on the back. "You did good," Al said.

The news of the murder was relayed to the fugitive bosses via an elaborate communications system. "We had particular pay phones and these set times for calls. And each phone had a number. So the message would be 'Phone booth two, two o'clock,' and you'd go to that phone and wait for them to call."

The designated phone booth that day was out on Long Island, on Glen Cove Road and Northern Boulevard. When the phone rang, it was Casso on the line. Al gave him the report. "He said he was pleased, and so was Vic. But he wanted to know why Joey Giampa had stabbed Mike in the throat. He says, 'Was there some particular reason why he stabbed him like that? Is it some kind of message?'"

Al didn't understand the question. He repeated that Giampa had said Salerno had been making noise. Casso said he still wondered about it. "If you want me to check it out, I will," Al said.

"Yeah, find out, will you?" said Casso.

Al dutifully called Giampa and cryptically asked him about the grisly detail. "Like I said, he was making noise," Giampa told him. Al reported back to the underboss. "Okay," said Casso.

It wasn't the last time the bosses worried over the iconography of their murders. The symbolism of the killings, Al was soon to learn, was almost as important as the killings themselves.

It took police a week to find Mike Salerno's body. The Giampa brothers had driven his car to a quiet residential block of two-family brick homes in the Wakefield section of the north Bronx, near where Mike Salerno had once ruled supreme at his tobacco shop headquarters.

Al had never asked Joey Giampa which of Mike's cars they'd used. It was his black Jaguar, a sleek four-door sedan with wire rims and white leather interior. It was registered to his daughter, Julia. No one had reported it stolen. The Jaguar sat abandoned on the street for several days. Everyone left it alone. It clearly belonged to someone important. Then a neighbor washing his own nearby auto noticed the smell. There was also a long dark stain on the street where something had oozed from the back.

When the police popped the trunk they found Salerno's decomposing body. He was wearing a tan sports coat and had on gold chains, bracelets, and rings. This time, mob protocol had been followed. The Giampa brothers had left him his jewelry.

The same week he was conspiring to kill the respected mob captain in the Bronx, Al had to help cover up someone else's sloppy killing.

Even by mob standards, this one was brutal and unnecessary. Worse, it was a civilian casualty, someone with no links to the armies of organized crime. He had died only because he'd made the mistake of trying to make peace between a pair of pigheaded young gangsters having an argument. One of them had a gun.

The victim was Ernest Abdul Mateen, a father of nine. An auto mechanic and part-time boxing coach from Bedford-Stuyvesant, Mateen, forty-three, was a black man who belonged to a local Muslim mosque. On a late Friday afternoon after attending prayer services, he had driven his wife to the Brooklyn Terminal Market in Canarsie to buy fruit and vegetables for the weekend. They bought in bulk for their big family, which often brought them to the open-air market that catered to restaurants and hotels around the city.

Mateen paused at stall number 22, Mediterranean Food Distributors, to examine the vegetables. It was a shop that Al had inherited when he took over the Canarsie crew. He was using it as a source of supplies for his restaurant, and as a base for scams at the market, including making sure all the nearby shops had one of the Joker Poker machines that he and Joseph were supplying.

That Friday, Mateen got to the stall in time to encounter an angry argument between two men. One of them was Nicholas Facciolo. Despite the different spelling, he was Bruno Facciola's younger brother. "Bruno had three brothers and Nicky was the youngest. They called him 'Nicky No Socks,' and he often hung around the stall. He wasn't a kid, he was in his thirties. But he acted like one."

When Mateen happened upon the argument between Nicky No Socks and Anthony Falsone, a part-time helper at the stand, it was getting physical. Mateen worked with youngsters who often wanted to settle things with their hands. He had trained his son, Ernest Jr., well enough to have won the *Daily News*'s Golden Gloves light heavyweight boxing championship the past two years in a row.

Mateen stepped between the two men. Facciolo pulled out a .22. He fired at Falsone. The bullet glanced off his elbow. Another shot caught Mateen square in the chest.

The boxing coach staggered to a nearby stall. The owner told him to sit down. "Help me," the coach said. He died before the ambulance arrived.

When police asked for witnesses, market workers went mum. The listed owner of the stall was a vendor named Anthony Fraggetta. His street name was "Tony Potatoes," and he owed loan shark debts to both Nicky No Socks and his brother Bruno. Fraggetta drove Falsone to Brookdale Hospital with his wounded wing. Tony Potatoes later claimed he didn't even know there was another shooting victim. He must have missed it because of his glaucoma and blurred vision, he told a *New York Times* reporter.

Falsone also initially declined to talk. Detectives eventually coaxed a name from him. Nicky No Socks. Except that Nicky Facciolo was nowhere to be found.

By the time the problem was presented to Al, the shooting had become a citywide incident. There were protest marches outside the market by members of Mateen's mosque denouncing the refusal of the shopkeepers to talk. Mayor David Dinkins was demanding to know when the DA was going to charge a suspect.

Bruno Facciola and his brother Louie came to see Al at La Donna Rosa. They conferred on the sidewalk in front of the pastry shop next door.

"I told them to hide that asshole brother of theirs, keep him out of sight. The mayor was getting involved. It was getting hot. We didn't need that nonsense. There was a stool pigeon in the market had given up Nicky's name. But if they couldn't find him, there was nothing they could do."

It was the same tactic the Luchese bosses were using. Stay out of sight until the heat dies down. It worked like a charm for Nicky Facciolo. He stayed on the run for eight years until he was arrested in a Queens pool hall in 1997. Convicted of manslaughter, he won a new trial on appeal. At his retrial, this time just on gun-possession charges, the man he'd been trying to kill in the first place, Anthony Falsone, suddenly had no memory of the incident. As he testified, Louis Facciola sat in court watching. Nicky No Socks won acquittal.

Ernest Mateen Jr. didn't allow his father's senseless murder to knock him off the tracks. He went on to win the light heavyweight title of the World Boxing Organization in 1995. "He was a nice, quiet kid," said Bill Farrell, a veteran reporter who ran the *News*'s Golden Gloves contests. Nicky No Socks's niece Carla won her own fame. She starred as one of the miniskirted young women in the VH1 reality show *Mob Wives*.

The other victim of the Luchese family's steadily increasing body count that spring was another civilian, but this one was hardly an innocent.

James Bishop had been the leader of the city's unionized painters for years. He was a burly ex-Marine from Queens who had won a Bronze Star in Korea. He had come home to get a job painting bridges, dangling dangerously high above the city's waters. A savvy backslapper, Bishop had risen in his union's ranks to become secretary-treasurer of District Council 9 of the International Brotherhood of Painters and Allied Trades. With six thousand members it was the city's third-largest construction union. Bishop's gift for politics also won him a slot as a local Democratic Party leader.

In his union post, he dangled just as dangerously as he did from the bridges. He was a regular visitor to Luchese consigliere Christy Tick Furnari's back room at the 19th Hole in Bensonhurst. There, the mobster gamed out bid-rigging schemes on public works projects, pitting Bishop's union against city painting contractors. It was the model later adopted by the windows racketeers.

In 1978, Bishop put himself even deeper in the mob's debt. His international union, weary of corrupt hijinks under Bishop's watch, appointed an outside trustee to step in and run things. Bishop asked Furnari to chase the trustee out of town. Big Pete Chiodo got the assignment. Along with two pals, Chiodo waylaid the trustee when he arrived at the union's West Fourteenth Street headquarters at six thirty in the morning. Beaten savagely with metal pipes, trustee Frank Wolford was hospitalized for three months. He left town as soon as he could.

But when Vic Amuso and Anthony Casso took over the Luchese family, Jimmy Bishop became one more redundant holdover from the old regime. They were much more taken with other family associates deeply embedded in the painters union. One was a wealthy former union official turned contractor named Frank Arnold. When Furnari was arrested in 1985 in the Commission case, Arnold had put up his $1.75 million mansion in Sands Point on Long Island's North Shore to get Christy Tick out on bail.

Another Arnold intimate was Leona Helmsley, feisty wife of New York real estate titan Harry Helmsley, whose empire was in need of endless coats of paint. Leona, dubbed the "Queen of Mean" by employees, got along so well with Arnold that she made him executor of her husband's will. Arnold made money even before the painters went to work. He had a deal with a Brooklyn paint supplier that earned the Luchese family a dollar for each gallon sold. Between his paint rake-offs and contract schemes, Arnold brought in $350,000 a year to the family, Casso told Al.

Bishop was indelicately pushed aside. Via Big Pete Chiodo, a message was passed to him that his grandchildren's lives would be in danger if he didn't step down. He quickly resigned his union post.

The ex-Marine's opportunity for payback came when the Manhattan district attorney's office and federal labor investigators began probing the union's mob schemes. Slowly, offering teasing morsels at first, he began to talk. Soon he was a full-fledged cooperator, testifying at a grand jury.

He was compromised almost immediately. Casso's well-wired law enforcement source soon passed word to the mob bosses that they had their own major leak.

Shortly before Casso and Amuso went into hiding, Al met with Gaspipe, Chiodo, and other Luchese members in a small room above a luncheonette at the corner of Utica and Flatlands Avenues. "Gaspipe had this piece of paper with the names of all the big painting contractors. He said Jimmy Bishop was cooperating. He said he was also worried that Frankie Arnold could go the same way."

Casso began to rant, like an emperor watching his kingdom spiral out of control. "Fuck Frankie Arnold and fuck James Bishop!" he yelled.

Al thought both men weren't long for this world. But Arnold's vast wealth bought him some extra time. Bishop's had already run out. Casso ordered Chiodo to scout out Bishop's daily routine. Al was told to retrieve three pistols armed with silencers that he had been given months earlier to hide for safekeeping. Jimmy McCann, Amuso's faithful assistant who had rescued Al in his daze after the murder of Mike Pappadio, came by to collect the weapons.

On the morning of May 17, 1990, the married Bishop was relaxing at the pool with his girlfriend at her apartment complex in Whitestone, Queens, overlooking the Throgs Neck Bridge. When he came out to get in his gray Lincoln Town Car, a hit team was waiting. Georgie Neck Zappola was the shooter. As Bishop climbed behind the wheel, Zappola stepped up and shot him with a .380 semiautomatic Beretta, one of the guns Al had kept stowed away for just such an occasion.

"I hit him ten times," Georgie Neck later boasted to his pal Joseph D'Arco. Despite the salvo of bullets, Bishop managed to throw his car into gear. The Lincoln rolled 150 feet before slamming into a fence.

The brazen daytime murder of a cooperating witness shocked even the veteran investigators chasing the painters union racketeers. Several suspects, including Pete Chiodo, were rounded up a day later. Manhattan DA Robert Morgenthau vowed to bring justice to Bishop's killers. At that point, no one imagined that law enforcement itself was a big part of the problem.

Two months after the bosses fled, Al had his first secret meeting with the men in hiding. The location was Dom Truscello's suburban home in Wayne, New Jersey. "Dom had a nice big house with a bar downstairs so that's where we had the first meet." Truscello was nervous about it, but he instructed his wife and family to be away that evening. "We were all

worried. Anything that happened, if we got found out and anyone got pinched, they're going to say it's our fault."

The bosses showed up unshaven, with two months of
beard, their faces hidden beneath baseball caps. As a business meeting, it was uneventful. The bosses ran through a
checklist of each captain's responsibilities. Amuso said they
were giving Joey Giampa the captain's post that had been held
by Mike Salerno. A $20,000 loan shark debt that Giampa had
owed to the veteran mobster was also wiped off the books.
Giampa's murder of his former friend had turned into a beneficial enterprise. Al was told to make sure they stayed on top
of the rest of the debtors in Salerno's sizable book of loans.
All of that money belonged to the bosses now, they decreed.

At the close of the meeting, everyone embraced, and then
the bosses left together, driving away in a black Jeep registered in Truscello's name.

Just a couple of weeks after the meeting in New Jersey,
Al was told that another message was coming in for him. The
designated phone booth was near the *New York Post*'s offices
on South Street, by Knickerbocker Village. The caller again
was Casso. "He is telling me he wants me to come out and
see them again, this time in Pennsylvania, near Scranton. He
wanted me to get an untraceable car and drive out there alone.
That I should stay at a motel down there."

The trip was complicated for Al. He didn't have a current
driver's license. He had let his license lapse since he was out
on parole. Any minor driving infraction, he feared, might
result in his being sent back to do the ten years he would
owe if he was found to have violated parole rules.

But he didn't argue. He got a car from another Luchese
associate and met George Zappola on Canal Street. Georgie
Neck gave him driving directions to where he was supposed
to go in Pennsylvania.

"I went up there at night, through the mountains. I'm
looking in the rearview mirror the whole way for cops."

He put up as ordered at a small motel called the Victoria.
The next morning he drove to his rendezvous spot, a supermarket parking lot. He sat there for an hour, waiting. "Then

I see this Jeep headed my way. It's Gaspipe. He had a full beard already."

Casso gestured for him to follow. They drove a couple of miles before the Jeep turned down a tree-lined street. Al saw Vic Amuso standing in front of a small house. His beard had grown in as well. It was the same color as his hair, a dark steel gray.

Al accomplished a big part of his mission right away. He had $50,000 cash with him that he had been told to collect from various Luchese family operations. He handed the envelope to Vic, who accepted it without a word. He also had a message for them from the Genovese captains who had already faced the music in the Windows case. "Benny Eggs Mangano was saying that each of the families involved was going to chip in $50,000 to hire an investigator to come up with evidence they'd need for the defense. He wanted Vic and Gas to join."

Amuso said they weren't interested. "He said to tell them they'd hire their own investigator. If their guy came up with anything useful, they'd pass it on."

During the discussion of the Windows case, Casso turned to Amuso. "We got rid of Sonny. What about Cakes?" he said. Amuso just stared back at his underboss, not saying anything.

Al wasn't sure who Sonny was, but he recognized the name "Cakes." It was the nickname for a Luchese associate named Joe Marion, a close pal of Amuso's who had been arrested in the windows scam.

Al acted like he hadn't heard. He broke the silence by asking how long they intended to stay on the run. Vic said the plan was to wait until the other defendants went to trial. "They figured that the evidence against them wasn't that great and they didn't want to be painted with the same brush as the others. They wanted to go to trial alone."

The three men talked for a while about John Gotti. The Gambino boss had been all over TV for months since his acquittal in the state case for attempted murder against the mobbed-up carpenters union official. His lawyer, Bruce Cutler, readily granted interviews lauding his client. Footage of

Gotti and his clique sauntering down Mulberry Street was a staple of the nightly news shows.

The Luchese bosses had plenty of time to watch TV from their hideouts, and the sight of Gotti's victory smile had reminded them of a long-unfulfilled pledge. The murder of Paul Castellano had been carried out without Commission approval. It was supposed to have resulted in a death sentence for Gotti. But aside from a 1986 car bombing that killed Frank DeCicco, Gotti's number two lieutenant, the other families had failed to make good on their vow.

At one point, Al had been asked to research bomb techniques with his contacts in Pittsburgh, where bombings were a frequent tool. "Vic said the plan was to make it look like the greaseballs from Sicily did it." An associate of Joe Sica was capable and willing to rig a deadly remote-controlled bomb. Al had reported back what he'd found out, but nothing ever came of it. The plot seemed to fall through the cracks. The mobsters in hiding were left glaring at their rival on television, unable to wipe the smile off his face.

What they could do, however, was eliminate their own internal enemies. And that list was growing.

A few weeks after his solo trip over the mountains to Scranton, Al was again summoned to one of the pay phones to get Casso's latest instructions. The message, delivered in mid-August, was that the bosses had discovered yet another rat in their ranks who needed to be exterminated. The offender this time was a man who had become one of Al's closest friends in his Canarsie crew, Bruno Facciola.

Al listened, dumbstruck at the pronouncement. Gaspipe presented it as something that had to be done for Al's own protection. Casso said that his law enforcement source had found out that California cops looking into Anthony DiLapi's murder had turned up a nickname of someone involved. The nickname, he said, was "Little Al."

"Who calls you Little Al?" asked Gaspipe. "Doesn't Bruno call you that all the time?"

Al had to admit that yes, Bruno called him that. A lot of

people did, but Bruno especially. He turned the idea over in his head. Unlike most of his crew, Bruno had never done time. He had prospered almost unmolested in his crime zone outside the Canarsie market. He was one of the the biggest loan sharks in east Brooklyn. He owned a demolition yard, a jewelry store, a riding stable, a restaurant, and who knew what else. Al went through the same dizzying see-saw of pros and cons that he'd wrestled with when Casso had told him about Mike Salerno's alleged infidelity to Cosa Nostra.

Unlike Salerno, whom he knew and admired mostly from afar, he knew Bruno well. "We treated each other like brothers. Our families got together. We ate together a lot." Part of the reason for the meals was Facciola's cooking. "His father was a fisherman, and Bruno knew his fish. I helped him remodel part of the pizza parlor, and afterward, he made this feast for us. He had the whole family, Dolores's father, the kids, to the restaurant and he cooked this big fish dinner."

He was also a commanding presence, a good-looking man with a full head of dark brown hair; people were drawn to him. He didn't have much education. Al suspected he couldn't really read or write. But he was the center of the action. His club at the industrial junction of Foster Avenue and Avenue D by the produce market was in a plain stucco-covered storefront with blacked-out windows, a few tables, and an espresso machine. But it was more than just a mob hangout. It was the main social center for men in the neighborhood with cash in their pockets. Its marathon card games were legendary, drawing players from around the city, including legitimate businessmen. Games would start on a Friday night and go all weekend. Players would go home, take a shower, and come back. Those who won weren't allowed to leave until they lost a few hands.

Al wasn't a card player but he enjoyed sitting around the club. You never knew who was going to turn up there.

In the early 1980s he had been sitting at a table with Bruno's brothers, Nicky and Louie, when a businessman from the neighborhood joined them.

"The guy's name was Schultz and he was often in the club

playing cards. He was a friend of Bruno's. His business was selling coffee filters. His biggest customer was Macy's. He had the downstairs store, where they sold the kitchenware. He said he had just come back from the West Coast, from Seattle, because he said there were these guys out there with two little coffee shops who were buying twenty times the amount of filters that Macy's was using. So he says, 'I had to go out there and see what this was all about.' And he said he went out there and they had these two little stores called 'Starbucks.' And he said him and his *landsmen* were putting up the money to buy the stores and expand."

The story appealed to Al's business sense. "I told him 'Good luck with it.' I should've asked if he wanted a partner." Starbucks owner Howard Schultz was raised in Canarsie, but a spokeswoman said he didn't have time to talk about any visits he might have made to social clubs in the old neighborhood.

Al and Bruno had even done a rare good deed together. They had been standing one afternoon outside the pizza parlor on Flatlands Avenue when a crowd of rowdy teenagers rushed into the street to surround a taxicab. "The driver was a black guy and they were shouting about him being in the neighborhood. They yanked him out of the cab and into the street and were beating on him and taking his money."

Al and Bruno ran over to pull the kids off the driver. "We were kicking at them, telling them to get the hell off the guy. Then Bruno yells, 'Watch out, Al, he's got a knife!' I spin around and there's this kid about to stab me. I knock the knife out of his hand and he took off." The rest of the attackers fled as well. The driver was helped back into his cab and drove away. A few minutes later a police squad car arrived. "They all knew Bruno at the precinct. The cop says, 'What's going on?' Bruno just shrugs. 'Nothing, far as we know.'"

In the past year, Facciola had been struck with cancer. He had lost most of his stomach to an operation. Al had visited his friend at home after the surgery. He often checked in on him to see how he was doing.

Despite his illness, Facciola remained a power to be reckoned with. "He had about twenty stickup guys around him, tough guys who knew how to take care of themselves." There was Ray Argentina with his fondness for guns and executions. Larry Taylor was a thief rumored to have killed a jewelry salesman whose wares he coveted. Facciola's brother-in-law, Al Visconti, known to all as "Flounderhead" for his awkward toupee, was another faithful follower.

Al wondered if maybe that was the real reason Bruno was now the next to go. Like Salerno, he was capable of pulling together a cadre of loyal and deadly shooters to challenge the absentee bosses and their own troops.

But his doubts were again trounced by the irrefutable accuracy of Casso's source. The windows indictments had come down exactly when he'd said. Jimmy Bishop had been a snitch. It was in the papers right after he was killed.

And Al remembered something else that had been nagging at him. A few weeks earlier, he and Bruno had again been on the sidewalk in front of the pizza parlor. Al had gone outside to help chase away a group of junkies who congregated on the corner. As he watched the junkies retreat, Al saw something out of the corner of his eye. It was Bruno making a chopping motion behind Al's back. "It was like a sign he was going to get me. I just caught it. When I looked at him he looked away. Afterward, I was thinking that Bruno can be devious, that I'd better watch him."

Now here was Casso confirming that vague suspicion, telling him he had to kill an old friend, a man who had saved him from being stabbed in the back. And the underboss again had specific instructions for the murder.

"Gas said that Vic wanted me to use Louie Daidone and Frank Lastorino, tell them they were supposed to be a team." And there was something else as well. "He says they should get a canary and put it in his mouth after they kill him. And to make sure he was found that way so everyone knew he was singing."

Al listened to his instructions. Symbols were important to them, he remembered.

* * *

He called Louis Daidone as soon as Casso hung up. He was at his bagel store in Howard Beach. They arranged to meet at the Seaview Diner on Rockaway Parkway, near the Canarsie Pier.

"We went for a walk. I told Louie he should get together with Frank Lastorino and make a plan." He also told him about the canary. Daidone listened. Louie Bagels went even further back with Facciola than Al. Bruno had been a Luchese soldier for more than twenty years, long before Casso and Amuso had received their buttons.

"I don't believe it," said Daidone. "I don't believe he's a rat."

Al didn't try to convince him. "They want it done," he said. It was the only argument that mattered. They needed a code word for Facciola. "Call him 'the Wing,'" Al said.

Daidone called Al later that day to confirm that he'd spoken to Lastorino. They had a plan, he said. There was something odd, Daidone added. Casso had called Lastorino separately, he told Al. "He already knew he was going to do it with me," he said.

A few days later, Daidone called again. The Wing had been dispatched. Al went out to Cross Bay Boulevard to get the details.

The dodge had been to tell Facciola that Daidone needed him to make a formal introduction to another wiseguy with whom he was dealing. Al was surprised that Bruno would fall for the bait. He had apparently not suspected anything until the last moment.

On the morning of August 24, 1990, Bruno drove to his own funeral. He picked up Daidone in his car and then followed his directions to a garage on McDonald Avenue in Brooklyn where Daidone said the meeting with the wiseguy was to take place. As they walked to the garage, Facciola began to sense something was wrong. "He was hanging back, he let Louie go in front of him."

When the door opened, Facciola saw Lastorino. Richard "Richie the Toupe" Pagliarulo, who had shot Sonny Morrissey, was standing behind him. Facciola realized what was happening.

Facciola bolted. "He made a run for it. Louie chased him. He used to play college football and he's pretty athletic. He ran out and tackled Bruno right in the street. He got all banged up doing it."

Facciola, weakened from his cancer operation, wasn't much of a match.

Daidone dragged Bruno back into the garage. Two men nearby stopped to gape at the fight. They didn't interfere. Inside the garage, Bruno cried out. "He was saying, 'Louie, let me see my daughter again. Let me go home one time.'"

They knocked him to the ground. Daidone held him down. Frank Lastorino had a knife. He stabbed him. The killers said that Facciola cried out in pain, begging to be shot. Pagliarulo stepped forward and obliged him, firing six shots into his head and chest.

Al listened to the cruel tale without flinching. "You're lucky the shots didn't bounce back at you," he said. "If it's concrete, the ricochet can kill you."

After Facciola was dead the killers rifled his pockets. Not for cash or jewelry, but for any evidence of his possible cooperation, another Casso order. They found no telltale notes. They took a small red Swiss Army knife that Bruno always carried as evidence that they had carried out their task. His body was dumped in the trunk of his 1985 Mercury sedan. Then they followed Casso's other command. Daidone had purchased a canary and killed it. He had kept it in his home freezer until he was ready. The little bird was stuffed into Facciola's mouth. The car was abandoned on a block on East Fifty-Fifth Street in Canarsie.

Like Mike Salerno's Jaguar, no one bothered the abandoned Mercury for almost a week, until the stench became noticeable.

A couple of days after his brother disappeared, Louie Facciola and a friend showed up at Daidone's bagel store. Facciola came walking slowly toward Daidone, his hand in his back pocket. Daidone spooked. He thought he was reaching for a gun. He dove to the ground. The men left without incident. Daidone made a panicked call to Al.

"They know, they know," he told him.

"Okay," said Al. "We'll handle it." He contacted Danny Cutaia and got a pistol. The two of them went to see Louie Facciola. They met at an auto lot on Utica Avenue. Al greeted Facciola. "I said, 'Louie, let's take a walk.'"

They walked down an alley alongside the car lot. "Louie, you know, things happen," Al told him. Both men knew what he was talking about. "I don't know what you're doing, but what have you got on your mind?"

Facciola didn't seem to know what to say. "I know, I know," he stammered. "It's nothing, nothing. Forget it."

"You're sure, Louie?"

"Yeah, I'm sure," he said.

But only his brothers cared. To the rest of the world, Bruno Facciola was just another mobster found in a trunk. No one had put together the pieces yet, or noticed that one more victim had run afoul of the new Luchese bosses, the ninth person to have vanished or been killed in the past eighteen months. Michael Pappadio and Sonny Morrissey were still just mysterious disappearances. Only the dramatic assassinations of the rebel carters and Jimmy Bishop had commanded any attention, and even that soon flickered away.

Part of the reason was that law enforcement was busy elsewhere. John Gotti and the nightly conventions at his Ravenite clubhouse on Mulberry Street remained the most intense focus of the media, and the FBI. Watching the comings and goings from the brick tenement, agents had figured out where to place their bugs. They had captured Gotti clearly on tape, conducting what he thought were secret strategy sessions in an upstairs apartment. Gotti had beaten the law three times in court. They now believed they had enough to put him away permanently.

Casso's crystal ball relayed word in early December 1990 that Gotti's arrest was imminent. Despite the less than warm relations between the families, the Luchese bosses tried to warn him. It wasn't completely altruistic. If they were ever going to kill Gotti, it would be easier to do so if he wasn't in prison.

Al was told to get hold of John Gammarano, the Gambino family veteran he had served time with at Lewisburg federal prison. "Johnny G was dealing with the labor-racketeering and Wall Street scams. He hung out in a bar in downtown Manhattan, Giovanni's Atrium on Rector Street. I went down there to tell him that Gaspipe had a message for Johnny Gotti, that he got information from the bulls that the pinch was going to come down and that they should take off."

Al found Gammarano in the restaurant. The two men walked out through the kitchen to West Street. "I told him, 'Anthony said to go now. Not to wait.' "

Gammarano seemed unconcerned. "He said John already knew, that he had his own thing going."

A few days later, on the early evening of December 11, agents arrested Gotti and his two top aides, Sammy Bull Gravano and Frank LoCascio, as they sat in the Ravenite. It was Gotti's last evening as a free man.

That same week, Al was summoned to another meeting with the fugitive Luchese leaders. The message was relayed through Patty Testa, whose brother Joey had been initiated as a soldier the same day as Joe D'Arco. Patty Testa owned a couple of Brooklyn car dealerships and had supplied the Jeeps that Amuso and Casso were using. He'd also taken on the role of messenger for the boss-in-hiding.

They spent a couple of hours driving through Brooklyn in Testa's Cadillac. "We were dry-cleaning ourselves, making sure no one could tail us." Testa finally parked on a street in Canarsie near an auto body shop on Farragut Road. The home belonged to Testa's elderly relatives. They were glad to have him and his friends enjoy their furnished basement. Testa told Al to wait in the car, then walked across the street to a small house. He reemerged about ten minutes later, beckoning Al inside.

"Don't make any noise," Testa whispered. He led him down a hallway to an entrance to the basement. Amuso and Casso were waiting downstairs.

The bosses still had their full beards. They did a run-through of family business. Al had another $60,000 for them. The money was still in Christmas wrapping paper, the same way it had been handed over by the construction executive who made regular payoffs to the family.

For a pair of men who had been in hiding for more than six months, the bosses seemed happy and upbeat. "They said they wanted me to throw a big Christmas party for the family. That I should spend what I had to, to make sure everyone knew we were doing good and still holding together."

The Luchese Christmas party was an annual tradition. They were lavish, spare-no-expense affairs, held at restaurants owned by members or friends. Tables loaded with lobster, shrimp, steak, and pasta were pushed together in the center of the room. It was too crowded for anything but buffet-style dining.

It was made members-only, a kind of meet and greet for the family's branches and crews. Everyone came, even the far-flung members from Las Vegas and the West Coast. Only the hosts, the two bosses, were expected to miss the party.

Al would have held it at La Donna Rosa. But it wasn't big enough. "It was also too hot, there were too many agents around."

But Al had a new restaurant he was helping to launch on Horatio Street on the far West Side in Greenwich Village. It was being run by his son John, along with a Chinese chef he'd met. The idea was Al's. "Everyone loves Italian and Chinese food, so I said let's put them together in one place." It was called Pasquale & Wong's. A wealthy Greek contractor from Astoria named George Kalaitzis who worked closely with Casso was the up-front owner of the place and was investing most of the money.

"I had one of our guys, Fat Mikey, get these rolls of green sparkling paper and put it over the windows so you couldn't see who was inside the place. Then we put up a big sign saying, 'Welcome Mediterranean Fruit Buyers.' That was our cover in case anyone asked what the party was for."

On the night of the event, Al had several associates serve as running valets. "Soon as guys would pull up in their cars, we'd drive them a few blocks away so no one could spot all the plate numbers."

Al cleared a special table for the family's old-timers. "They said it was the first time they'd been treated like that in years. Everyone was hugging each other. We had champagne all over the place."

Al interrupted the festivities to make a toast. "We tapped the glasses. *Bing, bing, bing.* I said, 'Merry Christmas to everybody, and let's not forget our friends who couldn't attend, you know? We wish them and their families a very merry Christmas.'" The room rang with cheers and applause.

The party broke up not long after midnight. "It didn't go late. It was just holiday spirit, that was the idea."

Within weeks, the absentee hosts were issuing orders to kill some of their yuletide guests.

A few days after New Year's, Al was called back to the home of Patty Testa's elderly relatives. It was snowing when Testa picked him up. Again, they carefully trawled the Brooklyn streets for surveillance before pulling up to the small home in Canarsie.

Downstairs, Casso and Amuso were seated at a table. There was a bottle of wine and several glasses in front of them. Casso spoke first. "Vic wants to tell you something," he said.

Amuso looked at Al. "You're now the acting boss of the family," said Vic. He reached for the wine and filled the glasses.

"*Cent'anni,*" said Vic.

"*Cent'anni,*" answered Al. They should live a hundred years. He wasn't sure what else to say.

"Just take care of the major things," said Amuso. "Let the little things go, and be careful." Then the boss added a restriction. "There'll be none of this," he said, pinching his finger. "And none of this." He pointed his index finger at him, thumb raised, like cocking a gun.

Al understood the sign language. No making new members. No killings, without higher approval.

Al was to keep things running, to be their eyes and ears. No one spelled it out, but it was clear they were satisfied with the way he had handled things so far. He had successfully helped dispatch five of their targets. He was already sitting in for them at meetings with other families.

He was also under no illusions. He had been Amuso's choice for the job, not Casso's. Vic was still grateful for past favors. His help back at Sing Sing when they were both starting out. His pep talks when Vic first took over the Luchese reins.

But he wasn't to run things alone. They had designated a full cabinet of acting officers to carry on in their stead. Anthony Baratta, the captain from East Harlem, would be acting underboss. Steve Crea, a soldier based in Yonkers and active in construction rackets, was acting consigliere.

Al was friendly with Crea, a good-looking man with gray hair and a massive chin who managed to make millions with his building firms while keeping a low mob profile. But he wasn't happy about having Baratta, known as "Bowat," as his number two. It was an old beef. "Paulie Vario told me Bowat hung with stool pigeons in Lewisburg. He had all these fancy airs about him, but his big thing was pushing *babania*." Baratta owned a swank restaurant on the Upper East Side. He also had a regular table at Rao's, the East Harlem restaurant on Pleasant Avenue that was now a chic dining spot for movie stars and politicians despite its longtime use as a hangout for the heroin dealers who had poisoned the city. Most of Baratta's crew members were actively dealing drugs. Al knew that Casso had done deals with him in the past as well.

"Nobody likes that fucking guy," Al told Amuso when Casso briefly left the room.

Amuso shrugged. "That's Anthony's guy," he said.

While they were talking Baratta arrived, escorted by

George Zappola. Amuso did the formal introductions, certifying Al's new rank. Baratta clapped Al on the back, congratulating him.

Al had another thick package of cash for the bosses, some of it Christmas gifts from the crews. Casso had asked for a breakdown. "He wanted to know who was giving what, to make sure he wasn't being shorted."

Al kept the itemized list in his own shorthand code, scratched out in tiny script as though it would make it harder for an outsider to decipher. He noted dates and figures. "$6,700 Bronx Lux," he wrote, signifying cash received from a Bronx home builder under Luchese protection. "John G. 3-way split" was Gambino capo John Gammarano, who worked closely on construction scams with the Luchese clan.

The payments ranged from $3,000 from a lawyer handling a Long Island Teamsters local, to $57,000 from the family's New Jersey faction, despite the ongoing feud. There were payments from trucking firms, contractors, and garment manufacturers. Altogether, the month's package came to more than $200,000.

Outside it was still snowing when they left. Baratta said good night and got into his small black Mercedes coupe with Zappola. Al crossed over to Testa's Cadillac. They chatted on the way back to the city. But Al's mind was racing. He couldn't resist the thought: What would Jimmy Alto say if he could see me now?

He wasn't sure what his own father would have said. It wasn't something they ever talked about. Even if the tough old bareknuckle prizefighter had asked, he couldn't have discussed it, any more than he could with any outsider. "He knew what I was. He knew that life. I didn't have to spell it out."

The old man was long retired, living in the cottage in Bayville on Long Island's North Shore with Al's mother. But Al had less and less time for family visits.

A few days after he was promoted, he had an urgent call from Joseph. Al's father had suffered a stroke. He'd been taken to the hospital. Joseph volunteered to go out to see them. Al thanked his son, and said he and Dolores would get there as soon as they could.

He raced out to Long Island, a couple of bodyguards alongside. He sat with his father for as long as he could before he had to go back to the city.

On January 25, 1991, his father suffered a second stroke. This one was fatal. His grandson and namesake was beside his hospital bed, along with Al's mother, when he went. The former Giuseppe D'Arco was eighty-one years old. He was a few weeks short of celebrating the seventy-seventh anniversary of the day he'd climbed off the SS *Verona* from Naples at Ellis Island clutching his mother's hand. He had captured every immigrant's goal, the American dream. His son was a big success in his chosen field.

15

MATAMORAS

What Al would have told his father, if he could have, was that he was now the acting chief executive of a heavily diversified, multimillion-dollar organization.

The core operations of the Luchese crime family remained gambling, loan-sharking, extortion, and theft. But beyond those mob staples, its business interests were wide and varied. They included air freight firms, bakeries, funeral parlors, roofing companies, car dealerships, building contractors, concrete suppliers, construction unions, produce vendors, and the garment shops that had been the cornerstone of the first semilegitimate fortune of the *borgata*'s founding fathers.

It was the job of acting boss Al D'Arco to see that all of those interests were protected, and to make sure that all revenues due and owing were collected. The job kept him busy.

He had considerable experience already with one of the family's top clients. In 1988, Amuso had asked Al to take on the task of stopping by the sprawling yards of the Quadrozzi Concrete Corporation near Jamaica Bay in Far Rockaway, Queens, to see the owner, John Quadrozzi.

The family's relationship with the firm went back to 1964 when Frank Manzo, the same Frank the Wop who had tried to block Al from becoming a Luchese soldier, had signed up the company. The Luchese family provided ongoing protection from other crime families and agreements with the various construction unions to give the firm operating leeway. It also promoted his product, pressuring other contractors to buy from him.

In exchange, Quadrozzi had agreed to monthly cash payments. By 1991, the tab was running at $20,000 per month, plus two bulk payments of $125,000 per year for extracurricular favors rendered.

Quadrozzi was sixty-two, a big gruff man with a brush mustache who spoke his mind. Al came to like him, often stopping by just to chat. "He was a good guy. I'd go into his office and he had one of those big brown leather doctor's satchels filled with cash. Always right there with him. When he opened it, you'd see it was filled to the top."

One reason for having all the cash around, Al learned, was that on Saturdays Quadrozzi offered a special cash-only discount on his concrete. "It was normally about $62 a yard, but on Saturdays he'd let you have it for $54 cash. The trucks would line up to get it."

The first time Al saw the bulging bag he asked Quadrozzi if he feared being robbed. The businessman grinned and pulled a pistol from the baggy pants he often wore. The two executives enjoyed discussing firearms.

"He was this big collector of rare shotguns. He collected this brand, Purdeys. If he heard about a Purdey shotgun for sale on the other side of the country, he'd fly out there to buy it. And those things went for $50,000."

The concrete supplier kept careful track of his payoffs. "He had a green ledger book he kept in a desk drawer. He'd pay me and then pull it out and write down the number in pencil in the book right in front of me."

Quadrozzi had prospered under the arrangement. He was the owner of ten separate companies and was president of a citywide trade group representing fellow suppliers, the Association of New York City Concrete Producers. His concrete was used for the city's largest projects, including massive sewage-treatment plants and the Cross Bay Bridge that his trucks traveled from the Rockaways to Queens.

His biggest coup was a con he pulled on the federal mob busters themselves. In 1990, Quadrozzi applied to purchase two concrete companies that had been seized by the federal government after they were found in the Commission case to be assets of the Genovese crime family. Potential purchasers had to undergo rigorous screening. After an investigation, then Manhattan U.S. attorney Otto Obermaier vouched to the court overseeing the sale that Quadrozzi was a legitimate businessman with no mob ties. He recommended that his purchase be approved.

But even as the review of Quadrozzi's records was under way in one room, Al was collecting the family's tribute next door. "I showed up one day and John tells me to keep quiet because Obermaier's guys are in the next room. He says, 'Don't let them see you.' "

Sometimes, Al served as Quadrozzi's bill collector. When another concrete firm that purchased its supply from Quadrozzi's yards fell $40,000 behind in payments, Al ordered the owner to show up in Little Italy with the cash.

Likewise, he went to bat for the company when firms with their own mob backers tried to underbid it. "There was this company Valente Concrete that was undercutting our company with their prices on all the jobs. The owner was with the Gambino family and the family out in Jersey, the DeCavalcante crew." The complaint was registered with the other families. When the price-cutting continued, the Luchese family threatened to up the ante. "We talked about killing Valente. But we worked it out."

Other times, he was a labor arbitrator. "I had to straighten out matters with the unions sometimes. The engineers would want three guys on a crane. So I'd have to convince them he was someone who deserved a break."

Al also assisted Quadrozzi with the union that represented his drivers, Teamsters Local 282. "When John bought the new companies from the government he didn't want all the workers in the union. So I went to see Johnny Gammarano from the Gambino family, which had the local, to straighten things out."

Local 282 was a sore subject with the Luchese family. It wielded enormous power over the construction industry, since its members drove the trucks delivering materials to building sites. The slightest slowdown on their part quickly disrupted production. Local 282 president Bobby Sasso was another visitor to Quadrozzi's office in Far Rockaway, with payments to the Teamsters leader noted in the ledger next to the initials "BS." The local had been under Luchese family control until Tommy Brown Luchese's daughter married Carlo Gambino's son. "Tommy Luchese gave the local to the Gambino family as a wedding present. He shouldn't have done that."

But the Luchese family had plenty of labor clout of its own. There were more than twenty union locals the family considered as its own property. They were off-limits to other crime groups, and their officers were subject to Luchese approval or veto.

"We had a lot of Teamster locals because Tony Ducks Corallo and Johnny Dio were close to Jimmy Hoffa. Back in the fifties, Hoffa gave them a bunch of union charters so he could control the votes on the Teamsters Joint Council."

Some locals were small but useful. Gerald Corallo, Tony Ducks's son, ran a Teamsters local representing employees at car dealerships. Once much larger, Local 239 had become essentially an insurance scam. Many members were the dealers themselves and their families, receiving Teamster health and pension benefits even though they were employers. It was a blatant violation of federal labor laws, but until a court-appointed union monitor stopped it, the scam ran for years. It was also a useful dodge for mobsters. "Jerry Corallo was the guy to see if you needed to put someone on the books who needed their medical, or who had to show they were working for parole. He'd get them a ghost job, then split the paycheck with them."

The most powerful Teamster unions in the Luchese portfolio represented workers at Kennedy Airport. Teamsters Local 295 had the truckers and warehouse workers. A separate union, Local 851, had airport clerical employees. Both were run by Luchese soldiers.

The family's stake in the airports stemmed from Paul Vario's tenacious claim struck in the 1960s. While members of Vario's crew like Jimmy Burke were hijacking their trucks, they had also moved in on the association of air freight companies created by the farsighted Hickey DiLorenzo while the Genovese mobster was still in full command of his faculties.

Overseeing the family's airport interests was Anthony Calagna, a gambler and horse racing enthusiast who had been inducted as a soldier in 1988 at the same ceremony as Joseph D'Arco. Calagna served as the top official of Local 295. Local 851 was run by Patrick Dellorusso, Louis Daidone's bagel business partner and a member of the hit team that took out Tommy Red Gilmore.

They were running a profitable empire. When Al was told to start collecting the payoffs, the monthly nut from various shakedowns ranged from $12,000 to $60,000, depending on the volume of business.

The Luchese family had been running the airport so long that it had its honored traditions. Negotiations were held at the Sherwood Diner on Rockaway Turnpike just east of the airport where the Canarsie crew had convened for planning meetings since the 1960s.

Some discussions got complicated. A major city freight firm called P. Chimento Trucking had long been under the protection of Pete DeFeo, the veteran Genovese capo from Little Italy. But when Chimento branched out to trucking at the airport, the Luchese family asserted its rights.

"Anthony Calagna and Patty Dellorusso came to me and said Chimento is running fifty trucks out there, doing a lot of airport work they shouldn't be doing unless they had a contract with our unions." The trucks were running out of a depot, or "barn" as truckers called it, near the airport. Calagna had offered the company a sweetheart deal covering only some of its employees, but it had refused to pay.

Al discussed the matter with Genovese leader Jimmy Ida,

without resolving the problem. After consulting with Amuso and Casso, Al decided negotiations had gone long enough.

"I told Anthony and Patty to put a strike on them. Just go down to their barn and block up all their trucks." The picket lines went up the same day. The brief show of labor muscle quickly resolved the matter.

"They settled. They agreed to pay $110,000." The only remaining hitch was that the company president said he needed help hiding the payoff in his books. Again, the Luchese racketeering network obliged. "We had him hire George the Greek's contracting company to do a little bit of work on the roof of his barn. That way they could pad the bill and draw the cash." Contractor George Kalaitzis got to keep $10,000 for his trouble. The rest went to the Luchese bosses.

The family also had a firm grip on an international air cargo firm called Amerford International Corporation that made regular payments for labor peace. It also put the mobsters' children on the payroll. Al's daughter, Dawn, worked there, as did a daughter of Sal Avellino.

Amerford officials sought an extra favor, asking Calagna to be allowed to replace their unionized clerical workforce with a nonunion subcontractor. Calagna relayed the message and the Luchese bosses said they'd be willing to oblige, for a price. The move saved the firm several hundred thousand dollars a year, and the initial payment Al saw was $100,000. There was more promised down the road. After the deal was cut, the company put thirty union members out on the street. When they complained to their union local, the leaders shrugged. There was nothing they could do, they said.

A few months later, Amerford hired a new director of labor relations. It was Luchese soldier Patrick Dellorusso.

At this point in his career, Al was something of a specialist at labor racketeering. His apprenticeship under Benny Ross and Lou Rich in the 1970s had taught him the art of winning sweetheart contracts, the careful mix of intimidation and financial persuasion required to get employers to sign with outfits that were unions in name only. The employees were usually the easy part. Shops tended to have a high turnover of low-paid workers either unaware of their rights, or fearful of asserting them.

The unions in the Luchese family's orbit operated on a much more sophisticated scale. Many were construction locals, divisions of the Laborers union whose members poured concrete, handled blasting and excavation, built roads, laid bricks, and hefted supplies around the work site.

These weren't the craftsmen of the construction trades. The Genovese family held the most sway with those unions, including the carpenters, plumbers, and engineers. But the laborers also enjoyed strong contracts with good wages and benefits, as long as they were enforced. Union officials also did well, commanding six-figure salaries, cars, and usually unlimited expense accounts.

The trick for the mob was to find the maneuvering room to arrange for favored employers to ignore the contract when it suited them. The scam was usually accomplished with newly hired workers paid less than union scale, or forced to work without overtime or paid benefits.

"The contractor wants to beat the workers. So he pays off the family-controlled unions to put nonunion guys on the job, or to skip on some of the benefits he's supposed to pay. He takes care of us and he's got no worries. He's got labor peace."

The other trick was to make sure schemes didn't collide with other crime families, each of which had its own satellites of construction unions and companies. Conflicts often arose.

In 1988, Al came up with an innovative management plan. Instead of obligating the bosses to sit down and hash out every jurisdictional dispute, why not designate crime family members with labor expertise to sit on a panel? It would be the Mafia's version of the National Labor Relations Board.

"There were too many fights, too many guys getting hurt. The idea was to settle things before they got out of control." The bosses liked it. In addition to himself, Al recommended

Dom Truscello, who was well versed in construction, and Steve Crea, who had his own contracting companies, as Luchese representatives.

The panel worked well. But sometimes conflict couldn't be avoided. In 1989, federal prosecutors in Brooklyn won a racketeering conviction against one of Paul Vario's nephews who had been serving as business manager of Local 46, a Queens-based Laborers local. The national union responded by placing the local under trusteeship. But the reform simply replaced one crime family with another. The new officers included close allies of the Genovese crime family.

Al registered the complaint. "They were trying to take over our local and we weren't going to let them." The matter was discussed at a series of meetings at the Elizabeth Street social club of James Messera, a Genovese captain.

The talks, however, failed. The clash escalated. "These guys were burning out the union. They were calling strikes and shaking guys down. They were out of control." Things came to a head at a sit-down at Little Charlie's, a clam bar on Kenmare Street around the corner from La Donna Rosa.

"It was me and Dom Truscello on our side, and Jimmy from Elizabeth Street and Jimmy Ida for the Chin. Later, Petey Vario showed up too."

The meeting got hot. At one point, Messera claimed that the local official now backed by the Luchese crew couldn't be trusted. "They wouldn't back down. They wanted us to pull out, keep their guys in control."

Al brought the matter to Gaspipe Casso. "He says, 'Hit them. Give them a good beating.'" The order was handed to Peter Vario for execution.

"Rugsy and one of his pals grabbed this guy Eddie and another guy who was with the Genovese crew from the local at gunpoint. They took them out and gave them a beating with ax handles. They put them in the hospital."

The would-be reformers limped away, ceding the local back to the Luchese family.

* * *

Violence was the core organizing principle for every business move the crime family made. Sometimes the mere threat was enough to accomplish the goal.

In 1989, a top official of a Teamsters local representing produce market workers committed suicide after being summoned to a sit-down with Luchese members. Edward Gallant was secretary-treasurer of Local 202, most of whose members worked for fruit and vegetable vendors at the Hunts Point Market in the Bronx. The union was briefly the focus of a dispute between the Luchese and Bonanno families as to which crime family was going to run it.

Al relayed the message that Local 202 was Luchese family property via Joey Giampa, head of the family's Bronx crew thanks to his murder of Mike Salerno, and Teamsters official Anthony Calagna, who knew most of those involved. Giampa already had a fearsome reputation in the market as a tough loan shark to cash-needy merchants. He welcomed the opportunity to expand his territory.

But at the time, no one was planning on hurting anyone. Al said his orders were clear: "I said to remind the union guys that they have a nice job with a nice expense account. Just remember the union don't belong to them."

Gallant had started out as a produce worker, and he had long bragged about his own mob ties. But after being summoned by the Luchese mobsters, Gallant told fellow local officer Warren Ullrich that he was terrified. "He said it was a fight among crime families and he was afraid he was going to be killed," Ullrich later told a *Daily News* reporter. "He shot himself. It was the day before Thanksgiving."

Ullrich's father, Charles, had been head of the local for twenty-five years before him. His dad had his own friends in the mob, including Tony Ducks Corallo. In 1955, when the union and vendors were still at the old Washington Market in lower Manhattan, two men entered Charles Ullrich's office and beat him savagely with pipes. The episode was seared in Warren's childhood memory, as was his father's insistence on remaining in his job after the beating. The son convinced himself that he too could ride out the storm. Even after losing an election to a new slate of officers, Ullrich kept visiting the market, hoping for a comeback.

This time, there was sentiment in the Luchese family for more than a beating. "Joey Giampa was telling me this guy Ullrich was going around the market saying he was still in control and he was making his own deals. He wanted to kill him."

Al decided that with Ullrich out of office there was no point, and it was not worth the risk. "I told him no. It would create all kinds of heat."

But Giampa persisted. "Joey comes back with this Ullrich's home address in New Jersey and says he wants to hit him. I said, 'No. If you want to give him a good beating you can.'"

Word of the threats reached the FBI. Ullrich got a knock on his door just as he was leaving his home in northern New Jersey to take his son to football practice. "It was the FBI. They said there was a contract to have me killed." The message was received. He didn't go back to the market after that.

There was one union that the Luchese family had claimed as its own for more than fifty years, but which was always difficult to tame. The Newspaper and Mail Deliverers Union represented delivery drivers at all of New York's big daily newspapers, as well as major magazine-distribution firms. But the union was always on the verge of mob-fueled chaos because so many members were themselves associates of organized crime. On every newspaper loading platform, drivers ran scams ranging from stolen bundles of papers to loansharking and gun sales.

It was an independent union with three thousand dues-paying members. At one point in the 1980s the Teamsters, its ranks replete with mobsters, contemplated affiliating with it. They decided against it. The NMDU was too mobbed up even for them, officials decided.

The Luchese claim to the union had originally been won through a wily mob associate named Irving Bitz. Known as "Itsy Bitsy," he had been a gunman for Lucky Luciano in his youth and was a prime suspect in the murder of bootlegger

Legs Diamond. He later graduated into high mob finance. In the newspaper-distribution business, he played both sides of the labor and management divide, arranging generous contracts for the union in exchange for bribes and timely loans to newspaper executives facing a cash crunch.

Itsy Bitsy was still going strong at age seventy-eight, the owner of two major news-delivery firms, when he disappeared in 1981. His body washed up on a Long Island beach a few weeks later. He'd been strangled, police said.

One of Bitz's protégés was the former president of the newspaper deliverers union, a fast-talking charmer named Douglas LaChance. Even after he was convicted in 1980 of selling out his own members by secretly dealing newspapers during a lengthy strike, LaChance remained a popular figure in his union.

When Al took over as acting boss, one of the management decisions he faced was what to do about him. The union leader was considered unruly and prone to cutting his own side deals without letting his mob chaperones know what he was up to.

LaChance had long been close to the DiPalermo brothers, who had multiple relatives on the payrolls at city newspapers. Al viewed him with skepticism. "He was close to Petey Beck. Then when Petey died, he was with Joe Beck. But he was always fooling around. Me and Vic talked about having to kill him one day because he was impossible to control."

Despite his past racketeering conviction, LaChance ran for reelection as president of his union in 1991. Al was leery of him. "The guy was still on parole but they let him run. What if he was a government agent?" He ordered Luchese members to steer clear of him.

But LaChance's opponent in the race was a Bonanno crime family associate. And whatever misgivings the Luchese bosses had, keeping the union in the family fold was important. It was a useful place for jobs for members and associates, and for shakedowns of businesses.

LaChance won reelection, celebrating his victory with a party at Forlini's, a restaurant on the edge of Chinatown and a favorite with both wiseguys and prosecutors from the nearby district attorney's office. Al dispatched Dom Truscello, whose son was a driver and member, and Anthony Tortorello, an old friend of LaChance's, to the party.

The Luchese men got there just in time. At the bar when they walked in LaChance was being toasted by a top Genovese family member named Ross Gangi, who had brought along other Genovese associates to add their congratulations. "They were making a play for him to come over with them and leave the Luchese family. Torty and Dom took him on the side and reminded him he was with us and he'd better remember it."

As tempting as it sometimes was, not killing people, Al understood, was usually the wiser business decision. The best example was a wealthy construction contractor named Joseph Martinelli.

An impressive figure with a shock of white hair and a wide mustache, Martinelli earned his way onto the Luchese hit list in 1989 when he started bucking Vic Amuso's demands for payoffs. Martinelli headed one of the city's largest concrete firms, Northberry Concrete. He had poured foundations for the Dag Hammarskjöld Plaza at the United Nations and hospital expansions on the Upper East Side. His firm was even tapped to help build the new federal district courthouse on Pearl Street behind Foley Square.

A major part of Martinelli's success stemmed from his membership in a mob-orchestrated bid-rigging club that divvied up all city jobs valued over $2 million. The result, lawsuits filed by state and federal prosecutors in the 1980s found, was that the price for each project was hiked up to 15 percent. That cost was then passed along to the public. It was one of the reasons New York City had the highest concrete costs in the nation.

Martinelli had forged his original pact with Christy Tick Furnari, who had helped send work his way in exchange for an annual payment of $100,000. That pledge fell by the wayside, however, when Amuso and Casso took over. The new bosses insisted on the payoffs, but neglected to forward any job referrals. The contractor resented being taken for granted. He stopped paying.

Amuso was furious. He designated both Al and Pete Chiodo to take care of it. "I made a meeting with Martinelli and Pete. I said, 'Look, you're getting all the benefits. We're protecting you.' I told him he was taking advantage of Vic's friendship." Al left the meeting thinking Martinelli had grudgingly agreed to go along. But a few days later, Amuso paged him.

"It was a Sunday and Vic was blowing his fuse. He said some guys in a Jeep had pulled up in front of his house in Howard Beach screaming his name and waving shotguns. They scared his wife and family. Vic said it was Martinelli. He said he was going to have him killed. He said he'd told Chiodo to take care of it."

The rebellion alone was intolerable to the Luchese leaders. Squashing it quickly became more important than any income they would forfeit from the contractor's demise.

Amuso and Casso hounded Chiodo to get the job done. But Martinelli proved evasive. At a meeting at a car wash on Flatlands Avenue shortly before Casso went on the lam, Al watched as Casso laced into Chiodo for the delay. "He says, 'Joe Martinelli is going to die of old age the rate you're going.'"

Chiodo finally took the direct approach. In the spring of 1990, he called Martinelli and told him that both Casso and Gambino underboss Salvatore "Sammy Bull" Gravano needed to see him over a complaint that had been lodged against Northberry. To his surprise, the contractor agreed to come.

Chiodo arranged to meet him near a video store in Staten Island. He put a gun in his pocket and instructed Richard Pagliarulo to follow behind from a safe distance in his car. Martinelli arrived in a Lincoln Town Car. Chiodo lowered his huge bulk into the passenger seat and directed the contractor to a secluded area in the wetlands of the island's South Beach section. When Chiodo saw that Pagliarulo was behind them, he told Martinelli to pull over.

They were in the middle of nowhere. Chiodo pulled

himself out of the car, telling Martinelli he'd take a look to see if Casso and Gravano were coming. Standing by the car, he reached into his jacket, pulled out a 9 mm pistol, and bent down to the open passenger-door window. Aiming at Martinelli's head, he squeezed the trigger four or five times. The gun only clicked.

"What are you doing?" yelled Martinelli, his face gone white.

Chiodo tried to laugh. "It's a toy pistol," he said. "I took it from my son because it looked too real."

Martinelli shook his head. "It does look real," he agreed. They sat in the car for a few more minutes until Chiodo said he'd better see what was keeping Casso and Gravano. They drove to a pay phone, where he pretended to make a call. "They spotted a tail—they're not coming," he said. Martinelli seemed relieved the meeting was off.

He dropped Chiodo back at the video store. When Pagliarulo pulled up, they drove back to the wetlands and inspected the gun. It had misfired because Chiodo hadn't pushed the magazine into place. Chiodo was embarrassed. Pagliarulo, whose own gun had jammed when he had shot ironworkers union leader Sonny Morrissey, reassured him. "Don't worry," said the loyal soldier. "I won't ever tell."

The contract on Martinelli was still in place when Al was designated acting boss. But Amuso and Casso were no longer asking about him, and Al had no interest in enforcing it. More important, Martinelli, thankfully still breathing, had gone back to making regular payoffs of $50,000 every few months. Handing the money to Amuso and Casso, Al explained where it had come from. "You'd think they would've said, 'Gee, good thing we didn't kill him.' But they never said a word about it."

Cooler heads also prevailed in an angry three-way dispute between crime families over the rights to a developer tapped by the City of New York to build affordable housing. The builder was a Pennsylvania-based firm called DeLuxe Homes, selected because its prefabricated town house-style units were cheaper and quicker to produce.

Designated to build in housing-needy neighborhoods around the city, the company encountered a different crime family at each location.

In the Bronx, Luchese member Steve Crea, a practiced contractor himself, was close to DeLuxe's superintendent, who agreed to funnel payoffs in exchange for mob favors. In Williamsburg, Brooklyn, where two-family homes were designated for a stretch of Kent Avenue near Al's old stomping grounds, Gambino underboss Sammy "the Bull" Gravano stepped forward with offers of protection and help. In Coney Island, where acres had been leveled for urban renewal since Al and Dolores had celebrated their wedding at Villa Joe's, a local associate of the Genovese family named Bartolomeo Nicholo, known on the street as "Barry Nickels," asserted his own rights to the firm.

Each family offered its own brand of the same package: relaxed union rules in exchange for cash and the use of mob-controlled subcontractors.

In Coney Island, Barry Nickels employed a well-practiced mob tool to get the builder's attention. He directed a local group of black construction workers demanding jobs to lay siege to the project. The group was one of many rogue off-shoots of a civil rights effort to integrate the construction trades. In the name of seeking minority jobs, so-called coalitions used violence and threats to win payoffs and no-show slots. It was a minor-league version of the Mafia's own hustle. Vincent DiNapoli, the Genovese family's creative construction expert, had been the first to recognize the coalitions as useful cat's-paws against developers hesitant to play ball.

Nickels's agent for harassing DeLuxe was a group called Akbar's Community Service, considered by police to be one of the most violent of the coalitions. It was headed by a former leader of a Brownsville street gang called the Tomahawks. Since then Derrick Ford, who grew up with boxer Mike Tyson, had morphed into Akbar Allah. He sported a gold front tooth with a large letter A stamped on it. At Nickels's urging, he sent his troops surging onto DeLuxe's job sites, doing his best to disrupt the project. "Yeah, we worked with Barry," Allah later told a reporter. "Sammy Bull too. We helped each other."

When a truck from the Luchese favorite, Quadrozzi Concrete, showed up to pour a foundation for DeLuxe, Barry Nickels personally showed up waving a pistol to chase away the driver.

After word of the confrontation reached Al, he convened a summit. In his view, Nickels had crossed the line. "You never pull a gun on a driver. He's got nothing to do with it. You can get killed for that."

An initial meeting in late 1990 was held at the 19th Hole in Bensonhurst. A tentative settlement called for Crea's superintendent to remain on the job, with the Gambino and Genovese families calling the shots. The Luchese crew got work for some of its subcontractors, plus a onetime payment of $550,000 to walk away from the company.

But the money wasn't forthcoming. A second meeting was called by Gravano, this one at Gargiulo's, the Coney Island restaurant where Amuso and Casso had reminded Al that his newly made son owed them greater allegiance than he owed his own father.

Al was suspicious. Coney Island was Gravano's home turf. His own construction company was not far away on Stillwell Avenue. "We heard Sammy had some of his shooters on standby in the neighborhood." As a countermove, Al had Joseph and another half dozen Luchese members and associates arrayed outside, armed with pistols and automatic weapons.

Al's suspicions increased when Gravano failed to arrive on time. Instead, John Gammarano, the Gambino family's delegate to the construction panel, showed up alone. "Johnny G showed up and said Sammy had seen heat in the neighborhood and wasn't coming." In a back room at the restaurant, Gammarano gave Al a peace offering, an envelope with $30,000.

The rest of the money, Gammarano pledged, would be coming shortly. But a few weeks after the near clash, Gravano and John Gotti Sr. were arrested. Payments slowed to a trickle. "They were paying in dribs and drabs. I was continually in conflict with them."

The one area of the construction business where the mob's talents were most in demand, even by otherwise law-abiding builders, was getting rid of the trash. What to do with work site debris was always a major challenge. Builders were knee-deep in it from the moment the job began. First, tons of rubble from the old structure had to be hauled away. That was followed by a steady stream of waste as the new building rose in its place. It was an especially tough problem during New York's massive building boom in the late 1980s and early 1990s, as new rules about how and where construction and demolition debris—C and D in the trade—could be dumped.

The nearest legitimate dumps were in western Pennsylvania and Ohio, long and expensive hauls. The pressure on contractors to get it done faster and cheaper was intense. No one wanted to know where the debris ended up, just that it was gone from the job site.

Enter the Mafia, which didn't much worry about rules. Al recognized the natural fit. "There was a lot of money in it. A lot of wiseguys got in the business."

Illegal dumping of construction debris was John Gotti Jr.'s first entrée into the business side of his father's empire. In 1988, a company tied to Gotti took over an old railyard site in Mott Haven in the south Bronx and opened the gates to construction companies looking to dump their debris. Investigators tracing illegal landfills said the line of idling trucks waiting to shed their loads backed up to the Triborough Bridge before the site was closed down.

Al got his own close-up look at the immense profits when he was dispatched by Gaspipe Casso to check out the dump in Matamoras, Pennsylvania, to see what Mike Salerno was up to out there.

The dump was located at a bend in the Delaware River,

near the borders of New Jersey and New York. It was an otherwise pristine location, just five miles north of the Delaware Water Gap National Recreation Area. The farmer who owned the land had a canoe and camping area at the other end of his property.

But it was also an easy shot from the city, some eighty miles if you took Interstate 84 from the New York State Thruway. It was a well-worn wiseguy path, about twenty miles southwest of where Chalootz Gagliodotto had done his own dumping of the bodies of Frank Tuminaro and Frank Gangi.

The landfill was essentially just a dip in the land, easily filled in with debris, then covered with a film of fresh dirt. The property owner had been assured that everything was on the up-and-up, with all permits secured and nothing but clean fill deposited on his land.

Actually, the site was in violation of a host of Pennsylvania environmental regulations. And no one was checking to see what exactly was being dumped. All they were doing was counting truckloads and cubic yards of debris to make sure truckers paid the right fees and that the Luchese bosses were getting their fair share.

Even that was tough work. Al's right-hand man, Shorty DiPalo, came back with a deep sunburn from the two weeks he spent keeping count of the loads. Al looked at him and laughed. "What, were you on vacation?" he wisecracked.

DiPalo, who depended on Al for everything from his rent to the car he drove, risked a rare nasty look at his boss. "You try standing on that platform," he said.

Even the intrepid Harpo Trapani, who had served Paul Vario as a loyal driver before Al recruited him as his own chauffeur, had a hard time at the landfill. Whatever was coming out of the trucks gave him headaches and nausea. "He said the smell was getting him sick. He asked to be taken out of there."

But everyone agreed they had seen more cash changing hands at the site than at most banks. Stacks of money paid by the truckers covered the table inside the small trailer that served as an office. Profits were supposed to be a three-way split: one-third for the property owner; one-third for Pasquale Masselli, a Luchese soldier who had come up with the plan, and his partner, a hustler named Donald Herzog; and one-third for the Luchese crime family. Some weeks, the family's earnings came to $30,000.

The Matamoras landfill was the envy of New York's mobsters. Gotti Jr., with his own Bronx dump shuttered, tried to elbow his way into the deal. At a meeting at a diner near Eighty-Sixth Street in Brooklyn with Casso and Al, Gotti offered $500,000 for a piece of the action, plus the right for his own trucks to dump at the site. Casso turned him down. He saw no reason to share his golden goose.

He should have taken the money. Neighbors downwind of the landfill had long complained of the same foul odors that sickened Harpo Trapani. They struck out with local officials who had been bribed to look the other way. But state authorities took an interest. When investigators showed up they ordered the site closed. No permits had ever been issued. A quick look determined that garbage and medical waste, in addition to construction debris, had been dumped in huge amounts at the site.

Al tried to fight back. He had John Zagari, an attorney who had done legal work for his cousin Joe Sica, the Genovese powerhouse in Pittsburgh, try to challenge the state's clampdown. Zagari did his best. He got engineers to file faked reports claiming they were cleaning up any contaminated waste in order to reopen.

The state wasn't convinced. Governor Robert Casey eventually leveled $933,000 in fines against the owner and operators. The dump had contaminated local groundwater and was likely to pollute the Delaware River, the governor said.

Al saw the shutdown as just a temporary setback. If demand was that strong, he reasoned, there would be other sites. It was a business worth investing in. Even though he couldn't stomach the smell, Harpo Trapani had the same idea. He suggested to Al that he buy into a carting company that provided debris containers for construction and demolition sites.

The firm Trapani had in mind was called A&M Carting, whose owners included a Luchese associate who was close to Canarsie crew veteran Pete the Killer Abinanti. A&M looked like a winner. The company already had a dozen pickup spots at New York City Housing Authority projects, a customer always good for the bill. Its containers were roll-ons: trucks would back up to the site, drop the container, then roll it back onto the truck when it was full. To handle even bigger loads, Al bought another company called Rhino Trucking. "It was two tremendous tractor-trailer trucks."

Like the rest of New York's private carters, the company's business plan was premised on the notion of "property rights." Mob trash haulers, like Ralph Masucci's brother-in-law, Angelo Ponte, who was one of the biggest, divided up the territory according to fiefdoms. Carters weren't allowed to poach customers by offering lower prices. Routes were the property of individual companies. They could be sold or bartered, but competition wasn't allowed.

It was the same practice that had helped make Sal Avellino Long Island's dominant trash hauler and a multimillionaire. The system was so sacrosanct that it had earned the death penalty for the rebel carters, Kubecka and Barstow, when they dared to break the rules.

There was also a rare opening in the business. A government conviction of a major Genovese-controlled firm in Brooklyn called Rosedale Carting had resulted in an auction of its routes. Al went to see his friend Jimmy Ida to see if he could work something out. Ida said he was agreeable, but any deal had to be approved by the Genovese family's carting broker, a mob elder from Brooklyn named Alphonse Malangone, who headed the Kings County Trade Waste Association. Thanks to eyesight problems, Malangone wore tinted glasses, a fashion statement that earned him the name "Allie Shades" among his wiseguy pals.

"Allie Shades had a book where he kept the records of every carting stop for the past twenty years. He used it to settle any disputes."

Malangone was also agreeable. "Allie Shades said okay,

as long as we cut the Genovese family in for part of our profits."

The problem of where to dump the debris was solved when Al learned that Mike Salerno had been partners in a second illegal landfill site, this one in the village of Hastings-on-Hudson in Westchester County. Salerno's partners there had been Vincent DiNapoli's brothers, Joseph and Louis. "Vinny and Louis were with the Genovese crew. Joe DiNapoli was with us, the Luchese family. They were pretty successful. They had their own carting company and were making a lot of money at it."

Since Mike Salerno had been a part-owner of the dump site, Al told the DiNapolis, it was only fair that his A&M trucks be allowed to dump there for free as a way of working off what they owed Salerno. It didn't matter that Al had helped engineer Salerno's murder. His mob-earned assets remained Luchese family property. "That was how it worked. What he had was ours."

But the Westchester dump site was also being targeted by angry neighbors. And for good reason. Some of the debris being deposited there was a toxic stew, worse than what had been found at Matamoras. Al heard the reports from carting company employees. "Some of the drivers said the tires on the trucks were melting when they drove into the dump from whatever was on the ground."

Again, state environmental investigators showed up. "We got a lot of tickets, and then they seized one of our trucks." For a few months, Al had to pay the insurance premiums on the trucks out of his own pocket. He was also shelling out for Harpo Trapani's salary when income failed to meet expenses. The plan to take over the Rosedale stops also collapsed after other Genovese-tied carters complained. The splendid business opportunity was becoming a money-losing headache.

Acting boss or not, Al was beginning to wish he'd never gotten involved in any of the landfill scams.

He would have seen his illegal-dumping venture as an even worse disaster if he'd known something else: thanks to his trips up to Matamoras, Al D'Arco was now the subject of intense FBI interest.

Tipped by an informant, agents went to take a look at the sprawling landfill by the Delaware River. The lead agent on the Matamoras expedition was Robert Marston, based out of the bureau's office in the Westchester suburb of New Rochelle. He was focused on trying to learn as much as he could about those who were allowing medical waste to wash up on beaches, and stuffing toxic-laced debris down abandoned mines in places like West Virginia and Ohio.

His informant told Marston that someone was making a small fortune at an illegal landfill on the New York–Pennsylvania border. Marston and his partner, Jim O'Connor, went up to look.

At first, they thought they might have been given a bum steer. They saw a long plain of rolling hills with a bulldozer pushing loads of dirt around. "It was right out in the open off of I-84, so you assumed they had a permit for it," Marston said of his first trip.

But a quick check found that wasn't the case. The agents put the site under surveillance. The intense activity and the long line of trucks enabled them to obtain a wiretap under Title III of the federal law permitting court-authorized snooping on private conversations.

Listening to the phone calls, they started sorting out the players. "There was an accountant, Donny Herzog, who seemed to be a guy in the middle. There was someone named 'Pat' who Herzog reports to."

Pat turned out to be Pasquale Masselli. Then there was someone named Frank Salerno who talked about his "Uncle Mike."

"We learn that 'Uncle Mike' was Mike Salerno. He was a longtime Luchese big shot from the Bronx who lived up in Ardsley. He had a diamond pinkie ring and a high-end Jaguar with his initials on it, a very well-known mob guy."

The agents had found something much bigger than an illegal landfill. And then things got dramatic.

"In the middle of our Title III, Mike Salerno gets killed."

Listening to the wiretap, the agents heard the landfill operators panicking. "They were saying, 'Mikey's missing,' and 'Mikey's dead.'" Fearing he could be next, accountant Donald Herzog fled the state for several days. He didn't come back until his partners pleaded with him. He had to come back, they said, to meet "Al."

Herzog, the agents learned, had been told to show up somewhere in Manhattan with his books showing the landfill's receipts and expenses. Someone named "Al" wanted to go over them. Marston wasn't sure yet who they were talking about.

"We knew he was a scary guy. We didn't have a picture of him and we never heard his voice."

The agents began trying to figure it out. Who was Al?

16

FINGERBOARD ROAD

Other law enforcement agents already knew who Al D'Arco was. They also knew exactly where he could be found.

In early January 1991, a pair of detectives from the Brooklyn district attorney's office went to the Little Italy Restoration Association apartment building at 21 Spring Street and took the elevator to the sixth floor.

Detectives Ken Santare and Matt O'Brien had a message for Al. They knew he'd be interested to hear what they had to say. And as long as they were doing him the favor of a personal visit to let him know what they'd heard, they also intended to ask him if he'd like to do one for them. Like maybe passing some information back.

They had no idea how he would respond. The DA's squad knew only that he was a rising gangland star with a nice restaurant and a crew of mob assistants. Other than that, they didn't know much about him. The closest they'd ever gotten to Al was when he had been spotted once out on Canarsie Pier talking to the now-missing Gaspipe Casso.

But it was worth a shot. It was part of their jobs.

On the way up to the apartment the detectives laughed about Al's residence. "You believe this guy probably has millions and he's living in this rent-controlled place?" said Santare.

They rang the bell on apartment 6P. No one answered. They waited for a couple of minutes, then went back downstairs. They walked around Little Italy for a while, then made another stab. Again no one answered. Santare was pretty sure that eventually Al would answer the door. They decided to try around dinnertime.

At 7 p.m. they made a third visit. After ringing the bell, they added a loud authoritative knock. There was a shuffling inside and then the door opened a crack. A handsome woman in her fifties with short dark hair flecked with gray peered out at them. The detectives identified themselves and said they were looking to talk to Al.

"He's not here right now," Dolores said.

Standing beside Santare, Matt O'Brien could see into the apartment. He saw a kitchen table with a plate of spaghetti, some bread, and a glass of wine. He didn't think Mrs. D'Arco was dining alone.

O'Brien piped up in a loud voice. "Look, tell Al we're not here to lock him up."

From within the apartment, they heard a door open. Al D'Arco appeared beside his wife. The detectives introduced themselves again. "We just want to talk to you," said Santare. "That's all we have to do."

"Okay, come in," said Al. They stepped just inside the apartment door. Al stood there, Dolores beside him, waiting to hear what they were going to say.

"Al, you want to excuse your wife?" said Santare. "This is something pretty important."

Al shook his head. "No, no," he said. "Whatever you have to say, she can hear it. She can stay here."

Santare shrugged. "Okay. Look, we have information that you've been targeted for assassination." He let that sink in for a couple of moments, waiting to see Al's response. Al didn't respond. He stood there stone-faced. His wife also didn't stir.

Santare continued. "And so have your son Joe and your son John."

Dolores looked up. The detectives saw her face color.

That was as much as they knew, Santare said.

Al acted shocked. "Me? Where is this coming from? You can't tell me anything else?"

Santare shook his head and grimaced as though to say he wished he could. He and O'Brien offered Al their cards.

"That's all we can say," Santare told him. "But if you want to discuss this further, you can give us a call and come into the office."

Al took the cards. "I ain't going nowhere," he told them with a laugh. "How about a drink?"

The detectives smiled. "Thanks, we can't right now," said Santare. "You've got our cards. Just give us a call." Then they said good night and walked back down the hall to the elevator.

Al closed the door behind the detectives wondering what else was going to go wrong. He was besieged with problems large and small that had dropped into his lap as a result of his promotion to acting boss. He was responsible to a pair of increasingly paranoid fugitive bosses whose list of demands and instructions was ever growing.

As for the news the detectives had brought to his door, he had a pretty good idea of what they were talking about.

Along with his appointment as the acting head of the family, Amuso and Casso had told him that they had additional murders for him to arrange.

The new targets were two of Bruno Facciola's closest associates, Larry Taylor and Al Visconti, who was married to Facciola's sister. According to Casso, the duo were planning on avenging their friend's murder. Casso said his law enforcement source had provided a tape recording, allegedly from a social club in Canarsie.

"Gas said he heard the tape and that these guys had a list. They were going to get Frankie Lastorino, Louis Daidone, Danny Cutaia, plus me and Joseph and John."

It was another of those moments when Gaspipe mysteriously knew everything from his "crystal ball." Al was hardly in a position to question Casso's source. But he was hesitant as well to embark on more murder for the same practical reason he avoided it in his business dealings. "Too much killing brings heat. These guys were always looking to kill the whole world."

But now here were the cops themselves knocking on his door to tell him they'd heard the same thing. He called Frank Lastorino and Louis Daidone.

They met in the parking lot of a Waldbaum's supermarket in Howard Beach. Al realized right away that Casso had again covered his bets. Lastorino already knew all about it, just as he had known ahead of time about the plan to kill Facciola. Al wondered again what was going on. Did the underboss think Al wasn't going to do it?

Lastorino had worked out his own plans for the hit. "He wanted to use his cousin, this kid Tommy Red Anzeulotto."

It was mob patronage, snagging a good job for a family member, regardless of his talent. Lastorino wanted his cousin to take part in the murder so as to give him a better chance of getting his button. Normally, it wouldn't have mattered. But in the case of Lastorino's cousin, Al knew there were doubts about him. "Tommy Red Anzeulotto had once told people that he wouldn't do time for nobody. Why would you do a murder with someone who says that?"

Daidone's candidate was his partner, Patty Dellorusso, the Teamsters official from the airport. Dellorusso was willing. The agreement was made that he and Anzeulotto would work together.

Taylor was the first victim. "Larry Taylor was very close to Bruno. They used to say he was like Bruno's son." The father-son relationship had blossomed amid multiple jewel robberies the pair had carried out together. "He was a stickup guy. His specialty was robbing jewelry salesmen."

The killers caught Taylor a couple of weeks later. On the night of February 5, he spent the evening partying. "They tailed him from the party. He was in a car with some girls and after he dropped them off they got him when he got to his house. They rolled up on him. Patty Dellorusso hit him with the shotgun, but he said Tommy Red held back. He hesitated and didn't come out of their car to help."

Dellorusso told Al he'd been furious. "He said, 'I almost turned the shotgun on him, too.' Finally the kid comes over and shoots Larry Taylor while he's already on the ground."

Police got to the scene shortly after the gunmen had fled. It was 10:30 p.m. Taylor, thirty-one years old, was lying between his car and the sidewalk in front of his home on Paerdegat Avenue in Canarsie. He was dead on arrival at Brookdale Hospital from wounds to his head and abdomen. He had apparently expected trouble. He had a .22-caliber still in his waistband.

Alfred Visconti was next. The motives for killing Bruno Facciola's brother-in-law were a little more complicated. Flounderhead Visconti was fifty-one years old. In his prime, he had been one of the city's most accomplished jewel thieves. Visconti was part of the team that robbed the Pierre Hotel in the wee hours of January 2, 1972, as guests were still recovering from New Year's Eve. It was one of the biggest hotel robberies of all time. The thieves, dressed in tuxedos and wearing false noses, stole $3 million in gems and cash from hotel safe-deposit boxes. It was a leisurely two-and-half-hour robbery as entering guests and hotel employees were bound and blindfolded.

"Flounderhead was a smart guy. He was a top-notch burglar. In prison he'd become a jailhouse lawyer. He was so good at it, he was still doing it even after he was out. Guys would bring him cases to work on for them."

But the story was later passed around among fellow ex-cons that while doing time for one of his arrests, Visconti had had sex with a black inmate. Vic Amuso had only heard the story from others. But he often called Visconti a disgrace, and referred to Facciola as a "*cornudo*" a cuckold for allowing his sister to stay with him.

Amuso had been talking about having Visconti killed since shortly after becoming boss. The alleged revenge plot renewed his fury. He had specific instructions for the murder. Flounderhead's brother-in-law had gotten the canary in his throat. Amuso ordered that Visconti get a more graphic symbol.

Amuso wanted them to get a cucumber, paint it black, and stuff it in the victim's rectum.

Al shuddered. They weren't just ordering killings. They were ordering perversion. "I told myself I ain't doing it. I wouldn't pass it on."

But he did pass on the message to have Visconti murdered. At Louie Daidone's car service, he met with Daidone and Ray Argentina. The able hit man had shifted his loyalties from his old captain, Facciola, to his new one, Daidone.

Casso had thrown another curve into the plans. This time, he had instructed Frank Lastorino to recruit his own separate hit team to kill Visconti. It was as if he wanted to see who could do it first.

"Gaspipe told Frankie not to tell anyone. But he was using his cousin, Tommy Red Anzeulotto, again, and Petey Argentina, Ray's brother. Petey Argentina didn't want to do the hit with Tommy Red because of what he'd said about not doing time for anybody." He asked Al what he should do.

Al told him to hold off, that he'd straighten it out. He tried to contact Amuso via his messenger, Patty Testa. Instead, Casso called him back. The underboss was angry. "He says to me, 'You don't want to talk to me anymore. You only talk to Vic.' We had a little argument. I said too many people knew about what was going on. It was getting out of hand."

Casso relented, telling him to use Peter Argentina and whomever he wanted. "He said just to do it right away."

They tracked Visconti down to a large apartment house where he was staying on East Forty-First Street off of Kings Highway in the Flatlands section of Brooklyn.

A hit team including the Argentina brothers and two other men waited for Visconti to come home on the evening of March 27. The victim was punctual. At 7 p.m. Visconti entered the building courtyard, where two of the shooters were lurking. Two others were waiting for him in the lobby. Shot four times, he died at the scene. Al had never passed on the order about the cucumber, but the shooters still got the message that Visconti was to be humiliated in death. One of the bullets was aimed into his groin.

Daidone reported the news to Al, who relayed it to the bosses in their hiding places. The message came back that they were pleased, but wanted more details. Who were the shooters? Who did what?

Al resented being asked. Standard mob practice was never to inquire about such things. Even bosses weren't supposed to know. Al hesitated, but made the inquiries. Daidone was nervous when Al told him what Casso had asked. "It was almost like Gaspipe was making some kind of report, that if he got caught he would turn it over."

But Al passed along the information just the same. No one was about to challenge them. "It was a pretty dangerous thing to start balking at that point."

Meanwhile, the steadily falling bodies had finally been noticed. And the key culprit, authorities were saying, was a mobster named Al D'Arco.

The day after Visconti's murder, the *Daily News* reported the killing as the third Luchese crew member to be slain in recent months. Citing law enforcement sources, the *News* said the murders were part of a purge ordered by D'Arco, "a little-known capo from Manhattan" who was the family's new acting boss.

D'Arco's rise to power, the paper stated, had "ruffled many mobsters." Bruno Facciola's brutal murder the previous summer had temporarily silenced his enemies. But Facciola's crew members had plotted retaliation. The *News*, with deep sources on both sides of the law, reported that the DA's men had warned Al that his life was in danger.

Three days later, the *News* was back again, this time with more confirmations of Al's role. It also ran a large photo, a fuzzy surveillance shot of him standing in a Little Italy doorway, looking relaxed but wary in a sports coat and slacks.

So now the whole world knew who and what he was.

A few days after Visconti's murder, the Luchese family paused from combat to replenish its ranks. New recruits, individually approved by the absent Amuso and Casso, were initiated as soldiers. Most had played a role in the recent bloodletting. The generals were handing out battlefield commendations.

Jay Giampa, who had helped his brother Joey dispatch Mike Salerno, got his ticket. So did Tommy Red Anzeulotto, just as Al had predicted. Rocco Vitulli, who had helped Frankie Pearl Federico kill the rebel carters, was also initiated. So was Patty Testa, Amuso's helpful messenger.

Even the two Bronx associates who had grievously fouled up the slaying of Johnny Petrucelli were on the list to be made. Unfortunately for Anthony Magana and Joey Cosentino, they couldn't be there. They were in jail, soon to be sentenced to twenty-five years to life for the murder.

As acting boss, Al presided over the ceremony. His one recruit was the faithful if hapless Pete Del Cioppo. "I felt sorry for him. I figured otherwise he's going to get killed for all his gambling debts. This way, no one could push him around anymore."

Ever mindful of health problems, Al bought special sanitary surgery pins for the occasion. He remembered how the blood had flowed at the prior ceremony as Bobby Amuso had gouged away with a heavy safety pin. He wanted to be careful. "The AIDS was going around heavy then." Best not to take a chance, he decided. "What are you gonna do? Make a guy and give him AIDS at the same time?" He also honored tradition, holding the ceremony in the basement of the Canarsie home of Peter "Rugsy" Vario, Paul's son. Vario kept a coop of pigeons in his backyard. The cooing could be heard during the ceremony.

In addition to the fugitive bosses, also missing from the induction ceremony was Big Pete Chiodo. The portly Luchese captain had never managed to climb out of the Luchese doghouse. If anything, he'd gotten himself into much deeper trouble.

Al had never been fond of Chiodo. The feeling was mutual. "I didn't like how he operated. He was pushy." But Al watched with sympathy as the lumbering Chiodo became a mob punching bag for the bosses.

Amuso and Casso had skipped town ahead of the windows indictments without letting Chiodo know he was facing arrest as well. A few weeks later, Casso had generously relayed a message from hiding to tell Pete to "lay low." Casso's law enforcement source had advised that Chiodo would be arrested as part of the state case involving the painters union shakedowns.

Chiodo quickly checked himself into a hospital, complaining of a heart attack. At four hundred pounds, it was easy to believe. He was arrested there anyway. To help Chiodo post bail, Al gave his attorney $8,000. Casso was furious when Al told him.

"Gaspipe tells me it's their money and why am I giving it up? He said Pete had taken enough of their money already to afford his own legal expenses."

It was a steady downhill slide from there. After his second arrest, the capo stayed close to home, a large Tudor house he was refurbishing in Staten Island's Grasmere section. "He was pretty leery. He was ducking."

Chiodo had good reason to be skittish. Among Amuso and Casso's several gripes with him was a major real estate matter. Chiodo had control of the property where the 19th Hole was located. The Luchese-run hangout on Eighty-Sixth Street across from the Dyker Beach golf course in Bensonhurst was where Amuso and Christy Tick Furnari before him had held court. The property had risen sharply in value and was now worth more than $400,000. The bosses wanted Chiodo to sign it over.

Under Furnari, title to the property had been held by his business manager, wealthy painting contractor Frank Arnold. In 1988, Arnold had transferred it to a friend and business partner of Chiodo's named Richard Tienken, a minor celebrity who ran a popular Manhattan comedy club where he'd helped discover actor Eddie Murphy. Amuso and Casso weren't impressed. They wanted the property. Chiodo, however, refused. "Pete said they owed him a lot of money. He wouldn't do it. They were mad."

Real estate was at the root of another dispute between them, but this one was deeply personal to Anthony Casso.

When he went on the lam, Gaspipe was building a palatial new home for himself. In 1988, he'd purchased a prized corner lot in Brooklyn's Mill Basin neighborhood. It was on the outer ring of a series of semicircular streets where million-dollar homes had sprouted on a peninsula in Jamaica Bay. Casso's site was an eight-thousand-square-foot lot tucked along a waterway called East Mill Basin. It boasted a long dock jutting out into the tidal channel, terraces, and a pool.

The property was initially listed in the name of the ever-helpful Frank Arnold. The painting contractor was rich enough so that no one would question his ownership of one more luxury home. But in the spring of 1990, as Arnold was facing charges in the Manhattan district attorney's painters union extortion case, title was transferred to a company called Highlite Development. It was owned by George Kalaitzis, the Greek contractor from Queens who worked closely with the Luchese underboss.

With Kalaitzis as the builder, construction of Casso's pleasure palace proceeded apace. To design it, he tapped a young architect named Anthony Fava, a partner with Pete Chiodo in several enterprises. Al had met Fava in 1987 and liked him well enough to ask him to help design his new restaurant in the Village, Pasquale & Wong's.

"He was a good kid. Pete brought him around and I gave him some work. He was working with my son John on designing a new burger joint, too. He'd come by the restaurant with his girlfriend. I wouldn't let him pick up a check."

Al's role in the project was to make sure the bills were paid from the steady flow of cash from Luchese family earnings. He was stunned by some of the expenses.

"Gas has George the Greek order two glass doors from West Germany that cost $44,000. He was spending hundreds of thousands of dollars on the place."

Building plans showed the three-story stucco home boasted a thirty-foot-wide master bedroom, an indoor gymnasium, and a solarium. It included two rooftop terraces, and a wide patio leading to the private dock. If he was ever free to live there, Anthony Casso would be residing in mob splendor.

Pete Chiodo was supposed to be overseeing the building of Casso's castle. Contracting was his expertise and the architect was his friend. Casso expected him to move things along.

But there were delays. One problem was that, like a lot of anxious new homeowners, Anthony's wife, Lillian, had changed her mind often about what she wanted. Another was that when the exorbitantly expensive doors arrived from Germany, they didn't fit. Work came to a halt.

Fava had his own complaints. The architect griped to Kalaitzis and Arnold that he wasn't getting paid fast enough. When the complaint reached Casso, he was irate. He also began to wonder how much he should trust the architect.

For his part, Chiodo wasn't paying much attention to the project. In addition to dealing with the indictments, he was doing extensive work on his own home. He built a high brick wall and a new apartment over his garage. His place was modest compared to the regal residence Casso was constructing, but Big Pete's place was also worth almost a million dollars. It sat atop a small rise with a backyard overlooking a pleasant little park called Bailey Pond.

It didn't help matters that Chiodo's home renovations were moving along swiftly while the Mill Basin mansion was stalled. Things got worse when Chiodo's wife went to see Lillian Casso about the problems. The two mob wives got into a fierce argument.

Al had to coax Chiodo to come to Manhattan for a meeting. They met on West Street, near where the burger stand had been. Chiodo showed up with a backup team including his father and uncle. Despite their differences, Chiodo vented openly to Al about his suspicions. As they walked, Chiodo brought up the killing of Bruno Facciola.

"Everybody is getting marked a rat," Pete said. "These

guys have a pattern. They are marking guys rats and getting them killed."

The two of them, Chiodo confided, were headed for the same fate. "I got information that you and I are going to be killed or hurt," he said.

Al listened. He had heard the threat already from the detectives who had knocked on his door. The possibility that Amuso and Casso could turn on him, as he had watched them do to others, had also occurred to him. But he wasn't about to express any of his own fears or concerns to Chiodo.

"Petey," Al said, "you are getting delusions. You are running away with yourself. Don't believe that. It's a money thing. You can always resolve a money thing."

Al figured that the disputes over the 19th Hole and the Mill Basin project could be fairly easily fixed. The other matter, though, was something to think about.

A few weeks later, Chiodo called Al to say that he'd decided to resolve the twin indictments he was facing. He would use his lawyer, Charles Emma, a Brooklyn attorney with close ties to the local Republican Party, to negotiate plea deals. He would have to do some prison time, but he'd have the matters settled.

Al told him it was all right with him, but that he needed to run it by Amuso and Casso. "What you do is your business," Al said. "But you have to get an okay if you are going to plead guilty. This involves the bosses and the other families."

Chiodo was already past talking. He first settled the state case, agreeing to plead guilty to a single count of second-degree grand larceny. In the more serious extortion charges contained in the federal Windows case, Emma negotiated a good deal for his client. Without being obligated to testify, Chiodo would serve up to six years in prison. He was just forty years old. Hopefully, he'd have a long life ahead of him when he got out.

To Amuso and Casso, it was treason.

Al was summoned again to the pay phone on Glen Cove

Road in Nassau County. The conversation was a replay of the last time the bosses had sentenced a member to death. Again, it was Casso relaying the order.

"Kill that fat bastard," Casso said. "He's a rat."

Al didn't have to ask whom he meant. He held the phone thinking how he'd told Chiodo he was imagining things.

"Use the kids," the underboss instructed. "Plus the Toupe." He had one more on his list. "And kill the architect," he added. "He knows too much."

Al found Richie Pagliarulo at his club, Café Sicilia in Gravesend, Brooklyn. The Toupe was dressed as though he was going out for a night on the town. He usually was. In addition to his dapper attire, Pagliarulo was so vain about his brown toupee that he had a hairdresser, Luchese associate Dino Marino, visit him three mornings a week to style it into place. The Toupe had long been one of Chiodo's most loyal aides. He had put some of the bullets into Sonny Morrissey and he had kept silent when Chiodo had botched the hit on contractor Joe Martinelli.

But when Al told him what he had to do to his captain, Pagliarulo was delighted. "Good," he said. "I've been doing all the work for him while he got all the credit."

Later, Al met with Joseph to tell him that Casso wanted him and his friends to reprise their performance from the Anthony DiLapi murder in California. Joseph had already heard. George Zappola had told him. Al wasn't surprised this time about the back channel. It was just one more curveball from the underboss.

The hunt began, but Pete Chiodo didn't make it easy. The big captain stayed close to home, rarely venturing outside. Frustrated, the hit team decided to try and get the jump on him by tapping his phone lines. A Luchese associate with expertise clambered up a telephone pole a few blocks away and found Chiodo's line. A cassette recorder was attached.

Every couple of hours, one of the team would climb up, flip out the old cassette, and insert a new one. It was a painstaking process. But on May 8, a Wednesday, they learned something. Joseph D'Arco listened as they played the recording.

"We heard Pete say he was getting on a plane. He was going to West Virginia." Talking to his father, Chiodo said he planned a couple of stops before he took off. He had to go to the doctor and stop by the bank. They also planned to pick up his father's car from the mechanic at a nearby gas station on Fingerboard Road.

Joseph immediately headed into Manhattan, where he retrieved a work car stolen earlier for use in the hit. He also picked up a pair of guns that Petey Del Cioppo had hidden, a 9 mm Smith & Wesson and a semiautomatic handgun. Both had silencers. With the weapons stowed under the seat in Del Cioppo's vehicle, Joseph followed him back to Staten Island in the work car. He wore gloves to avoid leaving fingerprints. When they got to the tolls at the Verrazano Bridge, Del Cioppo paid the toll for himself and his buddy behind him. Joseph didn't want anyone to spot the gloves.

"I was supposed to be in the shooter's seat. That was the original plan. Then Georgie Zappola says he got a message. They want me to drive instead."

Replacing him as the main shooter was a Luchese associate named Frank Giacobbe. Joseph had little faith in him. "Fat Frankie," as he was called, was part of Zappola's crew. He had taken part in several bank robberies, but he also had a heavy drug habit. On the way to the gas station at the corner of Bay Street and Fingerboard Road, Joseph eyed Giacobbe. "We're about one minute away from the station and this kid puts a cigarette in his mouth. He was shaking."

Joseph reached over and snatched the cigarette away. "What the fuck are you doing?" he said.

It was midafternoon when they got to the station. Joseph pulled up about twenty feet from the gas pumps. The second car, with the Toupe at the wheel, pulled sideways on Fingerboard Road, blocking traffic. George Conte, the designated secondary shooter, was beside Pagliarulo. Joseph saw Chiodo's Cadillac parked next to the gas pumps. Chiodo and a mechanic were busy looking under the hood. If they moved quickly, they could drop him easily, Joseph thought.

Frank Giacobbe opened the door and started toward his target. Climbing out of the car, he tripped. The gun in his hand went off. Joseph saw sparks shoot up from the concrete.

Instantly, Chiodo understood what was happening. He pulled his own gun and began firing back. "He was running backward, shooting." Giacobbe hid behind a large hoist. Despite his bulk, Chiodo moved surprisingly fast.

Joseph's instructions were not to leave the car. He opened fire from the car window. Then he leaped out, gun in hand, charging in Chiodo's direction. The two men pegged bullets at each other. Joseph felt time slow down. He was squeezing off rounds, aiming at Chiodo as he fled.

Joseph felt like he was seeing more clearly than ever before, that he could even see the stitching on Chiodo's shirt. He felt the rush of air as bullets whistled past his head. For a moment, he thought Chiodo had another shooter. But it was Fat Frankie. "He's shooting and he's coming closer to killing me than Pete."

He heard his own bullets thudding into Big Pete's massive frame. "He's giving out these yells as they hit. '*Umph!*'" Chiodo finally fell to the ground. He lay there on his back. Joseph approached, aiming his gun for one last shot. It jammed. He started to check what was wrong when he heard someone yelling his name. "Frankie is screaming over and over, 'Joe! Joe!'"

The rest of the hit team were in their cars. He didn't know what to think. He raced back to his vehicle, threw it into gear, and tore away from the station.

On the way back to Brooklyn, Joseph had just one thought: "He'd better be dead. He was looking right at me the whole time."

In Brooklyn, they began getting rid of the evidence. Joseph put his shirt and the guns into a plastic shopping bag. He handed it to someone to get rid of them. They made arrangements to have their two getaway cars, a Jeep and a Thunderbird, torched.

Luchese capo Frank Lastorino was at the Café Sicilia when they arrived. Lastorino advised Joseph to make himself scarce. He handed him $1,000 and told him to go with one of the Toupe's friends who lived on Long Island. "Stay over there until you hear from us," Lastorino told him.

On Long Island, Joseph called his father from a pay phone. Al had been anxiously paging his son, without response. He was on Flatbush Avenue when his own pager beeped. "Where are you? How come I can't get in touch with you?" Al asked when he reached Joseph.

Something had gone wrong, his son explained. Frank Lastorino had sent him out of town until things quieted down.

Al was enraged that Lastorino was giving his son orders. "Get back here," he told him. "The first thing the cops are gonna to do is look to see who's missing. They'll zero in on them first."

The news of the shooting was now on the radio. Chiodo had been taken to St. Vincent's Hospital in Staten Island in critical condition. Later reports updated his status. The victim of the attempted mob rubout in Staten Island was critical, but expected to live.

Joseph got a ride to Brooklyn, where he met up with his father. They embraced. He told his dad that Chiodo had to have recognized him. Al scolded him for not wearing a mask.

The question now was how to finish the job.

Plan B was to send Frankie Giacobbe, whose bumbling had put them in this fix, into the hospital. He would make his way to Chiodo's room, stab him to death, then walk out.

A nurse at the hospital, a friend of one of the plotters, was persuaded to help guide them. She had worked at St. Vincent's for years and could move about without being questioned. Her shift ended at 7 a.m. A reconnaissance run was planned for that hour when the hospital would be lightly staffed.

Wearing a set of doctor's white scrub clothes, a pal of

Giacobbe's named Frank DiPietro was led by the nurse down the corridor toward Chiodo's room. He couldn't even get close. As he approached, men in suits, clearly law enforcement, stood up to ask him where he was going.

Gaspipe Casso had no trouble coming up with a follow-up strategy. The order came to Al in a phone call to one of the designated pay phones.

"He says he wants me to send members to Pete Chiodo's parents' house. And to grab hold of them and threaten them with death if Pete cooperates." Casso knew exactly who he wanted to relay the threat. "He said to use Louis Daidone and Patty Dellorusso because they're big guys, intimidating."

Al listened, ticking off all the Mafia tenets violated by this order. "The rules of this life is that you don't threaten people's families. It's outside. They're innocents. It's wrong, especially with women."

But he didn't argue. The other rule of the Life was to obey without question. Daidone was even more irate when Al told him what Casso wanted him to do. "Grab the family? I won't do it," the bagel baker responded emphatically. Al was encouraged. Maybe they could find a way out of this, he thought.

But Casso had again covered his bases. He sent a backup messenger, George Conte, to see Daidone. "Georgie Conte tells him he's going to accompany them to the parents' house, make sure they do it."

It wasn't that bad, Conte told them. Casso wanted the parents to know they had a choice. If their son cooperated against the crime family, they would die. But if he didn't, then all was forgiven. He'd get a pass.

Reluctantly, Daidone and Dellorusso went to the home in Brooklyn. They camped outside, waiting for the couple to show. Casso was insisting that he be told as soon as the mission was completed. They worked out a code with Al. When his pager lit up with a string of 1s, it meant the threat had been made. Al would then relay the confirmation to the impatient Casso.

The intimidators waited for hours outside the house. It was

Chiodo's father who appeared. He and his wife had separated and he was seeing another woman. When the couple arrived, Daidone stepped out of the shadows. Chiodo's father, whom he'd never met before, turned and greeted him. "Hello, Louie, how are you?" he said.

Daidone hesitated, then spoke his piece in a rush. "If Pete cooperates, you both get whacked. If not, all is forgiven." Then he turned around and hurriedly walked away.

Pete Chiodo woke up on his way to the intensive-care unit at St. Vincent's Hospital following surgery. A pair of FBI agents were in the corridor watching him. John Flanagan and Lucian Gandolfo had tried to warn Chiodo that the Luchese bosses would try to kill him. Now they were taking no chances. Standing beside Chiodo's oversized gurney, dressed in hospital scrubs like the rest of the operating team, was an NYPD detective, Thomas Limberg, who was assigned to the FBI's Luchese squad, known as "C17." Limberg had been allowed to remain in the operating room during the procedure. There were serious concerns, the law enforcement officials told alarmed hospital officials, that the gunmen who had shot the patient might try to finish him off right in the hospital.

Gandolfo saw Chiodo slowly roll his eyes open. "He didn't really smile," recalled Gandolfo. "But his eyes suggested he was much happier to see us than the guys in baseball caps pointing guns at him."

The agents stood in the recovery room as the doctor told Chiodo that he had a dozen bullet holes in him. Five shots had passed right through him. Luck and his huge bulk had helped save his life, the doctor said. He had a long way to go, but he should recover.

As the doctor moved away, the agents glided over to Chiodo's bedside. "Your old friends made it pretty clear yesterday that you have nothing going with them anymore," said Gandolfo.

"There's no other way out for you," said Flanagan. "You know that."

Chiodo was too groggy to speak. Thanks to a combination

of poor eyesight and panic, he had no idea who the shooters were. Nor was he inclined to talk about it. But even if he did, he had little to tell them.

He knew that Amuso and Casso had ordered the attempt to kill him, just as he'd predicted they would weeks earlier. He also knew they weren't finished. He got the report from his father about Louie Daidone's murder threat if he cooperated. Another was delivered via his lawyer. Two men had rushed into the lawyer's Brooklyn office and yelled that Pete's wife would be next.

Charles Rose, one of the federal prosecutors working the Windows case, also came to the hospital room. It was the second time Rose had urged Chiodo to cooperate. Back in March 1990, Rose had warned him that the Luchese bosses intended to kill him.

He had waved Rose off at the time. He could take care of himself, Chiodo said. Now he looked at his two near-useless arms. He couldn't possibly protect himself right now, not to mention his wife and family.

Chiodo procrastinated as long as he could. "It's just the way I was brought up," he was later to tell a jury. After two months of being shifted between various hospitals and undergoing repeated procedures, he gave in. He'd cooperate, he told the agents.

17

PRINCE STREET

In the Luchese world, the air of sour suspicion that hung over every order from the fugitive bosses only grew thicker. Chiodo hadn't yet defected, but the assumption was that he would talk.

A few days after the failed attack, Anthony Calagna, the Teamster leader who had brought the family a fortune in payoffs from its airport extortions, showed up in Little Italy. He had his last package of payoffs to give to Al. He was due to surrender to begin serving a sentence for labor racketeering. He met Al at La Donna Rosa and they walked over to Kenmare Street. His envelope, thicker than usual, contained $25,000.

"Big Anthony had gotten pinched and he was headed to the can. I took $5,000 out and gave it to him. I said, 'Here, you're going away. Leave this for your wife.'"

As far as Al was concerned, it was standard mob etiquette. "If a guy's going away or he's just coming out, no matter what crew he's with, if you're doing good, you're supposed to help out. You run into him on the street, you take every dime you've got in your pocket and give it to him. Wish him luck."

When Al reported it to Casso, the underboss was furious. *"You gave away our money?"* he shouted. "You got no right to do that!"

Al felt his blood rise. He usually listened in silence to Casso's rants. "I was hot as a pistol. I said, 'Get the fuck outta here. Yeah, I gave him five thousand to give his wife. I got twenty thousand for you. The guy's going to the can. He didn't rat on you. He could've gone to the can and kept the twenty-five.' "

After Al raised his voice, Casso dropped it. But he could hear him smoldering at the other end of the line.

Money was now a steady source of discontent for the bosses. He had been told in no uncertain terms by both Amuso and Casso that he should pass George Kalaitzis as much money as needed for his investments, both in construction and for the gambling games he ran in the heavily Greek section of Astoria in Queens. "They said George is a good earner. Give him what he needs." That went especially for Casso's Mill Basin palace, a steady drain on the family's finances.

But the bosses did an abrupt about-face in the weeks after the Chiodo debacle. "Patty Testa comes to see me talking about how much I had given George the Greek. He says, 'Vic doesn't like people using his money.' "

The comment caught Al by surprise, especially coming from Testa, who usually only relayed information about meetings. "Pat, don't discuss Vic and money with me," he said. "I don't want to talk about that with you."

But Amuso told him the same thing in a phone conversation. "Give the money to Patty," he instructed.

Casso also questioned the accounts. He demanded a detailed list of all the money disbursed to Kalaitzis. Al laboriously copied it out by hand. It came to $680,000 since January. More than $230,000 had gone for the Mill Basin house alone.

The underboss demanded a similar balance sheet of expenses and revenue from the family's construction interests. Most of it was collected by Dom Truscello, who had taken over the Prince Street crew from Joe Beck DiPalermo after the habitual drug dealer was targeted in yet another narcotics case. The construction payments were a complex web of splits with other crime families who shared in the shake-downs.

Gaspipe scrutinized every figure. "Why'd you take a split here?" he asked, citing a $25,000 payoff from a Long Island contractor. A $300 payment that Truscello had kept was also challenged.

Al told him that had been the agreement. "If you want the money, we'll give it to you," he said. Casso said that would be a good idea.

Al thought about how things had changed. Before, discussion about the family's earnings had been the kind of detailed analysis any executive would expect. Now, every question carried a strong undercurrent of distrust.

John D'Arco got married that June. The wedding ceremony took place at St. Patrick's Old Cathedral on Mott Street. Al had been a steady supporter of the church. When the boiler broke, he had donated $25,000 for a new one. He attended the ceremony but stayed in Little Italy as the wedding party drove off for the reception at a deluxe Bronx catering hall, Marina Del Rey, overlooking Long Island Sound.

He didn't want to take a chance at a parole violation. Even though John had nothing to do with the mob life, members of his own crime family and representatives of the others would be in attendance, making generous wedding gifts. It was a tribute befitting the son of an acting boss.

He had noticed the agents parked on the block near his restaurant. They were hard to miss. One of them drove an olive-green Chevrolet with a maroon stripe. "He was pretty much on me all the time. I couldn't trust those guys. I figured, what's the sense of getting violated?" So now he was skipping his own son's wedding reception.

In early July, the bosses called for a meeting. Al got his initial marching orders while answering the pay phone on Glen Cove Road. Casso told him to meet Sal Avellino and Anthony Baratta at seven thirty in the evening at the cannon, the little park by the Verrazano Bridge where Gaspipe had teared up saying good-bye.

He was to get a car that couldn't be traced. He'd pick up Avellino and Baratta and take them to the parking lot at the golf driving range and batting cages on Flatbush Avenue near the Belt Parkway. Someone would meet them there.

A few hours later, Casso's personal messenger, George Zappola, showed up to tell him all over again. "I know, Georgie," he said wearily. "He told me."

The three men pulled up to the driving range around 8 p.m. It was across from Floyd Bennett Field, where Al had fallen in love with airplanes as a little boy. They didn't see anyone, so Al drove to the back of the large parking lot. A black Jeep with tinted windows was there with its motor running. Frank Lastorino was behind the wheel, grinning at them. "We left our car and went and got in with Frankie. I sat up front and Sallie Avellino and Baratta got in the back."

Lastorino drove through the streets for half an hour, making sure they didn't have a tail. "We went up and down the Belt Parkway, dry-cleaning ourselves. Then he heads over the Verrazano." In Staten Island, Lastorino stopped on a side street and turned off his lights. Al had no idea where they were. They sat silently on the dark street. A dog began to bark. They drove on.

They paused on another block, waiting to see if any cars stopped behind them. After a few minutes, Lastorino restarted the engine. He drove to a nearby house. It was behind a driveway blocked by an electric gate. The gate slid back as they approached.

Richie the Toupe Pagliarulo opened the door. They walked into a living room. Amuso and Casso were there. They had shaved off their beards. It didn't make them look any less like hunted men, Al thought. Amuso was glowering. "I says, 'Hey, it's good to see you.' He was just stony like."

Al sat down on a long sofa, Avellino and Baratta beside him. Amuso and Casso sat facing them, a coffee table in between. Lastorino sat off to the side.

"Vic was scowling. He says right away, 'There are no more

acting positions. Steve Crea is no longer acting consigliere. Dom Truscello is not a captain anymore."

Al was bewildered. They had made him acting boss just six months earlier. He had handed over every payment, carried out every assignment, no matter how distasteful.

He watched as Casso pulled a piece of paper from his pocket and unfolded it. Al could see he had some kind of list. Pen in hand, he started reading. Instead of an acting boss, underboss, and consigliere, they would now be part of a four-man panel. It would be Al, Baratta, Avellino, and Frank Lastorino. They were to meet every Tuesday to go over business.

Al looked at Amuso. "Vic wouldn't look at me. He's looking away."

Casso had more to say. Al would no longer have responsibility for the airports, he said. That would go to Sal Avellino, who would be assisted by Patty Dellorusso, the former Teamsters leader and a member of Al's crew. Lastorino would handle the gas tax schemes with the Russians. Baratta, a close friend of Sidney Lieberman, got the garment center.

Baratta seemed to like what he was hearing. He broke in to suggest that maybe it made sense to take Dellorusso out of Al's crew altogether and put him with Avellino.

Al was fuming. Taking someone from his crew, especially an efficient soldier like Dellorusso, would badly sap his strength. "No way," he barked. Everyone looked at him. Amuso was still staring into the distance.

Gaspipe eased the moment. "No, he'll stay with Al," he said. "He'll just do the airport with Sallie."

Casso stood up. There was coffee and food upstairs, he said. Al walked over to Amuso. "Vic, I want to talk to you," he said.

The boss shook his head. "I got to get someplace," he said. "I ain't got time now." Al stood there. "Vic," he repeated. "I need to talk."

Casso was watching them. "Go ahead," he told Amuso. "Talk to him."

They went into a bedroom. "Vic, what's up?" Al began.

He was thinking about what Patty Testa had said, how Vic didn't like people using his money. "Let me tell you something," he said. "I don't know what it is, but I never took a dime of your money. Never touched a dime."

Amuso didn't say anything for a moment. Then he began talking about the Prince Street crew. "I should never have listened to you about Dom. I should have left Joe Beck there."

Al was stunned to hear Vic accusing him. The move a few months earlier to pull DiPalermo down and replace him with Dom Truscello had been Amuso and Casso's idea, although Al had supported it. The eighty-four-year-old mobster was wanted in his latest narcotics case. There was no way he could run the crew.

The problem, Al was thinking, had to be the messengers. Testa and Zappola were spinning everything. "Vic, I don't think you're getting the right messages. It's all getting twisted," he said.

Amuso seemed increasingly uncomfortable. He still hadn't looked at Al. "I got to go," he said. He turned and walked out of the bedroom.

In the kitchen, the rest of the family's officials were dining on cold cuts. Al noticed George Zappola was there. He wondered if he'd been hiding inside the house when they arrived.

"Hello, Al," Zappola greeted him.

"Yeah, hello," Al muttered.

As they ate, Casso wondered aloud what Patty Dellorusso's cut from the airport money should be.

Al said that Anthony Calagna had received 25 percent. "We'll make it twelve and a half," said Gaspipe.

Amuso stood up. "We got to get out of here," he said.

Downstairs, Casso walked over to Al. He nudged him with his elbow. "Don't worry," he whispered. "We'll talk to you in a month, a month and a half."

Al watched them leave. "I was in the street a lot of years. I knew what that month and a half meant." It was just the beginning, he thought. They were taking things away, one by one. Just like they'd done to Pete Chiodo. Like they'd done to Mike Salerno. And Michael Pappadio.

It started even sooner than he'd expected. A week later, Al was home on a Sunday when he got a page from Patty Testa. He was at Prince and Mott Streets. "I'll come up and meet you," Al said.

Testa was standing on the corner when he got there. "I hate to bring you bad news, Al," Testa said. Al raised his eyebrows, waiting. "They're transferring Patty over to Bowat," he said. "You've got to tell him."

"*What?*" yelled Al. It was something he never did on the street. Testa tried to calm him down. "Look, Al—" he began. Al wouldn't listen. He turned and started walking away. Testa followed. "All right," Al said over his shoulder. "I'll do it tomorrow. Just get away from me right now."

Al was sure the bosses were needling him by the move. He had told Amuso what he thought about Baratta when he'd been made acting boss.

Still, he bit the bullet. He arranged to meet Baratta and Dellorusso the following afternoon on First Avenue near Bellevue Hospital. Bowat arrived in a small black sports car. He had Frank Lastorino with him. He probably heard about me popping my cork yesterday, Al thought.

He made a formal introduction. "Pat, this is your new captain," Al said, gesturing to Baratta. Dellorusso seemed confused.

"Hey, congratulations," Al added. "Now you'll be able to wine and dine in all those fancy uptown places this guy goes to."

Within weeks, the bosses had removed three more crew members from his authority. Pat Masselli, who had worked at the Matamoras dump, was reassigned. Frank Lagano and Anthony "Curly" Russo, whom Al had known for decades, were shifted to Sal Avellino's crew.

Anthony Baratta was in charge of arranging the panel meetings. He scheduled the first one for the East Harlem

apartment where he spent a lot of time. The apartment was
on the second floor of a building around the corner from
Rao's, the Mob-beloved restaurant on the corner of Pleasant
Avenue. Baratta could be found there almost every night,
the first table on the right. He was usually with his friend
and partner, Genovese soldier Louis "Louie Dome" Pacella.
The two were deeply involved in narcotic deals.

The first session was an expanded group. In addition to
the four panel officers, five other Luchese members were
present. One of them was Steve Crea, the now-ousted consigliere. He didn't look happy. Al asked him if he wanted to
get together for a cup of coffee.

"You bet," said Crea.

They met at a diner on West Twenty-Third Street in Manhattan. Seated across from Crea in the booth, Al said out loud
for the first time what he'd been thinking for weeks.

"They double-crossed you, and they double-crossed me,"
he said. "We didn't deserve it."

Crea nodded. They talked for a while about their mutual
suspicions. Then Al talked rebellion.

"I'm ready to go to war," he said. "What do you say? Could
you take out Bowat?"

Crea snapped his fingers. "Like that," he said.

"All right," said Al. "Put that on hold. We'll talk about it."
They shook hands and parted.

Things changed quickly. On Sunday, July 28, FBI agents arrested Vic Amuso in a shopping mall on the outskirts of
Scranton, Pennsylvania. It was not far from the house where
Al had visited him the year before. Amuso had just finished
speaking on a pay phone. The FBI said the arrest followed
an anonymous tip. The bureau noted that photographs of
Amuso were aired in March by the television show *America's Most Wanted*.

When Al heard the news, he wondered about the anonymous tip. But he moved quickly to see how he could help.

He drove with Dolores out to Howard Beach to see Vic's

wife, Barbara. The two women knew each other. Before he became a fugitive, Al and Dolores had attended parties at the house. "I knew the place was under surveillance so I didn't want to go up there." He handed Dolores an envelope with $30,000 in it. Barbara Amuso answered the door. Dolores just said hello and gave her the package. The wife seemed to be expecting it.

After Amuso was brought up from Pennsylvania to New York, Al met with the boss's lawyer, Martin Geduldig.

The attorney was at the restaurant, taking his son out to dinner before he began college. Al asked him if they could step outside to talk.

Out on the street, Al told the lawyer they had to try and get Amuso out on bail. Geduldig, a veteran criminal defense attorney who grew up on the Lower East Side near Knicker-bocker Village, shook his head.

"You're not going to get him out," the lawyer told him as they strolled. "He was on the lam."

Al asked if Vic had any message for him. Geduldig shook his head again. "No," he said. That can't be right, Al thought. "No, nothing," Geduldig repeated when Al pressed him.

Al then expressed his fears. "You know, he wants to hurt me," Al told him. The lawyer was surprised. Gangland figures didn't usually talk that way. He noticed how jittery Al was acting. "Al, nobody said anything to me," he said. "I don't think he wants to hurt you. He didn't give me any messages."

The government had a message for him, however. A few nights after Amuso's arrest, Al heard someone call his name as he walked through the Little Italy streets.

"Hey, Al, how you doing, buddy?" Al wheeled around. He was instinctively friendly, even though he didn't place the face.

"Hey," he responded. "How you doing, kid?" He looked closer. The man was solidly built. Then he realized where he'd seen him before. It was the agent with the olive Chevy.

"I just wanted to thank you for the information you called in," said the agent in a loud voice. "It was very helpful. We caught Vic Amuso in Scranton, you know."

"*Who the fuck are you?*" Al yelled.

"My name's Steve Byrne," he said. "I'm with the bureau."

Al looked around. It was a warm summer evening. The streets were crowded. Windows were open.

Al pointed his finger at the agent. "I'm gonna make a complaint against you!" he yelled. "You're trying to get me killed. You want everyone to think I'm a rat."

A member of the squad of FBI agents that had arrested Amuso, Byrne grinned. He had wanted to shake the tree a little. See what fell out. It was mission accomplished. Al stormed away down the street.

The message from Casso at the next panel meeting was that they should all keep doing what they were doing.

The meeting was at one of Baratta's favored restaurants, Sandro's on the Upper East Side near York Avenue. They went over the list of outstanding chores. After they were finished eating, they went to a nearby hotel where Baratta had arranged a room. There, they talked about one of the outstanding matters that Casso had urged them to accomplish, killing the architect, Anthony Fava.

Baratta and Avellino said they didn't even know him. Frank Lastorino volunteered to handle the contract.

"Frank said he had some documents with Fava's numbers and address on them. But the next day he says he can't find them." Lastorino had also changed his mind. He asked Al if he could take care of it. Al agreed to do so. But this time, he had no intention of carrying through.

His estrangement continued. "It was a whisper campaign. They were saying, 'Be careful with Al.' In other words, don't trust him."

Even his close friends were keeping him at arm's length. One was Dominic Truscello, the new captain of the Prince Street crew. "Dom used to call every night. He'd come over, we'd go out for a cup of coffee and talk."

They'd walk along South Street near the offices of the *New York Post*. "It was dark down there, we didn't have to worry about getting spotted. We talked about business, went over the construction rackets."

On his way back from Brooklyn one afternoon, he ran into Truscello in Little Italy. "Dom, what happened?" said Al. "You don't come around much anymore."

Truscello mumbled an excuse. "I've been coming in late," he said.

Al said they should get together later, head over to South Street. Truscello said he'd rather not go down there.

"Why?" Al asked. "What's wrong with South Street?"

"You know," answered Truscello. "Maybe it's hot down there."

Al didn't buy it. He doesn't want to be seen with me, he thought.

The same thing happened with Jimmy Ida, the Genovese family leader he'd been close with for years. "We used to meet two or three times a week, working things out between the two families. Jimmy was really running things for the crew."

The meetings were usually in the middle of the night, the favored time for the Genovese clan. The timetable came from Vincent Gigante, who kept out of sight during the day, confining meetings to the wee hours. His own members called him Dracula for his nocturnal habits.

"I'd wait up till two or three in the morning sometimes to meet with Jimmy. It was always the same thing. 'Vince' needed him."

But Ida also seemed to have lost Al's number.

Driving through the Little Italy streets one night with Joe Fiore, Al spotted Ida standing on a Broome Street corner, deep in conversation with another Genovese member named Nicky Frustace, known as "Nicky the Blond."

At the same time, Al spotted Ken McCabe, the ubiquitous investigator who had taken a beating outside the funeral for Paul Vario's son Lenny. McCabe was sitting at the curb in his white Chrysler carefully watching the Genovese members. Al directed Fiore to pull into a small parking lot in front of Ida, blocking McCabe's view. Al leaned out the window, motioning Ida over to the car.

"McCabe's on the corner," he whispered. "You're getting clocked." Ida looked over in alarm to where the agent sat watching him. "Come on, jump in," said Al. "We'll get out of here."

Al told Fiore to head to the Moondance Diner near Grand Street and Sixth Avenue, an all-night spot that Al often used for meetings. In the diner, he and Ida settled at one table. Fiore and Frustace sat a distance away at another.

"What's up?" said Al. "I haven't seen you around."

Ida seemed ill at ease. "I'm glad I ran into you, Al," he said. "Don't tell anybody, but I'm going away for vacation for like three weeks."

It struck Al as an odd thing to say, especially since he hadn't seen Ida in weeks. "All right, Jimmy," he said. "I won't tell anybody. But not for nothing, I got to be in touch. Something important comes up, who do we get in touch with?"

It wasn't a tough question, even for the notoriously suspicious Genovese family. Al had already been formally introduced to the family's acting administration, including Barney Bellomo, a young college-educated member from the Bronx who was serving as acting boss, and Michael Generoso, the acting underboss known as "Mickey Dimino." Ida was acting consigliere. "So, I'm thinking, the easy answer is 'See Mickey Dimino,' or something like that."

But Ida said nothing. He sat staring at Al for more than a minute as if he didn't know what to tell him.

"I'm sitting there and it's getting stupid. I'm waiting for an answer and he's just staring at me and I'm looking at him. And I'm thinking, So this is it. Something's going to happen to me in three weeks. Jimmy knows. He doesn't want to say anything because the word is out that I'm no good. He's thinking maybe I'm wired. And he was just spotted with me so he's likely to get asked. They'd pick him up for questioning."

Al finally let the tongue-tied consigliere off the hook. "You want me to get in touch with Mickey?" asked Al. Ida still said nothing. But he bobbed his head forward in an awkward nod of agreement.

There wasn't much more to talk about. Outside on the

street, Al asked Ida if he wanted a ride back to the neighborhood. "No," he said, "I'll walk." Al watched his old friend and Frustace walk away.

Right after Labor Day, Pete Chiodo, still weak and undergoing rehabilitation, made his courtroom debut in the Windows trial. He was the final government witness. The trial was moved from Brooklyn to the White Plains federal courthouse to make the trip less arduous for him.

He was the first sworn member of the Luchese family to publicly break his vow of *omerta*. His right arm trembled and his voice was shaky at times. At one point, he complained he felt dizzy and asked the judge for a break. But he held up pretty well during three days on the stand testifying against the nine defendants, including leaders of the Genovese, Colombo, and Gambino families. There was every reason to expect he'd be in better shape when Vic Amuso's trial rolled around in the spring.

III

—

The Outlaw

18

THE KIMBERLY HOTEL

Wednesday, September 18, 1991, was a Jewish holiday. It was Yom Kippur, the Day of Atonement. Schools were closed and many New Yorkers had the day off. The mobsters handling the operations of the Luchese crime family hoped that law enforcement had it off too. They scheduled a business meeting for that afternoon.

Despite the many recent setbacks and the fears permeating their ranks, their marching orders from the boss in jail and the underboss still in hiding remained unchanged: no letup on their enemies, no slacking off on their criminal enterprises. Vic Amuso and Anthony Casso had blossomed into full-blown fanatical despots, prepared to take everyone down with them. They were ruling now purely through terror, ready to execute any who disappointed them.

The meeting began at a fashionable Chinese restaurant called Chin Chin tucked away on East Forty-Ninth Street. It was another favorite of Anthony Baratta, the Upper East Side dining connoisseur and narcotics marketer. Al had Joe Fiore drive him uptown to the restaurant. He arrived promptly at 1 p.m.

When he arrived, Baratta was out front with Frankie Pearl Federico, the drug-dealing assassin who had grappled with carter Robert Kubecka. Baratta told Al they were waiting for representatives of the Bonanno crime family. They wanted to discuss a beef about a bookmaking problem.

Al gave a silent groan. He knew exactly what it was about. He thought he had already resolved the dispute. Frank Lagano, one of the crew members taken away from him in recent weeks, was accused of stiffing the Bonanno family on a hefty debt. Lagano and his pal, Curly Russo, would be there as well.

After a few minutes, Anthony Spero, the acting Bonanno boss, arrived. With him was acting underboss Sal Vitale and a craggy-faced capo in his seventies from Bensonhurst named John Faraci, known to everyone as "Johnny Green."

Al respected Spero as an old-school gangster. And he was fond of Johnny Green, who had landed at Normandy on D-day. But he wasn't looking forward to the debate. Lagano was given to raving and rambling. And he knew the Bonanno crew was seriously bent out of shape over the matter.

They sat at a table in the front of the restaurant. Al noticed right away that Baratta seemed nervous. He kept looking at his watch. At one point he called over Federico. "Tell the hotel we're on our way," he told him.

Federico's job was to be the walker. "He's the guy who takes you to the meeting, since it's supposed to be a secret where it is until you get there." Al knew exactly where they were going, however. They had used the Kimberly Hotel around the corner on East Fiftieth Street before for meetings.

When Federico returned, Baratta gestured toward the Bonanno crew members. They followed Frankie Pearl over to the hotel. In silence, Al waited with Baratta. Bowat seemed distracted, he noticed again, still looking at his watch and tapping his feet. There was no small talk.

When Federico came back, Al followed him out to the street. Baratta said he would wait for Frank Lastorino. "On the way out I see Frankie Pearl turn around and look back at Bowat. He makes this little gesture with his hands, like, 'Where do you want me to take him?' And Bowat points toward the hotel. I caught that, too."

Federico seemed edgy as well. "We're walking up Third

Avenue. I know Frankie a long time. We were in prison together and the guy usually talks a mile a minute. Now he's not saying anything."

Federico turned onto East Fiftieth Street and paused in the middle of the block in front of the Kimberly. Next door was a French restaurant with green canopies. Federico pulled out a slip of paper with the room number on it. "It's 29B," Federico said. He stayed on the sidewalk as Al entered the hotel.

The lobby was surprisingly empty. The clerk behind the reception desk, a short man with close-cropped hair in a dark blue uniform, nodded to Al as he headed for the elevator bank. The room was on the hotel's top floor.

Sal Avellino opened the door. The Golfer looked tired, like he didn't want to be there. Al told him that Baratta and Lastorino were on their way. It was a two-room suite. He entered down a short hallway past a bathroom. Beyond was a sitting room with two couches, chairs, a TV, and a bar. To the left was a bedroom with its own sitting room and another bathroom. The Bonanno family officials were back there with Lagano and Russo, already haggling over the money.

The issue centered on a major gambler who was close to Frank Lagano. The gambler had lost $400,000 with one of the Bonanno's bookmaking outfits. "They claimed Frankie's guy beat them for some serious money." Al had tried to work out a settlement a few months earlier, but Lagano had failed to follow through.

It was a lengthy discussion. Baratta and Lastorino arrived in the middle of it. Al did his best to defend his former crew member. It was a losing cause. "Frankie Lagano wouldn't listen. He was raising his voice all over the place. I had to remind him that he was speaking to an acting boss, Anthony Spero." The final verdict was that Lagano would have to pay $135,000 to wipe out the debt.

As the Bonanno members got up to leave, the conversation turned to Pete Chiodo and his performance on the witness stand a few days earlier. There were no Bonanno family members in the case, but Spero was seething. There was only one way to deal with the problem, he said. "All the family members of those who become rats should be killed," he said with venom. "Women, children, everything. Murder them."

Al listened to the speech in shock. Anthony Spero had been around a long time. If he was talking that way, Al thought, then the Life was changing. So were the men at the top.

It was already 4 p.m. The panel members still had a long agenda. "We went over construction deals, loan shark collections, gambling. We talked about what to do for Vic. It was a lot of stuff."

An hour later, Baratta called downstairs to Federico to bring up coffee and sandwiches. Al watched his every move. He kept thinking something was off. Lastorino and Baratta seemed to be exchanging little smiles, passing remarks. "Maybe things will be better soon," Lastorino said at one point, looking at Baratta as he spoke. Baratta smiled and nodded. It was an inside joke of some kind. Al looked at them. Did they think he didn't notice?

Lastorino kept going into the bathroom by the entrance. Al counted five trips. It was like his kidneys were floating.

"What'd you do?" Al asked when he came back and sat down. "Drink too much last night?" Lastorino, a big man with a head of dark curly hair, ignored him. He sat back down at the end of the couch.

To Al, everything the men did in the room became increasingly ominous. Every little action was magnified. Lastorino kept reaching inside his shirt, scratching his chest. He might be hiding a weapon, thought Al. He's trying to get me used to it, so I won't notice when he grabs it.

Baratta stood up and began walking around the suite collecting used glasses, cups, and plates. Al swiveled in his chair, watching him move about the room. What's he doing that for? Al wondered. The guy's not a waiter. He's running a crime family. Al's mind was racing. Maybe he's getting rid of anything with fingerprints on it. That must be it, he decided.

Al was sitting upright in his chair. Behind him was a large armoire. There was a long coffee table in front of him. Even the discussions weren't making sense to him anymore. It sounded like mindless babble. They were filling up time, he decided. Waiting for something to happen.

Al looked out the window. It was getting dark. He checked the clock. It was 7 p.m. Suddenly, Baratta announced he had to leave. "Frank, I have to make that appointment, remember?"

Lastorino looked up. "Oh right, you got to go, right, Anthony?"

They sounded like actors talking on a stage, Al thought, as though they'd rehearsed that little exchange. But it was an opening for him to leave as well. He wanted to get out of there as soon as he could. He'd been there too long already.

Al stood up. As he rose, Lastorino came halfway off the couch, his hand stretched out. "Al, wait a minute," he said, sounding excited. "Don't go yet. I got Big Mike downstairs. He wants to talk about that thing with the Koreans and the corrugated cardboard."

Now Al was on full alert. No one had said anything about Mike DeSantis, the Luchese soldier who had helped bury Sonny Morrissey, being there. He was the owner of an auto body shop on McDonald Avenue in Brooklyn with interests in waste-carting firms. The cardboard scheme had been broached a few weeks earlier. Like the garbage rackets, the idea was to squeeze the hundreds of Korean produce stores to get control of the tons of cardboard their shops generated.

Al wanted to tell them to forget about it. He could almost feel the menace in the room. But he didn't want to sound panicky. "All right," he snapped. "But we're like all day here already." Lastorino promised it would be quick. Al sat down again, still alert, his back not touching the chair.

A few minutes later, DeSantis stalked into the room. Al did a double take. A big man, DeSantis was walking stiffly in blue jeans and heavy black boots. Despite the late-summer warmth, he had on a thick blue sweatshirt. Underneath was a heavy material that made him look several sizes bigger than he already was. He was carrying a plastic shopping bag.

He's walking like Frankenstein, Al thought. He stared at

DeSantis's sweatshirt. He realized with astonishment he was wearing a bulletproof vest.

"Hiya, fellas," said the big man. He walked over to where Avellino was seated and placed his plastic bag beside a small table. Avellino, who had been tuning out of the meeting for the past hour, suddenly jumped.

"Oh, a bag!" he said.

Al watched DeSantis put the bag on the floor. As he leaned over, Al saw a large lump under his sweatshirt. The shape came into focus. It was the butt of a pistol tucked into the back of his pants.

You don't bring a gun to a meeting unless you're looking to use it, Al thought. It was one of the oldest rules on the books. It meant you had bad intentions. Al now knew he wasn't being paranoid. They had brought DeSantis up there with a gun for one purpose. They were going to kill him right there in the hotel room.

"I got to take a leak, guys," DeSantis announced as he straightened up. He stepped into the bathroom near the entrance door.

Al got up again. He looked around the room. Lastorino was staring at the hallway leading to the exit. Avellino seemed out of it. If he isn't part of the plot, Al decided, he must be another target. They're going to hit us both, he thought.

Any minute Mike DeSantis would come out of the bathroom with his gun in his hand. "I was thinking I'd run right at him, try to tackle him. Claw at his eyes. Anything I could do."

He stood there waiting. Lastorino was now talking about the cardboard scheme, but to Al it just sounded like garbled nonsense. He was hardly listening. DeSantis is in there a long time, he kept thinking. Lastorino is talking just to distract him.

He tensed as he heard the door of the bathroom open. DeSantis emerged. There was nothing in his hands. DeSantis walked back over to the bag he'd left by the table. He leaned over to take something out. The lump on his back was gone.

He hid the gun in the bathroom, Al told himself. He hid it

in there and when Frankie goes in to take one more leak, he's going to come out blasting.

DeSantis offered Al a piece of paper he'd taken out of the bag. "Here," he said. "You want to look at that?" It was a brochure of some kind about the cardboard business. Al noticed DeSantis was avoiding looking at him.

He thrust out his hand. "Hey, Mike, howya been?" Al said suddenly. The move startled DeSantis. His eyes flickered on Al's and then immediately looked away. He slowly extended his hand to shake. It was ice-cold and clammy.

When DeSantis turned away, Al took a half step back and jammed his own hand into his pocket. It was the oldest of tricks. All he had in his pocket was his beeper. But he was desperate. He thought he might be able to fool them into thinking he too was armed.

He flung the brochure back at DeSantis. "I don't want to look at this," he snapped. "What do I know about corrugated cardboard? You got the best guy in the world right here. That's his game," he said, nodding at Avellino. "I'm leaving, I been here too long already. I got Joe Cuz waiting for me all this time."

He took three long strides toward the hotel room door.

"Al!" said Lastorino loudly, rising out of his seat. Al turned at the door, his hand still in his pocket. "Al, don't you want to say good-bye?"

Lastorino was looking at him, then looking at the bathroom. He was trying to figure out if he should make a reach for it, Al decided. He didn't think he had the nerve. Al walked quickly back into the room. He pumped DeSantis's hand again. "Good-bye Mikey," he said. He nodded to Avellino. "Good night, Sallie."

He took the same three long strides out the door. Lastorino followed. "Al, am I going to see you Thursday?" he asked in the corridor. His voice was high-pitched and anxious. There were plans to get together to split up some of their earnings. "Remember? We got to meet tomorrow."

Al looked at him. "Frankie, you want me to come back up?" He said it with a threatening edge. He wanted Lastorino to understand that if he came back up, he would be ready to fight.

"No," said Lastorino. "No, that's okay." He seemed deflated.

Al punched the elevator button. He watched Lastorino until the doors closed. Alone in the elevator, he let out a long breath. "They were going to fucking kill me in there," he said out loud.

Out on the street, Joe Fiore was nowhere to be found. Al walked quickly to Second Avenue. He hailed a cab headed downtown.

"Bowery and Spring Street," he told the driver. He sat back in the seat trying to think what he should do next.

He found Joe Fiore standing on Prince Street in front of Ray's Pizza. "I thought you didn't need me anymore," Fiore said.

Al scolded him for leaving, but told him to get the car out of the garage on Elizabeth Street. "I want to get to Joseph's place in Brooklyn, fast," he said. He paged his son to let him know he was coming.

Joseph listened to his story as they walked along Paerdegat Basin near his apartment. "Once they got me, they'd be coming for you next," Al told him. He asked Joseph if he wanted to come back to the city with him, to stay on Spring Street. "No," said Joseph. Louise wasn't feeling well. "I'll stay here. I'll come in and meet you tomorrow morning."

Joseph said he had a pistol in the house. "Load up," Al told him. "Don't answer the door. Anybody comes up the stairs, start shooting."

He hugged his son and walked back to where Joe Fiore was parked. "I was trying to think. I was really nervous. I was hot and nervous."

Thursday morning, he paged Sal Avellino. He punched in the number for the pay phone at Kenmare and Mott Streets. A few minutes later, the phone rang. It meant he was still alive.

He asked Avellino if he'd realized what had been going on in the hotel room.

"Yeah," said Avellino. He sounded shaky.

"They were going to kill us."

"Yeah," he repeated.

"Look, you're my friend," Al told him. "I'm telling you and your brother. Don't keep any more appointments. Lay low."

Avellino didn't say anything. Al knew what he was thinking. That a shooting war was about to start and he was trying to decide which way to jump.

"Look, we'll talk," Al said. He hung up.

He was waiting for Joseph when he got a page from Louie Daidone. "Al, I have to see you," Daidone said. "You passing by Brooklyn?"

Al wasn't going to offer any more targets. "You want to see me, I'm at Kenmare and Mott," he told him.

"I'll meet you," said Daidone. "Be there in about forty minutes."

He was on the corner when Daidone and Patty Dellorusso pulled up. He was glad to see them. If he was going to fight back, Daidone and Dellorusso would be key. "I figured they'd be able to help us do our damage."

Dellorusso stayed in the car. Daidone came over to Al. He was carrying an envelope. They walked along the street.

Daidone had been bumped up to acting captain of the Canarsie crew after Al had been made acting boss. Daidone was in charge of collecting from members. He told Al he had the money from a shakedown that Ray Argentina was running on an asbestos-removal firm.

Al looked at him. He doesn't know anything about it, he decided. They were standing on Spring Street in front of Guidetti's funeral parlor. He decided to trust him.

When he had finished the story he waited to hear what Louie had to say. If they decided to push back hard, Daidone would be Al's strongest ally.

After a pause, Daidone spoke. "It blows my mind," he said.

Al looked at him. "That's it? It blows your mind?"

He'd been expecting a different response from the big ex–football player.

"Yeah, it blows my mind," Daidone repeated.

Al sighed. He told Daidone to go ahead. He'd see him later. They walked back to Kenmare Street, where Dellorusso was parked. Two less allies, he thought as he watched them drive away.

A little while later he got another page that confirmed it. It was Daidone again telling Al he was going out with his wife that evening, but he was available if Al needed him.

"You're going out with your wife?"

"Yeah," Daidone said. "We're going to Radio City Music Hall."

"Forget about it, Louie," Al told him. He didn't try to hide his anger. "I don't need you." He slammed down the phone.

He stood on the corner, trying to count the people he could rely on if he mounted a fight. He didn't get very far. There was Joe Fiore, Pete Del Cioppo, a few others maybe. And there was Joseph of course, who had arrived in the city in the late morning. His son was urging his father to rally his troops to fight. He had a plan.

"I can get Georgie Neck Zappola," Joseph said. "We can force him to show us where Casso is hiding, and we can take him out."

His son John was also beside him, even though John had never been involved in his mob affairs. He'd never wanted him to be. He believed that, unlike Joseph, it wasn't in John's blood.

Joseph's pager buzzed. He looked at the number. "It's Frank Lastorino," he told his father.

"Call him," Al said. "See what he's saying."

Joseph dialed from the pay phone. Lastorino picked up.

"What's up?" asked Joseph.

"Tell your father, Joey. We trunked the architect," Lastorino said.

Joseph looked at his father. "I'll tell him," he said.

"They killed Fava," he said after he hung up. "He said to tell you they 'trunked the architect.' "

Al felt a wave of disgust. He had hoped the contract Casso

had issued on the young designer would be forgotten, the way other fits of rage by the Luchese bosses had faded over time.

"He was an innocent kid. An architect. He wasn't a threat. He wasn't part of our life. What did he ever do? There was no reason to kill him."

He told his sons it was time to go home. His own rage had ebbed. The notion of turning the tables on his enemies and seizing power in the family suddenly seemed like nothing he wanted to do.

"I asked myself, What are you fighting for? To be boss of what? I realized there is going to be treachery like this forever. It wasn't worth it."

Forget about it, he told himself. He felt disgusted with the life he had chosen, even more with the people running it.

"They marked me a rat, and I wasn't a rat. That's an even worse thing to do. I had gone along with it too. Mike Salerno's a rat? Bruno gets a canary in his mouth? I believed all that stuff. I saw the whole stinking mess. It was like looking in a mirror. I didn't want it anymore."

Friday morning, Joe Fiore knocked on his apartment door. Al stood cautiously to the side. "Who is it?" he asked.

"It's me, Joe Cuz."

Al didn't open up. "Joey, go down to the restaurant. Wait for me there," he said.

As he waited to make sure Fiore had left, the phone rang. Dolores answered. They used it only for their own family members.

"It's Mr. Veltre, from parole," she said, covering the mouthpiece with her hand.

Al took the phone. "Yes, Mr. Veltre," Al greeted his parole officer. The two men always addressed each other formally.

"Mr. D'Arco," he said, "the FBI called me to say that they've learned there is a contract on your life."

Al felt himself tighten. So even the FBI knows, he thought.

"Would you like to speak to someone there?"

Al cut him off. "Mr. Veltre, I don't want to speak to any-body."

"Well, Mr. D'Arco, this is serious. It's not something to sneeze at. The FBI has called me a couple of times about this. I can give you the number."

Joe Veltre had been Al's parole officer almost since he got out of prison in 1986. On his end of the phone, he had the sense that Al heard the genuine alarm in his voice.

"I don't want any phone numbers," said Al. "Look, I'm not going anywhere, but are you going to be in your office in a few hours?"

Veltre said he would be there.

"Well, I'll walk down to see you, and whatever you got to tell me, you can tell me then. But I don't want to speak to anyone from the FBI."

"Okay," said Veltre.

Al hung up the phone. He could take care of himself. But his family was now a target as well.

"We got to start packing up, right now," he told Dolores. His two younger daughters, Tara and Dawn, were home. They all heard the panic in his voice.

"Why? What's going on?" they asked.

He ignored their questions. "You got to get out of here and that's it," he said. He started throwing things into boxes, grab-bing clothes, and putting things into bags.

The girls were sobbing.

"Look, there's bad stuff going on," he yelled. "Joseph knows about it. John knows about it. Just do what I say."

His house was chaos. Dolores knew without being told what was happening. But she was also distraught.

He tried to ignore the crying. He told John to go to a travel agent. "I want you to get airline tickets and make reservations for you, your mother, and the girls," he said.

"To where?" John asked.

Al was briefly stumped. "Hawaii," he said finally. The fam-ily had been there a couple of times before. Dolores had friends there.

They packed most of the afternoon. At 5 p.m., Al realized

he had forgotten to visit the parole office. He dialed Veltre's number. He was still at his desk.

"Mr. Veltre, I said I'd get back to you. I'm still here but I want you to know I am packing up my family. I am getting them out of town."

"I think that's a good idea," Veltre said. "Why don't you come in?"

"No," said Al. "If anything happens, I know how to reach you. If I make any decision, I'll let you know."

After he hung up, his own words echoed in his ears. What decision?

Joseph tried to talk him out of it. They could still win, he told him. If he could get to Gaspipe, he could also get to Frank Lastorino. Joseph said he had a way to get into Lastorino's home.

"It would be, 'Hello, Frankie?' Boom. He's gone," he told his father. As for Anthony Baratta, they could get Steve Crea to make good on his offer to take him out.

But Al had reached a turning point. Winning no longer counted. He had broken none of the rules of the street. The rules had been broken against him. What counted now, more than anything else, was keeping his family safe.

"Fuck the street, fuck the mob. My family comes first. I wasn't worried about Joseph. I knew he could take care of himself. But say I try to stick it out, and they catch up with my daughter? They catch up with my son John? I can't do it alone. I'm only one person. There was only one way."

Saturday morning, he got Dolores, John, and his daughters off safely. He and Joseph drove out to Long Island, to his mother's house in Bayville.

Sitting on a porch that Joseph and Al had helped his own father build when they first moved out there, they continued the discussion.

"What are we going to do, Dad?" Joseph asked him.

Al didn't answer right away. He took a breath. "We're going to call the FBI," his father said. "We're going in."

They sat there for a few moments thinking about what had just been said.

Before he knew it, they were both crying.

"You got to decide for yourself, though," Al told him.

"I don't know if I can do it," Joseph said. "But I'm staying with you. I'll do it for now."

Al had refused to take the phone numbers parole officer Joe Veltre had offered him. But he knew that his lawyer, John Zagari, had been bothered by agents after the Matamoras landfill deal fell apart. He had to have the number of someone to call.

He reached Zagari at home in Pennsylvania.

"You're talking about the witness protection program," the lawyer said after Al told him what had happened.

"I guess so," said Al. "What do you think?"

"It's a good idea," the lawyer said.

"Make the call for me, John," said Al.

"I will," said Zagari. "Stay by the phone."

19

TRUMBULL

He threw his gun behind the house. The agent on the phone, Bob Marston, had told him to be sure not to have any weapons on them when they arrived.

The little house was on a dead-end lane on a neck of land extending into Oyster Bay. Long Island Sound was a couple of blocks away. The house was empty except for Al and Joseph.

Al told the agent they would meet them outside. "It's a dark street," Al told him. "We'll be out by the streetlight so you can see us."

He made a point of telling Marston that he expected to see him there, not some other agents. "I will come with *you*," Al told him. "Don't be sending no one else."

Marston promised. He described himself so that Al would know him. "Six foot two, glasses, brown hair, 180 pounds. Medium build." He would be with his partner, Jim O'Connor, he said. They would also have other agents there as backup, just in case.

Standing on the porch at midnight, Al and Joseph heard nothing but crickets. Then the street erupted.

"All of a sudden, there's cars shooting up and down the block, racing around."

A blue Buick sped past the house. Marston was in the

passenger seat, his notebook with the directions he'd gotten
from Al open on his lap. O'Connor was driving. "I think we
just missed the house," Marston told his partner. O'Connor
jammed on the brakes and backed up at full speed.

Another agent following them raced past, stopped at the
end of the block, then backed up and blocked the road. A third
car pulled up with a squeal of tires, the driver cutting the
wheels so that the auto was sideways in the street. Another
agent's car jerked to a halt behind it.

On the porch, Al and Joseph looked at each other. "We
couldn't figure out what they were racing around like that for."

Marston and O'Connor got out of their car. They stood on
the curb. They saw two men come down off the porch and
start walking toward them. A shorter, balding older man was
wearing a dark blue windbreaker. He had a small gym bag
in his hand. The younger man beside him was wearing a Mets
baseball cap.

"Mr. D'Arco, I'm Bob," Marston said, extending a hand.
He introduced O'Connor.

"This is my son Joseph," said Al. Everyone was guardedly
polite. Marston asked Al if he was armed.

"No," said Al. "We got rid of them. I just got some clothes."
He hefted the small gym bag. The agents took his word for
it. Thinking back on it later, Marston was surprised that they
didn't pat them down or look in the bag. He realized he had
already started to trust Al D'Arco.

"Let's get going," the agent said. He opened the back door
for them to get in. Al and Joseph hesitated. Neither father nor
son had good memories of rides in the backseats of cop cars.
They had certainly never done so voluntarily. After a moment,
Al clambered inside. Joseph followed.

No one said much in the car. Their first stop, Marston announced, leaning over the front seat, would be his office in
New Rochelle. They'd have a chance to use a bathroom and
get coffee or a drink of water. They drove in a four-car cara-
van across the Throgs Neck Bridge into the Bronx, then up
Interstate 95 to Westchester County. The trip took about an

hour. In the back, Joseph seemed to nod off. Al stared out the window.

The FBI's offices were located inside a Ramada Hotel right off the highway. Basically a substation of the far larger New York office, the New Rochelle outpost was known as a "resident agency," where agents covering Westchester and next-door Putnam County were based. When they arrived, several of Marston's colleagues were there waiting for them, including his supervisor, Craig Dotlo.

While Al and Joseph used the bathroom, the agents consulted with their boss. It was one thirty in the morning, but calls would have to be made, they agreed. There were several people who would want to know right away that the acting boss of the Luchese crime family had voluntarily placed himself in FBI custody, even if they were deep asleep when the call came.

Dotlo called FBI headquarters in Washington. The alert was immediately passed to bureau director William Sessions, a former federal judge named by President Reagan to head the agency in 1987.

Marston knew who his first call should be. He sat down at his desk and dialed the home number of Anthony Siano, the prosecutor handling the Matamoras landfill case. Siano, forty-three, was a veteran of the Brooklyn Organized Crime Strike Force, the federal prosecutors who had made Al's former captain, Paul Vario, a special target a decade earlier. Siano had often told the story of how they had sent Vario to prison, never to return, with the help of their then star witness, Henry Hill. The case wasn't much, Siano admitted, a perjury rap for lying about Hill's no-show job.

Marston smiled to himself as he dialed. Henry Hill had been the mob equivalent of a team batboy. Al D'Arco was like landing Casey Stengel.

Siano was asleep when the call came in. "Tony," said Marston, "I'm sorry to wake you, but I thought you'd like to know I am here at the New Rochelle office with Al D'Arco. He's with us now."

It took Siano a moment to grab ahold of what he was

hearing. Al D'Arco, the acting Luchese crime family boss they'd heard about on the landfill wire? Was in custody? Siano was known for his own tart-tongued sense of humor. He immediately had the same suspicion Marston had had several hours earlier. "Is this your idea of a bad practical joke, Bob?" he asked.

Marston laughed. "No, he's here. He's come in. We're going to get to a safe location. I'll call you first chance I get after that."

Siano tried to absorb the news. No one this high in the mob had ever defected before. There was no playbook on how to handle it. He put his hand on the phone, debating whether he should wake up his own boss, Howard Heiss, chief of the organized-crime unit in the Southern District of New York. The debate didn't last long. Siano imagined the questions he'd be likely to face if something went wrong: "Just when exactly were you planning to tell me that you had the acting Luchese boss in a hotel room in Westchester?"

His call woke up Heiss's wife. Siano introduced himself with apologies. Heiss greeted him with a tone suggesting that if this wasn't something really important, Siano should forget about going to work on Monday.

"We've got Al D'Arco, the acting boss of the Luchese crime family, in custody," Siano said. "He's flipped." He heard only silence on the other end. After a pause, Heiss spoke.

"All right, what are you doing?"

"We're trying to settle the situation and make sure he's safe," said Siano. "But he's going to need a lawyer."

"Okay, keep me posted," Heiss said. Then he hung up.

Siano looked at the phone. As the wiseguys say, he told himself, now I'm on record. They can't say I didn't tell them.

In the New Rochelle office, Marston was trying to figure out where to take his new companions. He needed a place that was both safe and convenient. He didn't have to look far down the road to guess that this was going to take up most of his time for the coming weeks, if not months. If he wanted to be able to see his family, he'd be wise to get a place nearby.

There was a Marriott Hotel off the highway in Trumbull, Connecticut, about fifty miles east of the office and not far from where Marston lived. He woke up a friend who worked in the hotel chain. The friend helped arrange three adjoining rooms on the top floor for them.

He had driven his own car to New Rochelle to hook up with O'Connor, so they decided they would drive separately to Trumbull. That way, they'd have two cars available. Al went with Marston. Joseph got in O'Connor's car.

Marston chatted with Al beside him in the passenger seat. They talked about Al's family. The agent told him a little about his own. "I don't live too far from here," Marston said as they drove along the Merritt Parkway.

At the hotel, Al and Joseph shared a room. Marston and O'Connor were down the hall in rooms of their own. Neither slept the first night, however. They still didn't know what they were up against. A couple of other agents arrived to keep a watchful eye on the hallway.

In the morning, the situation got complicated right away. Joseph was sick. Al took Marston aside to explain his son's ailment. He needed methadone, Al told him. He was hooked. He hadn't replenished his supply in a few days.

Getting methadone for a potential witness was another new experience for Marston. But he figured that someone in the bureau would have experience with it. He was right. The New York office had a small medical unit attached to it. An agent went to the city to retrieve a prescription.

Once medicated, Joseph felt better. But he was largely silent, often sitting on the bed in the hotel room, saying little.

His father was the opposite. Al was already bouncing off the walls, second-guessing himself and worrying about the next move by his former mob allies. He warned Marston that the Luchese bosses had sources inside law enforcement. "I don't think they understood how much these guys knew. I was trying to tell them they shouldn't sell them short."

Both he and Joseph still had their pagers with them. They buzzed in a continuing chorus, the numbers lighting up on the small screen with the codes showing various mobster pals reaching out for them. The agents wanted to ask about the calls, but Siano gave strict orders. They shouldn't make any effort to question or debrief the D'Arcos until they had legal representation, he said.

That presented another major problem.

Al insisted that he already had a lawyer, John Zagari, the Pittsburgh-based attorney he had called the night before looking for help in reaching the FBI. "That's the guy I trust," he told Siano and the agents. "That's who I want representing me."

It fell to Marston to tell Al that Zagari couldn't be his lawyer. Worse, he couldn't tell him exactly why not.

What they couldn't tell Al was that Zagari himself was a target in the illegal-landfill case. He was likely to be indicted. In fact, they had more solid evidence against the lawyer at that point than they had against Al, whose role in the landfill scheme they were still trying to determine. But since it was still possible that Al might decide against cooperating and walk out of the hotel, they couldn't tell him that, either. To do so would have put Zagari in jeopardy.

Al reacted with suspicion and rage. "You're telling me I don't have the right to have my own lawyer represent me?" he thundered.

The decision confirmed all the fears and doubts he had about his new alliance. They were screwing him, he thought, just as he should've known they would do. He was in the hands of men who had been his sworn enemies just forty-eight hours before. Someplace out there, his former friends were trying to find him and kill him. He had just moved his family far away. Now he was being told he couldn't have the backup of the one person he thought he could trust.

Marston asked Al to take a walk with him outside. They couldn't go far, so they simply walked around the hotel parking lot. The agent tried to cool him down. He could have any other lawyer of his choosing, Marston told him. They would give him a list of court-approved attorneys, eligible to be reimbursed for their work by the government. He just couldn't have John Zagari. There was a conflict, he told Al as they walked around and around in the lot, one that would hurt both Al and Zagari down the road once the problem surfaced.

Meanwhile, Siano scrambled to come up with a list of attorneys who could represent Al. They needed someone knowledgeable about organized crime who wouldn't have a conflict of his own, having represented members of the Luchese family in the past. He worked his way through a short list, making calls to find out if the attorneys were interested and available.

He ended up with just three names. One was an Italian American. Siano put that name at the top of the list. He went to the hotel to hand it to Al. The first name was James De-Vita. A former prosecutor in the Southern District, DeVita had become a white-collar defense attorney in private practice. DeVita's specialty wasn't organized crime, but he had a couple of other attributes Siano thought would help. He was from Brooklyn, and he was Italian.

Al still suspected that he was being conned. But he noticed the ethnic connection. "I'll try him," he said, pointing to DeVita's name.

Nothing was simple, however. They couldn't just tell De-Vita to meet them at the Marriott. Elaborate security precautions were taken for each meeting. Siano reached DeVita at home and told him he had a potential client who would like to interview him as his possible lawyer. He gave DeVita a location. "Meet us there tomorrow afternoon," he said. "You'll be picked up."

Agents drove the lawyer on a circuitous route, looping back on themselves, and pulling over on the side of the highway. They were scrubbing off, the same way Al and the Luchese gang did when they tried to make sure that law enforcement couldn't tail them.

An hour later, they finally deposited the attorney at a large parking lot. Cars filled with heavily armed agents were posted at the entrance and exit. Siano introduced Al to DeVita and then left them alone. He watched as the two men wandered around the lot. They were feeling each other out.

"Where are you from?" was Al's first question.

"I grew up in Brooklyn," said the lawyer.

"Yeah, what part?"

"By the Navy Yard, Fort Greene area," DeVita said.

Al felt a twinge of hope, his first in weeks. If he couldn't have the lawyer he knew, then the next best thing, he figured, would be to have a lawyer from his own neighborhood. A *paisan*, to boot. Al posed a number of other questions and then asked DeVita if he would represent him. He'd be glad to do it, DeVita said. But if he was going to fashion a cooperation agreement for Al, he needed to know everything he'd done, his entire criminal history. They walked and talked for a couple more hours.

Later, speaking to Dolores on the phone in Hawaii, Al told her about the lawyer from his old neighborhood. "His name's DeVita. He grew up on Clinton Avenue."

DeVita, Dolores reminded him, was the name of the doctor who delivered John and Tara. The doctor's office was on Clinton Avenue.

The next time he saw the attorney, Al asked him about it. "That was my father," DeVita told him. "He was an obstetrician. He had his office right there in our house."

Al grinned. His lawyer's father had delivered his kids. Now the son was going to try and deliver him.

Marston and Siano thought they were over the hump. Once Al had an attorney, they could commence working out a plea agreement. As soon as that was reached, they could proceed to the task both men were anxious to get started on, getting Al to tell them the many mob secrets he harbored.

But they had again underestimated Al's deep suspicions. They assumed that Al understood that he and Joseph would have to have separate attorneys representing them. Both had separate criminal liabilities. A judge might well question the independence of a single attorney claiming to represent the best interests of both father and son.

Al was outraged all over again. It was another trick, he insisted. "You're trying to pit us against each other. You want to split us apart," he said.

He announced he was leaving. He packed the few belongings he had in his small gym bag and began heading out the door. Marston rushed to block his way.

"Al, let's talk about this," he said. "Let's take another walk and just talk."

There was nothing to talk about, Al said. He tried to push past him. Marston planted his hands on Al's shoulders. He towered over the shorter man, but he wasn't sure how long he could restrain him, or what he'd do if D'Arco tried to fight him off. "Wait, Al," he pleaded. "Let's try and talk this through."

Al was finally convinced to take another walk through the parking lot. If he didn't trust anyone, Marston told him, he would be all alone. He had to trust someone, he said.

"I got friends," Al spat back. "I got people I trust. I can handle it on my own."

He vented steam as he paced. Marston mostly listened. The more they walked, the calmer Al became. After more than an hour of walking, Al had agreed not to leave.

Back upstairs in the hotel, Marston called Siano to tell him what had happened. "You know if he wants to leave, we can't stop him," the prosecutor told him. "He's not charged with anything. We've got nothing to hold him on."

DeVita recommended a former colleague from the U.S. attorney's office named Vincent Bricetti to serve as Joseph's lawyer. Joseph was willing to go along with whatever his father decided. Al relied on DeVita's judgment. If he liked Bricetti, he figured, his son would be well represented. As it turned out, both lawyers drove hard bargains for their clients.

Al's agreement was a dense four pages. He agreed to plead guilty to a criminal information charging him with racketeering. His crimes, he acknowledged, included both homicide and mail fraud. He would have to testify truthfully before any grand juries or criminal cases at the government's request.

For its part, the government agreed that it wouldn't seek a sentence of more than twenty years against him. He could get less, depending on the level and quality of his cooperation.

Or he could get more, up to life imprisonment if the sentencing judge so ordered. The government also agreed to admit him and his immediate family into the witness protection program.

For Joseph, Bricetti demanded complete immunity. He would cooperate, and testify if asked. But there could be no threat of any prison time. The demand put Siano in a tough spot. He knew that Al D'Arco's crimes had to include murders. As an acting boss, his testimony was potentially invaluable. He knew nothing about Joseph's activity or his potential value as a witness.

"He wants a total immunity bath for the kid," Siano complained to Marston. "But we don't know anything about him."

Before he agreed, Siano said he wanted to find out what else the FBI knew about Joseph. "I want to make sure I'm not giving away the store."

He asked the bureau to query all the supervisors following the five crime families to see what they knew about Joseph's criminal activity. He waited for a response. The answer was blunt and dismissive. "He's a nobody," Siano was told. "He's nothing but a hamburger flipper."

Fair enough, Siano decided. In that case, we have nothing to lose. He ran the offer up the chain of command to Howard Heiss and Heiss's boss, U.S. Attorney Otto Obermaier. The decision was to agree to Bricetti's terms. Joseph D'Arco would have immunity.

At his first debriefing session, Joseph told Siano and the agents about how he had killed Anthony DiLapi in California. He also told them that he had been the one to put most of the bullets into Big Pete Chiodo earlier that year.

Siano was stunned as he listened. "We were each thinking the same thing," said Siano. "Some hamburger flipper."

On September 26, five days after he had quit the mob, Al D'Arco began telling the story of his lifetime of crime.

DeVita was in the room for the first session, as was Siano. Marston took the notes. Jim O'Connor and a third agent, William Confrey, were there as well.

The agents and prosecutor were impressed with Al's intense focus. It was the same industriousness that he'd applied to his criminal activities. He told them he was willing to work just as hard for his new boss as he had for the last one.

The first memo was six pages long. It was recorded on an FBI form used for potential witnesses known as an FD-302, the first of more than seven hundred that Al would generate over the following two years. It contained a shorthand version of Al's career with the Luchese family, from his 1982 initiation to his promotion as acting boss in January. He made no attempt to glorify his role. Amuso and Casso had designated him as their "prick," he told them, the one they called upon to do "something unpleasant" when ordered.

He told them about the internal bickering and scheming that had consumed the family after Amuso and Casso had gone into hiding. He described the nighttime meeting in Staten Island in July when he had been demoted, and where his old friend Vic Amuso wouldn't look him in the eye. It had been followed by a growing realization, he said, that he was being set up for his own assassination.

In a quick count, he cited the murders in which he had played a role, including his personal participation in the slaying of garment center tycoon Michael Pappadio. He told them about the senseless killing of architect Anthony Fava, carried out just two days before he quit the mob.

Who else, Marston and Siano asked, was on the Luchese hit list?

Al named four members of the New Jersey faction who were still targets of active murder plots. He told them that Amuso and Casso had also vowed to kill Neil Migliore, the veteran Long Island mobster who had made a fortune in the construction business. And then there was his own former associate, Pete Del Cioppo. "I think Petey definitely has something to worry about," Al told them.

The information triggered an automatic FBI response. Any time the bureau learned of a possible murder conspiracy, agents were obligated to warn potential victims, just as word had been passed to Al via his parole officer.

It was always a tough sell. The targets were inevitably more suspicious of the agents giving the warnings than of their fellow mobsters. One way to enhance their credibility was to convince them the tip had started with one of their own, the missing Al D'Arco. No word had leaked yet that the former acting Luchese boss was with the FBI. Presumably, the Luchese mob still wasn't sure what had become of him.

Marston decided to take a photograph of Al holding his official FBI credentials. It would serve as a "vouch photo"—proving that Al really was cooperating. They posed him in one of the hotel rooms, against floral-patterned curtains kept drawn day and night. In the photo, Al was still wearing the same blue-and-white, collarless short-sleeved shirt he'd had on the night he was picked up in Bayville. He looked directly into the camera, the credentials held chest high by his fingertips so that Marston's name and official picture were clearly visible. The expression on Al's face was sober and serious. "This is for real," he seemed to be saying.

After the initial debriefing session, a new crisis erupted. The agents told Al that Joseph had to go into a drug detox program. The bureau couldn't continue to feed his methadone habit, they said. In the meantime, Al would be moved to a safe house in upstate New York.

Al erupted in fury. "They were trying to break us up again, split us apart." He didn't dispute that his son needed help. He'd never been able to persuade Joseph to kick methadone. Part of the problem, Al knew, was Louise. Joseph's wife still battled her own addiction. In the days after Al and Joseph had decided to cooperate, she had generated new anxiety by hesitating to join her husband. "I don't know if I can do this without her," he told his father.

Al fumed and cursed. He insisted that he needed to be with his son. Marston again performed his role as counselor, gently trying to talk his witness down. They did more tours of the parking lot, Al venting as they walked.

Despite his protests, Al knew there was no way out anymore. He had cast his fate with the government. There was a picture now to prove it. Even as he paced the hotel lot, federal agents were warning Pete Del Cioppo and Neil Migliore about the threats to their lives. As proof, they were showing them the photo of Al D'Arco holding Bob Marston's FBI credentials.

Before they parted, he sat with Joseph in their hotel room. "We said we would get through this, and be together again, the whole family. That we had to stay strong for everyone else."

He watched his son walk down the hotel corridor with a team of agents. He was all alone now, he thought.

The safe house was a large, comfortable home on the edge of the woods. There was a swimming pool, a tennis court, and a fireplace. Al didn't want to walk in the woods. "They got ticks and stuff in there," the city gangster told Marston. It was chilly the first night. Al watched as one of the agents tried to build a fire. "He didn't know what he was doing. He kept throwing wood on it, almost burned the place down." Al, who knew something about setting fires, took charge. "You gotta give it a chance to catch," he told them.

In the FBI, he was now a star. An almost daily parade of high-ranking agents arrived to interview him, each with his own line of questions to ask. Marston admired Al's ability to size up the people who sat across from him. "We'd go for a walk out on the tennis court afterward and he'd say, 'You know that guy really has a big ego,' or, 'I'm not sure I'd trust that one.' And he'd usually be dead-on. He had a great ability to read people very quickly."

But his suspicions had not disappeared. He tensed up when the room grew crowded and the questions were unrelenting. One day he interrupted an interview with a group of agents and beckoned Marston to follow him into a bedroom next door. Al closed the door behind them.

"Listen, I know about the thing with the finger," Al whispered.

Marston had no idea what he was talking about. Al pointed to his index finger. "You know," he continued, "when they take the blood test in prison. I know what they do to guys."

"I'm not following, Al," Marston said.

Al looked at him grimly. "The cancer," Al said. "When they give guys cancer in prison."

Marston still thought he was missing something. "What do you mean they give them cancer, Al?"

He spelled it out for him. "When we get arrested, and they prick your finger to take your blood and they put the cancer in," he said. He began listing mobsters he knew who had gone to prison in perfect health, only to contract cancer within months of their incarceration.

"And you think they give them cancer on purpose, Al?"

Al looked at him. "C'mon, Bob," he said.

Marston didn't know what to say. Here was a man he'd come to view as intelligent and perceptive telling him that he believed there was a government plot to give cancer to mob convicts. He tried not to insult him. "I don't think that happens," he said.

"Okay," said Al. "Well, anyway, I wanted you to know I know."

Later that night, the agent thought about the huge chasm that lay between Al D'Arco's view of the world and his own. In the war against crime, law enforcement could rightly be suspected of sometimes tilting cases, planting evidence, or lying on the witness stand. Those abuses occurred. But plotting to poison inmates? "It was like they saw us as Hitler and themselves as the Jews. They thought we were capable of anything." What was even more striking, he thought, was the window it opened on Al D'Arco's desperate state of mind. He had jumped from one group plotting to kill him to another he saw as having equally sinister intentions.

It wasn't Al's only fear. In the big house near the woods, surrounded by armed agents, he still felt haunted by the world he'd left behind. Some nights he awoke from nightmares. He was being chased by Gaspipe Casso. Other nights Chin Gigante was after him. He did his best to fight them off, but they kept catching up.

* * *

Ten days after he vanished from the Little Italy streets, the news that Al was now a federal informant made the newspapers. D'Arco was "the highest-ranked mobster to violate *omerta*," reported the *Daily News* on October 3. The story, on page 3 of the paper, carried the same grainy photo of him in the dark shirt and light jacket. It also reported that Joseph D'Arco was cooperating. An unnamed underworld source told the paper that the defections had the Luchese hierarchy "going absolutely crazy now."

High-level FBI officials did their best to spin the story away from his cooperation. New York's top organized-crime agent was quoted in a *New York Times* article the same day saying that D'Arco was "on the run," having fled to avoid execution by fellow mobsters.

The story confirmed one of Al's many suspicions. The FBI could tell its own lies when it thought it would help.

20

IN AMERICA

He spent six weeks in the safe house near the woods being debriefed about the mob life. He detailed the meetings, the schemes, the murder plots, the byzantine feuds between and within the crime families.

Agents marveled at his capacity for detail, his knowledge of crimes large and small, his insights into the world he had mastered.

Some tales were simply startling. The mobbed-up makers of the porn film *Deep Throat*, Al told them, had been gunned down by Colombo family shooters in a feud over the movie's $25 million profit. A shot that went wild killed a former nun standing behind her front door in the Brooklyn neighborhood where the hit took place.

Others offered a simple road map. If they checked the second floor of Genovese capo Anthony "Tough Tony" Federici's popular Park Side Restaurant in Corona, Queens, they'd find a gambling operation complete with satellite dish TVs.

Anyone wanting to eavesdrop on Genovese consigliere Jimmy Ida talking business should consider his favorite Mulberry Street dining spot, La Mela Ristorante. There, Al said, Ida stood in a small alcove off the rear hallway leading to the backyard.

Luchese captain Steve Crea, he informed them, preferred

to meet by his pigeon coop atop the roof of a Bronx construction firm owned by close associates. Crea so favored his pigeons that he often claimed to be going out of town so that he could spend more time with his birds.

Other stories were almost comic. Actor Burt Young, famous for his role in *Rocky*, was so starstruck by his mobster pals that he asked Vic Amuso if he could become a made member. Stick to your acting job, Amuso told him.

The agents filled their notebooks, then dictated them for transcription into the 302s. The writing was in the stilted, bureaucratic style that had been J. Edgar Hoover's facts-only preference. But sometimes the pathos of the scene slipped through.

"Facciola begged to see his daughter before he was killed," they wrote as Al described the wrenching murder of his friend Bruno.

Even before he appeared before a single jury, the former acting boss's decision to quit the Mafia was having an effect.

In early November, gangland was rocked by a new defection. Gambino family underboss Salvatore "Sammy Bull" Gravano was led out of the Metropolitan Correctional Center. He had been awaiting trial with his boss, John Gotti, on charges that could lead to life in prison. After hearing the FBI's secret tapes of Gotti bragging about his crimes, Gravano had reasonably concluded he didn't have a chance.

The Gambino underboss had closely followed D'Arco's own move. On the day Al's switch was reported in the papers, Gravano's attorneys had rushed to the MCC to tell their client about it. It had apparently got him thinking.

Elated agents told Al he had helped set the stage for the latest crossover.

Sometimes the applause rang hollow. He was still subject to temper tantrums. A real or imagined insult from an agent or a prosecutor could send him charging out to the tennis court, where he would stomp about in anger. Marston and O'Connor were now accustomed to their part-time jobs as social workers. They would tag along behind, trying to soothe his bruised feelings.

He did his best to relax. He cooked his *zuppe de pesce* and other specialties for the agents. In between the formal debriefing sessions, he regaled them with stories about characters he had known and his travels.

One evening, the movie *Goodfellas* was on TV. Al had seen it before. "Almost realistic" was his appraisal. He sat on the couch, talking about the characters depicted from Paul Vario's old crew. They watched the wisecracking gangster played by Joe Pesci and modeled on Tommy DeSimone insulting a nightclub table full of wiseguys. "Yeah, I was sitting right over there," Al said. "No one was real surprised when he got whacked."

Marston and the other agents grinned at each other, shaking their heads.

Stories and movies aside, he often felt lost and alone, like an exhibit on display. The news from Joseph was mixed. His son had made it through the drug rehabilitation program and was being relocated to his own safe house in New Jersey. But his wife had bolted from the witness protection program. After her initial reluctance, Louise had agreed to join him. Then she'd changed her mind again. "She said she just couldn't do it," Joseph told his father.

So they were both alone. In a gesture of solidarity, Joseph bought a gold medallion and had it inscribed to his father. He asked one of the agents to deliver it.

Al read the inscription. "Dad—My father, my brother, my best friend. Love your son Joseph."

Al's newly adopted family announced its plans for him. His maiden voyage as a witness for the prosecution, he was told, would be later that spring. He would be testifying against another old friend, Vic Amuso.

The trial would include the extortion and labor-racketeering charges in the Windows case that Amuso and Casso had fled two years earlier. But prosecutors intended to add new charges based on Al's information. They would make it a murder trial.

It would not be an easy case to make, however. Unlike the John Gotti indictment, soon to go to trial in Brooklyn federal court, there were no devastating wiretaps or bugs catching the defendant talking about secret plans for murder. There was also little other corroborating evidence. The jury would have to be convinced based on the strength of the testimony.

Prosecutors already had Pete Chiodo. He had done well in the first Windows trial, but there were more acquittals than convictions. They were determined that Amuso shouldn't get away.

They wanted to size up their new star witness. The first meeting took place at a motel in Tarrytown, about thirty miles north of the city on the Hudson River. Windows case prosecutor Greg O'Connell drove up from Brooklyn with Lucian Gandolfo and John Flanagan, the Luchese squad agents who had stood guard over Pete Chiodo. They took the usual circuitous route, stopping, looping around, scrubbing off.

At the motel, Al assured them he was looking forward to confronting Amuso. But he was worried that they were treating Casso, who was still at large, too lightly. He turned the tables on the prosecutor, asking him what kind of security would be in place for the trial. "You can't underestimate this guy," Al warned them. "He's got sources."

The FBI was already furiously hunting for Casso's "crystal ball." Pete Chiodo had told them about the Luchese underboss's uncanny inside knowledge about law enforcement activities. Al had confirmed it.

Sometimes, Al told them, Casso called his sources "agents." Other times, they were "bulls" or "cops." With Gaspipe, he told them, it was all disinformation, an effort to throw everyone off track. He was likely to say "agents" if they were cops, "cops" if they were agents.

Whoever they were, the tipsters made a lethal combination with Casso. No targets were off-limits.

There was grim proof a few weeks later. On the morning of March 10, 1992, masked gunmen shot Pete Chiodo's sister as she was returning from dropping off her son at school.

Patricia Capozzalo had just pulled up outside her home on West Seventh Street near Kings Highway in Gravesend, Brooklyn, when the shooters jumped out of a stolen black Plymouth van. One of the gunmen tripped getting out. The noise alerted Capozzalo, who ducked beneath the dashboard. The shooter fired five times through the window and fled.

One bullet lodged in her neck; another glanced off her back. Capozzalo, thirty-eight, survived, her life saved by the same nervous stumbling on the part of the gunman that had spared her brother at the gas station in Staten Island.

The day of the shooting, her brother was in Detroit being readied for trial by O'Connell and his partner in the Windows prosecution, Charles Rose. Gandolfo and Flanagan were there as well. They had just wheeled the witness, still disabled and confined to a wheelchair from his own shooting, into a hotel when they looked up and saw Chiodo's face on a wide-screen television in the lobby. The newscaster was reporting the attempt on his sister's life. Agents and prosecutors huddled around Chiodo in an effort to hide him and quickly got him up to their suite.

The next day's newspapers were filled with law enforcement officials and academic experts bemoaning how the mob's rules had changed. "They do this in Italy, they do this in Colombia," said one criminology professor. "They don't do it in the United States."

They did now. Like her parents, Capozzalo's only crime was being related to Big Pete Chiodo. She was a mother of three, the president of her local PTA. As soon as she was ready to travel, she and her family were moved into witness protection.

Three weeks after the attempt on Chiodo's sister, another of Al's warnings proved correct. Neil Migliore, the wealthy Luchese mobster who had been shown the "vouch" photo of Al holding Marston's FBI credentials in a bid to alert him that he was on the hit list, was shot.

The attempted hit was another botched effort, showing how stretched-thin and overanxious the Luchese ranks had become. It also displayed their indifference to civilian casualties.

Migliore was seated at a table in the front window of a crowded restaurant in Westbury, Long Island, attending a birthday party for a friend's four-year-old granddaughter. A passing car slowed down as a gunman armed with a shotgun blasted away at the fifty-nine-year-old mobster.

Migliore survived. Despite his severe wounds, he rejected the FBI's invitation to join D'Arco and Chiodo on the other side.

The brazen shooting came a day after another mob milestone. On April 2, John Gotti was convicted on all counts in Brooklyn federal court. Among them were six murders, including the execution of his predecessor, Paul Castellano. It was the government's first win against the Gambino boss after three failed prosecutions had earned Gotti his media tag of "Teflon Don."

At a postconviction press conference, FBI agents and prosecutors cheered Brooklyn U.S. attorney Andrew Maloney and assistant FBI director James Fox. "The don is covered with Velcro," Fox told reporters. "Every charge stuck."

In the crowd, prosecutors O'Connell and Rose assured each other that they'd soon be standing next to Maloney celebrating the conviction of another mob boss, Vic Amuso.

They faced stiff odds. From the prosecution table, they'd be asking a jury to take the word of two admitted mob killers, Pete Chiodo and Al D'Arco. The government was cutting both turncoats a break for their own crimes in exchange for their help. Both had good reason not to like the defendant. One blamed Amuso for his recent shooting. The other was convinced he'd narrowly escaped the same fate.

Making those points from the defense table would be one of America's criminal defense stars. Gerald Shargel, a suave man with a goatee, was considered a legal prince of darkness by many prosecutors. He had won acquittals for both Sammy Gravano and John Gotti. He'd been barred from representing Gotti at his last trial when the judge ruled that Shargel was a "house counsel" to the Gambino crime family. Other clients had included Anthony Casso and Paul Vario's prized hijacker, Jimmy Burke.

At Gotti's state trial for ordering the shooting of a union official, Shargel had demolished the state's star witness. Vincent "Fish" Cafaro, the Genovese captain who had annoyed Al at the MCC back in 1986, had become a highly prized mob defector. But Shargel nailed him in repeated inconsistencies. The Amuso prosecutors had considered using Cafaro at their own trial, but dropped the idea after seeing the damage Shargel had inflicted.

As backups for Shargel, Amuso retained two other top criminal defense attorneys. Alan Futerfas was an expert on complex racketeering cases. Michael Rosen was a cagey veteran who had started out as partners with Roy Cohn, the ex-prosecutor turned mob legal ally.

O'Connell's task was to brief Al on what to expect. "Just lay it all out there," the prosecutor told him. "Don't try to minimize anything. If it's true, just say 'yes.'"

There was a part of the job for which there was no real preparation, O'Connell knew. Witnesses had to admit their own crimes in public, in front of strangers, with a judge watching, and reporters in the courtroom taking it down. It was an embarrassing and scary prospect. There was no telling how different people would react.

Al insisted he was ready for the fight.

The trial opened on May 18. Presiding was Eugene Nickerson, a tall, soft-spoken former Democratic politician from Nassau County. Nickerson had presided at John Gotti's first federal trial, one that had ended in a stunning acquittal that propelled the Gambino boss to fame. A stickler for defendants' rights, Nickerson had been the first federal judge to block objections to jurors based on race. In this case, the prosecution asked for the jury to be anonymous and sequestered. The FBI had uncovered evidence of jury tampering in the first Windows trial, they said. Shargel argued it would prejudice the jury against his client. Nickerson sided with the prosecutors.

The panel included eight men and four women. At the defense table, Amuso didn't look like much of a threat. He was shorn of his fugitive beard, and his gray curly hair was neatly trimmed. Dressed in a gray suit and red tie, he had reading glasses perched on his nose as he took copious notes on a pad in front of him. He looked more like the garment executive he listed as his occupation than a mob boss. He was a far cry from the dapper John Gotti, a constant preening presence at the same Brooklyn courthouse during prior months with his silk pocket squares and tailored suits.

In his opening argument, prosecutor Charles Rose pointed at the defendant. This "deadly don," said Rose, had conducted a "reign of terror." Amuso hadn't carried the gun, Rose said, but he had given the orders.

Shargel warned jurors that they would hear a fantasy concocted by "two psychopathic killers." Chiodo and D'Arco were trying to dodge their own guilt by invoking a classic excuse. "They'll tell you 'Vic made me do it,'" said Shargel.

Chiodo went first. He testified from his wheelchair, his left arm in a brace and his right leg in a cast. He told about the order to have Sonny Morrissey killed and four other slayings he had participated in with the crime family. He described the shooting at the gas station just a year earlier that had almost cost him his life and had left him an invalid. He knew why they had tried to kill him, he said. "I had become a liability."

During cross-examination, Shargel accidentally kicked Chiodo's oversized wheelchair. It was the most damage he inflicted on the witness.

The trial broke for the Memorial Day weekend. Al took the stand the following Tuesday.

"I looked right at Vic when I sat down. He made out like he was busy, writing things as if he was the lawyer. He wouldn't look at me."

A newspaper reporter covering the trial saw what Al missed. *Newsday*'s Pete Bowles spotted Amuso sneering at D'Arco as he entered the courtroom. The defendant, wrote Bowles, "shot him a look of contempt."

The courtroom was filled with reporters and columnists

eager to see how the highest-ranking turncoat in mob history fared. Jimmy Breslin, the columnist whose sons Al had helped protect from Joey Gallo's kidnapping threat, now writing for *Newsday*, came to watch. So did Mike McAlary, author of a hard-boiled column for the *New York Post*.

Amuso's wife, Barbara, and other family members lined one side of the gallery. Defense attorneys, investigators, and prosecutors, many of whom expected to deal with D'Arco in their own cases sometime soon, filled the rest of the seats.

They heard Al, his Brooklyn accent slow and somber, describe his criminal career. He offered an account unadorned by excuses or complaint. His trade had been "murder, hijacking, burglary, arson, gambling, and yes, narcotics," he said.

He described his first encounters with Amuso, at the bustout near the Navy Yard and when he'd offered him a fellow inmate's helping hand at Sing Sing. He told about the drug deals Amuso and Casso had engaged in, and walked the jury through his own murder conspiracies. In chilling detail, he described his savage attack on Mike Pappadio.

"I hit him a few times and he still stood on his feet, and he was saying, 'What are you doing that for?' and he called my name out," he testified.

He described the meetings and telephone conversations when Amuso and Casso had instructed him in conducting the family's affairs, naming the location of the designated phone booths, even the telephone numbers. He told of the dog barking at him and his fellow gang members as they sat on a quiet Staten Island street the night Amuso had removed him as acting boss.

His narrative of events at the Kimberly Hotel spilled out in long takes, mostly uninterrupted by defense objections. Even Amuso's attorneys seemed fascinated.

O'Connell glanced at the jury. They were engrossed. "He had the jury, he had the judge, he had everybody in the courtroom," O'Connell said later.

The prosecutor asked D'Arco about the handwritten lists he had compiled in his cramped, tiny print in response to Casso's demands for an accounting of all income and expenses.

The paperwork, now sealed in plastic and labeled with evidence tags, had been retrieved from Al's Spring Street apartment by the FBI a few days after he had fled.

He ticked off the names of the contractors who had paid regular tribute to the Luchese family in exchange for favors rendered. It was the first time the payoffs and the businesses, many with major government contracts, had been mentioned in public. Reporters scribbled furiously to keep up. Within days, both company executives and city officials were scrambling to explain their dealings.

Then there was the mob family's internal bookkeeping. Al interpreted his shorthand, recalling each one. There was $500 for flowers for Anthony Baratta's mother's funeral, $15,000 for the lawyers for the shooters of John Petrucelli, and rows of Christmas tribute payments by the crews to the bosses.

"Al, Christmas," he read from one document, "representing myself and my crew. We gave Vic Amuso and Anthony Casso $12,000."

"In cash?" asked O'Connell.

"Yes, we did," said Al.

He glanced at the defense table. Amuso's steady glare was now a sarcastic smile as he looked at Al. The boss silently mouthed the words "Thank you." Al looked over at the jury. They had caught it as well.

Agent Lucian Gandolfo watched the two former friends in the courtroom. "Al was pumped," he said. "This was his chance to set the record straight." Amuso seemed forlorn. "He sat there by himself. Never said a word. Rarely looked up. When he did, he was expressionless."

Al had been on the witness stand for four days when O'Connell asked him about his decision to turn himself in to the FBI.

He recounted the phone call from his parole officer, Joe Veltre, confirming that there was an active murder plot against him. He described the turmoil in his home as he told his wife, daughters, and son John that they had to leave immediately. He paused and wiped away tears that had sprung to his eyes as he told the story.

He said he and Joseph had together pondered their next move.

"He said, 'Dad, what are we going to do?' "

Shargel had been quiet during the story. He rose to object.

"No, I will allow it," said Nickerson.

"So we got marked rats," Al continued. He now gave the speech that had been running through his head for months, the one he'd been waiting to deliver to his former friend.

"We weren't rats. I says, 'A guy that calls a guy a rat and the guy is not a rat, he's worse than a rat.' That's the saying in our life. I says, 'They set guys up before. They are doing the same thing to us. We ain't even got a chance.' "

He looked at Amuso as he spoke. The head of gray curls remained bent over his notepad, the pen moving across the paper. The boss never looked up.

Shargel lived up to his reputation. His cross-examination began with a lancing attack on Al's sympathetic description of a close family terrified by threats of murder. The defense lawyer wanted the jury to forget about the tears they had just seen.

Hadn't Al submitted false documents to the managers of 21 Spring Street that he wasn't living with his wife in order to hold on to a government-subsidized apartment?

The question surprised Al. Amid all the other crimes he had confessed, he hadn't remembered that one. Shargel showed him the records.

"Yes, I did," he said after looking at them.

"While you were on the streets of New York, selling dope and killing people, the government subsidized your living, right?" Shargel asked.

"Yes," Al answered quickly. O'Connell objected and Nickerson sustained him, but the jury had already heard it.

In his new life, he was still subsidized by the government, the defense lawyer pointed out. He had simply shifted from one agency to another.

Al offered no argument. It was true, he acknowledged.

Shargel next moved to drugs. After his own conviction in the heroin sales case, his own children had become addicts, wasn't that true? A son, a daughter, and a daughter-in-law all had drug problems?

Yes they had.

"Did you sell heroin to your kids?" Shargel asked.

Al breathed slowly, resisting the bait. "No, I did not," he said.

Over the next two days, the lawyer tried similar sorties, all blunted by Al's frank acknowledgment of his criminal past.

"Did you choke up with tears when you told those two people to go out and take a human life?" Shargel asked of one of the murders.

"No, I did not."

In his closing argument, Shargel noted that the government had offered only the words of its cooperators as evidence of Amuso's guilt in several of the murders charged. That shouldn't happen in America, he told the jury.

The trial lasted a month. The jury needed just seven hours to find the Luchese boss guilty on all counts. *Daily News* reporter Frances McMorris noted that the jury foreman barely glanced at the eleven-page verdict sheet as he answered guilty to each of the fifty-four charges.

Amuso, chewing on a mint, stared straight ahead, showing no emotion.

Just two months after Gotti's conviction, Brooklyn U.S. attorney Andrew Maloney got to tell another press conference that his office had notched another major win against organized crime, convicting the boss of yet another crime family.

D'Arco's turn on the witness stand was crucial, the prosecution team agreed, complementing Chiodo's testimony. "Pete gave you the substance of the conversations," said FBI agent Lucian Gandolfo, who worked with both men. "Al would give you the name of the place, the cross streets, who was sitting where, the color of the tablecloth, what everybody ate, and what they said."

"He told stories from the heart," said O'Connell. "He didn't apologize for his life of crime, in all its ugliness."

* * *

A week later, New York got a good look at that ugliness. June 23 was the date of John Gotti's sentencing. It was a given that he was going away for life, and his fans showed up in large numbers to protest outside federal court on Cadman Plaza in downtown Brooklyn.

Gotti's sentencing, alongside his loyal consigliere, Frank Locascio, who was convicted with him, took just ten minutes. Under strict guidelines, U.S. district judge I. Leo Glasser said, he had no choice but to send both men to prison for their natural lives. Gotti stood silently, a slight smile on his face. Locascio proclaimed his innocence, adding that he was guilty only of being Gotti's friend.

The real action took place outside. The protesters arrived in buses. A crowd of nearly a thousand mostly young white men rallied in the park across from the courthouse. "Free John Gotti!" shouted a leader who had brought a bullhorn. "We want a new trial. The government stinks!" It was the first organized pro-Mafia demonstration since Joe Colombo's Italian American civil rights rallies more than twenty years earlier.

The crowd surged past a line of police in riot gear. They overturned a federal marshal's car, and smashed windows in another. Seven protesters were arrested. Eight police officers were injured, one of them bloodied from a punch to the face.

Gotti saw none of it. Hustled out of the courthouse, he was loaded that afternoon on a specially chartered flight to the federal penitentiary at Marion, Illinois, then the most restrictive prison in America. The feds wanted to get him away from his crime family as soon as possible. They also drew special satisfaction at giving Gotti an exceptionally uncomfortable day. The fearless godfather of crime was terrified of flying.

Al also took to the air. He was in the hands of the federal marshals himself now, having been accepted into the Witness Security Program, its official name.

He was a frequent-flying commuter, traveling to out-of-the-way locations. Known as "neutral sites" in the lingo of the WitSec program, they were places where Al could be debriefed in safety by prosecutors and agents.

He had quickly become a popular figure on the organized-crime circuit. Thanks to his performance at the Amuso trial, prosecutors were eager to use him. His dance card as a cooperating witness already held a half dozen trials where he would testify. More were expected. Unlike Sammy Gravano, who had won a cap on how long he could be used as a witness, Al D'Arco had pledged to testify as long as the feds needed him.

It was a grueling schedule for all concerned—deputy U.S. marshals, agents, prosecutors, and the witness. Tony Siano and Bob Marston were along for many of the rides. Their own case regarding the Matamoras landfill was put on hold so that Al could first appear against more prominent mob figures. They accepted the situation. But as the federal officials who sponsored D'Arco into the program, one or the other of them was present whenever he was being questioned.

Siano was steadily impressed with Al as he watched the debriefing sessions. "He knew chapter and verse, but the best part was that he would not tell you something unless he knew it was true. There would be an agent asking him about what so-and-so said to him in the basement of La Donna Rosa when it was just Al alone with their target. All Al had to do was say 'Yes, the guy said that,' and the guy was going to be indicted. Al would say, 'I know what you want but I can't help you.' He was fabulous."

FBI organized-crime supervisor Michael Campi noticed the same thing. "He'd sit there and think about it when I asked him a question," said Campi. "He wanted to be right."

Beyond his accuracy, Campi was amazed at the breadth of his knowledge. "He understood the streets, the mentality, the protocol. He also understood the treachery."

The trips didn't allow for much recreation, and the marshals often kept their witness on a short leash. But when allowed, Al tried to scout out Italian restaurants wherever they landed. He'd chat up the owners, delighted when he found someone from a part of Italy he knew.

In Billings, Montana, he pushed Siano to get permission from the marshals to take a ride out to Little Bighorn Battlefield

National Monument. The history buff wanted to see the site of Custer's Last Stand. The marshals gave permission, and Al and Siano drove to the site on the vast western plains. At the park center, they looked at the diorama and listened to the rangers describe the battle. Then they wandered over to the memorial.

There was a small fenced-in area, tombstones, and an obelisk. Al walked up to the marker and read the long list of names of the fallen soldiers. Suddenly, he called out to Siano. "The bugler was an Italian!"

Bob Marston had his own adventures on the road. He and Al spent several nights at a motel in a small city on the edge of an Indian reservation with a group of prosecutors and agents. One night Al wanted to go for a walk. It was still his way to unwind from the lengthy and intense sessions.

They had gone just a couple of blocks, talking as they went, when Marston looked up to see a half dozen men moving menacingly toward them. The agent looked around. The street was deserted.

The men formed a half circle around D'Arco and Marston so they couldn't pass. It was clear they'd been drinking. One of them stepped forward and put his hand inside his jacket, as though reaching for a weapon. Marston began to sweat, his own hand moving toward the Glock he carried at his waist.

"I'm standing there thinking this is really bad. We're not even supposed to be out here. How am I going to write this up if I have a shoot-out, with the most important witness in protective custody in jeopardy of being shot?"

As Marston watched the man's hand, Al stepped up. He was several inches shorter and many years older than the group seemingly intent on robbing them.

"You okay, buddy?" Al asked, looking up at the man. Al had his chin raised, and was speaking calmly. "We're out taking a walk here. Why don't we keep going this way, and you go that way. You okay with that?"

Marston watched in wonder. It was like two dogs sniffing each other out, he thought. "It was all body language on Al's part. It was the way he stood and talked."

The man nodded and moved on, the group tailing behind.

They seemed almost embarrassed. "Maybe it was the accent. But they realized they were picking on the wrong guy."

Al was dismissive when asked about the incident. "Ah, it was a bunch of drunken bums. Nothing to worry about."

In October, Vic Amuso appeared for sentencing. Like Gotti, he wore a fixed smile into the courtroom. Like Gotti, his sentence was a foregone conclusion. Convicted on all counts, including nine murders, federal sentencing guidelines dictated a life term.

In a navy-blue suit, he stood beside his attorney, who spoke for his client. "Mr. Amuso stands before you," Gerald Shargel said. "He maintains his innocence."

From the bench, Judge Nickerson shrugged. "I guess I have to impose life in prison," he said.

Again, the action was outside. Barbara Amuso stood in the hallway outside Nickerson's sixth-floor courtroom, waiting for the prosecutors to exit. *Daily News* reporter Frances McMorris stayed to watch.

"There's been an injustice done!" the wife yelled when Charles Rose came out the door. "You should hide your head in shame. You intimidate women and children."

Rose stopped and faced the mobster's wife. "The only women and children I think about are the wives and children of the men your husband had killed," he said.

Mrs. Amuso wasn't finished. "You show your guns and your badges to young children. That's what this government is all about," she said.

Rose opened his suit jacket. "I don't carry a gun, I don't carry a badge," said the prosecutor, who turned and walked away.

Over the next eight months, Al testified at six trials. They yielded ten convictions. Just days before Christmas, his testimony helped send yet another crime family leader, acting Colombo boss Vic Orena, to a life sentence. Two weeks later, in a separate trial, he helped convict Patty Amato, one of Orena's top lieutenants.

In Manhattan, he took the stand against Luchese soldier Joey "Bang Bang" Massaro and an associate charged in a brutal murder case. They too were convicted.

Back in Brooklyn, he testified against a deadly associate of the Bonanno crime family named Vincent Giattino. A brawny man with a billiard ball dome, Giattino was known as "Kojak." A proud hit man, he had bragged to Al about his numerous killings, both as assignments and as favors for mob bosses. Prosecuted by Greg O'Connell, it was another case where witness testimony was paramount, since there were no tapes. The jury returned convictions on eleven counts.

In state court in New Jersey, Al finally rid the Luchese family of the leaders of its outlaw faction there, the goal that had long eluded Vic Amuso and Gaspipe Casso. His testimony won convictions of Anthony "Tumac" Accetturo and four other members of the Jersey crew.

The convictions caused more Luchese dominos to fall.

Facing thirty years in prison, Accetturo also decided to change sides, becoming a cooperating witness. Hard on his heels were two other members of the New Jersey faction who also called it quits with their crime family.

But Joey and Jay Giampa, the brothers from the Bronx who had readily carried out orders to kill their former captain, Mike Salerno, walked out of a Manhattan federal courtroom as free men. Al told the jury in his usual painstaking detail the tale of how he had relayed Casso's instructions for the murder. He described his walk through Little Italy a few days later as Joey Giampa told him the deed was done.

But then one of the prosecutors asked him to make a reach. Did the number "607.16" that was found on scraps of paper in Giampa's pocket mean anything to him? Al initially said no, he had no idea what it meant. During a break, he spoke to the prosecutors. When he returned to the stand, he changed his testimony. The figure might be a disguised reference to $607,000, he said, since that was the amount of money they found in Mike Salerno's loan shark book after he was killed.

He was wrong. Joey Giampa's attorney, James LaRossa, a skilled practitioner who had been Shargel's mentor, later put

Giampa's rent receipts from his apartment into evidence. The rent was exactly $607.16 per month. D'Arco, LaRossa told the jury in his closing statement, was just a "trained seal," willing to say whatever prosecutors wanted. The jury acquitted Giampa and his brother in just thirty minutes.

"They pushed me to say something I wasn't sure of," Al said. "It was a big mistake."

He wasn't the only one making mistakes. Anthony Casso slipped up as well. After almost three years on the run, he had settled down in a girlfriend's home near Budd Lake in New Jersey, a rural area fifty miles west of New York City. Neighbors had noticed the split-level home being fixed up. A swimming pool, a hot tub, and new decks were added. The house was purchased for $250,000 after Casso went into hiding, and an added $100,000 was spent on improvements. The residents kept to themselves.

Investigators at the Brooklyn district attorney's office, utilizing new technology to trace cell phone calls, checked to see where Frank Lastorino was calling. They soon homed in on the Budd Lake area. They brought their suspicions to the FBI. Richard Rudolph, a key agent on the Windows case, went out to poke around.

"It didn't take long to find out where he had a house," said Rudolph. "But it was so remote we couldn't do surveillance."

Instead, they got warrants to tap the phone. Listening in, they heard Casso's voice. On January 19, 1993, the fugitive underboss was arrested as he was coming out of the shower.

Casso was taken to the MCC. Under an indictment won while he was on the lam, he was charged with fourteen murders, plus the old Windows racketeering counts.

The agents were elated to finally catch Casso. They were also intrigued by what they found in the New Jersey house. In addition to $340,000 in cash, a rifle, and a stack of FBI reports that had been provided to Amuso's defense attorneys, they found the same kind of paperwork that Al had told them he had laboriously prepared at the underboss's direction.

Rudolph recognized it immediately. "Here were the same

documents that Al had told us about that he wrote." For some reason, Casso had held on to them.

The documents were a potential treasure trove of evidence. But the FBI had to figure out what they meant. Rudolph and fellow agent John Kapp met with Al at one of the neutral sites to go over them.

Even Al was astonished at the degree to which Casso had committed the family's secrets to paper. There were monthly tabulations of how much the bosses had hauled in from each of their criminal concerns. Casso had also squirreled away the lists of Christmas tribute money, as if he needed them for future comparisons. There was a neatly typed list of proposed new Luchese members, made up to look like wedding guests, listing the inductees as "Mr. and Mrs."

Al knew why he had kept his own records. He didn't want to be accused of stealing. What was Gaspipe worried about?

Even with both top Luchese bosses now finally behind bars, their wave of terror continued. Two weeks after Casso's capture, Pete Chiodo's uncle was found dead in the trunk of a car. The body of Frank Signorino, sixty-eight, was frozen solid by the time police responded to complaints on February 2 of an abandoned auto in Brooklyn's East New York section. He had wounds to his forehead and a black plastic bag wrapped around his head.

Ten days later, someone torched a garage attached to the home of Chiodo's ninety-five-year-old grandmother. After the blaze, Annette Signorino fled her house on Avenue V in Brooklyn's Gravesend.

Even Big Pete was surprised by that one. In a comment relayed via the FBI, he said he "couldn't believe someone would try to harm an old woman."

At least Al's family was safe. Dolores and the rest of their children remained with friends in Hawaii for eighteen months, waiting for Al to finish ping-ponging around the country for his debriefings and courtroom appearances.

The marshals who ran the WitSec program came up with

a location where the reunited family could settle. No one was completely satisfied. It wasn't New York. An Italian restaurant meant the Olive Garden chain. But they were secure and together.

Joseph didn't fare as well. His wife, Louise, never kicked her own habit. She bolted from the detox program and went back to her old haunts in the city. She visited Joseph periodically in the fall and early winter of 1992 and 1993 in his secret locations. It was a violation of the WitSec rules, but he didn't care. He wanted to see his wife.

When the marshals found out about it, he had to be relocated once more. It was a breach of security. If Louise knew where he was, then so could the Luchese gang. After he was relocated, they broke the rules all over again.

But Louise wasn't in good shape. Doctors diagnosed her with primary pulmonary hypertension, an often fatal cardiac ailment, worsened by her drug addiction.

"She was always a little bit of a thing," said Joseph. "She was four foot-eleven inches and weighed a hundred pounds. But she had the heart of a lion." She didn't complain about her illness, he said.

"We spent Christmas together and she looked good. Then all of a sudden she started turning blue." They were in a small city in South Carolina at the time. At the hospital, doctors said the reason for her rapid deterioration was that she was ten weeks pregnant. An abortion might save her life. Louise refused. Joseph was holding her in his arms when she died on January 26.

The death was a tragedy for Joseph and a thorny problem for the marshals and prosecutors. Louise's body was shipped home to New York to her family. Joseph insisted on attending the wake. Since Louise's father was in the Life, there was no question that wiseguys would be present.

Tony Siano pleaded with him. "Joey, please, you're going to get killed," he told him. The marshals were sympathetic and scrambled to find an alternative. Could they get a warrant for the body? they asked Siano. If so, they could take the casket out of the funeral home and bring it to a safe spot where

Joseph could have a private viewing. Siano considered the question. Kidnap a corpse? It was a novel idea, but not impossible. They'd have to get the application to the right judge, he said.

Siano was puzzling over the language for the warrant when the marshals called. Never mind, they said. Joseph had been convinced. He would visit Louise's grave later.

The main event looming on the organized-crime calendar was the trial of Gaspipe Casso. O'Connell and Rose were preparing the prosecution. They wanted as much witness firepower as possible. To that end, O'Connell approached Sammy Gravano, who had dealt with Casso frequently as a fellow crime family underboss, and who had been a devastating witness against his own former chief, John Gotti.

Nothing doing, said Gravano. He wanted no part of taking the stand against the unpredictably lethal Anthony Casso. Gaspipe might be in the MCC, he reasoned, but his disciples were still out there, actively trying to terrify witnesses like Chiodo into silence.

"He was afraid of what Gaspipe might do to his family," said O'Connell. Gravano's federal handlers declined to press him to change his mind. The decision was to keep him for cases against his former Gambino cohorts, not to spread him too thin. Part of the danger to any witness's usefulness was overexposure. Any time one took the stand he risked a foul-up, like the mousetrap that had snared Al at the Joey Giampa trial. Better to save a witness for the ones you really wanted.

For his part, Al said he couldn't wait to testify against his former friend. "I was looking forward to seeing Gaspipe sitting there. I wanted him to hear what I had to say just like I got to say it to Vic."

FBI agent Lucian Gandolfo believed he understood Al's motivation. "He thought he was standing for what was right, but also for the old values that had been abandoned by the mob."

O'Connell saw the same thing. Gravano and D'Arco had dramatically different motives for cooperating, he realized.

"For Sammy, it was a good move," said O'Connell. "For Al, it was a mission."

The next move was Anthony Casso's. In late February 1994, recognizing that testimony against him by D'Arco and Chiodo was likely to sink him the same way it had Amuso, Gaspipe sent word to Richard Rudolph that he too was ready to flip. It was another unthinkable desertion for the Mafia.

The new witness was quickly shipped to the federal prison at La Tuna, Texas, near El Paso on the Mexican border for debriefing. He was placed in a two-room prison cell with a special place in the history of mob informants. It was the "Valachi Suite," where the first defector had told his own secrets.

Rudolph took part in the initial sessions. Casso began with a joke. "Every time I stepped out of the house I committed a crime," he said. "You expect me to remember all of them?"

Start with the "crystal ball," the agents suggested.

Casso named a pair of NYPD detectives. He said he paid them from $3,000 to $5,000 a month for a steady flow of law enforcement secrets. They had even carried out hits for him. He had paid hefty bonuses for assisting with murders.

One of the "cops," as Casso called them, was Stephen Caracappa, who had been part of the city and federal task force assigned to organized-crime investigations. As such, he'd had access to files where wiretap and surveillance information was stored. The other was Louis Eppolito, a burly former weight lifter with a chest full of decorations for his police work. Eppolito had also worked mob cases. But he had long been looked at askance by some police officials thanks to his family's own Mafia connections. Both his father and an uncle had been mobsters. Both detectives had retired after more than twenty years on the force.

O'Connell and Rose flew to El Paso. They sat in the little sitting room in the Valachi Suite. Casso offered a wealth of information, detailing schemes and naming the mobsters he had conspired with, including the other remaining key Mafia target, Vincent Gigante.

He confessed that he had schemed to have Charles Rose

assassinated, even sending hit men to scope out what they thought was his residence. He had also plotted to have Judge Nickerson killed. The judge's death, he hoped, would delay his trial.

But the prosecutors found it hard to separate the truth from the spin. Casso initially owned up to a dozen murders. Pressed for details, he admitted to two dozen more.

The gangster insisted the cash found at the house in Budd Lake was all he had. But search warrants executed on banks near Casso's Brooklyn home found $200,000 in a Milk-Bone dog biscuit box in one safety-deposit box. A flawless ten-carat diamond worth $600,000 was in another.

He denied any involvement in the murder of Pete Chiodo's uncle and the torching of his elderly grandmother's garage. He insisted he had had no plans to whack Al D'Arco.

But both agents and prosecutors were already starting to wonder. Casso had lied about several killings, they believed. He was given a lie detector test. He flunked.

On top of that was the growing sense of unease they had sitting with him in the little room at La Tuna. His eyes were lifeless, O'Connell noticed. "There was no smile, no twinkle. Just malevolence, just scheming."

With apparent delight, Casso described the murder of a young man who had worked aboard a boat he had used for marijuana smuggling. The murder took place in the Florida Everglades.

"I shoot him and he falls back against my car," Casso told them. "There's blood all over my car. It's a fucking mess. I don't have a towel so I take off my shirt and put it in the water to wash off the car." Laughing as he spoke, Casso paused in his story and looked at O'Connell. "Then, Greg, you won't believe what happens next. We dumped him in a grave we dug. And then he *sits up*!"

"What did you do then, Anthony?" asked O'Connell.

He watched Casso's face contort. "I took a shovel with some dirt, I stuck it in his mouth, and held him down while we buried him."

O'Connell and Rose read each other's thoughts. The story would probably not go over too well with a jury.

There was some apparent truth telling. Casso said the reason for ordering Mike Salerno's death was because he believed the Bronx capo was envious of him and Amuso. He didn't trust him, Casso said. He said nothing about Salerno being a rat. Al had been right to wonder.

The prosecutors flew back to New York convinced that it didn't matter how well versed their new witness was in mob secrets. "It gets to a point where somebody is just too evil to put on the stand," said O'Connell.

The decision not to use Casso before a jury left D'Arco as the main workhorse for prosecutors on organized-crime cases. He continued his tour of witness stands, testifying at seven more trials.

In Atlanta, he gave evidence in a murder case against a member of the Aryan Brotherhood charged with carrying out a mob hit.

Twice he appeared against Vincent Gigante, the Genovese boss cloaking his mob leadership behind a pretense of mental illness. At a hearing to see whether or not Gigante was competent to stand trial, Al was asked if the boss's act was common knowledge among wiseguys.

"Yes," he said. "He would babble to himself, urinate in the street, things like that."

If the Chin were truly mentally ill, the prosecutor continued, what concerns would the leadership of Cosa Nostra have about him?

"He would have a terminal illness right away," said Al.

"What?" said the judge.

"They would kill him, your honor. Terminal illness. They call it a mercy killing."

He cited examples from ancient and recent mob history. "Way back, there was Willie Moretti. He had syphilis. He was talking too much. Saying family things. So he was killed."

The same thing had happened to Al's friend Hickey

DiLorenzo. "He was all out of line. He didn't know what he was doing." He too was put out of his misery, Al explained.

Gigante's crazy act was ruled "an elaborate deception." At his trial in 1997, Al told of the times that Vic Amuso had described his meetings with "the Robe." Discussing their plan to kill John Gotti with a remote-controlled bomb, Amuso had assured him Gigante was on board. "He says, 'Don't worry about it. The Robe knows about it.'"

The unfulfilled Gotti murder plot was one of the counts on which Gigante was convicted on July 26, 1997. The "Odd-father," as the tabloids dubbed him, was given twenty-four hours to report to prison. He was to die there eight years later.

Most cases never went to trial. Nineteen Luchese members and associates pled guilty rather than face the tag team of Al D'Arco and Pete Chiodo on the witness stand. Among them were capos Sal "the Golfer" Avellino, George "Georgie Neck" Zappola, Steve Crea, and Frank Lastorino.

Al's description of mob penetration of labor unions was compiled in lengthy affidavits filed in successful civil racketeering cases alleging mob corruption. The Manhattan district attorney drew on his expertise to make the case that the newspaper drivers union was mobbed up. Federal prosecutors did the same for the Teamsters, carpenters, laborers, and hotel workers unions.

But Al might have been trying too hard when the Matamoras landfill case finally went to trial. Al found himself in the witness chair looking at a row of eight defendants, including three of his former aides. Pete Del Cioppo, glum as ever, was there, along with Shorty DiPalo and Harpo Trapani. All had been Al's close friends. All of them, he believed, had deserted him when he had been falsely labeled a rat.

Despite his long wait, Tony Siano knew it was going to be a tough case. The highest-ranking mobster in the scheme, Mike Salerno, had been killed with Al's help. The case's top indicted mobster, Patsy Masselli, had died before trial. That left Al, a former acting boss, testifying against lower-level members and associates.

"They were all painted as nobodies," said Siano. "Jurors

want you testifying up. They don't want the chairman of the board of Chase Bank testifying against tellers. It's fundamentally unfair."

Al had built up a special venom for his old pal Petey Del. "I know he was out in Bayville looking for my sister after we went in. They seen him knocking on the door there." He also heard that Del Cioppo had claimed he had given heroin to Al's daughter.

But the jury was unconvinced. In a switch from usual verdicts, it acquitted the mob figures and convicted accountant Donald Herzog and attorney Alfred Christiansen, who were running the landfill's business operations.

In 2001, he helped send one more boss to prison. The defendant was Anthony Spero, the Bonanno crime family chieftain whose angry words had so struck Al that night at the Kimberly Hotel. Spero had railed that the only way to discourage cooperators was by killing their entire families. What happens when they accuse someone who's innocent? Al had wondered at the time.

The Spero trial was another rematch with defense lawyer Jerry Shargel. Before taking the stand, Al met with the prosecutor, an assistant Brooklyn district attorney named Chris Blank, who had been specially designated as a federal prosecutor for the trial. Blank asked his witness if he was prepared for a new round of withering questions and accusations from Shargel. Al assured him he was. Shargel could call him any name he wanted, D'Arco said. "I know what I am," he said. "I'm still a mobster. But I'm an outlaw, that's all. It's not like they throw you out of the mob when you flip. You're just considered an outlaw. That's what I am. An outlaw."

A year later, the responsibility for deciding Al D'Arco's fate fell to the judge who had presided at the Matamoras landfill trial. The judge was an imposing figure with a bald head, a bow tie, gold spectacles, and a large brush mustache out of the Old West. His name was Charles Brieant and he looked something like Judge Roy Bean, the legendary Texas hanging judge. Brieant had been on the federal bench since 1971, a nominee of the original law-and-order president, Richard Nixon. He had won a reputation as a tough judge when it came to sentencing. Brieant could basically give Al whatever sentence he felt he deserved. As Al said repeatedly on the witness stand when pressed about his likely sentence, he could get anything from "zip to life."

It had been eleven years since he had signed his agreement with federal prosecutors. The letter evaluating his service, known as a "5K letter" for a section of the federal sentencing guidelines, was written by deputy United States attorney David Kelley. He submitted it in the name of his boss, the then top Manhattan federal prosecutor, James Comey, who had been named to his post by the latest law-and-order Republican president, George W. Bush.

It detailed Al's criminal history, including his roles as captain of a Luchese crew and as acting boss of the family. It listed twelve separate murders and murder conspiracies to which he had pled guilty. It was a bloody record that began with Red Gilmore and ended with the architect, Anthony Fava. Included were the attempted murders of contractor Joe Martinelli, Pete Chiodo, and New Jersey mobster Anthony Accetturo.

It went on to tick off Al's track record as a government witness: more than a dozen trials, more than fifty convictions.

The letter was quietly effusive. D'Arco had "committed to the terms of his cooperation agreement as if it were a full-time job," Kelley wrote. He had shared his mob knowledge with agents and prosecutors from around the country, including Boston, Newark, Detroit, Memphis, Miami, Chicago, Kansas City, Las Vegas, and Los Angeles. D'Arco's cooperation had been "extraordinary," wrote Kelley, "establishing a track record that stands alone among the many cooperators who have helped the government eradicate organized crime over the past decade."

"From day one," Kelley added, "D'Arco's information has been on the money, and for the past eleven years D'Arco has never wavered from his commitment to the government."

The sentencing itself took place in an unannounced session

in Brieant's courtroom in White Plains, New York, on October 10, 2002, at the unusually early hour of 8:30 a.m. Al couldn't make it. At age seventy, he was ailing and couldn't make the trip. From a government office near where he had been relocated, he spoke into a video camera that projected his voice and face onto a screen on the wall of Brieant's courtroom.

On his own monitor, Al could see the judge and the other men in the room. Kelley was there with another prosecutor, Andrew McCarthy, along with Jim DeVita, Al's attorney. So was Kenneth McCabe, the tireless investigator who had once haunted Al on the streets of Little Italy. The two men spoke often over the years, the mob watcher and the old mobster comparing notes. It was the last time Al would see McCabe, who died in 2006 after a yearlong battle with cancer at age fifty-nine.

The hearing didn't take long. DeVita spoke first. Al had fashioned himself into "a one-man crime-stopper," he said. He urged the judge to recognize his contributions and the turnaround he had made in his life.

Al spoke next. He thanked Kelley and DeVita "and many individuals I can't name." They had helped him turn his life around, he said. "They really helped me keep on the straight and narrow, and so has my family." He would never let them down, he added.

Brieant also had little to say. D'Arco had been under constant supervision since his plea and had broken no laws. He sentenced Al to time served. It meant he was free to go.

After his sentencing, he could have ducked the last request for his testimony. He had recently undergone extensive surgery to remove a tumor. But when asked in 2006 to testify in the long-delayed trial against Casso's police detective informants, he said he wouldn't miss it. "I was cut loose, but I was glad to do it."

Essentially, he was doing Gaspipe's job for him. The best wiseguy witness against the detectives would have been Casso himself, who could have detailed their dealings and conspiracies. But Casso was thoroughly damaged goods by then. In

1997, prosecutors ripped up his cooperation agreement. He'd been caught in too many lies, and had continued to commit crimes, even behind bars, bribing guards and assaulting other inmates. A year later, he was handed a combined sentence of 455 years in prison. He was fifty-six years old. He would do as many of them as he could.

Sammy Gravano would also have been able to talk about Casso's law enforcement source. But he had also washed out of the witness protection program. After being caught peddling Ecstasy pills to teenagers in Phoenix, Arizona, where he had been relocated by the government, he was sent back to prison.

Of the three top New York mobsters who had crossed over in the early 1990s, Al was the last one standing.

The key witness was Casso's go-between, an aging former drug dealer named Burt Kaplan who had passed the messages and the payments.

The case was a sensation from every angle. Notoriously dubbed the "Mafia Cops" in the city's media, the defendants were the first New York City detectives ever accused of serving as mob hit men. Their murderous chores for the underboss were staggering. They had kidnapped two victims, delivering one to Casso for torture and execution, and killing the other themselves.

As another favor to Gaspipe, they had shot a John Gotti capo named Eddie Lino after using their police shields to pull him over on a Brooklyn highway. Lino had dined at La Donna Rosa with Al and Joseph just three days before he was killed.

The police ruse violated Al's sense of mob fairness, as did all of Casso's dealings with the detectives. "It was dirty pool, using the cops to get Eddie. Where I grew up, you're not supposed to bother even talking to them."

He had never met ex-detectives Steve Caracappa and Lou Eppolito. But he had been on the receiving end of repeated tips that Casso told him came from his "bulls."

He described those conversations in testimony on the first day of the trial. Then he buckled down for cross-examination by Eppolito's hard-charging lawyer, Bruce Cutler. An un-abashed admirer of his former client, John Gotti, Cutler was known more for courtroom bombast than stealthy questioning.

Al knew Cutler from his days on the Little Italy streets. The lawyer was a Mulberry Street regular, often dining with the Gotti crew at their favorite restaurant, Taormina, just up the block from Davie Petillo's old club.

When Cutler began shouting at Al on the stand, the witness gave as good as he got.

"Do you want to keep talking forever, Mr. Cutler?" said Al as the lawyer shot rapid-fire accusations at him. "Like you did in Taormina when you sat down with all the crew in there and drank with them and ate with them, and never picked up a tab? You lived it up."

Judge Jack Weinstein intervened. A no-nonsense jurist with fluffy white eyebrows that sprouted like wings from his forehead, Weinstein, eighty-five, had already scolded Cutler about his own shouting. He seemed to enjoy seeing the lawyer get a small taste of his own medicine. But then he warned both witness and lawyer that they faced contempt if they kept it up. A few minutes later he abruptly terminated Cutler's cross-examination.

After the monthlong trial, the jury deliberated for ten hours over two days, convicting the ex-detectives on all counts. The former cops were sentenced to life imprisonment.

During a break between his trips to New York courtrooms, Al took a trio of FBI agents on a guided tour of his gangland geography and history.

The agents tucked him into the backseat of their car, a hat covering his bald head for disguise. One agent sat next to him, with two up front.

Al kept up a running patter as they drove, filling them in on the history of crime on the streets of New York.

They started on Cleveland Place, where he pointed out La Donna Rosa. He showed them Dom Truscello's Café Giardino up the block.

They went over to the Lower East Side, "the Fourth Ward"

as Al still called it. He showed them the entrance to Knickerbocker Village off of Cherry Street that Jimmy Ida used when he visited his girlfriend. They passed the K & K Luncheonette and he pointed out the seafood store on Madison Street run by Luchese members Anthony Tortorello and Frank Tortorello.

They drove across the bridge to Brooklyn, past the streets of his youth near the Navy Yard. They took the Belt Parkway to Sheepshead Bay, where Al pointed out Joe's Clam Bar on Emmons Avenue. Anthony Casso's daughter was engaged to marry the owner, he told them.

Farther down the avenue, in front of Randazzo's Clam Bar, a black Rolls-Royce Corniche with Florida plates was parked. It belonged to Carmine Lombardozzi, a veteran Gambino family moneymaker.

Around the corner on Nostrand Avenue, he showed them a yellow-brick apartment house where Gaspipe kept a spare apartment.

A couple of blocks away was a motel, Angels on the Bay, long controlled by Casso and Amuso. It had been a major moneymaker, especially after the city placed homeless families there.

There was Canarsie Pier, and the restaurant, Abbracciamento on the Pier, where Bonanno acting boss Anthony Spero brought his boat, and where Casso and Amuso often met.

In Flatlands, he pointed out the Walnut Bar, where Vic Amuso and his brother Bobby had presided. Nearby were homes of Sonny Bamboo and Danny Cutaia. A pink Cadillac was parked in front of Patty Testa's house.

At the Brooklyn Terminal Market, he showed them the stalls where Joker Poker machines were stored, and the social club frequented by Petey Vario and the Argentina brothers. Across the street was Bruno Facciola's old social club, where card games had gone all weekend. A few doors away was Jerry & Pepe's barbershop, where he had advised Gene Gotti to go on the lam.

Farther down Flatlands Avenue was the home of a wealthy Luchese associate named Fat Ralphie who ran a local cater-

ing hall. A white Rolls and a black Jaguar were in the driveway.

On Cross Bay Boulevard in Howard Beach, he showed
them Louie Daidone's Bagels on the Bay. Over there was Russo's on the Bay, another mob favorite. Down the street were
a couple of Vic Amuso's properties. He was ready to keep
going on his mob excursion, but the agents had had enough
and decided to call it a day.

It didn't occur to him at the time, but it was his last look
at the life he had left behind.

"I know where I'm going next," Al said in the spring of 2012,
interrupting a long tale of his gangster deeds. He was seated
in a two-room hotel suite not unlike the one that night in midtown Manhattan where he'd spotted the pistol tucked in the
back of Mike DeSantis's belt and known his mob career was
over.

He was wearing a tan windbreaker, blue jeans, and white
sneakers. He was holding a baseball cap he'd been wearing.
For a seventy-nine-year-old man who had spent time in hospitals in recent years, he looked pretty good. He still hits a
heavy bag he keeps at home.

"Yeah, I'm going down there," he said with a grin, pointing
to the floor with his finger. "I know I ain't got a chance. But
I had some times."

He was covering his bets nonetheless. One day FBI agent
Lucian Gandolfo, whose father was a minister and who later
became one himself, suggested to Al that he ask God for for-
giveness. "I want to do that," Al said. Gandolfo led him in
prayer.

At home, he still prayed every night, he said, the reflexive
habit drilled into him by his Nonna back on Kent Avenue.
And ever since he stopped having to spend his days tending
to mob affairs, he accompanied Dolores to mass at a local
Catholic church. "She never misses church so I never miss it
either." A few years ago, after becoming friendly with the
priest, they renewed their marriage vows after more than fifty
years as a couple.

The family has stayed largely together with their new names in a new location somewhere in America. There have been tough times of the kind most families endure. But they gather for meals most Sundays. Joseph lives nearby. He and his dad often go for drives together. Al, the ex–truck driver, still drives as well, but he often gets lost, even after living in the same town for more than fifteen years. "Not that there's anywhere to go around here," he complained.

Did he have regrets? he was asked.

"How could I have regrets for something I was part of? The mob was all around me. I wish I never knew any of this, but it was in my family, in my neighborhood."

He offered the same image he had invoked on the witness stand. "It was like a forest around me. I can't regret it. I would have eventually wound up doing life or in the chair, the death chamber. But as far as living day to day? I take that life any fucking day of the week."

He paused to reflect. "I could be back to crime now, if I wanted it. Crime is crime. You don't forget how to make a living. But I won't go back to it because I got Dolores. And I got my family. My life ain't that important when it comes to them."

He shook his head and slapped the baseball cap against his knee. "When I tell the FBI that I'm through with crime, I'm through with crime. If I'm starving, I won't go back to it. I gave my word."

The crime life still pursues him though, often late at night. "I still dream about that life. Guys chasing me, I'm chasing them." He laughed. "Maybe they'll get me yet."

AFTERWORD

As of 2015, here's the status of the major players in Al D'Arco's life of crime:

Vic Amuso, 80, is serving a life sentence for his conviction for racketeering and murders, currently housed at a federal prison in Cumberland, Maryland.

Benedetto Aloi, convicted of labor racketeering in the Windows trial, was released from prison in 2009. He died of natural causes in 2011 at the age of 75.

Thomas "Tommy Red" Anzeulotto, 51, was convicted at trial of loan-sharking and other crimes and served an eight-year prison term. He was released in 2001 and has no arrests since then.

Ray Argentina, 60, is in a federal prison in Danbury, Connecticut, for racketeering charges including bank fraud, assault, extortion, and narcotics trafficking. He is due to be released in 2024.

Carmine Avellino, 70, was arrested on extortion charges in 2014, ten years after he was released from prison following a 10-year prison term he received for helping the Luchese family control the private sanitation industry on Long Island.

Salvatore "the Golfer" Avellino, 79, was released from prison on October 13, 2006 after serving two racketeering convictions for murder conspiracy, extortion, and arson, to maintain control over the crime family's private carting interests.

Anthony "Bowat" Baratta, 76, was released from prison in March 2012 after serving time for three separate convictions for racketeering and drug dealing, including one for scheming to sell heroin while he was behind bars for a prior drug rap.

Jimmy Burke died of natural causes in 1996 while serving a life sentence for the 1979 murder of a drug dealer who owed Burke $250,000. He was convicted while doing time in federal prison for his role in the Boston College point-shaving case. He was 64.

Anthony "Gaspipe" Casso, 75, is serving a life sentence for racketeering and 14 murders. He is currently housed in an undisclosed state facility in Minneapolis.

Peter "Big Pete" Chiodo, 64, was sentenced to five years' probation in September 2007. He is living under the federal witness protection program somewhere in America.

George Conte, 55, was sentenced to 22 years in prison for racketeering and several murders, including the 1991 slaying of Anthony DiLapi in California. He was released in March 2014 and relocated to the state of Arizona.

Steven Crea, 67, is currently viewed as the boss of the Luchese crime family. He was released from prison in 2006 after serving three years for labor racketeering.

Ralph "Raffie" Cuomo was released from prison in 2002 for his last drug-dealing conviction. He died of natural causes in 2008. He was 71. Ray's Pizza closed its doors in 2011.

Domenico "Danny" Cutaia, 78, has served several short stretches behind bars for loan-sharking and other schemes in the past two decades. He was released from a federal prison hospital in October, 2013.

Peter "Petey Del" Del Cioppo, 80, was acquitted of all charges relating to the Matamoras landfill indictment in 1995.

Louis "Louie Bagels" Daidone, 69, is serving a life sentence for the murders of Bruno Facciola and Red Gilmore, currently in Allenwood, Pennsylvania.

Patrick "Patty" Dellorusso, 54, served a 10-year prison term for labor racketeering, and then an additional year for violating the terms of his supervised release. Released in 2004.

Michael DeSantis, 61, was sentenced to 21 years in prison for racketeering and several murders, including the killing of Sonny Morrissey. He was released from custody on June 28, 2010.

Angelo "Shorty" Dipalo, 86, was acquitted of all charges relating to the Matamoras landfill indictment in 1995.

Frank "Frankie Pearl" Federico, 87, pleaded guilty to the murders of private carters Robert Kubecka and Donald Barstow and was sentenced to 15 years in prison. He is scheduled for release on February 20, 2016.

Joseph "Big Joe" Giampa, 74, was released from prison in 2001 after serving two years in prison for a racketeering conviction in New Jersey.

Santo "Jay" Giampapa died of natural causes in 1994, two years after he and his brother Joseph were acquitted of the murder of Mike Salerno. He was 57.

Frank Gioia Jr., 48, became a cooperating witness. He served seven years behind bars and is now in the federal witness protection program.

John Gotti died of cancer on June 10, 2002, in federal prison in Springfield, Missouri, while serving life in prison. He was 61.

John A. "Junior" Gotti, 51, was tried four times on racketeering, murder, drug-dealing, and kidnapping charges, resulting in mistrials.

Matthew "Matty the Horse" Ianniello was released from a prison hospital in 2009 after a 15-month stretch for labor racketeering. He died of natural causes in 2012. He was 92.

Jimmy Ida, 75, was convicted of racketeering and the murder of Hickey DiLorenzo. He is slated to spend the rest of his life behind bars.

Thomas "Tommy the Greek" Kapatos was murdered in New York on January 27, 1977, by Genovese gangsters.

Frank Lastorino, 76, was released from prison in December 2008 after serving 14 years for racketeering and several murders, including the slaying of painters union official James Bishop.

Gioachino "Jack" Leale was murdered in 1991 after one of the bodies he had been told to make disappear was recovered from a park in Queens, New York.

Sidney Lieberman, 87, was convicted of labor racketeering and served four years in prison. He was released in 1998.

Venero "Benny Eggs" Mangano, 93, was convicted of labor racketeering in the Windows trial. He was released from prison in 2006.

Frank "the Wop" Manzo pleaded guilty to labor racketeering at Kennedy Airport and was sentenced to 12 years in prison. He was released from prison in 1994. He died of natural causes in 2012 at age 88.

Richard "the Toupe" Pagliarulo suffered a heart attack and died in Lewisburg Federal Penitentiary on January 15, 1999, after serving six years of a life sentence for murder. He was 50.

Anthony Spero died of natural causes in a prison hospital in North Carolina after serving seven years of a life sentence for racketeering and murder. He was 79.

Frank "Harpo" Trapani, 63, was acquitted of all charges relating to the Matamoras landfill indictment in 1995.

Dominic Truscello, 81, was released from federal prison in 2006 after serving two years behind bars for engaging in a labor-racketeering scheme with Steve Crea.

John Zagari, 56, pled guilty to racketeering charges in the Matamoras landfill scheme. He served two months of home detention and a year on probation. He is a practicing attorney in Pittsburgh, Pennsylvania.

George "Georgie Neck" Zappola, 56, was sentenced to 22 years behind bars for racketeering and several murders, including the 1989 slaying of Mike Pappadio. He was released from federal prison in March 2014.

ACKNOWLEDGMENTS

Many people helped us write this book. We thank them all, starting with Alfonso D'Arco, the kid from Kent Avenue who rose to run the Luchese crime family and then helped bring it tumbling down. He said he would answer every question, and he was true to his word. Dolores, his bride of fifty-eight years, helped fill in many blanks. Joseph D'Arco also shared his recollections and was crucially open about his own hard times.

Many current and former members of the law enforcement community gave invaluable help. Heading the list are former FBI agent Bob Marston and former federal prosecutors Tony Siano and Greg O'Connell. All three were there as Al D'Arco evolved from a dedicated mobster into a dedicated government witness. We thank them for taking the time to share their insights, as well as the high points and low points they encountered along the way.

Mike Campi, Lou Gandolfo, John Kapp, Joe Ponzi, and Eric Seidel also provided unique assistance about a variety of topics.

Detective-investigator extraordinaire Kenny McCabe gets a special mention for help he provided the authors before he died. So do the late former prosecutors Mario DiNatale and Charles Rose, who worked together on the Windows case, and the great private eye Lawrence Frost, also gone much too soon.

We also express appreciation to the folks who helped us, but explicitly asked us not to mention them. They know who they are. Others who helped along the way include: William Bastone, Chris Blank, Ellen Borakove, Stephen Byrne, Dan Castleman, Jim DeVita, Lou DiGregorio, Mark Feldman, John Flanagan, Martin Geduldig, Roger Greenbank, Elie Honig, Ed McDonald, Daniel McGillicuddy, Sal Miciotta, Wells Morrison, Alfred McNeil, Jim Margolin, Matty O'Brien, Jim O'Connor, Vinny Panzarino, William Rashbaum, Murray Richman, Dick Rudolph, Ken Santare, Jeff Schaffler, Jerry Shargel, George Terra, Angela Troisi, Joseph Veltre, and Joel Winograd. Some in this last group were wise enough never to have actually spoken to us. But we include their names here because their work in one way or another helped us tell the story.

We also thank the many friends and family members who supported us and put up with us—and our absence—while we worked, especially our respective mates, Barbara Capeci and Susan Mastrangelo.

Big thanks to St. Martin's Press honcho Tom Dunne and his talented team, including Rob Kirkpatrick, Nicole Sohl, and Joe Rinaldi. Attorney Ellis Levine kept us in check.

Lastly, thanks to our ever-upbeat literary agent, Ed Breslin, who kept on pushing to make this happen.

INDEX

Index